Modern Records, Maverick Methods

Modern Records, Maverick Methods

Technology and Process in Popular Music Record Production 1978–2000

Samantha Bennett

BLOOMSBURY ACADEMIC
NEW YORK • LONDON • OXFORD • NEW DELHI • SYDNEY

BLOOMSBURY ACADEMIC
Bloomsbury Publishing Inc
1385 Broadway, New York, NY 10018, USA
50 Bedford Square, London, WC1B 3DP, UK

BLOOMSBURY, BLOOMSBURY ACADEMIC and the Diana
logo are trademarks of Bloomsbury Publishing Plc

First published in the United States of America 2019

Copyright © Samantha Bennett, 2019

For legal purposes the Acknowledgements on p. vii constitute an
extension of this copyright page.

Cover design/illustration © Jason Anscomb

All rights reserved. No part of this publication may be reproduced or transmitted
in any form or by any means, electronic or mechanical, including photocopying,
recording, or any information storage or retrieval system, without prior
permission in writing from the publishers.

Bloomsbury Publishing Inc does not have any control over, or responsibility for,
any third-party websites referred to or in this book. All internet addresses given in this
book were correct at the time of going to press. The author and publisher regret any
inconvenience caused if addresses have changed or sites have ceased to exist, but
can accept no responsibility for any such changes.

Library of Congress Cataloging-in-Publication Data
Names: Bennett, Samantha (Music professor) author.
Title: Modern records, maverick methods : technology and process in popular
music record production 1978-2000 / Samantha Bennett.
Description: New York, NY : Bloomsbury Academic, 2019. |
Includes bibliographical references and index.
Identifiers: LCCN 2018039904 | ISBN 9781501344107 (hardback) |
ISBN 9781501344091 (pbk.)
Subjects: LCSH: Popular music–Production and direction–History–20th century. |
Sound recordings–Production and direction–History–20th century.
Classification: LCC ML3470 .B452 2019 | DDC 781.64/14909–dc23
LC record available at https://lccn.loc.gov/2018039904

ISBN: HB: 978-1-5013-4410-7
PB: 978-1-5013-4409-1
ePDF: 978-1-5013-4412-1
eBook: 978-1-5013-4411-4

Typeset by Integra Software Services Pvt. Ltd.

To find out more about our authors and books visit www.bloomsbury.com
and sign up for our newsletters.

Contents

List of Illustrations	vi
Acknowledgements	vii
Introduction	1
1 Constructing Records: Sound Recording and Production Technologies at the Turn of the 1980s	19
2 The Sound of Technology: Machines and Formats That Transformed Mid–Late 1980s Popular Music	37
3 Technological Hybridity: Conflations of Analogue, Digital, the Cutting Edge and the Vintage in the 1990s	55
4 Maverick Methods: Tech-Processual Unorthodoxies in Contemporary Record Production	75
5 Sound Recordists in Flux: The Diversification of the Recording and Production Role	93
6 Sound Minds: Mapping Recordists' Attitudes	111
7 Analysing Technology and Process in Popular Music Recordings: A Tech-Processual Methodology	133
Conclusion	173
Notes	184
Records Cited	210
Bibliography	217
Filmography	234
Index	235

List of Illustrations

Figure

6.1 Attitudinal matrix depicting tech-processual standpoints of sound recordists in the 1980s and 1990s   114

Tables

I.1 Matters of technological and processual potential impacting on popular music recordings   3
I.2 Recordist autobiographies and biographies since 1979   12
4.1 Music recording technologies deemed 'standard': 1970s–1990s   79
4.2 A breakdown of tech-processual unorthodoxies in contemporary record production, 1980s and 1990s   85

Acknowledgements

I would like to thank the following individuals without whom this book would not have been possible. First, thanks to all the recordists and recording industry professionals who contributed by giving their time, thoughts and experiences. I am very grateful to Phil Harding, Tony Platt, Mick Glossop, Steve Levine, Melvyn Toms, Chris Sheldon, Dave Harries, Malcolm Atkin, Steve Culnane, David Mellor and Steve Albini for their generosity of time. My thanks also to Penny Rimbaud of Crass for his time and thoughts.

I thank my fellow academics for their support and willingness to listen, bounce ideas, share experiences and offer advice. I am eternally grateful to Professor Mark Butler, Professor Paul Draper, Associate Professor Phillip McIntyre, Professor Albin Zak, Dr Eliot Bates, Professor Andy Bennett, Professor Rob Toulson, Professor Simon Zagorski-Thomas and Dr Justin Morey. Additionally, I am indebted to Professor Allan Moore for all his mentorship and guidance, particularly at the beginning of this book. Many thanks to Leah Babb-Rosenfeld at Bloomsbury Academic for her support in the publication of this book.

Special thanks to my wonderful, supportive colleagues, formerly at the University of Westminster and currently at the Australian National University. And, of course, my eternal gratitude to my friends and family for all their love and support.

Introduction

Music recording and production is not a magic trick; musicians do not disappear behind a curtain and emerge sometime later having miraculously produced a recording of their works. Yet, if we consider scholarly discourse until the late 1990s, it might appear that way. Until the turn of the millennium, popular music studies and popular musicology have focused almost entirely on composition, performance and reception, with a large portion of scholarship dedicated to cultural and contextual analysis. Of the textual analyses that exist, many including those by Philip Tagg,[1] Allan Moore[2] and David Machin[3] focus on song structure, lyrical content, semiotics and meaning. Musical elements and stylistic attributes are the focus of analytical works by Walter Everett,[4] and work on micro aspects of rhythm and groove has been the point of focus for scholars including Mark Butler[5] and Anne Danielsen.[6] John Covach[7] has focused on aspects of rock song form, and scholars including Sheila Whiteley[8] and Lori Burns[9] have analysed the female voice, lyrics and musicality in a variety of contemporary recordings. Where the sound recording is the analytical reference point, the question as to how that musical work made it there in the first instance is rarely asked, as Warner[10] recognized in *Pop Music, Technology and Creativity* and Moore[11] noted in *Rock: The Primary Text*. Perhaps, until very recently, it was deemed unimportant. As Stephen Cottrell rightly pointed out in *Recorded Music*, we have seen the 'rise and rise of phonomusicology'[12] in recent years and it is not before time.

At this early stage, I want to define three key terminologies and, in turn, the three areas of focus I use regularly in this book.

As used by Albin Zak throughout *The Poetics of Rock*, the term **recordist** is used to describe those individuals who are in some way responsible for either part or whole of a recording process. This book is intended to build on Zak's work by extending the era of focus into the 1980s and 1990s. As such, I continue to apply the term 'recordist' as an 'umbrella term' to incorporate producers, sound engineers, programmers, tape-ops, as well as conflations of the artist-engineer/artist-producer role. This is not intended to be a 'one-size-fits-all' term – in Chapter 5, for example, I discuss this term and look at the role of the recordist in more detail – but Zak uses the term in a particular context to discuss sound recording and production roles and agency more efficiently. Next, I use the word **technology** to describe systems routinely featured and applied to a commercial popular music recording and production workflow, including music production technologies such as synthesizers, samplers, sequencers (both hardware and software) and MIDI (Musical Instrument Digital Interface) systems; sound recording technologies including analogue and digital tape recorders, hard-disk recorders and computer-based recording systems; sound processing technologies to include mixing consoles, pre-amps, dynamics and time-based signal processors, multi-effects processors and other sound manipulation systems. I also use the word 'vintage' to describe pre-1975 technologies implemented after 1985 and 'precursor(s)' to describe technologies implemented in recording and production processes that were made and/or used between five and ten years prior to technologies available at the time of the recording in question. I use the term 'cutting edge' to describe professional-level, then newly released recording and production technologies. Musical instruments – acoustic and electronic – are also music technologies, but these are not the focal point of this book. Finally, the word **process** is used to describe recording techniques and gestures implemented by a recordist in order to capture, process and record sound. Process includes: microphone placement; use of multitracking and overdubbing; sampling, looping and sound editing techniques; recording 'orchestration' to include position of acoustically or electronically recorded or programmed instrumentation in the overall mix according to volume; the spatial positioning of aforementioned instrumentation in the overall mix; applications of dynamics and time-based signal processing; applications of technologies in ways not originally intended; manually controlled and automated spatial, volume and processing gestures; and mastering. Communication and interaction with musicians and other agents are also part of many recording processes, although that is not the focus of this book. I use the term 'processual' to describe aspects of recording practice pertaining to process, as described in the above definition. In this book – and in other publications[13] – I use the term 'tech-processual' (where 'tech' is short for 'technology') as a methodological descriptor, which encapsulates the specific aspects of a recording I am most interested in illuminating when analysing popular music recordings. I am interested in the space(s) existing between performance and reception: the oft-overlooked matters of technological and processual potential that impact on what we eventually hear on a record (see Table I.1). The term 'record' implies a physicality that has not been as prevalent in recent years, as the dominant music formats are not formats at all but an array of digitized codecs: *carriers* of documents. The study of music documents and artefacts and the transition of recorded music documents from physicality to virtuality have been expertly dealt with, particularly by Richard James Burgess.[14] Whilst it is acknowledged here that the aforementioned continuum of recorded music artefacts to file formats is one of the biggest areas in our discourse, this book is focused on the era between 1978 and 2000, and therefore, vinyl and CD recordings are the reference formats.

Whilst I am interested in the technological aspects of popular music, I am not attempting to separate the tech-processual matters away from their musical contexts; popular music and record production are inextricable. To that end, I am not promoting a dedicated discipline of study: this work bridges popular music studies, as it situates the aforementioned analyses within the contextual frameworks of technological development and recordist agency, and popular musicology, as it deals with the textual

Table I.1 Matters of technological and processual potential impacting on popular music recordings

Technological	Processual
Microphones	Recordist attitudes, visions and aesthetic intentions
Mixing consoles	Recordists' 'gestures'
Analogue tape recorders	Recording techniques
Digital tape recorders	Recording workplace
Hard-disk recorders	Mixing techniques
Hardware samplers	Microphone choice and placement
Hardware sequencers	Automation
Dynamics processors	Manipulation of frequency content
Time-based processors	Spatial positioning of instruments
Samplers	Application(s) of processing
Music technologies: computer-based music devices, synthesizers, sound modules	'Established' or 'standard' working practices
Digital audio workstations (DAWs)	'Unorthodox' working practices

analysis of commercially available, recorded popular music tracks. The intention here, therefore, is to *illuminate* the tech-processual attributes of popular music recordings as playing an important role in the construct of popular music and as having a significant impact on what we eventually hear. Also insufficient is to acknowledge the role of technology, recordist and workplace on sound recordings without lifting the lid on these oft-overlooked influences and unpacking the all-important *why*? In his seminal methodology *Song Means*, Allan Moore suggests the 'what?' in popular music studies has for too long been the rather superficial line of questioning in the discipline. Moore suggests we should be more concerned with the 'so what?'; I agree, and in *Modern Records*, it is my aim to unravel the influence of technology and recordist upon what is eventually heard. One way of doing that is to flip the analysis on its head and ask: What would X recording sound like without the presence of Y technology or Z recordist? Can we imagine Frankie Goes To Hollywood's *Welcome to the Pleasuredome* (1984) without the Fairlight CMI or Trevor Horn at the helm? Dr Dre without an AKAI MPC? U2's *The Joshua Tree* (1987) without Brian Eno? Any 1980s Michael Jackson record without Quincy Jones? The point is that the recordist and the tech-processual means by which a popular music recording is constructed is absolutely central to our understanding(s) of it. I am, however, not for a moment suggesting I am the first to figure this out. Since the turn of the 1980s, four distinct areas of investigation have formed essential cornerstones of studies in record production. Those being:

- the design, choice, implementation and mediation of sound recording and music technologies on/in the recording process;
- recordist(s);
- the role(s) and interaction(s) of recordists with the aforementioned technologies, as well as musicians, performers and business men or women in the recording and production process; and
- the workplace in which those technologies and personnel operated in order to achieve the documentation of the audio/musical event.

This is now an established discipline with burgeoning sub-disciplines resulting in a steady increase of academic studies since the turn of the millennium. One of the earliest published articles, 'The Producer as Artist', was written by Charlie Gillet in 1977[15] – an auteurist proposition that was particularly forward thinking for its time. This paper focused entirely on the role of the recordist, as Gillet drew parallels between the tasks of a record producer and those of a film director. More recently, auteurist studies have been critiqued – record production is, by nature, a collaborative event – but the significance of Gillet's article was to draw attention away from the composer, the composition, the musician, the performer, the *performance*, and any sort of audience or reception analysis and move the spotlight onto the recordist and production process. Another key turning point came around 1990, which was a significant year for recording and production scholarship: Andrew Goodwin's widely cited 'Sample & Hold' was published in *Critical Quarterly. Popular Music and Society* dedicated a special edition[16] to technological and processual studies of recording and production, with notable articles on recording technology by Steve Jones[17] and on the role of the producer by Jari Muikku.[18] Jeremy Beadle's 1993 book *Will Pop Eat Itself?*[19] brought the cultural significance of the sampler into the scholarly domain, quickly followed up by a number of what have now become benchmark studies in this discipline: Paul Théberge's 1997 text *Any Sound You Can Imagine*,[20] Mark Katz's 2004 book *Capturing Sound: How Technology Has Changed Music*,[21] Timothy Warner's 2003 text *Pop Music, Technology and Creativity*[22] and Albin Zak's 2001 benchmark study *The Poetics of Rock*.[23] In addition, the past decade has seen key works deal with the historical, contextual and analytical voids in the area of sound, music technology and production and the influence of sound recording on popular music in particular. In his book *Stage to Studio*,[24] James P. Kraft traces the impact of an emergent and proliferating recording technology on musicians, labour and culture in the late nineteenth century and into the first half of the twentieth century, focusing on how musicians negotiated the transition from performance to recording.[25] Notably, Susan Schmidt Horning's 2013 book *Chasing Sound*[26] is one of the most insightful historical texts in recent years, tracing the development of sound recording from Edison's invention of the phonograph through to the LP. This meticulous text deals with sound recording as a key turning point in music history, as well as the significant impact of multitrack tape recording, studios and personnel through the early-to-mid twentieth century. Additionally, Schmidt Horning deals with the oft-mentioned but rarely analysed aesthetics of high-fidelity audio. Another major contribution to this field lies in Simon Zagorski-Thomas' *Musicology of Record Production*.[27] This book traces the study of record production as a discipline before critically examining key themes including the development of audio technology and performance, communication and practice in the studio. This comprehensive tome also considers the role of the consumer and the business of recorded music, thus presenting record production study at the point between performance and reception and dealing with record production in the context of both. In an ambitious work documenting many of the discourses present in the *Art of Record Production* forum,[28] Zagorski-Thomas consolidates his earlier work in an essential text. Further edited collections, particularly by Greene and Porcello,[29] have filled an important void in anthropological studies of the recording studio and studio practice. *Wired for Sound* traces recording and practice via a number of – until then, overlooked – cultures, including indigenous Australia, Native America and Indonesia. Broadening this discipline further, the edited collection *Critical Approaches to the Production of Music and Sound* – a comprehensive overview of global sound and music production, to include focus on aspects of gender, indigeneity and virtuality – was published by the author and Eliot Bates early in 2018.[30]

These important studies, to an extent grappling with the wider sociological, legal and musicological meaning of new technologies, have laid immense groundwork – academic studies in many areas of record production now flourish. We now have at our fingertips a wealth of great work by even greater scholars, many of whom have studied the role of the recordist in detail and from a range of angles in dedicated texts, which has certainly brought great weight to the argument that the recordist plays a vital role in the way that records are made and, more importantly, in the way that records *sound*. Few scholars, however, have tackled the work of contemporary recordists. Warner's book on Trevor Horn, *Pop Music, Technology and Creativity*, is particularly significant, pulling recordist discourse out from its 1960s hiding place and into the late-twentieth-century realm of digital recording practice. Mark Katz deals with the sociopolitical ramifications of the sampler and other technologies in *Capturing Sound: How Technology Has Changed Music*, with some insightful study on Norman Cook and Chuck D as artist-producers. Scholars from the global *Art of Record Production* forum have made up for lost time with eight journal issues, a book and a conference in its twelfth successful year – enough substantiation that this area of study is finally gaining recognition as one of the most important areas of popular music studies. Furthermore, this area of discourse epitomizes contemporary academic interdisciplinarity; as an editor of the *Journal on the Art of Record Production*, I have reviewed articles and conference papers taking scientific, anthropological, ethnographic, cognitive, musicological, analytical and sociological approaches – all equally valid and valuable.

Record production discourse is not just present in the scholarly domain. Indeed, the topic remains a frequent point of discussion for music journalists. Topics on recording studios and technologies have made their way into broadsheet newspapers and even into the film industry, with recent documentaries such as Dave Grohl's 2013 film *Sound City*[31] garnering much critical acclaim. However, such popular cultural documentations of technology, recordists and workplaces are often superficial, biased and sentimental accounts relying upon practitioners' oral histories and hindsight. Furthermore, they often contain a skewed version of events that unhelpfully mythologizes recording practice and perpetuates discourses of 'magic', 'alchemy' or 'black art' – exactly the type of mythological discourse this book seeks to address and dispel. Using the aforementioned example of *Sound City*, whilst Grohl enlists a remarkable array of discussion from former recordists and musicians who frequented the studio, the narrative is that the workplace was 'magical' and the Neve console 'unique'. A logical perspective on the often banal goings-on in a recording studio is provided by one of the few female contributors Stevie Nicks, who read out a letter written to her parents from the studio in 1972 saying, 'I'm getting very tired of sitting around listening to 12 hours of music per day.'[32] *Sound City* is a good example of what Alan Williams has called the 'canonization of process',[33] depicted no more or less mythologically throughout the *Classic Albums* documentary series.[34] This collection of largely 1970s classic rock 'making-ofs' features plenty of illuminating anecdotes from the musicians and recordists involved. Yet the series features multiple skewed accounts, reinforces mythologies and, in many cases, presents records in neatly framed packages that, in some cases, skirt matters of fact. Take the episode *Never Mind the Bollocks ... Here's the Sex Pistols*.[35] At one point, we see footage of John Lydon recording vocals to 'God Save the Queen'. *Never Mind the Bollocks ...*, to include the aforementioned single, was recorded in Wessex Studios by Chris Thomas and Bill Price. Yet the recording has been synched to footage not from the Wessex sessions but from earlier demo sessions at Gooseberry – a much smaller, 'dingier' basement project studio. Perhaps no filming took place at the Wessex sessions. Regardless, a clear attempt has been made to depict the Sex Pistols recording in a culturally appropriate setting; after all, the elite Abbey-road lineage recording personnel, then cutting-edge recording technologies and newly acoustically treated recording rooms at Wessex hardly sits comfortably with punk aesthetics. I am very grateful to Liam Watson (Toerag Studios, London) for pointing out another inconsistency in the *Classic Albums* series.[36] In *Paranoid*,[37] an episode on Black Sabbath's 1970 album, a similar anomaly occurs. We see recordist Tony Allen behind a large-scale mixing console continually solo'ing and muting individual tracks of the original recording. *Paranoid* was, however, recorded at Regent Studios to a 4-track recorder. In the documentary, we see the original 1″ tape boxes with the Regent Studios label and the '4-track' box ticked. Yet Allen is able to solo a perfectly clean drum mix and a similarly clean bass guitar. Later in the documentary, Allen solos drums, bass and guitar from 'Electric Funeral'.[38] However, the footage then cuts to the musicians performing the track in a recent studio setting. So, Allen is not soloing and muting the original recordings, but *re-recordings*. Why this was deemed necessary is unclear; arguably the accomplishment of recording *Paranoid* to 4-track is more worthy because of the limitations they faced. Again, perhaps this is about cultural representation. 4-track is associated with the 1960s; the 1970s was the time of larger consoles and 16- to 24-track recording. The issue with these (mis)representations is that the presentation of technological and processual attributes of record production in widely received, general interest media is, at best, idealized and, at worst, fabricated. These documentaries may be entertaining, but over time, such small, yet important factual inconsistencies build into mythologies; it is no wonder that scholars and cultural commentators alike discuss tech-processual matters and recording workplaces in terms of 'magic', 'alchemy' and 'black art', all of which are discussed at length in this book.

Such mainstream documentations of recording practice, workplaces and recordists negotiate record production history through rose-tinted glasses: it is a sepia-toned, nostalgic, schmaltz-laden version of events that presents the 1960s/1970s recording industry as being a 'golden age'. I am not suggesting this is wrong – there is a large audience for such entertaining accounts and at least some recognition is given to recordist, workplace and tech-processual matters, however warped they may be. Additionally, a focus on the 1960s and 1970s dominates entertainment, cultural commentary and academic studies of rock record production. This book shifts the focus to the 1980s and 1990s: an era equally rich in diverse, creative and non-standardized modalities of record production and yet to be fully investigated. At this stage I should mention genre. *Modern Records* does not focus solely on rock, pop, hip-hop, dance or any other genre. It neither promotes nor discourages an aesthetics of genre but looks at commercially successful, popular recordings and their technological and processual attributes. Therefore, I am equally as interested in Dr Dre[39] as Phil Ramone[40] as Sylvia Massy.[41] I am just as concerned with the working practices of Brian Eno[42] as I am with Tim Simenon.[43] John Loder[44] is given just as much thought as Liam Howlett.[45] I also wish to acknowledge that this book focuses entirely on recordists and technologies of the 1980s and 1990s and as such the overwhelming majority of recordists featured in this book are men. As scholars such as Paula Wolfe,[46] Simon Zagorski-Thomas[47] and cultural commentators such as Mark Savage[48] and Steve Haruch[49] have noted, at the turn of the 2010s, women comprised less than 5 per cent of commercial music recordists and that number was even lower during the period dealt with in this book. As a scholar working in phonomusicology and not sociology, cultural or gender theory, I am not fully equipped to address this shocking disparity head-on. This book does, however, focus on numerous female artists – including Blondie, Madonna, Salt N' Pepa, Alanis Morrisette, amongst many others. Additionally, this book features a focus on one of the leading recordists of the 1990s, Sylvia Massy, and her innovative work with both Tool and System of a Down. Of course, this does not deal with, answer to or otherwise reason as to the lack of women present in audio and recording. I can only hope that, as a female author, this book addresses, albeit in a small way, a common misconception that women do not engage in technical aspects of music production. Ultimately, this is a study of the technologies and processes that can be traced via commercial popular music recordings, largely focused in the era between 1978 and 2000.

Technology

The advent of digital technology in the early 1980s marks the beginning of what may be the most fundamental change in the history of western music since the invention of music notation in the ninth century.

Timothy Taylor[50]

The invention of sound recording in the late nineteenth century – as noted by many scholars including Schmidt Horning,[51] Morton[52] and Katz[53] – can be thought of as a transformative moment in the history of music. So too is the advent of multitrack recording at the turn of the 1950s, as described by Cunningham[54] and Milner.[55] Taylor recognized the beginning of the 1980s as another significant 'turning point' in the history of music and he is absolutely right; the CD format (1982),[56] MIDI (1984)[57] and Sony's professional DASH recorder (1982),[58] all hit the audio and music industries at this point in time. However, the emergence of digital music technologies in high-end, professional recording studios can be traced back slightly earlier to 1978, when Sony released its PCM-1600 digital audio recorder,[59] the first digital master recording system for professional recording studios. Such developments were consolidated in the music technology domain, as the New England Digital's (NED) 'Synclavier Synthesizer System' (1978)[60] and the Fairlight CMI (Computer Music Instrument) (1979)[61] emerged as two of the first digital sampling, synthesis and programming devices. The sound of these new devices manifested in the music of the era: recordists and studio owners working with emergent new-wave, post-punk and new romantic artists, as well as established rock musicians, embraced these new devices, resulting in a sonically discernible shift in commercial popular music. Whilst artists such as Kraftwerk shifted the sound of popular music away from 'natural' performances and towards almost entirely electronic composition with albums including *Autobahn* (1974) and *The Man Machine* (1978), by the turn of the 1980s, the mainstream charts in both Europe and the United States were dominated by *both* analogue and digital synthesis-constructed recordings, including benchmark records such as Tubeway Army's *Replicas* (1979), The Buggles' *The Age of Plastic* (1980) and Duran Duran's *Duran Duran* (1981). Therein lies a part justification for this book's starting point: the aforementioned conflation of analogue and digital synthesis at the turn of the 1980s illuminates one of the main arguments in this book, that of the onset and proliferation of digital systems at the turn of the 1980s and the resulting effects on tech-processual practice and, ultimately, on commercial popular music. I am, therefore, concerned with the advent of digital technology in the late 1970s, the 'fundamental change' further developments had on popular music into the 1980s and subsequently, the breadth of recording, music and format technologies used in 1990s record production. Remarkably, this pivotal era in music technology has been somewhat overlooked. Whilst plenty of scholarship exists on the technological, cultural and legal implications of the sampler,[62] few sources specifically address other important developments of the era.

The advent of what can be described as 'the digital age' has had a profound effect on popular music and the ways in which it is performed, produced and consumed. New, predominantly digital sound recording and music technologies from the late 1970s onwards have often been recognized as bringing about significant changes on popular music.[63] Yet digital technologies did not change recording practice overnight – analogue recording remained central to many professional and semi-professional workplaces until the turn of the millennium. Intriguing, then, that amongst the recording industry, music industry and in academic studies an 'analogue vs. digital debate' has ensued.[64] Whilst this has been useful in scientific studies focused on listening and psychoacoustics, it is an unhelpful paradigm in which to frame historical, technological and cultural accounts for a few reasons. First, as new digital technologies emerged around forty years ago, they did not suddenly present musicians, recordists and workplaces with a 'one or the other' choice of sonic domains in which to work. Moreover, such technologies were integrated, with varying degrees of urgency, into existing workflows and workplaces. For some workplaces, those who had the financial means to do so, new devices were integrated almost as immediately as they became available. For others, the advent of new technologies meant a decrease in the second-hand market value of precursors; thus, the previous elite generation of cutting-edge technology became more accessible only when superseded with a newer technology. Secondly, there appears to be no definition or set understanding as to what is being discussed under these conflations of decades of technological development we so casually label 'analogue' or 'digital'. What is meant by 'digital' when used in relation to music and technology? 8-bit? 192 KHz? 128 bps? Are we talking about hard-disk recording and storage capacity? MIDI? CDs? AIFF files? Computers? The conversion process? Nyquist theorem? Interfaces? No, these different technological thematics are often conflated into one 'umbrella' word, then pitched against another, equally indefinable terminology, leading to an entire discourse then being built upon it. That is not to say there is not some value in comparative studies of individual technologies. For example, Austin Moore's analysis of the UREI 1176 tube compressor and its Universal Audio digital skeoumorphic counterpart[65] is a very helpful study in contemporary recording and technological iconicity.[66] Thirdly, it is vital to acknowledge the inextricable nature of technological application with aesthetic musical intention. For Trevor Horn, for example, the inclusion of the latest digital technologies into his workflow was essential, due to the cutting-edge new-wave music he produced. For John Loder, owner of North London's 'Southern Records' and studios and producer of anarchic punk such as Crass, a Fairlight CMI would have been not only unaffordable but also irrelevant to the aesthetic direction of the music he produced. Finally, thus far, it has not been possible for digital audio to accurately reproduce an analogue sound waveform identically. Whilst sampling rates are far more accurate than in the past – and computer processing power has simultaneously improved in order to facilitate such high overall data rates – to compare diametrically opposed sonic domains is, to a large extent, like comparing apples with pears. The reality is that most recordists and workplaces assimilate technologies from both domains into the same workflow. At this stage I want to foreground a key argument: this book has no intention of perpetuating the so-called 'analogue vs. digital debate', since I am arguing that more is revealed by focusing on the great diversity of practice present amongst 1980s and 1990s recordists who conflated technologies from both domains; it is this conflated, *hybrid* workflow that I have identified – and am most interested in unpacking – in this book. Yes, there are sound recordists working wholly within the analogue domain today: Steve Albini,[67] Liam Watson,[68] Lewis Durham[69] and Pete Hutchinson[70] are just a few who remain dedicated to a purely analogue workflow. Conversely, recordists working, or who have worked, wholly in the digital domains, such as Steve Levine,[71] Eliot Mazer[72] and currently Liam Howlett, are equally as successful with their outputs. And the latter are certainly more prevalent than the former. Yet if we take all these example recordists' technologies and attempt to 'oppose' them in some sort of sonic battle, it falls at the first hurdle: the aesthetic intentions, choice of technologies, attitudes towards technologies, rosters of artistes as well as 'place' in the music industry are unique to each circumstance, thus rendering the opposition deeply flawed, if not, irrelevant. In reality, the majority of commercially successful sound recordists fall somewhere between these two dimensions: during the 1980s and 1990s, many commercially released popular music recordings were made using analogue *and* digital technologies in conjunction, as integrated into the same workflow, as illustrated in all examples featured in Chapters 3 and 7. Such technological hybridity in the production process therefore forms a central thesis of this book: I argue that, between 1978 and 2000, commercial popular music production rarely aligned exclusively to one sonic domain or another. In reality, the majority of recordists blended technologies from both domains into their workflows, which also featured individualized production techniques, or what I term *maverick methods*.

In saying that, recognizing recordists such as Albini and Durham working wholly in the analogue domain long into the twenty-first century also raises a strong counter-argument to technological determinism. One point made repeatedly through this book is that the rate of technological change and introduction of 'cutting-edge' technologies through the eras does not precisely, nor consistently or conveniently, correlate to technologies applied to commercially successful recordings made in corresponding eras. Let's take a random year – 1987 – and consider some of the recordings. U2's *The Joshua Tree* was tracked via a vintage, 1972 Neve console and recorded to analogue tape. Concurrently, Stock, Aitken and Waterman (referred to from here on as SAW) were using Sony's then cutting-edge DASH system as centric to their 'factory' output. Robert 'Mutt' Lange constructed Def Leppard's *Hysteria* via a 48-channel SSL console. John Loder tracked a Roland TR-909 Drum Machine to a Studer 8-track on Big Black's *Songs About Fucking*. The point is, these diverse recording aesthetics are strongly aligned to *musical* aesthetic intention. *Hysteria* would not have sounded anything like *Hysteria* had Loder recorded it to his 8-track in the independent, punk-oriented Southern Studios. *The Joshua Tree* would not have sounded at all like *The Joshua Tree* had SAW programmed it with a LinnDrum and Publison into a Sony DASH. The choice and application of technologies to the recording process is, therefore, equally as important as the choice of musical instruments; the sonic alignment of sound recording and production technology to the aesthetic musical intention is so important to the overall integrity of the record, and it is precisely these factors that neither popular music studies nor popular musicology has addressed in any great depth until very recently.

The aforementioned recordists achieved significant commercial and independent success in 1987, illustrating that the applications of technological precursors and 'vintage' systems were at least equally important to recording sessions as the so-called 'cutting edge'. Once again, the notion of aesthetic intention is pertinent.

Modern Records is not a claim that technology alone affected popular music of the era. Rather, the intention is to trace how technology, recordists, processes and attitudes changed during this important era in record production. Additionally, the book recognizes an eclectic technological landscape in the 1990s and how new modalities of record production emerged as a result. Popular music recording in this decade was certainly unique in terms of tech-processual practice, due in part to new, DAW[73]-based recording, the continued use of the precursors of the 1980s and integration of pre-1980s vintage systems into contemporary record production.

Recordists and canon

Scholars of Western Classicism have turned the study of the composer canon into a significant, established discourse: Who belongs there? And why? And who *says* so?[74] Of course, there has been decades of scholarship on the Viennese School,[75] with thousands of analyses, historical contextualizations and musicological (re)interpretation of score reinforcing the notion that such composers belong in a 'special' group. As notions of 'genius' and 'contribution' and 'meaning' are made by one scholar after another, a canon emerges: the perpetual compounding of reinforcement(s) elevating that select group above everyone – *everything* – else. Sooner or later, it becomes widely accepted that Mozart and Beethoven are better, higher and more important than other composers, whether the reasons behind such assertions are clear or not. Such compositions are pushed to the forefront of educational curricula and orchestral production,[76] offering emergent musicians and audiences alike an ever-narrowing pool of repertoire to both perform and consume.

Popular music is no different. In fact, it has taken scholars and cultural commentators far *less* time to categorize their artists and performers into a multitude of categories and (sub)genres and to judge their talents by oft-unsubstantiated barometers of 'authenticity'. Wyn Jones has written on what she identifies as the rock canon,[77] which is reinforced by the presence of male, Anglo-American, commercial recording artists of the 1950s through 1970s in both rock historiography and popular music academic studies.[78] The 'list' has become one such essential mechanism for organizing popular music. Whether it involves 'Biggest selling singles of the year' on Radio 1 or 'Desert Island Discs' on Radio 4, 'Top 100 tracks of the 1980s – as voted for by YOU!' in Q magazine or 'The Pitchfork 100 Independent releases of the 1990s', it is our way of making sense of our culture, separating the artistic wheat from the proverbial chaff. Where we are faced with an ever-increasing quantity of music, canonization simply helps us navigate it. There are, however, problems with canonization. As selected artists are elevated above others, the contributions made by those excluded are obscured. Scholars including Helen Reddington have astutely noted that where music reporting, reviewing and criticism are largely documented by male journalists and commentators, women are excluded and, as a result, under-represented in rock historiography.[79]

As with Western Classicism and popular music, scholarly tendencies to canonize have not stopped at the entrance to the studio door. Whilst few recordist biographies exist, the ones that do situate accounts of their tech-processual practices as secondary concerns. Many, including those by George Martin and Glyn Johns, document anecdotes of working with well-known musicians, thus foregrounding musician agency and musical practices. In these cases, what is documented is

Table I.2 Recordist autobiographies and biographies since 1979

Recordist	Title	Year
Phil Brown	Are We Still Rolling?	2010
Geoff Emerick	Here, There and Everywhere: My Life Recording The Beatles	2005
Phil Harding	From the Factory Floor	2011
Glyn Johns	Sound Man	2014
Quincy Jones	Q: The Autobiography of Quincy Jones	2002
Daniel Lanois	Soul Mining: A Musical Life	2010
George Martin	All You Need Is Ears	1979
Mixerman	The Daily Adventures of Mixerman	2009
Mark Opitz	Sophisto-Punk	2012
Phil Ramone	Making Records	2007
Ken Scott	From Abbey Road to Ziggy Stardust	2012
Mike Stock	The Hit Factory	2004
Pete Waterman	I Wish I Was Me: Autobiography	2000
Crouch & Crouch	Sun King, The Life and Times of Sam Phillips	2009
Wade & Picardie	Music Man – Ahmet Ertegun	1991
Repsch	The Legendary Joe Meek: The Telstar Man	2000

less an account of the recordist's own tech-processual practice and more social and experiential accounts of working with well-known artists. Existing recordist biographies do, however, paint an interesting picture of the 'place' of popular music recordists in wider popular music. As we can see from Table I.2, of the few that exist, the majority of recordist autobiographies have been released in the last eighteen years, with only two released prior to 2000. This is not an exhaustive list, but much can be construed from what is both present and absent: all these recordists worked with high-profile, commercially successful recording artists in the United States, UK or Australia; all are male and the vast majority worked with rock musicians.

The problem with biographical studies representing recordists in popular music historiography lies in their 'behind the scenes'[80] or 'backstage'[81] role. Few recordists are prominent enough to be equally as renowned as commercial, performing artists. So forms a canon whereby recordists are more revered by their association to well-known artists than for their recording and production practice carried out on a day-to-day basis. For example, George Martin is synonymous with the work of the Beatles, regardless of his work as recordist in the 1980s and 1990s. Later studies by Kehew and Ryan[82] and Lawrence[83] reinforce Martin's Beatles association further, and thus his later work is under-represented. Paradoxically, we have a case in British recordist John Loder, whose work with Crass, Jesus and Mary Chain, Ministry and Big Black amongst hundreds of other artists created a sonically identifiable, punk and post-punk sonic signature over a period of more than three decades. Yet aside from the sole article by Bennett,[84] not a single interview, scholarly article or biographical account exists where Loder's work has been acknowledged, either in the time Loder was alive or posthumously. It serves as a lesson to all scholars working in this fascinating subject area that we face a significant challenge in contributing to the representation of recordists in popular music historiography.

A pattern already emerges: from the biographies in existence, it is as if the only two UK studios that ever existed were EMI at Abbey Road and PWL at Borough. What this does is reinforce a type of *workplace* canon. Scholarly studies on sound recording history, such as Milner's *Perfecting Sound Forever*[85] and Cunningham's *Good Vibrations*,[86] also concentrate heavily on the Abbey Road engineers of the 1960s, as well as US luminaries such as Phil Spector and Sam Phillips. 'Shock' documentaries, including 'The Agony and the Ecstasy of Phil Spector' (2009) and Al Pacino's depiction of the producer in the HBO biopic (2013), as well as Mick Brown's book *Tearing Down the Wall of Sound* focus on the more sensational aspects of Spector's character as a violent and unpredictable dictator, as opposed to his work as a record producer. The 1960s UK engineer Joe Meek has been similarly portrayed in posthumous studies. *The Legendary Joe Meek* (2001) by John Repsch[87] and the 2008 film *Telstar: The Joe Meek Story*, both focus on the engineer's closet homosexuality, alleged schizophrenic episodes and later murder/suicide, although *Telstar* does go some way in accurately depicting Meek's idiosyncratic production processes. Yet in Cunningham's *Good Vibrations* (1998), Ted Fletcher, a one-time colleague of Meek's and to some degree his posthumous legacy-builder, paints a different picture of Meek as 'shy and retiring ... a very quiet bloke'.[88] Historical studies of popular culture have focused more on the characters and crimes of these individuals than their body of works and perhaps rightly so. In both these cases, it is difficult to separate out the groundbreaking works of these men without acknowledging their crimes; an example of this is found in Alexis Petridis' article 'Phil Spector and the Myth of the 'Mad' Record Producer'.[89]

Regardless, popular culture has created mythologized versions of Spector and Meek in particular and it is not my intention to reinforce that. *Modern Records*, whilst at times acknowledging historical contexts, refocuses the discourse on a later point in popular music history – from 1978 to the turn of the millennium. In order to illustrate what I mean by the mythologization of sound recordists and their misrepresentation in historiography, let's turn the spotlight onto a modern-day recordist: Steve Albini. I am by no means the first to recognize the vast contribution this US recordist has made to Anglo American independent and alternative music; works by O'Hare[90] and Sheppard[91] illuminate Albini's contribution to a great extent. Indeed, Jaques Attali's 'Recording is power ...'[92] quotation from his seminal text *Noise* could have been written with Albini in mind, considering the independent sonic signature Albini has created into a benchmark of rock recording since the late 1980s. Let us look for a moment at Albini's perception of himself as a recordist:

- 'It's [producer] such a pejorative term, one I associate with a mode of thinking, a way of life, that I shun and abhor.'[93]
- 'I absolutely refuse to call myself a producer.'[94]
- 'The producer is responsible for artistic decisions on the record, and I am not.'[95]
- 'I am not a producer.'[96]

Let us now look at how Albini is depicted in cultural commentary and in academia:

- ' … enfant terrible producer Steve Albini … '[97]
- ' … the band hired producer Steve Albini'[98]
- ' … the choice of Steve Albini as producer … '[99]
- 'Steve Albini had produced both records … '[100]

Over the course of his career, Steve Albini has continued to assert his position as a sound recordist and not a producer. Yet in both academic studies and journalism, Albini is routinely depicted and discussed as a producer, and the works he has been involved in recording are routinely referred to his productions. Steve Albini has, therefore, been regularly cited as possessing and implementing a skill set he does not possess and never has possessed. It is, therefore, precisely this kind of misrepresentation that our discipline needs to address and avoid reinforcing any further.

Analysing recordings

Close readings of popular music have taken many forms. In 1982, Philip Tagg's analytical model put forward a hermeneutic-semiological methodology of seven musical expressions, to include aspects of time, melody, orchestration and texture. At this embryonic point in the history of popular music studies, Tagg recognized dynamics, acoustics and electromusical/mechanical aspects of the music to be of equal importance to traditional musical elements and form.[101] Tagg's work outlined popular music studies as a 'sociocultural field',[102] and the majority of work in this discipline is firmly fixed to this cultural theoretical and/or sociological starting point.

Popular music analytical readings have tended to focus on arrangements, often using excerpts of musical score as a reference point, thus illuminating the popular song in a way that only those trained in such musical theory can understand it. Score can be helpful in that it illustrates matters of orchestration, time signature, key signature, melodic and harmonic progressions, tempo and structure, as Tagg,[103] Moore,[104] Cook[105] and others have demonstrated. It is, however, limited – almost useless, in fact – when it comes to highlighting the presence of the technological, recording-processual and acoustical properties of a sound recording. There is no way of marking use of equalization (EQ) or panning on a traditional stave. Neither can we deduce dynamics – as inherent to the sound recording as opposed to the music – or time-based processing, volume automation or distortion. Alternative, visual means of depicting sonic characteristics are more useful. William Moylan's *Understanding and*

Crafting the Mix,[106] David Gibson's *The Art of Mixing*[107] and Dockwray and Moore's work on the 'Soundbox'[108] present the mix as a multidimensional, virtual cuboid where instruments are positioned. Gibson's visual guide suggests mix organizations are genre-specific. Dockwray and Moore's study focused on analysing recordings between 1968 and 1972. Both these studies are significant and important contributions to our discourse since they recognize – at least to some extent – the multidimensional extra-musical aesthetics of the recording. Other scholars have recognized elements of sound processing in recorded music and have theorized the effect such processing aesthetics has on recorded song. Particular attention has been given to the voice in recorded music. Nicola Dibben, for example, stated that '… contemporary popular music recording techniques such as reverb, delays, filters and overdubbing help "stage" voices … '.[109] Serge Lacasse described the effects of such sound processing as examples of 'mise-en-scéne of voice', using case-study examples and listener response data to illustrate a range of processors as sonically discernible on record. For example, Lacasse argues the amplification of aggression by means of applied distortion and the potential of expressiveness via applications of echo.[110] Another important area of discourse concerns the fabrication of environment via time-based signal processors. Peter Doyle has considered the construction of space in pre-1960s recordings in his seminal book *Echo and Reverb*.[111] Anne Danielsen and Ragnhild Brovig-Hanssen have taken this concept one step further and looked at extremities of space fabrication that can be considered surreal, using examples by Prince, Suede and Portishead.[112] Studies on recording analysis are still uncommon and this is in no small part due to the entirely different sets of terminology and descriptors present in the musical and sound recording domains. Albin Zak has quite rightly critiqued this dependence on music-based analytical method, as he states:

> Among the problems inherent in establishing an academic discipline aimed at illuminating record production, then, is the need for a fundamental aesthetic reorientation as well as new modes of analytic description. We must resist reducing musical meaning to matters of musical syntax, which stipulates a de facto hierarchy of aesthetic value.[113]

Where my methodology builds on those of Dockwray and Moore and others is that it situates the analyses in their concomitant tech-processual contexts, to include intention, recordist agency, apparent technologies and workplace(s), before analysing the presence of these factors in the text itself. I should be clear at this stage about what it is I am *not* trying to achieve with this methodological proposition. First, I am not attempting to separate the technological and processual attributes of popular music recordings away from their musical aspects. In fact, I remain unconvinced that this is possible, nor indeed necessary. As has been demonstrated in studies relating musical performance to recordings,[114] linking sociocultural factors to recordings[115] and matters concerning audience/reception, the study of the recording and production process is inextricable from front-end matters of compositional, arrangement and songwriting potential to end-user reception and interaction. So, I suggest that this is a vital matter for *illumination*, and my aim is to highlight the technological and processual attributes of recordings and not to champion a separate mode of study altogether.

Modern Records

Having outlined this vital area of discourse and established some of the significant scholarship within it, the purpose of this book and its potential contribution to the now-established field of studies in record production is addressed. Many scholars, including Zak,[116] Taylor[117] and Katz,[118] have acknowledged the early 1980s as a significant era in popular music history, but *Modern Records* attempts to unpack why the 1980s and 1990s era is so important and for what reasons.

The aims here are threefold. First, the intention with *Modern Records* is to analyse the importance of new technologies on popular music recordings from the late 1970s onwards, approaching the development of technologies in the analogue and digital domains as not in opposition, but as concurrently developing and often used in conjunction. Using a largely ethnographic methodology drawing upon first-hand interview material with many 1980s and 1990s recordists and changes in working practices during these eras are highlighted. I have undertaken extensive ethnographic work with members of the predominantly UK recording industry, including recordists Chris Sheldon, Steve Albini, Stephen Street, Steve Levine, Mick Glossop and Tony Platt, and industry personnel including Melvyn Toms, Dave Harries, Steve Culnane, Malcolm Atkin and David Mellor. In total, the views and oral histories of these individuals are assimilated into the discussion and serve as important components in the wider theoretical positions put forward throughout the book. All these individuals worked extensively at the height of the commercial recording industry at some point between 1978 and 2000. Many were immersed in the workplaces, technologies and recording practices that informed some of these decades' most revered sound recordings. As such, all interviewees were in a strong position to reflect on the era and the ramifications of its various technological and processual developments.

Secondly – and with reference to the all-important 'so what?' – ways in which such changes in working practices 'fed back' into standard modalities of record production are illuminated. It has been acknowledged that technological change in the 1980s 'split' recordists into two broad ideological 'camps' – the traditionalists, those sticking with 'tried and tested' methodologies, and the technophiliacs, those with tech-utopian views, often involved in cutting-edge, technology-driven record making.[119] However, the reality is a far more complex web of attitudinal patterns pertaining not only to technological preference but also to views on music and musicians, aesthetic directions, performance as well as the music industry as a whole. Such attitudes are analysed in relation to the impact on the recordists' technological and processual decision making.

Thirdly, the aforementioned technological and attitudinal factors are exemplified via six recording analyses. Furthermore, the choice of analyses presents a dichotomy for technological determinists: all recordings were made using a combination of then new, precursor and 'vintage' technologies by recordists using non-standardized modalities of record production. Using an analytical template that considers the technological and processual factors as primary considerations, scaffolded with contextual matters of intention, workplace, technology and process broadens the analytical focus of recorded music analyses. Using musical descriptors as only secondary points of reference, the implications of technology and process as heard on contemporary recordings are exemplified.

1

Constructing Records: Sound Recording and Production Technologies at the Turn of the 1980s

In *The Poetics of Rock*, Albin Zak stated:

> British recordings of the early 1980s marked a turning point in terms of both sound and public awareness. With an abundance of sound processing, new electronic instruments, and resurgent experimental attitudes, the distance between the natural sound world and the sound of records increased markedly.[1]

Zak makes a critical observation in terms of both the prevalence of non-'natural' sounding records and the period of time when such sonic characteristics became more noticeable. This chapter begins slightly earlier in the late 1970s, charting many significant digital music and recording technologies that emerged and discussing them in relation to commercially released records on which they featured. This is a key era in recorded popular music due to the influx and potential of digital recording, synthesis, sampling and carriers. Such technological development serves as important precedent to computer-based music recording and production and as such makes for an ideal starting point. Extending Zak's observation, I assert that the late 1970s signified a musical 'fork in the road' between records featuring live, acoustic and electric instrument performances and those featuring music heavily 'constructed' from programmable devices. This may be interpreted as a generalization and of course records were made that featured both acoustic and electronic programmed instrumentation. However, if records *in general* sounded sonically opposed to the natural sound world in the early 1980s, some records were even further removed from that point, to the extent that they resembled nothing that had been heard before. Suffice to say this period of technological development was intense, political and resulted in major musical and cultural impact.[2] Technological development did not, however, occur only in the digital domain. Multiple developments in the analogue domain, including larger and more sophisticated mixing consoles, tape machines, drum machine development and programmable, analogue synthesis-based devices emerged and proliferated. The late 1970s is a good starting point for other reasons. Until then, recording technologies followed a 'more of the same' trajectory; recording to analogue tape was the only option, regardless of the number of available tracks. To that end, many recordists and recording houses assimilated increased track tape recorders as and when they were released; the technology, operational aspects and maintenance, whilst varying from machine to machine, remained largely the same throughout the 1960s and 1970s. In saying that, there was certainly a large degree of aesthetic choice as to how those technologies were implemented; historically, analogue tape machines have been used in ways other than intended to create extraordinary effects – such practice dates back to European *musique concréte* and, in particular, the work of Pierre Schaeffer.[3] That the introduction of new, predominantly digital music technologies led to both utopian and pessimistic standpoints in the audio and music industries is well documented.[4] However, whilst plenty of work exists on the music of the era and less so of the recording technology and workplace environments of the era,[5] connections and synergies between these two domains have rarely been acknowledged. It is fair to say that concurrent to the Western economic boom, the 1980s was a time of technological and processual excess: professional audio and music recording technologies were more expensive than ever, technological development – particularly in the digital domain – increased markedly, competitiveness between manufacturers was rife and record company recording budgets ever increasing. Whilst the lines I am about to draw between technological change and impact on music could be interpreted as deterministic, I am not espousing technological determinism. Indeed, recordist agency is critical to this discussion and is considered in more detail later on. It is not possible to chart every technological development or record of the era, and this book does not attempt to do so. The aim of this chapter is to deal with some of the most *significant* developments in sound recording and music technology of the era and to consider the embodiment of such systems in popular music recordings.

The Fairlight CMI – technology and politics

> In the pioneer field of sound sampling, the American loses ground to the Australian; Synclavier does not yet have the same capability. It has thus attracted a less favourable attention from the electronic music academics at the BBC, who have for instance tended to plump for the Fairlight.
>
> Giles Dawson[6]

Developed in Sydney, Australia, during the early to mid-1970s, the Fairlight CMI (Computer Music Instrument) is one of the most influential music technologies in the history of music recording and production. A bold claim perhaps, but this groundbreaking device was – along with New England Digital's Synclavier – at the very nexus of that sonically discernible 'fork in the road',[7] as described in this chapter's introduction. How could one machine have made such an impact?

During the early 1970s, Sydney-based electronics engineer and synthesis enthusiast Peter Vogel began experimenting with the potential of digital synthesis along with friend and analogue synthesist Kim Ryrie. Almost simultaneously, Motorola consultant Tony Furse began work on his Qasar M8 synthesizer, a hybrid analogue–digital synthesizer featuring an 8-bit microprocessor. After synergizing their respective expertise – and with a licensing deal from Furse – Vogel and Ryrie built the first computer-based digital synthesizer with on-board sampling capability. Released in 1979, the original Fairlight CMI I featured an 8-bit analogue-to-digital converter, dual 8″ floppy disk drives and pre-programmed sets of sound timbres, setting a global precedent for digital sampling, synthesis and sequencing capability, all contained within a single music production system. Initial take-up of the Fairlight CMI I was enthusiastic, particularly amongst artists associated to avant-garde and/or art rock musicalities including Mike Oldfield and Peter Gabriel, producers including Richard James Burgess and Trevor Horn and synthesists such as Iva Davies. The Fairlight consisted of a digital sampler with 1MB floppy drive for storage, a dedicated software sequencer and keyboard. Heavy, cumbersome and initially utilizing a basic 8-bit microprocessor, the Fairlight was the first sample-based synthesizer that brought the possibility of waveform editing to a generation of professional recordists. Of particular note was the 'light pen' attached to the side of the monitor, with which the user could 'draw' waveforms on the screen. At between $25,000 and $36,000, the Fairlight – like the Synclavier – was out of reach financially to the majority of musicians and recordists. In saying that, its sound is widely recognized across a wide range of synth-pop, new romantic and pop records throughout the 1980s, primarily due to the large number of commercial recording artists who accessed the few machines in existence. The original model was released in 1979 through 1980 and an updated series II (1983) incorporated MIDI ports. The last Fairlight model was released in 1985; the series III was priced at more than $70,000. At the turn of the 1980s, the updated Fairlight CMI II was the most sophisticated computer music instrument available, consisting of a computer, keyboard and monitor with the Fairlight's unique 'light pen' attached. The Fairlight CMI II featured two 8″ floppy disk drives, one for hosting the system disk[8] and the other for data disks containing sounds and storing sequences. The user interface – a low-resolution green colour displayed on the Fairlight's video monitor – operated in 'pages'. Each page allowed users to perform specific tasks: for example, Page 2 allowed for the management of disk files; Page 6 enabled users to draw or alter harmonic content in a waveform; Page 8 allowed for the recording of samples; and Page D displayed the voice waveform in a three-dimensional image. Perhaps the most groundbreaking feature was the Fairlight's Page R: a 'Real-Time Composer' editing window displaying one bar of music programming on up to eight tracks. This *visual* representation of multitracked sound sources pioneered music programming and sequencing as we know it today. Thus, the Fairlight can be considered a forbearer of the DAW; the impact of screen-based waveform depiction on computer-based devices is fully realized in today's production systems.

Whilst the Fairlight was used to sample original sounds, such as in Peter Gabriel's 'Shock the Monkey' (1982), it could also be used to sample and programme instrument sounds, such as the drum patterns throughout Def Leppard's *Hysteria* (1987). The Fairlight featured pre-programmed sound banks of standard instruments and effects. One of the most popular of these was a patch called 'Sararr' – a breathy, voice-like instrument that became a focal-point sound in the 1980s synth-pop genre. The patch can be heard across Jean Michel Jarre's *Zoolook* (1984) and in Yazoo's *You and Me Both* (1983), but perhaps features most prominently in Tears for Fears' *Songs from the Big Chair* (1985) and is particularly foregrounded on the single 'Shout' (1984) – the effect is heard throughout the song and the instrument itself features prominently in the accompanying video. These pre-programmed sounds were also used to create memorable, atmospheric song introductions; perhaps the most famous of these was the synthesis-driven introduction to Stevie Wonder's 'Happy Birthday' (1982) and the dark, percussive introductory loop to John Farnham's 'You're the Voice' (1986). The Fairlight was also used to create memorable television and movie themes, including 'Theme From Miami Vice' (1984) by Jan Hammer, thus integrating itself into the aural fabric of 1980s popular culture.

Timothy Warner's book *Pop Music, Technology and Creativity* charts Trevor Horn's use of the Fairlight on notable records, including Frankie Goes to Hollywood's 'Relax' (1983) (*Welcome to the Pleasuredome* 1984), Grace Jones' 'Slave to the Rhythm' (*Slave to the Rhythm* 1985) and The Art of Noise's debut album (*Who's Afraid of?*) *The Art of Noise!* (1984). This study illuminated common musical and technological motifs in Horn's production, largely due to the sampling and sequencing methods he employed on the Fairlight CMI. One of the earliest of these was Horn's production on Dollar's 'Give Me Back My Heart' (1982), as Horn described:

> One of the first really interesting things we did that blew me away, was we sampled Thereza Bazar going 'aahhhh' and 'la! la!' And we used that on Dollar's 'Give Me Back My Heart' and it worked perfectly. What was clever about what we did, though, was that Thereza Bazar didn't just sing into the machine, we made up the samples. We 16-tracked her for every note. This was still in the days of analogue tape, and we bounced it down so we had a beautiful bed that was 16 tracks of her, across the range of an octave or whatever.[9]

Here, the foregrounding of technological intervention on a musical performance is acutely evident, and it was precisely these techniques that situated Horn at the very forefront of 1980s music production. I do not wish to cover the same ground that Warner expertly dealt with in his book, but further uses of the Fairlight CMI series II are worth noting.

Emergent digital technologies were not always met with approval by members of the recording industry. On the contrary, as much as technologies could be embraced and celebrated, they could also be divisive and used to make powerful political statements. In early 1980, Kate Bush began work on her album *The Dreaming* (1982), incorporating the kind of 'cut-and-paste' recording techniques more in keeping with avant-garde composition. Bush took on the multiple roles of artist, producer and Fairlight CMI I programmer, having acquired the first incarnation of the instrument in 1980. The title track, 'The Dreaming' (1982), is particularly significant. Lyrically and conceptually, 'The Dreaming' deals with Indigenous Australian rights, referencing the plight of Indigenous Australians following British colonization. Bush has sampled a Digeridu[10] and looped it within the Fairlight to form the underpinning of the entire record, thus utilizing and conflating Australia's most ancient and cutting-edge musical instruments.

Let's consider another The Art of Noise[11] track, that of 'Close (To The Edit)' (1984). In this track, the Fairlight has been used to sample various vocal and 'found sound' motifs, programme those samples and to create rhythmic and melodic sequences, which form the underpinning of the track. But the Fairlight's presence is not simply technologically or sonically discernible. The song title itself features a reference to a key feature of the Fairlight, that being its editing functionality. The rhythmic underpinning has been created from a sampled motorbike sound. A synthesized pulse acts as the track's bassline as other vocal and melodic samples are programmed in on top. The instrument's 'machine' presence is further reinforced in the accompanying video, which is set in a disused, graffiti-covered, decaying railway passage as various acoustic instruments lay, apparently rotting, along with burned-out oil cans and other discarded debris. A ceramic bust of Mozart lies on the tracks, along with a corroded saxophone, cello, violin and piano. A young girl dressed in punk clothes gathers and then tosses large quantities of musical score, trampling over the paper strewn across the floor. Three members of The Art of Noise appear in the video alongside her; the beginning of the film has been edited so the musicians appear and disappear in time with the music. Whilst the Fairlight itself does not feature, its musical presence is replaced by power tools: that of a large, electric chainsaw, a jigsaw and a large pair of metal cutters, which are later replaced with a circular saw. The Art of Noise proceed to use these tools to destroy the acoustic musical instruments present in the scene: large serrations, sparks and strikes are synchronized to the music. This created a powerful, metaphorical commentary on the Fairlight's sample-sequenced compositional potential as 'destroying': traditional musical instrumentation (as depicted by the decaying, later destroyed instruments); structure, arrangement and form (as depicted by the musical score); and Western Classicist music tradition and canon (as depicted by the Mozart bust). This aggressive situating of the Fairlight's potential – as a musical, compositional and recording device – as the destroyer of traditional music was indicative of wider technological pessimism surrounding the machine (and other digital music devices) from some factions in the recording and music industries and well addressed in scholarly discourse.[12] The Art of Noise – and their satirical film that played on then rife technological pessimism – were unapologetic and carefree in their representation of such feeling, but others used the Fairlight *not* to suggest it was necessarily the future of music, but in answer to accusations of inauthenticity and the absence of live performance.[13] The use of the Fairlight CMI was so controversial and divisive that it became the focus of a music industry backlash, particularly from the Musicians' Union, who feared the proliferation of such an instrument would destroy the livelihoods of musicians. Whilst the Fairlight CMI was not the first electronic instrument the Musicians' Union felt threatened by, it symbolized the proliferation of programmed – and programmable – digital music devices that threatened traditional modes of performativity. To that end, some musicians felt compelled to publicly confirm the *absence* of the instrument on their records. For example, Phil Collins's *No Jacket Required* (1985) featured the liner note 'There is no Fairlight on this record',[14] although this acknowledgement may have, at least in part, been due to Collins's former band mate Peter Gabriel's extensive use of the machine.

The Synclavier

> The 80s was a decade of seemingly limitless possibilities in electronic music and sound production. It was the decade of the Superstar, synthesisers, computers, the CD and decadence. Wall Street, The Yuppie, Dallas, Dynasty.
>
> Steve Hills[15]

Hills's commentary on 1980s tech-utopianism is particularly relevant to this chapter. In situating professional audio and music technological developments in the wider, excess-celebrating popular culture of the era, he recognizes the Synclavier – and other digital technologies – as aspirational and as a status symbol. The technological similarities between the Fairlight CMI and Synclavier ensured the two systems remained at the forefront of computer-based music production system design between 1978 and 1986. This did, however, result in tension between the two companies; NED, for example, accused Fairlight of 'gimmickery' in regard to its 'light pen' technology.[16]

Hills's conflation of 1980s technological development with then commercial symbols of economic power epitomizes the aspirational and inaccessible nature of some music and recording technologies of the era. Undoubtedly, the Synclavier[17] was one of the most technically advanced and prohibitively expensive music technologies of its time, positioning it beyond the reach of most musicians and recordists. A 1973 prototype named the 'Dartmouth Digital Synthesizer' could make 'beeps and whistles'[18] and was intended for hearing test applications, as well as electronic music composition. The Synclavier I was not fully realized until after the development of a further technology: a 16-bit processor card named the 'ABLE' computer. The 1975 'ABLE' became NED's first product; it sold mainly to university academics who used the sophisticated computerized system for data collection applications.[19] The Synclavier I consolidated both technologies – the original, Dartmouth synthesizer and the 'ABLE' processor – along with FM synthesis (on license from Yamaha) into a commercially viable product intended for musical applications. This early version featured a 16-channel keyboard-less synthesizer and 32-track digital sequencer: a pioneering design that caught the attention of musician Frank Zappa and recordist Mike Thorne.[20] However, the Synclavier II released in 1979 was widely recognized as the first music production workstation system: an 8-bit FM synthesizer accompanied by – and controlled from – a wooden keyboard (named 'ORK', from 'Original Keyboard') featuring military-specification controls and its trademark silver control wheel. Slightly later, it was possible to incorporate the DEC VT100 monitor terminal; for the first time, a *visual* as well as aural representation of musical patterns was realized. Mike Thorne was one of the first recordists to fully realize the potential of the Synclavier II. In programming the piano sound central to the musical arrangement of Soft Cell's 'Tainted Love' (1981),[21] along with two early Roland synthesizers, the commercial success of the single was undoubtedly a turning point in the sound of popular music.

The original Synclavier II came with 'factory' preset sounds,[22] many of which emulated traditional instruments used in classical, jazz and popular music. These sounds were originally presented as 'timbre banks' on floppy disks and could be controlled, operated and edited from the keyboard. Along with recognizable instrument sounds such as harpsichord, oboe, xylophone and drums, the Synclavier's presets also included timbre presets referring to musical genre (Funk 1–6, Disco, Honky Tonk), analogue synthesis (Sine, Triangle, Square) elements, including 'water' and 'wood', and even unclassified sounds, including 'music box', 'zap', 'gaggle of squeaks' and even 'weird sound'. Such presentation of sound sources blurred the lines between the specificities of acoustic and electronic instrument timbres, genre aesthetics, analogue synthesis, foley sound effects and emergent, unidentifiable sounds. The Synclavier II's development period intensified and an updated 'Sample-to-Disk' model was released in 1982; its groundbreaking disk-based sample-streaming system allowed for increasingly sophisticated editing and reshaping of sounds. The Synclavier II could be programmed with sampled sounds, adaptations of sounds and/or presets from its ORK keyboard. A popular preset was the percussive, hollow, synth-gong sound used as an introductory motif on Michael Jackson's 'Beat It' (1982) with other preset and adapted sounds heard throughout the *Thriller* (1982) album from which 'Beat It' derived.[23] Many Synclavier sounds formed atmospheric, as well as rhythmic, underpinnings to the popular music of the era. In Genesis' 'Mama', for example, we hear the Synclavier II's 'Strange Voices' preset lending the track a dark and ambient texture.[24] Conversely, programmer Keith Miller used the system to create a unique, groove-oriented, upbeat pop aesthetic throughout Culture Club's debut album, *Kissing to be Clever* (1982). Such music was indicative of large-budget, Anglo-American major label output at the turn of the decade, and the link between the Synclavier and such artists is certainly not coincidental. In 1984, the Synclavier dropped the 'II' and released its most technologically sophisticated model yet: the PSMT. This upgraded version featured a new, Velocity Pressure Keyboard ('VPK') and an upgraded, Model C ABLE processor, resulting in faster programming and what was the first hard-disk recording system. Additionally, the upgrade incorporated MIDI, enabling the control of multiple MIDI-compatible systems. It was this version that was used extensively throughout the 1990s across much commercial popular and rock music and was one of the most sonically distinctive sounding machines of its time. Nile Rogers, for example, programmed the Synclavier PSMT on Madonna's 'Material Girl' and 'Stay' from her *Like a Virgin* (1984) album. The Synclavier was also used to compose entire albums: Frank Zappa's *Francesco Zappa* (1984) was one such recording realized entirely on a Synclavier. Yet the instrument was not only used in predominantly electronic pop music. Paul Simon integrated the Synclavier on 'I Know What I Know' and 'Gumboots' – two tracks featured on the South African music-inspired *Graceland* (1986). These Synclavier-driven albums were some of the most sonically distinctive records of the decade; however, one record in particular came to epitomize the realization of the Synclavier, that of Eurythmics' *Savage* (1987). This record featured multiple instances of Synclavier production. Recordists Dave Stewart and Olle Romo incorporated pre-programmed sounds, further sounds that had been left on the machine by its previous owner Jack Nitzsche and sampled rhythmic sounds including 'banging on wooden tree stumps and young tall Bamboo in a Japanese forest', which were applied to tracks throughout the record.[25] Inevitably, the Synclavier became the main competitor to the Fairlight CMI, although by 1992 NED went into receivership and stopped producing technologies. At a cost of over $200,000 for a full hard-disk Synclavier II and monitor, the system was far beyond the reach of the vast majority of musicians. However, it was widely used in professional circles and became synonymous with the 1980s work of Prince and Michael Jackson.

A key record where the Synclavier features prominently is on Jackson's *Bad* (1987). Produced by Quincy Jones, engineered by Bruce Swedien and programmed by Christopher Currell, *Bad* represented the realization of almost an entire album created with one computer-based musical instrument. The Synclavier was, however, implemented in unusual ways to create distinct rhythmic patterns and notable musical motifs. For example, in pre-production stages, Currell programmed instrument patterns and grooves that would be presented to Jackson for selection. Once in the studio, musicians were appointed to recreate the rhythm and melodic lines with instruments. Jackson insisted he preferred the sounds of the Synclavier and as the recording sessions progressed, the Synclavier became the generator of the majority of the instrumentation.[26] Additionally, the Synclavier was used to sample sounds to be used as creative effects. A recording of Jackson's heartbeat was sampled into the Synclavier and used in the introduction to 'Smooth Criminal' (1987) (0.01–0.10). In 'Speed Demon', we hear a synthesized racing car shifting through gears and synchronized with the rhythm track (1.58–2.07). Here, the majority of musical, instrumental and foley elements were largely conceived, composed and produced via a single piece of technology. This then cutting-edge conceptualization was coupled with another recording innovation. The album implemented Bruce Swedien's 'Acusonic Recording Process' technique, as featured on Jackson's previous album *Thriller* (1982). Such terminology represented the tech-utopian discourse prevalent in the professional audio industry throughout the 1980s, but also indicated the desire of leading commercial recording artists to align themselves with the most cutting-edge recording and production techniques and the very highest fidelity recordings. Swedien's process did, however, mean little more than the synchronization of multiple analogue and/or digital tape recorders, as he explained:

> Acusonic Recording Process describes the way that I work with digital and analogue multi-track tape machines and SMPTE time code to generate a virtually unlimited number of recording tracks. Initially, I designed the system specifically for the projects that Quincey and I did together. It wasn't very long before I was using this system on every project.[27]

In the era before digital audio workstations, synchronizing multiple tape recorders was common practice and, therefore, it is difficult to attribute the 'invention' of this technique to Swedien alone. However, in naming the technique, not only did Swedien position himself at the forefront of tech-processual innovation but created a seemingly high-fidelity authentication that could be attached to his recordings: Jackson's *Bad* album featured the liner note: 'Recorded and mixed using the "Acusonic Recording Process".[28] This innovative coupling of the Synclavier and digital tape synchronization epitomizes working practice at the cutting edge of commercial record production in the 1980s.

Digital tape recorders

Early digital tape recorders were prohibitively expensive and as such rendered them the tools of a recording 'elite'. This section considers the introduction of such technologies to the recording workplace, referencing interview material from workplace owners and recordists of the time who frequented concomitant elite recording houses.

The introduction of digital tape recorders to the professional audio market was one of the most controversial developments of the decade. Initially, Sony's video-based PCM-1600 (1978) was one of the first 16-bit digital recorders. Using a U-Matic video cassette for storage and playback, this device was later updated to the 1610 and 1630 models that remained standard CD mastering machines into the twenty-first century. However, these machines were intended for broadcasting and mastering; the main digital tape recording systems used in professional studios were Mitsubishi's ProDigi and Sony's DASH machines.[29]

In 1980, Mitsubishi introduced the X-80 recorder, a reel-to-reel mastering machine in direct competition with Sony's PCM-1600. Later in 1982, Mitsubishi followed up with the X-800 ProDigi – a 32-track machine, which almost instantly became the leading digital tape recorder. This digital multitrack utilized 1" tape, supported splice editing and had a switchable sampling rate from 44.1 KHz to 48 KHz. It could be argued that in the ProDigi system, Mitsubishi initiated one of the key technological developments in the 1980s. However, coinciding with the ProDigi's release, and therefore in direct competition, Sony brought its multitrack DASH machines to the market in 1982. Available in 2-track, 24-track and 48-track models, the reel-to-reel machines ran on ½" tape (1/4" for the 2-track models) and – like the ProDigi – had changeable sampling rates from 44.1 KHz to 48 KHz. There were many similarities between the ProDigi and DASH, but by the mid to late 1980s, the DASH became the format of choice in many professional recording studios and by 1986, 300 machines had been sold worldwide.[30] It is important to note that both the DASH and ProDigi were digital audiotape (DAT) standards that were also adopted by other manufacturers. Studer, Matsushita and Teac adopted the DASH standard into its own digital recorders. Otari and AEG incorporated the ProDigi, thus creating a standardization divide in the professional audio industry. In fact, the divide was so entrenched that by the mid-1980s, *Billboard* magazine declared the 'digital format controversy [is] still in full bloom' and referred to a 'war' between 'Mitsubishi's ProDigi camp' and the 'Sony/Studer/Matsushita side'.[31] This points towards a technological 'arms race' of sorts present in the professional audio industry that was, to an extent, mirrored in the commercial music industry. I address this 'technological arms race' later, suffice to say that professional audio technological development was a highly competitive industry – as it had been since the 1960s. OMD (Orchestral Manoeuvres in the Dark) and New Order recordist Stephen Hague regularly used the Sony DASH 3324 machine throughout the 1980s. He suggested the digital recorders allowed for a more flexible recording approach than their analogue counterparts:

It was great for moving things around or for doing major structural edits. What's more, there was a rehearse mode on the master machine, whereby you could drop in to any or all tracks on the master machine from the offset slave machine, and preview the results without actually going into record. That way, if you wanted to adjust the in or out point of the drop-in onto the master machine, you could just nudge those parameters.[32]

As the next case study illustrates, these then cutting-edge devices presented multiple issues with workplace integration, data access time and synchronization. One record that epitomized technological and processual excess in the early 1980s was Dire Straits' *Brothers in Arms* (1985). Recorded at AIR Montserrat – George Martin's luxury recording studio built on the tiny Caribbean island – *Brothers in Arms* was recorded over a period of five months. This record would feature a number of technological 'firsts': the first commercially released recording to have been recorded to digital multitrack tape; one of the first commercially released compact discs (CD); and the first release to feature the 'DDD' SPARS code.[33] Such digital aesthetics are bound up in the music of the record. In 'Money for Nothing', for example, a sharp, glossy overall tonality is imbued in the recording, the result of multiple stages of digital recording, mixing, mastering and production. At over eight minutes long and featuring Sting (another regular AIR Montserrat recording artist), 'Money for Nothing' is a lengthy, progressive rock-inspired track featuring a maximized stereo field and wide dynamic range, particularly in the introduction, which takes more than two minutes to fade in against a sparse, synthesis-laden background; this particularly long introduction, slowly increasing in volume, mirrored CD's heightened dynamic range. However, recording sessions were fraught with difficulties, particularly surrounding the digital tape recorders. AIR Montserrat technical manager Malcolm Atkin described his first encounter with a Sony DASH machine as recording sessions began for Dire Straits' *Brothers in Arms*:

> AIR did *Brothers in Arms* by Dire Straits. We did it in Montserrat. I got a call from Damage Management saying, 'Can you go down and see the band? Sony have thrown this digital tape machine at them and they want to record with it.' I didn't know anything about digital – nobody knew anything about digital! It was a hand-made machine. Looked amazing. We took it to Montserrat. It died about 3 weeks in. It threw a complete wobbler. I took all the flack for it and they had to fly to New York where the only other digital machine on the planet was and they had to transfer the tapes onto that machine then bring it to the West Indies to finish the album. You couldn't do anything to it as you'd do with an analogue tape machine. Don't even think about touching the azimuth! Don't go there! For the first time ever, a tech team on site didn't know what it was doing and didn't have the tools, the machinery or the knowledge to service this thing.[34]

Atkin cites a number of key points: the pressure placed on globally successful commercial recording artists to adopt the latest technologies, the pressure on elite recording houses to buy into such systems and subsequent disruption (and undoubtedly substantial cost increases) to the recording process. Atkin's comments also point towards a loss of control over technological change. Whilst the Sony DASH multitrack recorder looked and behaved similar to an analogue tape machine, its technological, operational and storage features were altogether different. This greatly impacted on the professional industry's maintenance tools and personnel skill sets of the era, leading to a shift in both technological application and recording and production roles. Former BBC and AIR Montserrat maintenance engineer Steve Culnane worked as a professional audio maintenance engineer before, during and after this era:

> During the 1980s, it was an extremely exciting time for digital audio, but also an extremely frustrating time for anyone who was around at the time. Now, I've got a Prism analyser and I can look at the jitter, the word clock. I've got scopes that can look at the data rates. [In the 1980s] I couldn't even see the data rate on the scope we had at Tape 1 [AIR studios]. You were literally out in the dark. You ended up with a load of in-built aural tools to try to work out what the hell was going on, because you couldn't quantify anything, you couldn't measure anything. There was nobody to phone up. Neve would say it was a problem with the Sony, Sony said it was a problem with the Neve.[35]

This uncertainty and lack of understanding surrounding the operation of digital audio systems is corroborated by Melvyn Toms, a senior maintenance engineer at Abbey Road Studios, throughout the 1970s and 1980s:

> We knew what we were dealing with, with analogue stuff and we could hear it. We could test for distortion and there were distortion analysers, phase checking systems, we could look at analogue waveforms and test them. You couldn't do that with digital unless the equipment manufacturers – like the Sony's and JVC's of this world – built it into their systems for you. And a lot of the time, they didn't. That was the crux of what we were dealing with as technical engineers, we couldn't actually prove what we were hearing and that's where this big black area came about with the questionability of digital sound.[36]

Toms cites the inability to analyse at a digital signal as being the catalyst leading to questions surrounding digital audio as a medium. Audio industry personnel and their attitudes towards technologies are examined later on, but the initial problematic nature of integrating and maintaining early pieces of digital equipment quite possibly led to wider scepticism.

By the end of the 1980s, DASH and ProDigi were the digital tape recorders of choice in the professional industry. Such machines retailed at over $150,000 each and stayed within the professional audio industry's realm, but the development of budget digital audio recorders was on the horizon. The Sony PCM-501ES, for example, released in 1984 was one of the first semi-professional, 16-bit digital audio recorders that, priced in the range of $900, was one of the first accessible digital audio recorders.

One of the key benefits of digital tape recorders was the expanded high frequency range and perceived hi-fidelity. Compared to analogue tape, digital tape recorders were more robust in that they eliminated generation loss and brought a 'sharp', 'clean' clarity to recordings not heard prior to their induction. To that end, it is unsurprising that digital tape recorders were most popular with high-profile pop music recordists and recording workplaces: Gregg Rubin (Harry Connick Jr) Giorgio Moroder (Donna Summer, Phil Oakey, Berlin), Phil Ramone (Frank Sinatra, Billy Joel) and Frank Zappa were just a few recordists who pioneered the implementation of the Sony DASH recorder. Nile Rogers used it to notable effect throughout the recording of Madonna's *Like a Virgin* (1985) in the synergized programmed and performed elements. I consider the work of SAW later on, suffice to say that they were one of the first production teams to incorporate multiple digital tape recorders in their workplace. Despite the elite recording industry take-up, due to the prohibitive cost – some machines cost in the range of $150,000 – only 300 machines were in operation during the late 1980s. Once again, this demonstrates the exclusivity of high-end, professional digital recording of the era. Digital tape recording was a minority sport, accessible to an elite group of recordists and recording workplaces. Interestingly, despite being superseded by the late 1990s by hard disk recorders, a number of recordists and workplaces continued to use digital tape machines long into the 2000s. For example, brothers Chris Lord-Alge[37] and Tom Lord-Alge[38] both used a 48-channel Sony DASH machine for more than two decades. Sony ceased manufacturing digital audiotape in 2007, and therefore by the 2010s, the DASH format was used by a minority of recordists.

Digital effects processors

The sound of 1980s commercial popular music featured prominent use of then cutting-edge digital effects processors. Indeed, many artists of the era used such emergent devices to such a degree that they became part of the 'signature' sound. This can be heard to notable effect on Joy Division's *Unknown Pleasures* (1979), Siouxsie and the Banshees' *Hyaena* (1984) and The Cure's *Disintegration* (1989). These albums are three such examples whereby the main sonic trope was a heavy, reverberant soundscape. Development of digital effects processors began in the 1970s, during a time when reverbs were created either with natural room ambience or plates, such as EMT plate reverbs. Indeed the prevalence of such constructed reverbs proliferated further into the 1980s, moving far beyond what Peter Doyle referred to as the 'fabrication of space'[39] and by the 1990s into the realm of surrealism.[40]

Glossy, expensive and digital, these systems quickly became status symbols in the professional audio recording domain. For example, during the 1980s US industry publication *Billboard* published a bi-weekly segment titled 'Sound Investment', detailing professional recording houses' most recent equipment acquisitions. Almost every week from 1982 onwards, a high-end workplace acquired either a Lexicon 224X or 224XL, Eventide Harmonizer or AMS RMX-16

Digital Reverberator. Whilst there were many other systems available throughout the 1980s and into the 1990s, the aforementioned three were key then cutting-edge digital processors used prolifically throughout commercial music production of the era. Whilst they were often used in conjunction, the individual machines – and the specificities of their presets – became signature tropes in contemporary record production.

Developed by Antony Agnello for US company Eventide, the 910 Harmonizer was one of the first digital effects processors brought to the sound recording market in 1975. Its two main features – delay and pitch shifter – were predominantly used on vocals and drums. By today's standards, the Harmonizer was primitive, featuring just four delay time settings and one semi-tone of pitch shift capability. As the Harmonizer was not widely available during the late 1970s, it remained a tool of an elite guild of recordists. Tony Visconti was one such recordist, who used it to dramatic effect on David Bowie's *Low* (1977), amongst other recordings. In late 1977, this was a unique sound; upon listening to his recordings, Visconti's peer group could not understand how such effects had been achieved, as he stated:

> It was a radical sound, especially on the drums. I had the second Harmonizer in Europe and I guessed it would be a matter of time before other producers figured out what I was doing. But when the album (*Low*) came out the Harmonizer still wasn't widely available. I had loads of producers phoning me and asking what I had done, but I wouldn't tell them. I've heard hundreds of 'Low sounds' on other records since.[41]

The Harmonizer can be heard on other, elite recordist/workplace-made records of the late 1970s, including Sex Pistols' *Never Mind the Bollocks …* (1977), where it is the most audible delay on 'Sub Mission',[42] and AC/DC's *Back in Black* (1980), where recordist Tony Platt used the Harmonizer to 'fatten up the sound' by feeding 'a gated snare signal into an H910 detuned to about 93 with the feedback and anti feedback up'.[43]

However, despite being used in such innovative ways on classic rock records of the late 1970s, the Eventide Harmonizer did not proliferate until well into the 1980s, largely because the cost of the device prevented widespread adoption. One of the most recognizable uses of the Harmonizer came in 1983 during the recording of Duran Duran's *Seven and the Ragged Tiger* (1983), also recorded at AIR Montserrat. On this record, the pitch-shifting component of the Harmonizer was used to extraordinary effect across Simon Le Bon's vocals, exaggerating the nasal-like delivery and creating a dehumanizing effect. The pitch shifter created a signal shifted up to a semi-tone higher or lower that when combined with the original signal resulted in a slightly robotic, 'phasing' type effect. This effect is foregrounded in 'The Reflex' (1984), one of the biggest-selling commercially released singles of 1984. Le Bon was renowned for being a 'character' vocalist as opposed to a technical singer; recordists Ian Little and Alan Sadkin initially used the Harmonizer's pitch-shifting capability to mask Le Bon's out-of-tune performances, as Little stated:

He is not a naturally gifted singer, and ... he doesn't have great pitch. It's not unusual for him to sing out of tune, so when I worked with him we would use quite a lot of effects on his voice; mainly Eventide Harmonizer with a very small percentage pitch-shift up or down or both, in addition to the normal step delays and reverbs and possibly even some chorus. Remember, these were the days before *Auto-Tune*. By making the pitch ambiguous, the Harmonizer helped disguise the fact that his singing was flat.[44]

Whilst the intention here was to mask less than optimum performances, Little and Sadkin did more than simply correct performance 'mistakes'. In 'The Reflex', they constructed an innovative, instantly recognizable 'voice' for Le Bon, resulting in one of the most sonically distinctive vocal recordings of the era. Subsequently, the Harmonizer would be the catalyst for pitch-shifting devices throughout the 1980s and 1990s, ultimately resulting in the development of the Antares Autotune by 1997. Eventide's Harmonizer was, however, one of the most revolutionary digital technologies and preceded the Antares by more than two decades.

In 1978, Lexicon – a US effects processor manufacturer – released its 224 digital reverb unit. The device was unique: small, white, with a 'miniature mixing console'-like appearance and red digital display. The reverb settings quickly became integrated into the pantheon of fabricated acoustic spaces: chambers, rooms, concert halls and plates were the 224's main simulators in a compact, easy to use system that was regularly pictured sitting atop consoles in 1980s recording session photographs. At almost $8,000 it became an essential piece of 'outboard' equipment in many professional recording studios throughout the 1980s. Lexicon updated the 224 in 1986 with the 480L, one of the most widely used digital effects processors in the professional industry, which cost upwards of $10,000. The 'Lexicon sound' is believed to be heard on 'more than 80 percent of the world's most successful music albums'.[45] The 224 was used prolifically throughout the 1980s, perhaps most notably on U2's *The Unforgettable Fire* (1984). Here, recordists Brian Eno and Daniel Lanois created a heavy, lush sonic soundscape from a Lexicon 224 Hall setting, using auxiliary returns on the console to foreground the reverb channels. This is most notable on '4th of July' where the seemingly endless reverberant tails on the organ create a vast soundscape with depth of field rarely heard before.

Whilst the Lexicon 224 was renowned for its use in classic pop and rock records of the 1980s, one of its most innovative applications was on Frank Zappa's recordings of the London Symphony Orchestra in 1983. The LSO performed many of Zappa's compositions, including 'Sad Jane', 'Pedro's Dowry' and 'Envelopes'. Historically, orchestras are recorded live in concert halls; the recording is a transparent 'true' capture of that performance with its nuances, audience coughs and footsteps intact. On this occasion, Zappa recorded the LSO at the Twickenham Film Studios, an acoustically 'dead' space. Additionally, this would be the very first recording of an orchestra to multitrack digital tape. Zappa attempted to 'close mic' each instrument separately, using hyper-cardioid microphones to separate each instrument out and avoid overspill. However, despite this attempt and unsatisfied with the result, Zappa positioned sheets of plexiglass between parts of the orchestra in order to obtain as much separation as possible. His treatment of the orchestral recordings at mix stage was particularly innovative, considering that technological intervention in classical recordings was, at the time, uncommon outside of avant-garde composition, although it is important to acknowledge the influence of such music and recording techniques on Zappa's work. Featuring hundreds of edits and multiple fabrications of acoustic space, *The London Symphony Orchestra: Zappa Vol. 1* is an entirely constructed and unorthodox classical music recording. This construction of sonic spaces is particularly audible on 'Strictly Genteel' where the instruments are bright, separated and lack the cohesion of classical orchestral recordings. This creation of separate spaces was achieved via the application of different presets on the Lexicon 224XL; the percussion in particular is foregrounded in an altogether different space, as Zappa stated:

> When we mixed it [LSO], as partial compensation for the ugliness of the room, we decided that each section in the music would be treated as a different 'SCENE', and that each 'SCENE' could occur in any kind of imaginary ambience that was appropriate to its mood (sort of like stage lighting). At this point the DEAD ROOM became a blessing in disguise – we could go from scratch, building 'artificial acoustics' with digital impunity. So, a collection of imaginary environments was created with a Lexicon 224-X[L] [*sic*] digital reverb processor. Each imaginary world had a different set of characteristics. We mixed each section of the music as if it had occurred in its own personalized acoustical space.[46]

As Lexicon effects proliferated, the industry also adopted AMS systems at the high end. Widely regarded as the first microprocessor-controlled digital delay line, AMS released the DMX 15-80 model in 1980. The unit, a rack-mountable sized system with 90 dB of dynamic range proved extremely popular, particularly when later 1980s models included sample and trigger functionality. AMS reverbs were the main competitors to the Lexicons and by the mid-1980s the two most commonly used reverb units were the AMS RMX-16 Digital Reverberator and the Lexicon 224.

The AMS RMX-16 featured a calculator-style interface with nine preset reverb programs stored in the system: Ambience, Room A1, Hall C1, Plate, Hall B3, Chorus, Echo, Nonlin (non-linear) and Reverse. Like the Harmonizer, the RMX-16 was often used on drums and vocals. Perhaps the most recognizable – and well documented – use of the system is heard on Phil Collins's 'In the Air Tonight' (1981) whereby the 'Nonlin' patch can be heard on the toms, even though the drum recording was largely a result of recordist Hugh Padgham's manipulation of ambient microphone recording techniques and the talkback control on the then cutting-edge SSL 4000 mixing console.[47] The RMX-16 was also used on Prince's 'Kiss' (1986), where the 'reverse' patch is applied to the kick drum. So recognizable was this effect that in a rereleased plug-in version of the AMS RMX-16, a preset was entitled 'Kiss Kick'.[48]

Whilst the RMX-16 could be heard on many classic pop and rock records of the era, it was also embraced by UK post-punk, indie and alternative genres, particularly in the creation of excessive, seemingly endless reverberant soundscapes. Widely acknowledged[49] is the use of reverb to create isolated, sometimes cavernous spaces to allude to social isolation. In *White Boys, White Noise*, Bannister comments on the use of excessive reverb generally in the context of 1980s indie and emergent 'shoegaze' artists, 'Jangle and drone plus reverberation create a contemporary equivalent of Spector's "wall of sound" – a massive, ringing, cavernous noise … '.[50] This very trope can be heard throughout key records at the turn of the 1990s, including Ride's *Nowhere* (1990), My Bloody Valentine's *Loveless* (1991) and Lush's *Spooky* (1992).

The positioning of instruments amongst large, fabricated, reverberant sound stages was arguably pioneered by Martin Hannett and his use of both the AMS RMX-16 and AMS DMX-1580 delay line, particularly on the music of Joy Division. Having just purchased the DMX-1580 in 1978, Hannett took it to Cargo Studios in Rochdale to use with the then unknown Joy Division on their first record. In fact, the application of these then brand new effects on the band's music was so prominent, the band named one of their earliest songs 'Digital' (1978)[51] in recognition of the sound of the processor. Hannett's constructed spaces for Joy Division resulted in such a distinctive sonic trope that multiple alternative artists emulated it throughout the 1980s. For example, John Loder used the AMS RMX-16 to construct 'cavernous' spaces for the Jesus and Mary Chain; the brittle, yet distant ambient constructions are heard throughout *Psychocandy* (1985),[52] but particularly on the single 'Just Like Honey' (1985). Even at the turn of the 1990s, the RMX-16 was being used to create dark, industrial-rock soundscapes. This is particularly audible on records such as Nine Inch Nails' 'Something I Can Never Have' (*Pretty Hate Machine*, 1990), where the RMX has been used to create an ambient sound stage for the entire track.

However, simultaneously a comparatively budget digital effects processor emerged as an unlikely but direct competitor. Yamaha's SPX-90 (1985) was another key development in the digital effects processing market. Incorporating both time-based and dynamics-based effects processing, the SPX-90 was – and still is – regarded as a classic system in professional studios, despite the substantially lower cost than the Lexicon or AMS.

Summary

Having considered some of the groundbreaking technological development at the turn of the 1980s, we start to understand why it was such a critical turning point in music technology – as well as popular music – history. Until the mid-1970s, commercial sound recordings presented us with representations of human performances on acoustic and electronic instruments. Yes, until then we had been used to hearing the 'presence' of technology, particularly artificial reverberation, the use of tape editing and effects, such as echo chambers and plate reverbs, as well as early analogue synthesis. And in many avant-garde influenced recordings, that technological presence was certainly exaggerated. The difference between pre- and post-late 1970s commercial popular music is the presence of computer microprocessors in digital processors and digital synthesis, programmed sound effects, samples and synthesized representations of acoustic instruments.

Evidence of computerized technologies (a) applied to the compositional process and (b) aurally prominent and discernible in popular music recordings for the first time placed machines in the very foreground of popular music recordings. To that end, the 1980s witnessed the 'foregrounding' of machines, preset and programmed instrument sounds and fabricated environments like no other decade before it. With every passing year, new sounds and effects made their way into workplaces and recordist practices thus generating an altogether new pantheon of tools and techniques.

It is, therefore, perhaps not surprising such rapid technological development was met with delight as to the potential of it, as well as scepticism surrounding the implications for traditional music and musicians, as well as recording processes. This is discussed to a greater degree in Chapter 6, suffice to say not all workplaces and recordists embraced these new systems as may have been implied through the discussion of technologies in this chapter.

One criticism of 1980s commercial popular music was its similarity;[53] whilst the systems featured in this chapter existed in few numbers – 300 Sony multitrack DASH machines and around 300 Fairlight CMIs were manufactured – their presence in elite recording houses ensured they would be encountered by a regular stream of high-profile artists and recordists with large recording budgets. Long into the 1980s, high-end music technology users could still influence the future direction of products. For example, the Synclavier's updates were based on existing user feedback. This also reinforces the existence of an 'elite' industry: those with these expensive and, therefore, exclusive tools of the trade ensured they were only accessible to the very highest profile artists. It is unsurprising, then, that the Fairlight, Synclavier, digital tape and digital effects processors featured across Michael Jackson, Dire Straits and Madonna records: these were three of the biggest selling commercial recording artists of the decade. The next chapter considers music and sound recording technologies as they headed into the 1990s, as well as applications of what were considered by then 'precursors' and the effects of technological iconicity.

2

The Sound of Technology: Machines and Formats That Transformed Mid–Late 1980s Popular Music

In this chapter, significant music recording and production technologies in the mid-late 1980s are identified and situated in the context of commercial record releases on which they feature. Here, the focus is on mixing consoles, then new music technologies including MIDI devices, as well as the proliferation of digital formats. The technological landscape in which mid-late 1980s records were made is particularly fascinating: commercially successful records of the era were not all made using the then latest technologies nor did commercial record production comfortably align with the rate of technological development. Additionally, largely self-produced records from emergent dance and hip-hop artists began to compete with the output of the established commercial record industry. In certain markets, music technology manufacturers were not only the companies behind such new musical devices; by the mid-1980s they became *brands*. The ubiquity of drum machines, such as E-Mu's SP-1200, Roger Linn's LinnDrum and AKAI MPC, as well as samplers such as AKAI's S-900 and E-Mu's Emulator II, resulted in some of the most recognizable commercial music of the decade. Furthermore, the accessibility of such devices redrew the boundaries of the recording workplace, as well as redefined recording and production roles. Indeed, the impact of MIDI, samplers, sequencers and digital synthesis was profound,[1] yet such cutting-edge technological systems were not implemented across the board: plenty of examples of resistance and tension are found amongst both recordists and workplaces. Starting with the high-end consoles in widespread use throughout the decade, moving through drum machines, MIDI and computer-based software sequencers, this chapter considers the technologies that impacted so dramatically on the recording and production workplace, role and popular music of the era and beyond.

Consoles

From the late 1970s and throughout the 1980s, SSL and Neve became the two major console manufacturers that dominated the professional market.[2] This technological rivalry overshadowed the 1970s companies MCI and Cadac and brought console development to a whole new level with 'in-line' models, increased channels, on-board processing and computer-assisted memory. As a result, MCI suffered and was quickly bought out by Sony in 1982, rendering its JH-600 console a 'vintage' piece by the mid-1980s. Dave Harrison of the Nashville, US-based Harrison consoles was instrumental in designing the 'in-line' models that were the precedent to the later large-scale Neves and SSLs.[3] The SSL 4000 E-Series (1981) brought 'total recall' into the professional recording domain.[4] This feature enabled mix engineers to save mixes and recall them via an on-board computer, thus eliminating the reliance on human memory or indeed channel strip notes jotted on pieces of paper. The console was updated with the G-series in 1989; however, SSL did not release fully automated consoles until 1991 with their 8000-G model. In the 1980s, developments in console technology impacted significantly on artists, engineers, producers and studio personnel. Neve's position in the 1970s as professional console suppliers was further secured with its development of the 'AIR Montserrat Desk', based on its highly successful 1970s model, the '804812'. This custom-built, 56-channel professional console was initially specified by George Martin and installed in AIR studios Montserrat during 1979 and was used prolifically throughout the 1980s.[5] Only three were ever made and the 100 KHz frequency response arguably set a new precedent for console manufacturing. Neve then released the V-Series console line in 1985, which proved the main rival to the SSL-4000. However, Neve was instrumental in developing some of the key console technologies of the era. Necam (Neve Computer Assisted Mixdown) set a moving fader, automation standard that SSL would later capitalize on. In the 1980s, APRS (Association of Professional Recording Services) chairman Malcolm Atkin and former EMI Abbey Road engineer Dave Harries both worked at the UK's most renowned recording facilities including AIR Lyndhurst and AIR Montserrat. Both recall a time when Neve and SSL – and their concomitant functionalities – dominated both the recording workplace and the sphere of recording practice generally. Malcolm Atkin illustrates the difference between Neve and SSL consoles as perceived by the recording industry, 'The pros saw Neve's for recording, because of the headroom and SSL's for mixing. The two companies spent decades trying to move their company image.'[6] The SSL console became a high-end recording brand by the early 1980s, the name becoming so renowned to the point where it would be demanded on sessions, even by those who had no idea what it did. Former AIR and current British Grove studio manager Dave Harries explains:

> The 'must have' by the end of the 1980s was an SSL. We used to have people at record companies phoning up saying 'have you got an SSL?' but they didn't know what it meant. So if you didn't have one, they wouldn't book you. Because it was the first desk that let you have a true, proper recall. What they forgot about was that there was loads of outboard gear mixed into it that didn't have recall.[7]

Malcolm Atkin goes on to explain how the functionality of the SSL in being able to recall a mix in order to change it was an attractive prospect to A&R personnel who wanted to make amendments once the mix had been completed:

> Total recall. Studios loved it! Why? Because we could make more money out of it. It meant the A&R man could have some power back, or he thought he could have

some power back. 'I love the mix boys, but can you just change such-and-such'. What he didn't realise, was that we had to charge another hour's studio time. What he didn't realise, was it was only doing it on the desk. What he didn't realise, was that all the outboard gear was not doing it. It went on for years and years that trick. I don't think A&R men did clock that we were laughing all the way into our sleeves the whole time.[8]

Atkin highlights the financial benefit to the studio if a mix took longer because of recalls. He may well have been laughing, but Steve Culnane points out the pressure placed on studios that didn't have a 'recall' console:

From a studio owner's point of view, the SSL recall system was extremely and deservedly controversial, mainly because the A&R departments were willing to accept anything. You could take two SSL's and within a year they would sound completely different, depending on how much care had been taken over them. But the A&R departments believed it and they then put pressure on owners of other desks, like Neve and MCI, that they wouldn't get the work because they didn't have an SSL and they didn't have recall. The way they were embraced by A&R departments was extremely ignorant on their part.[9]

The sonic characteristics particular to Neve, MCI and SSL consoles may well have been subjective and attributable to individual preference, but consoles remained a recording facility's biggest and most important purchase. It is unsurprising that the console, as big and imposing – even intimidating – as it was, became the central focus of the studio during the 1980s. Former EMI Abbey Road maintenance engineer Melvyn Toms acknowledged the importance of console choice, as he stated:

The choice of console was extremely important. Not only the functionality of it, the size of it, the manageability of it, the sound of it, but it would also determine to a certain extent what artists you would get through the studio doors. We started to find out that some artists, producers and engineers would not work on a SSL or they would not work on a Neve. Therefore, you had to choose a console, not just on technical reasons. It was perception and it was the most expensive part of the studio.[10]

Toms makes a vital point in that console choice was often made on matters of perception and industry fashion as opposed to sonic quality. This substantiates the points made by Atkin, Harries and Culnane, in that during the 1980s the SSL console became a brand.

A good example of 1980s large-scale mixing console production is Robert 'Mutt' Lange's work on Def Leppard's *Hysteria* (1987). Here, the potential of increased console functionality, such as the introduction of gating on each channel and multiple routing and processing features, was fully realized, resulting in the musical foregrounding of technological intervention as never heard before. Def Leppard, a UK rock band originating from Sheffield, featured five musicians: a vocalist, two guitarists, a bassist and a drummer, yet dozens of vocal tracks and guitar motifs are heard throughout, suggesting multiple overdubs and extensive multitracking. This is particularly audible on the single 'Animal' (1987), as drummer Rick Savage pointed out: 'We'd take what we recorded in the first verse [guitars] and fly it in to the second verse. There's nobody playing the song all the way through.'[11] A key feature of the track is the vocals, particularly in the chorus (0.48); the lead is tightly compressed, de-essed and edited of breaths, pops or any other performance nuances and then double-tracked. Further, group harmonizing backing vocals are positioned at the extremities of the stereo field. The resulting vocals feature such heavy processing that they are dehumanized, sounding almost entirely electronic. The use of editing, overdubs and panning is brought to the fore in the second verse (1.20). Multiple guitars including lead guitar lines, e-bowed guitars, semi-acoustic strummed chords and single 'dive-bomb' notes have been panned around the stereo field, creating an expanse sonic canvas. Due to drummer Rick Allen suffering an arm injury resulting in an amputation prior to the recording sessions, most of the drums on *Hysteria* were programmed from a Fairlight CMI, resulting in a record that was entirely constructed from instrument programming and performance snippets, as opposed to performances from start to end. Long before the era of DAWs and processors such as Autotune, this record demonstrated the potential of technological intervention on recorded music to such an extent that it resulted in the proliferation of the term 'overproduction'.[12]

The LinnDrum machine

Another important 1980s development was the advent of the drum machine, in particular, models manufactured by Roger Linn, as Mark Vail points out:

> In this day of 16- to 24-bit arrogance, mention the word 'great' in reference to an 8-bit device and you're bound to raise a few cynical eyebrows. But if it weren't for an 8-bit marvel known as the Linn LM-1 – with which Roger Linn introduced a number of drum machine features taken for granted today – it might have taken us a lot longer to reach this enlightened age of the digital drum machine.[13]

The ubiquity of the first LM-1 machine amongst commercial record production was such that it defined the sonic character of chart pop music of the decade. The 8-bit Linn LM-1 featured a rounded, yet hollow and 'airy' kick drum pad, as well as a sharp, whip-like, reductive snare drum pad. This combination featured across many hit pop records of the early 1980s, including Prince's *1999* (1982), Madonna's *Madonna* (1983) and Michael Jackson's *Thriller* (1982); the latter album features a particularly prominent LM-1 pattern underpinning the single 'Wanna be Startin' Something' (1983). Subsequently, LinnDrum machine sounds were associated to the commercial success of the most popular, prolific and materially successful US artists and were, therefore, an aspirational instrument in then current music production. As the instrument proliferated, the drum machine's sounds were foregrounded in mixes to unusual degrees. The sound of the

LinnDrum machine can be traced throughout the early to mid-1980s, but the sound became increasingly foregrounded as the decade progressed. For example, on the work of both Phil Collins and Genesis throughout the 1980s, the updated LinnDrum (LM-2) is particularly prominent throughout *Genesis* (1983), *No Jacket Required* (1985) and *Invisible Touch* (1986). The emphasized drum programming created a particular sonic signature for Genesis and Collins's 1980s work and gave them the means of assimilating their established 1970s progressive rock into the broader sonic canvas of commercial 1980s pop. Another example of a particularly prominent LinnDrum sequence is heard on the single 'Human' taken from Human League's *Crash* (1986). This track features a LinnDrum sequence positioned louder in the mix than Phil Oakey's lead vocal and panned to such an extent that it is the feature instrument.

Indeed, the LinnDrum machine was an exclusive instrument: there were only 500 LM-1 (1980) drum machines initially made by Linn, but it was to be the updated LinnDrum machine (1982) with many more cymbal patterns and changeable sound chips that became one of the defining music technologies of the decade. The final Linn product, the Linn9000 (1984), featured a full multitrack MIDI sequencer. Only 1,000 were produced and, possibly due to large amount of competition from other synthesizer manufacturers, Linn dissolved as a company in 1986. At over $7,000 for a Linn9000, the drum machines were again only accessible to the professional industry. David Mellor remembers such inaccessible price points, as he points out:

> The Fairlight was fiendishly expensive, the Synclavier was fiendishly expensive, the Emulator was only hugely expensive, but they were way, way out of reach of the small scale operator. You'd know of all this stuff going on at the high end like Trevor Horn producing Frankie Goes To Hollywood and making a whole record without using tape. You'd be aware of those things going on and think 'I want to get on that bandwagon.'[14]

As previously described by Synclavier technician Steve Hills,[15] Mellor's comments exemplify the aspirational nature of such technologies and the competitive nature of technological ownership. The aforementioned LinnDrum examples all feature similar sonic qualities: the rhythm patterns are foregrounded in the mix; the beats are used as both foundation sequences and sonic motifs; they are often used in conjunction with particularly glossy vocal productions and other synthesized instruments. To that end, the resulting sound is an electronic, dehumanized (ironic in the case of The Human League), entirely constructed form of pop music featuring minimal natural performance.

MIDI: Synthesizers, samplers, sequencers

One of the first major digital technology developments, announced in 1982 by Sequential Circuits and Roland, was the MIDI protocol. The Musical Instrument Digital Interface was a digital data connection device, enabling multiple systems to be connected together in order to communicate as part of the same set-up. With one MIDI unit acting as a 'controller' with the facility for up to 16 'slave' devices, this universal digital bus gave the user previously inconceivable options. When a MIDI-compatible synthesizer was connected to a sequencer, multiple patterns or sequences of musical data could be programmed without the need for continual playing and, quite controversially, without the necessary need for musical ability. This development had many consequences: firstly, both musical and recording systems could be integrated as one set-up, in a small space, with a relatively small budget; secondly, MIDI sequences could be programmed one note at a time, meaning that a user could potentially recreate a symphony without having any playing ability; and thirdly, the system was universal, appearing as standard on many synthesizer, sampler and sequencer manufacturers' systems by the mid-1980s. Indeed, this combination of musical and programming capability was a key factor in MIDI's success.

By the mid-1980s, Japanese companies Roland, Yamaha, Korg and AKAI were four significant manufacturers producing a range of MIDI-compatible items including samplers, synthesizers, keyboards and sound modules. Many accessories accompanied the main devices, including interfaces, 'thru' units, cables and sound modules. Alesis concentrated on producing drum machines and cheap effects processors along with other companies such as Evolution Synthesis. Significant technologies included the Roland TR-909, the company's first venture into a MIDI-compatible rhythm composer, based on the earlier TR-808. This programmable drum machine was a more affordable and therefore accessible system than the Linn. Indeed, MIDI ports became essential connectors on synthesizers and whilst MIDI systems were not recording technologies per se, their integration with samplers and sequencers positioned them more centrally in the recording process. Interestingly, the MIDI-less TR-808 grew popular long after manufacturing ceased and became an essential tool in early house and hip-hop programming through the late 1980s and beyond and one of the only non-MIDI devices to increase in popularity through the decade.

Aside from drum machines, the 1980s was perhaps most synonymous with digital synthesizers. Models such as Yamaha's DX-7 (1983), Roland's Juno-106 (1984) and D-50 (1987), Ensoniq's Mirage (1984) and later, Korg's M1 (1988) were used extensively in the pop, dance and hip-hop genres by musicians and producers alike. However, despite the decade's music being dominated by the sounds of digital synthesizers, arguably the most significant technological development of the 1980s was the sampler, as Coleman suggested:

> AKAI made sampling accessible to the average musician, offering short memory on affordable machines such as the iconic AKAI S-1100 sampler. These machines empowered an entire wave of British pop in the 1980s, not to mention American R&B.[16]

Building on the bulky, cumbersome and low-memory Fairlight CMI, many samplers were manufactured – both at the high-end and budget markets – as more compact devices. Samplers were also convenient and portable, with streamlined interfaces and MIDI capabilities, not to mention cheaper. Before AKAI's domination of the market, one of the first such systems was E-Mu's Emulator (1981), a floppy disk-based sampler.

One of the most significant hit records of the decade was made using an Emulator, that of Paul Hardcastle's '19' (1985). Well over a decade on from Jimi Hendrix and Jim Morrison's Vietnam War protest songs, Hardcastle flipped the discourse on its head and brought the issue of post-traumatic stress disorder amongst war veterans to the fore. Composed using the E-Mu Emulator II, the track is a collage of blended material, sampled narration from the 1984 documentary *Vietnam Requiem*, including interview excerpts from war veterans, as well as sampled crowd noise.[17] The use of repetitive sample-triggering on the word '19' was a means of emphasis, not only to reinforce the average age of US soldiers in the Vietnam War but to highlight the lengthy remainder of these soldiers' lives spent living with post-traumatic stress disorder. The impact was multifaceted: Hardcastle spoke of Vietnam veterans sending letters of their experiences and thanks for raising awareness of their predicament. '19' was one of the only sample-based compositions to win an Ivor Novello award for songwriting and despite being composed from almost 100 per cent prerecorded material, the 'n-n-n-n-nineteen' hook created from sampler triggering was a feature motif that became assimilated into the broader sampling technique toolbox.

The Emulator II was manufactured in 1984, this time fully MIDI-compatible and with an additional hard disk option. The Emulator II would prove one of the most prolifically used and recognizable technologies throughout early to mid-1980s pop and was often used in conjunction with the LinnDrum machine. The Emulator II featured multiple interchangeable disks containing sound banks of sampled instruments including brass, drums and piano. One of the most famous disks was 'Marcato Strings', a large, string ensemble sound that captivated musicians and recordists working in mainstream popular music. Like the LinnDrum kick and snare sounds, the Emulator II's Marcato Strings proliferated amongst chart music of the era and are notably featured on some of the most recognizable tracks of the era, including Pet Shop Boys' 'West End Girls' (1985), which was constructed almost entirely from Emulator II patches, and INXS' 'Never Tear Us Apart' (1988), which featured a prominent 'Marcato' string motif, foregrounded at the song's introduction.

Despite the success of the Emulator II, the company began to fall behind in the sampler market by the end of the 1980s, mainly due to the rapid development of AKAI's S-series samplers. In 1985, AKAI released its 12-bit S-900, a compact, rack-mountable sampler with floppy disk drive and integrated MIDI ports. The following S-1000 (1988) and S-1100 (1990) models became ubiquitous in the late 1980s, used amongst professionals, hobbyists and musicians alike. Furthermore, AKAI continued its S-series line long into the 1990s with the highly successful S-3000, which significantly reinforced its position as leading sampler manufacturers. In 1988, AKAI released perhaps its most influential technology. The MPC-60, a 12-bit/40 KHz sample-sequencing device, was the first in a long line of such systems. The MPC series was developed as a collaborative effort between AKAI and Roger Linn. When in 1986 the Linn Electronics Company ceased operations, Linn joined AKAI to create sample-programming products based on his 'LinnDrum' and 'Linn9000' models. The MPC-60 became one of the most prolifically used systems in the late 1980s and on through the 1990s, particularly in modern R&B and hip-hop genres. MPCs are still used today – so prolific was their use during the so-called 'Golden Age' of hip-hop that they have become a marker of rap authenticity: for example, inside the gatefold sleeve of Dr Dre's *2001* (1999) album is a photograph of the producer in front of piles and racks of vinyl and an AKAI MPC, depicting the technological cornerstones of the record.

E-Mu and AKAI were not the only sampler manufacturers. At the high-end, French manufacturer Publison introduced a sample-based computer in 1983. A 16-bit system that could sample stereo audio, as well as add many effects such as compression, delay and reverb, the 'Infernal Machine 90 – Stereo Audio Computer' was simply known as the 'Publison sampler' in the professional industry. At a cost of almost £15,000, it was a system more prevalent at the high-end and was a key technology in the work of SAW. In a 2009 interview with me, SAW's remix engineer Phil Harding described creating a club house classic on the Publison sampler – the 12" 'Pain Remix' of Depeche Mode's 'Strangelove' (1987):

> I played the 'pain' sample with the Publison to the tune of David Bowie's 'Fame'. There's quite a spread in that melody, yet it's all in time with that track because of what the Publison did. I believe it was the first MIDI machine that allowed you to change pitch without the time. I think it took until the early 1990s for something else to match that, when Steinberg developed 'Time Bandit' where you could change the pitch without affecting the speed or change the speed without affecting the pitch. We all take that as standard now, but back then it was revolutionary.[18]

Harding's experience highlights a number of issues: firstly, the divide between functionality of budget samplers (featuring mono sampling capability and limited memory) and more expensive systems (featuring relatively large memory and stereo sampling capability) and, secondly, the alignment of such expensive music technologies to elite record producers and recording houses. Harding also refers to the pitch-shifting capability of the Publison, which enabled PWL to produce pop records with signature musical motifs. The Publison is, therefore, a good example of an exclusive 1980s music technology, highlighting the correlation between high-end music technologies, professional recordists and hit records: 'Strangelove' was a UK top-20 hit and a US Billboard number 1 hit.

Yet budget MIDI systems also made their way into the professional recording domain. This will be illustrated further later on, but I would suggest that the *musical* capabilities of MIDI as opposed to its *programmable* features were a key factor in this 'cross over'. Indeed, Warner suggested that:

> One result of this (inexpensive home recording equipment) has been a breakdown of amateur/professional status in the production process. And this breakdown is also evident in the equipment itself: manufacturers now rarely distinguish between 'professional' and 'domestic' products.[19]

This is a good time to bring in an example of a hit record made with budget MIDI equipment. In mid-1988, Gerald Simpson – a former member of UK acid house trio

808 State – recorded the best-selling independent single of that year: 'Voodoo Ray'. The track, a 3 minute 30 second, largely instrumental acid house track, featured a combination of Roland SH-101, TR-808 and TR-909 programmed rhythm with sampled female vocals. The lead vocal motif, *voodoo ray*, was in fact a sample taken from Peter Cook and Dudley Moore's *Derek and Clive (Live)* (1976) 'Bo Dudley Sketch'. The original line spoken is *voodoo rage*, but the AKAI S-900 sampler used to capture it did not feature enough memory to hold the entirety of the second word, hence the lead vocal sample – and track title – 'Voodoo Ray'.[20] Simpson programs another sketch sample 'later', as well as vocal snippets sung by his friend Nicola Collier, repetitively triggering patterns of 'oohs' and 'ahs', some of which are less than a second in length. The result is a sonically sparse and minimalist soundscape featuring melody lines entirely pieced together by sampled vocals. The track, recorded and produced in Manchester's small project Moonraker Studios, became the best-selling independently released track of 1988, reaching number 12 in the UK charts.

Early computer-based sequencers

In 1985, Atari, a home computer and video games console manufacturer, developed the 1040ST computer model with fully integrated MIDI ports. This enabled the connection of multiple MIDI compatible devices, which ultimately facilitated a full production chain. Synthesizers and modules loaded with prefabricated sounds, samplers enabling the editing of such sounds and software MIDI sequencers – when run on the Atari 1040ST – became the central workspace for music production workflows that, in some instances, could compete with the established professional recording industry. Such sequencers available in the mid to late 1980s included early versions of C-Lab's Creator and Notator software. Steinberg's Pro-16 and Pro-24 (with an updated 24 available MIDI tracks) for the Atari and Commodore were also available by 1986. Steinberg went on to release its full MIDI sequencing package, Cubase Version 1, in 1989, which would revolutionize MIDI programming and elevate the potential of dance music production even further. MOTU was one of the first companies to bridge the professional and semi-professional gap with its Performer software. Having released the score printing software 'Professional Composer' for the Apple Macintosh in 1984, the company built on that initial success with Performer, a MIDI sequencing package for both the Apple and Atari platforms. It was not until the early 1990s that MOTU's Digital Performer, a fully integrated audio and MIDI sequencing package, was brought to the market. David Mellor explained the appeal of the Atari:

> I found out about the Atari and I wanted one because it had that graphic environment rather than dealing with text. Cubase was infuriating because it seemed to have a lot of bugs in it. Although it had this graphic display so it had these blocks and a cursor passing through the screen. At the price the Atari cost, it really was a great price for the functionality. In terms of the value, it did seem like

really, really good value. Where the Atari was about £600, the Macintosh was about £3,500, so that was just a different level.[21]

A good example of the potential of early sequencers is found in Bomb the Bass' 'Beat Dis' (1988) from the album *Into the Dragon* (1988). The track, an upbeat house-inspired electronic dance music composition, was constructed almost entirely from samples by Bomb the Bass' founder and only member, the then 21-year-old Tim Simenon. Simenon pieced together 'Beat Dis' from more than seventy samples, including motifs from the *Thunderbirds* theme, Geoffrey Sumner's 'Train Sequence' from *A Journey into Stereo Sound* (1958) and the main 'Beat Dis' motif from Afrika Bambaataa and Soulsonic Force's 'Looking for the Perfect Beat' (1983). 'Beat Dis' is a classic example of the potential of sample-based sequencer compositions that were prevalent amongst both UK dance music and US hip-hop of the era and was produced on then budget equipment, including an Atari 1040ST running Steinberg's Cubase precursor Pro-24 software. Simenon sequenced his own drum and bass patterns from sampled TR-808 and TR-909 sounds stored on AKAI disks; he would not use sounds from sound libraries or presets, as he explained:

> If you buy a library you have to sit down and listen to it all. I mean, how boring is it to listen for a whole afternoon to snare sounds or bass drum samples [laughs]? Also, I don't put days aside to go sampling snares or something. What happens is that whilst I'm working at sessions I'll sample things that sound good. So my library is constantly updated.[22]

Unsurprisingly, the capabilities of software sequencers run on budget Atari 1040ST's appealed to young, electronic musicians and recordists of the decade, such as Simenon and Simpson. However, older musicians more associated to 1970s rock genre also experimented with the system. For example, the 1040ST was used to programme Mike Oldfield's synthesis-laden *Earth Moving* (1989), a major sonic departure from his early, performance-centric albums such as *Tubular Bells* (1973). Perhaps the most unlikely use of the Atari ST was Mick Fleetwood's use of sequenced drum samples and synth lines throughout Fleetwood Mac's *Tango in the Night* (1987), as he stated:

> I've learned I can integrate MIDI into my music and really use it in a very human way. I've learned you can apply it to whatever you want. If you want it to sound like a bloody robot, it will. But on the other hand, you can really do some wonderful things with it that are very organic.[23]

The tightly synchronized drum patterns heard throughout tracks like 'Big Love' and 'Little Lies' brought a glossy, cutting-edge pop sound to Fleetwood Mac's middle-of-the-road songwriting style. Amongst the new hip-hop and dance music of the era, *Tango in the Night* was perhaps out of place, yet the use of the Atari and sampled drum patterns effortlessly assimilated the 1970s band into the sonic canvas of late 1980s mainstream pop.

Samplers

Never before or since has a music technology development challenged notions of musical authenticity, reimagined musical instrumentation or transformed genre; the digital sampler confronted existing understandings of authentic musical performance, provoked legal and moral debates surrounding intellectual property and created divides in the western music and sound recording industries. Much has been written about the use of samplers[24] and the implications for intellectual property,[25] copyright law and the wider music industry.[26] The functionality of samplers was such that when used in conjunction with a synthesizer and/or sequencer, they could be used as musical, compositional and production tools, blurring the lines between these processes. To that end, the potential of sampling practice was realized in some of the most 'collaged' tracks in popular music history: Public Enemy's *It Takes a Nation of Millions to Hold Us Back* (1988) and The Beastie Boys' Dust Brothers-produced *Paul's Boutique* (1989) are two examples of records almost entirely constructed from samples.[27] Undoubtedly, the sampler and associated sampling practice resulted in new intertextual forms during the late 1980s, although due to the surrounding legalities, the foregrounding of extensive sampling practice in popular recordings was short-lived.

One record epitomizes the intertextual potential of samplers more than any other: De La Soul's *3 Feet High and Rising* (1989). The record, largely constructed with AKAI S-900 and E-mu SP 12 samplers, is a sample collage quoting a breadth of genre from 1970s prog rock, funk, soul and AOR, disco and blues. The record was lauded by some as representing the dawn of a new musical era; an example of how sampling could push creative musical boundaries; the epitome of 'sampler as musical instrument' in its own right.[28] Others questioned the artists' claim to authorship, the legality of such quotation: the authenticity of a record featuring little original musical performance.[29] *3 Feet High and Rising* reinforced the established funk and soul canon, whilst simultaneously referencing obscurities and introducing comedy skits between songs. It could be argued that *3 Feet High and Rising* was hip-hop's first concept album: a painstakingly assembled sample mash-up preceding mash-up genre by two decades. 'Cool Breeze on the Rocks', for example, blends dozens of 'rock-themed' snippets: Michael Jackson's 'Rock With You' (1979), Ashford & Simpson's 'Solid' (1984), The Trecherous Three's 'The Body Rock' (1980) and Jefferson Starship's 'Rock Music' (1979) were just a few.

UK dance acts such as Coldcut, Bomb the Bass and M/A/R/R/S exemplified late 1980s 'cut and paste' sample collage specialists, drawing from musics past and present, documentary film, found sound effects and maximizing the potential of cheaper samplers. Erik B and Rakim's 'Paid in Full' is a great example of late 1980s sampling aesthetics, retrospectively lauded as a 'benchmark' album in what Alex Ogg termed 'The Golden Age of Hip Hop'.[30] The original album title track is, in itself, a sample collage, the underlying rhythm taken from the Soul Searchers' 1973 instrumental 'Ashley's Roachclip' from *Salt of the Earth* (1974) and the iconic bassline taken from Temptations' lead singer Dennis Howard and Siedah Garrett's 'Don't Look Any Further' (1984). Yet the commissioning of UK dance music duo Coldcut to provide the '7 minutes of madness remix' propelled the track to new heights; Coldcut utilized a Casio FZ-1 sampler and early computer-based software sequencer C-Lab (a precursor to Emagic's Logic software) to remix the original, drawing on an eclectic range of sample material. Vocals taken from the Salsoul Orchestra's 1983 track 'Ohhh, I Love It' gave the remix its instantly recognizable intro. Additional vocal samples, taken from Israeli singer Ofra Haza's version of traditional Hebrew song 'Im Nin' Alu', were wound in to the mix creating a unique hybrid hip-hop/dance/globalized hip-hop track. Coldcut also took the 'pump up the volume' sample from Eric B and Rakim's earlier hit 'I Know You Got Soul' and the 'This is a journey into sound!' proclamation from British actor Geoffrey Sumner. The remix resulted not only in increased exposure for all the sampled artists but in the formation of a then unprecedented sample canon: Ofra Haza not only became a household name following the remix, but 'Im Nin' Alu' was later sampled by Public Enemy, Delerium, Vanilla Ice and Fabolous.[31] The bassline to 'Don't Look Any Further' was later used by Tupac Shakur, Lil Wayne, Nate Dogg and Warren G, and the drum break in 'Ashley's Roachclip' became one of the most sampled rhythm phrases in hip-hop, later underpinning Milli Vanilli's 'Girl You Know It's True' (1988), PM Dawn's 'Set Adrift on Memory Bliss' (1991) and Lloyd and Lil' Wayne's 'Girls All Around the World' (2008). Key motifs from the Salsoul Orchestra's 'Ohh I Love It' later appeared in Madonna's 'Vogue' (1990). In this example, Eric B and Rakim have not only created their own record but introduced a collection of recordings from which others in hip-hop have continued to reference. To that end, 'Paid in Full' can be considered a benchmark recording in terms of sampling practice, as well as signifying the establishment of a future bank of canonized samples informing a continuum in both sampling practice and hip-hop genre.

Let's take a look at another significant – yet overlooked – record from the mid-1980s. Salt N' Pepa's 'Push It' (1986) is a good example of multi-intertextual hip-hop form as realized by sampling and sequencing practice. Although acknowledged in feminist discourse as a rare example of female empowerment in male-dominant African American hip-hop genre,[32] there is plenty to be said about the intertext itself. The track is underpinned by a sampled motif from Coal Kitchen's 'Keep on Pushin (1977)', yet most of the other samples of Salt N' Pepa themselves. We hear classic sample trigger effects; the girls' voices, particularly 'Salt and Pepa's here!' are sampled, spread over a MIDI keyboard, then triggered – with the classic 'chipmunk' and time stretched effects audible as the 'Salt' is retriggered up and down the keyboard. Throughout, Salt N' Pepa repeat two key phrases, 'Pick up on this' and 'There it is!'; both are examples of quotation. 'Pick up on this!' is the introductory phrase from James Brown's 'Greedy Man' (1971) and 'There it is' from James Brown's 'There it is!' (1972). Once again, we see hip-hop artists paying their dues to the African American funk and soul canons, but there is more going on in this track. Hurby Luv Bug – a DJ and Push It's producer – MC's throughout, his heavily delayed vocal interjections a homage to Caribbean dub producers. He also alludes to Morris Day and The Time's 'The Bird' (1984) – a track taken from the then recent *Purple Rain* (1984) movie soundtrack – with the line 'This dance ain't for everybody, only the sexy people'. Finally, having rapped only a few originally penned lines, Salt N' Pepa's 'Push It' pay-off, 'Boy, you really got me goin'. You got me so I don't know what I'm doin", is an allusion to The Kinks' 'You Really Got Me'

(1964) – referencing this influential 'British Invasion' track along with obvious funk motifs and a recent film soundtrack maximized 'Push It's sonic familiarity and is a good example of sample collage techniques in widespread use towards the end of the 1980s.

Technological tension and the presence of performance

So far, I have focused on music of the mid-to-late 1980s that reflects a changing, progressive technological landscape. This is not to say that the aforementioned examples are indicative of how *all* commercial, popular music was made during this time or even that the technology alone was responsible for this shift. Indeed, the agency of the recordist is discussed in detail later on, but there were plenty of commercial recordings made during the mid to late 1980s that did not feature the sound of new digital technologies. In fact, there were significant records of the era that could be interpreted as an active stance *against* such technological intervention, which, arguably, led to greater success. To put it another way, there were many records of the mid to late 1980s that were sonically notable for what they did *not* feature, their performance-led aesthetics standing out as the exception rather than the rule. One such record was U2's *The Joshua Tree* (1987), made with little to no then current music or recording technologies, as recordist Brian Eno stated:

> It's not coming from a 1980s mentality. It's coming from somewhere completely different. [*The Joshua Tree*] was self consciously spiritual to the point of being uncool. I thought being uncool was a very good idea then, because people were being very, very cool.[33]

The intention of both band and producers was to capture a performance. The recording of the band playing live as a group suggests that despite having technology available that allows for 'drop-ins' or overdubs, this path was rejected in favour of past techniques. Guitarist The Edge and bassist Adam Clayton's use of vintage instruments adds to a distinctive sonic tonality, consistent with traditionalist recording. However, by opting for a more traditional approach, Eno and Lanois also opted for many potential problems that they would not have had if using more modern technologies, as recordist Daniel Lanois stated in *Sound on Sound*:

> We had it in mind right from the beginning to record as much performance live off the floor as possible. That was pretty much a unanimous decision 'cos, as you know, studios can be a pitfall if you live in the land of promise and rely on overdubs to pull a track together.[34]

Recorded live to analogue tape via a vintage Neve mixing console, one of the most successful singles from the album, 'Where the Streets Have No Name' (1987), illustrates such live performance capture techniques. The performances feature timing fluctuations throughout (indicative of the absence of a click track), large variations in dynamic range, particularly in the vocal performance (signifying the absence of 'harder' compression styles of the era) and reverb consistent with a natural, live room as opposed to digital effects processors. The decision made to consciously subvert then current technology and processes resulted in one of the most sonically recognizable and, simultaneously, one of the most commercially successful recordings of the decade.

A unique example of hybrid production techniques at the end of the 1980s lies in Soul II Soul's *Club Classics Volume One* (1989). This soul fusion record, featuring African roots, US R&B, reggae and neo-Soul influences produced a UK number 1 hit in 'Back to Life (However Do You Want Me)' (1989) and a Billboard number 1 in 'Keep on Movin" (1989). Yet the record possessed a unique sonic identity and featured none of the new digital technology aesthetics present in so many commercially released records of the era. Situated on Harrow Road, Addis Ababa Studios was a small recording studio in London that regularly featured independent British reggae, roots and emergent 'new jack swing' recording artists, including Warrior's Dance, Aswad and Mikey Dread. UK soul collective Soul II Soul recorded their debut album *Club Classics Volume One* (1989) at Addis Ababa, as well as larger studios including Britannia Row and Lillie Yard, blurring the project and professional studio domain. Incorporating 2″ analogue tape recording and editing/splicing techniques, a then precursor AMS digital delay, as well as creating rhythms with an E-Mu SP-1200 drum machine and Moog synthesizer, then mixed on a then cutting-edge SSL G-series console, Soul II Soul created one of the most sonically discernible records of the decade, as lead songwriter-recordist Jazzie B stated:

> we were going for this different dimension sonically. In those years, we were using variations of compressors and the first G series SSL board as well. We were going for a harder, colder sound, which we tried to make warmer. It's incredible what the compression of oxide can do in a recording. These are all elements that made up the end product.[35]

Like Eno and Lanois, the intention from the outset was to subvert the sonic canvas of the era and to create something altogether different. The conflation and application of both analogue and digital, cutting-edge and vintage technologies to the production process resulted in a unique record, sonically and aesthetically removed from the homogenous commercial mainstream, yet simultaneously appealing directly to it by way of sonic differentiation. *Club Classics Volume One* went on to be one of the most critically acclaimed records in British popular music history.[36]

Digital formats

Another important development in the 1980s was the advent of digital formatting in the guise of DAT and CD. These new digital formats became instant competitors to the sonically polar vinyl and cassette formats that had dominated the pre-recorded format market until the mid-1980s. Using the PCM coding/decoding system developed in the late 1970s, the CD was eventually brought to the market in 1982, as Morton states:

The complex electronics of the original Sony PCM coder/decoder of 1977, for example, had to be recreated as a set of small, inexpensive integrated circuit chips. Further, a laser device cheap enough to install in a consumer disc player and capable of being mass-produced was not available until about 1981. With these key technical hurdles out of the way, the two companies unveiled the CD in 1982.[37]

Sony and Phillips' introduction of the CD as a consumer format culminated in pressures on the professional recording industry to record, mix and master with the signal being kept in the digital domain for the entire chain. The US industry organization SPARS (Society of Professional Audio Recording Services) developed a code for identifying which parts of the CD had been recorded, mixed and mastered in the analogue or digital domain. This code was stamped on the reverse side of the CD in a three-letter format: AAA, AAD, ADD or the much-coveted DDD. The SPARS code was adopted between 1984 and 1991; a marker of the tech-utopian ideology of digital recording of the 1980s, the SPARS code was certainly a sign of the times.

This was further substantiated later in the decade when Sony released its DAT format. A 48 KHz/16-bit technology, DAT was to CD as the cassette was to vinyl, a small, compact and potentially noise-free digital tape. David Mellor explained its instantaneous appeal:

> I think it was about 1987 when DAT came out and that was a revolution. It was so exciting. It wasn't just me, it was everybody! It was 16-bit; you could make a CD quality recording. The first machine that Sony brought out cost £1,000. I used it until I wore it out. It was a miracle. An absolute miracle. The reason it didn't become a successful consumer format was because the record companies in the US resisted its introduction. They didn't want people copying CD's and making copies that were as good quality as the CD.[38]

Indeed, the DAT was controversial in some areas of the professional audio industry. Not only did the DAT cause a significant copyright controversy in the United States but also led to widespread confusion as to its use, with many in the professional industry questioning it as a professional mastering format. Dave Harries explained, 'I've known whole classical albums done on DAT. Mastered on DAT. 120 piece symphony orchestras on a tiny piece of tape the size of a couple of postage stamps. Frightening. Terrifying!'[39] Melvyn Toms highlighted the error rates present on DAT tapes and how that decreased their reliability as a format, as he states:

> DAT was a nightmare. It was basically a very affordable, cheap form of digital recording for artists. The error rates on DAT's were enormous. A lot of people were turning up with – sadly, some EMI producers had gone overseas and spent a lot of money in a wonderful location recording somewhere very exotic, with a very high profile artist and come back with a DAT as a master! Some very questionable product came as a result of that. It was misunderstood. It wasn't a professional format.[40]

Toms points out the confusion that existed amongst members of the industry with regard to how DAT should be used, yet he also recognized that some professional engineers used the format regularly. This implies that Sony attempted to market DAT as a useful format to a wide range of consumers. Boasting a sample rate of 48 KHz – an improvement on the 44.1 KHz of CD – DAT was promoted as a high-end mastering format, but the US industry in particular refused to adopt it, concerned that such a hi-fidelity 'digital cassette' would provide consumers with a means of re-recording and sharing high-quality digital audio. The format was so controversial that Sony addressed the divisive industry response in an advertisement entitled 'Fact/Fiction'.[41] The advert depicts a number of newspaper clippings bearing highly sceptical headlines about the DAT format under the word 'Fiction'. The DAT machine itself illustrated under the word 'Fact'. The paragraph beneath the imagery contains statements such as 'Quality must always be king' and 'Forget the hype. Ignore the controversy. DAT is highly convenient and it works.'[42] The paragraph ends with 'You've read the fiction and you've got the facts. Now buy the product. There's no turning back.' Such terse statements illustrate how Sony, an audio industry stalwart, struggled to market DAT with tech-utopian ideology in the face of industry pessimism.

Whilst these practitioner quotes substantiate a technological divide in the 1980s, they highlight other issues. Mellor references the US music industry's copyright infringement concerns in their resistance to DAT; however, this was ultimately overcome by a 'Serial Copy Management System' or 'SCMS', a code integrated into the DAT data stream allowing only one copy to be made.

The copyright implications of digital audio recorders were debated for many years, before the United States finally passed the Audio Home Recording Act in 1992 (five years after DAT's release). The act featured a clause stating that all new digital recording devices include SCMS as standard. However, one reason the Home Recording Act took so long to pass was due to the resistance from computer companies, which argued that everyone had the right to back up their hard drive data onto CD-R. The main resistance came from Apple computer that eventually won an exemption. However, in the time it had taken the US industry to adopt the DAT in order to minimize copyright infringement, the technology had been superseded.

The decline of analogue synthesis

With the rise of MIDI systems in the 1980s, one aspect of manufacturing suffered. The highly competitive digital synthesizer market resulted in declining demand for analogue synthesizers including large audio manufacturers such as Moog and Oberheim, both of which went out of business, as Tom Rhea pointed out:

> You notice that Yamaha screwed up for a long time before they hit on the DX-7 [1983]. They could afford to keep trying. In a company like Moog, ARP, Sequential and Oberheim, you're living from one NAMM show to the next. If you don't have a hit at one show, you'd better at the next, or you're dead.[43]

In 1981, ARP synthesizers, which had previously dominated the 1970s analogue synthesizer market, went into liquidation. Moog Music followed suit and filed for bankruptcy in 1986. Oberheim, a successful manufacturer in the early 1980s with their DMX drum machine, also went into liquidation in 1986, eventually being bought out by the Gibson Guitar Corporation. Yet a 1980s technological anomaly came in the form of one of Roland's most successful synthesizers: the Jupiter 8. This colourful, programmable synthesizer made between 1981 and 1984 was a polyphonic analogue synth featuring two voltage-controlled oscillators per voice. Its robust structure and unique sound cemented its place in 1980s synth culture at a time when digital synthesis had all but wiped out its analogue counterparts. Significantly, the sound of the Jupiter 8 was one of the most sought after in British new wave and popular music and can be heard throughout Duran Duran's *Rio* (1982), Talk Talk's *It's My Life* (1984) and Go West's debut album *Go West* (1985), amongst many others. These technological anomalies – the well-documented Roland TR-808 and TR-909 and others – are examples of a handful of analogue devices that existed and proliferated through an era of predominantly digital commercial music production. Perhaps the most surprising instance was the case of Sequential Circuits. Having spent the late 1970s developing the MIDI protocol to widespread industry acclaim and commercial success, as well as releasing the highly regarded Prophet-5 synthesizer in 1978, the company dissolved in 1987 and was bought out by Yamaha. Clearly, these one-time heavyweights of 1970s analogue synthesis had fallen prey to the digital synthesizer market. This decline epitomized the 'out with the old, in the new' tech-utopian philosophy of 1980s music production in both amateur and professional domains.

Summary

The era between 1984 and 1990 was one of the most transformative in popular music history, in no small part due to the proliferation of new, flexible and largely digital music technology devices that infiltrated both amateur and professional recording domains. The impact of such technologies, particularly console recall in the high-end of the market and MIDI sequencers at the mid-low end, altered popular music composition and arrangement techniques to the point where entirely new forms, such as the 12" remix, emerged. The potential of remixing, along with composite digital sample editing techniques of the late 1980s, resulted in entirely new genres and sub-genres of popular music. The epitome of sampling practice was found in late 1980s hip-hop[44] and house music, whereby new intertextual forms dominated the commercial mainstream: in the clubs, in the charts and into popular music historiography.

The competitive nature of music technological progress was beginning to show, not simply in recording studio discourse but in the ever-present foregrounding of technological intervention in the popular music of the era: the presence of the LinnDrum as the loudest instrument in particular pop mixes; the obvious sequencing patterns and samples present in hip-hop; and the dramatic sonic canvases created by automated mixing. This created a commercial music mainstream dominated by the sound of pre-programmed sounds, digital synthesis and large-scale record construction, the likes of which had never been heard before. It is, therefore, unsurprising that 1980s commercial popular music brought with it accusations of much of the output 'sounding the same'. Whilst a great number of new digital technologies were brought to the market during the era, the tonal qualities of 8-bit samplers, synthesizers and sequencers were such that when used in combination, it often resulted in a slick, polished and 'constructed' sound with little dynamic range or form variations.[45] The mid-to-late 1980s was a time of complex changes in the nature of studio record production. No more could studio maintenance engineers troubleshoot workflows by traditional means. The established roles of tape operator, engineer and producer became blurred with the advent of the programmer, remix producer and DJ, not to mention more 'production-aware artists'.[46] Ultimately, by the end of the decade, the popular music landscape had transformed with the output of project studios and semi-professional recordists, DJs and programmers jostling for chart positions with the output of the established professional record industry.

3

Technological Hybridity: Conflations of Analogue, Digital, the Cutting Edge and the Vintage in the 1990s

So far, the trajectory of sound recording and production technologies through the 1980s and its influence on commercial popular music of the era have been traced. The turn of the 1990s saw yet another marked technological shift in sound recording and production technology, as well as a notable change in the wider recording and production workplace. High-end digital tape recording that proliferated in the elite recording industry during the mid-1980s continued long into the 1990s with many workplaces committed to the DASH or ProLogic multitrack formats. This is not to say that analogue technology was replaced overnight. In fact, digital recording did not overtake analogue in both the high-end and consumer recording industries until the end of the decade. Until the early 1990s, there remained a notable 'split' between home studio set-ups, often featuring budget MIDI equipment and professional recording workplaces, whose main technology specification still revolved around large-format mixing consoles and analogue or digital multitrack tape recording. If the Atari ST signified the beginnings of the so-called 'democratisation of technology'[1] in the late 1980s, the introduction of the ADAT digital multitrack recorder by US manufacturer Alesis in 1991 was another key turning point in both the history and cultural practice of recording, as Jonathan Sterne pointed out:

> Despite a host of economic and cultural factors, the ADAT/Mackie combination came to symbolise the rise of the amateur recording and a whole 'semiprofessional' realm of small studios, often located in homes, or other less-than-optimal acoustic spaces.[2]

This early 1990s 'tipping point'[3] signified a change in the accessibility, utilization and application of technologies. By 1995, the influx of cheaper digital recording technologies, including the ADAT, into the sound technology market and its subsequent impact on recorded music were such that industry magazine *Billboard* ran a front-page article entitled 'Budget Studio Gear Breaks Barriers'.[4] In it, Paul Verna claimed the technology had 'transformed the record-making process in recent years, allowing artists and labels unprecedented flexibility and forcing top recording studios to diversify their product mix'.[5] However, the mid-1990s saw a poignant pause for reflection in the wider audio industry, as sound recording and production technology's recent past began to catch up. In his 1996 Audio Engineering Society keynote address entitled 'Technological Change: The Challenge to the Audio and Music Industries', John Strawn reflected upon the decade's digital format changes:

> The point is that as digital technology swept across society, the audio industry did not steer how the technology would be adopted. Instead, it waited until the technology was stable, then adopted the technology as best it could.[6]

Of course, this is just one individual's perception of the rate of technological change into the 1990s, but it is certainly indicative of an industry-wide feeling. Yet the word 'sweeping' points to the ubiquity and widespread use of cheaper and, therefore, more accessible production tools in the marketplace. Dave Simons also recalled a kind of digital technology malaise by the turn of the 2000s:

> Back in the early 1980s, proponents couldn't say enough great things about digital technology: how quiet it was compared to tape; how digital storage eliminated the problem of archiving; and how it made editing child's play. All still valid points, a quarter-century later. However, it was easy to overlook one very noticeable shortcoming: digital didn't always produce the most pleasing tones.[7]

As discussed earlier, technologies like the Fairlight CMI and Mitsubishi ProDigi were distributed in the hundreds of units, such was the prohibitive cost of the machines and their intended use in the elite recording industry. By the early 1990s, sound recording technologies were distributed in the thousands, ensuring increased availability and, therefore, accessibility by a wider range of users. The perceived inability of the industry to 'steer' digital sound technology is indicative of a loss of control and certainly of technological determinism; that the recording industry was, by the late 1990s, apparently operating in such a disorderly technological landscape and unable to control its use is certainly suggestive of a technological takeover of sorts. The knock-on effect on the music industry was notable. By the 1990s, the ubiquity of cheaper sound recording equipment resulted in many home studio recordings competing with those of the professional industry for sales, chart places and industry accolades, including Grammy awards.

The diversification of 'product mix' as also noted by Verna[8] was indicative of the technological hybridity present in recording workplaces. More studios featured mixtures of computer-based recording systems, digital recorders and analogue technologies than ever before: a result of twenty years of digital technological development and the lingering presence of analogue tape machines. As discussed later, this technological mash-up of sorts was largely down to recordists' attitudes and their personal technological preferences. Complete new studio builds and refurbishments were uncommon in the 1990s.[9] Instead, newer technologies – particularly computer-based software systems such as Digidesign's Pro Tools – were integrated into the workplace alongside existing devices. To that end, it was common for recording workplaces to feature high-end digital and analogue machines of the 1980s. By the 1990s, high-end machines of the previous decade were accessible via the second-hand market. The price of these devices plummeted, thus placing the elite industry's cutting-edge tools of the 1980s in the hands of an altogether different demographic by the 1990s. Additionally, systems such as the Sony DASH and Mitsubishi ProDigi were considered outdated by the late 1990s – even obsolete[10] – thus, a great deal of what were by then technological precursors and other systems considered 'vintage' brought about an era of technological hybridity and unique workflows. This chapter considers some of the key developments of the decade, as well as the origins and value of technological precursors.

ADAT

In 1991, US manufacturer Alesis introduced its ADAT (Alesis Digital Audio Tape) recorder at the annual NAMM (National Association of Music Merchants) convention. This small, rack-mountable digital recording device utilized S-VHS tapes as its storage medium and featured up to 67 minutes recording time on 8 tracks with 44.1 KHz/16-bit digital multitrack recording capability. A unique feature of the ADAT recorder was its modular format. Up to 16 recorders could be easily synchronized together to create up to 128 tracks of digital multitrack recording. Many in the industry have referred to the introduction of the ADAT format as 'revolutionary',[11] and this was, perhaps, more due to its lower cost than its technical specification. At $4,000 for an 8-track machine, a 24-track recording facility was now available at a fraction of the price of a 24-track Sony DASH,[12] thus placing professional digital audio recording in the hands of a new demographic of recordists and workplaces. The repercussions on the wider music industry were significant. The audio fidelity of demos increased, with recordings made on an ADAT machine comparable in quality to those realized in professional workplaces with elite recording equipment. Additionally, S-VHS tapes were cheap; at $15 each, these were less than half the price of analogue or digital multitrack tape, thus creating an accessible format that, due to its small size, was also transportable. By late 1992 – just one year after the machine was introduced – more than 20,000 units had shipped worldwide, and the introduction of the machine is widely considered to be responsible for the proliferation of project-sized studios. As Petersen suggested, the impact was far-ranging:

> The repercussions of ADAT were far reaching indeed. Was it mere coincidence that, as the first ADATs were delivered to retailers, the Society for Professional Recording Services recommended that record labels drop the ADD, DDD ... ? After years of 'educating' consumers to look for that all-important 'DDD' tag, was the decision to abandon the code based on affirmation of analog ... as a viable medium, or was the availability of low-cost digital a perceived threat to the allure of a DDD sticker?[13]

This recognition of the ADAT's impact, and the simultaneous decline in the aspirational qualities of digital audio, is corroborated by recordists and other members of the audio industry, who identify the ADAT as being a divisive system. Significantly, the machine was embraced by alternative, 'indie' and hip-hop artists in both the United States and the UK and empowered small labels by allowing them to create small recording facilities. For example, independent New York label Zero Hour Records created Ground Zero Studios in the early 1990s. Recordist Joe Lambert commented on the accessibility of the ADAT:

> The ADATs are great because they're affordable. Our bands don't have the budget to spend $130 for tape. Also, this allows them to work bit by bit. Because we have 5 machines, if one of our bands needs to take one home they can.[14]

This combination of affordability and portability aligned the ADAT with independent record creation and the empowerment of artists through recording technology. On the one hand, this was something to be celebrated. Within three years of its release, an ADAT-recorded single – 'Stay (I Missed You)' (1994) by US folk artist Lisa Loeb – became a Billboard number 1 hit. At the time, Loeb was an unsigned artist and the track was recorded to ADAT in a home studio by her then boyfriend and aspiring producer Juan Patiño. By the time Loeb signed to major label Geffen Records, the company decided to continue her home-recording sound on her debut album *Tails* (1995), as A&R representative Jim Barber explained: 'We managed to make ADAT work for us in a way that gave us all the technological capabilities we needed, and we didn't have the expense of working in a 24-track facility.'[15]

Another example lies in the recording of Alanis Morrisette's multi-platinum selling debut album *Jagged Little Pill* (1995). Renowned songwriter Glen Ballard recorded Morrisette's record at his small home studio in San Fernando, the United States, using ADAT recorders and a Euphonix console. Significantly, all Morrisette's vocals were recorded through a 1954 AKG C-12 electrostatic microphone and vintage limiters and tube preamps,[16] lending the record a classic, past-era sonic familiarity and thus differentiating it from other rock records of the era. This combination of budget digital recording with vintage devices and processing is a good example of technological hybridity in the 1990s recording workplace. Ballard's assistant engineer Christopher Fogel described the particular 'sound' of the ADAT recorder thus:

> I wasn't sure I'd made the right decision doing the drums initially on ADAT, as I thought maybe they were sounding a bit brittle, a bit harsh. And I still think to this day that they do – but that lends itself to the character of the record.[17]

Perhaps the best example of an ADAT hit record is found in 'Regulate' (1994) by Warren G and Nate Dogg. This track, produced by Warren G and mixed by Greg Gertzenauer at Track Record Studios in Los Angeles, utilized multiple ADAT recorders to realize one of the most accomplished examples of multi-intertextual form in hip-hop. Here, multiple, disparate samples and digital synthesis lines are integrated into a cohesive track that, unlike sample-based hip-hop records of the late 1980s, featured little to no obvious signs of sampling or 'copy and paste' techniques. Conversely, the main rhythmic loop, taken from Michael McDonald's 'I Keep Forgettin'' (1982), was consolidated with a synthesized string pad and the central melodic 'whistling' hook from Bob James' 'Sign of the Times' (1981). Replayed motifs[18] including 'let me ride' from Parliament's 'Mothership Connection (Star Child)' (1975) and 'where rhythm is life and life is rhythm' from The Evasions' 'Wikka Wrap' (1981) were strategically alluded to. Perhaps most significant is the treatment of the introductory sample. Taken from the film *Young Guns* (1988), a short monologue spoken by the character Charlie Bowdre is cut in to the song's introduction. Yet the sample has been edited with precision, fading in and out in between the spoken lines so as to minimize any background noise from the original film and to keep the words prominent. This is a stark contrast to many hip-hop records of the late 1980s, which often featured more obvious signs of sampling with harsher edits, time stretching and easily identifiable collage techniques due to hardware sampler's low RAM and disk memory. Warren G attributes the success of 'Regulate' – a Grammy-nominated, platinum-selling Billboard rap chart number 1 – to having produced the track in his home studio set-up on the ADAT machines:

> These [ADAT's] right here, inside the machine, were the tapes I recorded 'Regulate' on. I got smart and understood I could save money by recording right at the house. I set up a studio. The closet was the vocal booth. I did 85% of ['Regulate'] at home.[19]

On 'Regulate', a slick, professional result has been achieved: the ADAT's multitrack, auto-locate and loop functionality enabling the seamless consolidation of multiple samples into a cohesive, original track.

Another example of minimalist record construction lies in *Endtroducing* (1996) by US producer DJ Shadow. This entirely sample-constructed album was created using only a turntable, an AKAI MPC60 and an ADAT recorder. He explained the reasons behind this technological choice: '*Endtroducing* was recorded to ADAT because that was all that we could afford back then.'[20] Clearly, by the mid-late 1990s, multiple, multi-platinum and critically acclaimed records were made on ADAT devices, both demonstrating and realizing that big hits were possible on budget equipment. However, not everyone in the industry embraced the device. The lower cost came at a larger price – as well as unreliability and technical faults. ADAT heads would often wear out and the S-VHS format was considered cumbersome and unreliable by many, particularly due to an unreliable tape transport mechanism. For example, in *Vibe Merchants*, Hitchins suggested Jamaican recordist Errol Brown steered clear of the ADAT:

> Errol Brown claimed that the ADAT digital recorder and other modular recording systems were not considered dependable enough for the industrial demands of the professional recording studio, which operated on a round-the-clock basis. It was therefore the owners of home, or small recording facilities who pioneered the transition to digital multi-track recording in Jamaica during the early 1990s and not the established recording studios.[21]

The professional audio industry's disdain at the influx of such accessible and easily operated digital recording devices is epitomized in the reaction of some members of the Audio Engineering Society. Just one year after John Strawn's aforementioned keynote address, a statement on cheap digital devices was made at the 1997 convention, as Jonathan Sterne noted:

> At the 1997 convention of the Audio Engineer's [sic] Society ... a controversial sculpture appeared on the convention floor. Entitled 'Shit on a Stick', it featured an ADAT recorder and a Mackie mixer impaled on a four-foot metal spike.[22]

The ADAT was, however, not the only digital recording device to shift the technological and processual landscape in 1990s record production. At the professional end of the industry, the Otari RADAR overhauled recording and production practices in both the professional and semi-professional recording spheres.

Otari RADAR

In November 1994, Japanese audio company Otari unveiled their hard-disk recorder at the AES (Audio Engineering Society) Convention in San Francisco. The system was designed and built by Canadian manufacturer Creation Technologies of Vancouver and distributed worldwide under an exclusive licence by Otari. Featuring 1.2 GB of hard-disk recording space, the RADAR was a truly revolutionary device and featured many components designed to save time during recording sessions. Indeed, the cutting-edge design lay in the acronym: RADAR standing for Random Access Digital Audio Recorder. For example, due to the absence of tape, edits could be made almost immediately via spot-point editing and without having to rewind/forward to a selected point. It was, therefore, legitimately marketed as a time-saving and portable device. Additionally, the machine allowed for backwards recording and playback, as well as non-destructive editing and instant 'undo' features, cut-and-paste editing and 99 cue points, thus simultaneously increasing the speed and functionality of digital recording, as Langford points out:

> This non-linear editing process allowed editors sample-accurate editing and the ability to select, cut, copy, paste, and move sections of audio without any physical process at all, and, best of all, this was the start of the ability to undo the edits if they either weren't done correctly or simply didn't have the desired effect.[23]

Additionally, the Otari RADAR was compatible with ADAT, allowing users to link multiple ADAT machines together and therefore increase their system capability. With recording sample rate options between 32 KHz and 48 KHz, the Otari RADAR was the first hard-disk recording system that offered the same recording fidelity as the Sony DASH and Mitsubishi ProDigi, but at a fraction of the cost. Costing $24,000 for a 24-track system, the price point positioned the RADAR within the reach of both professional and project recordists and workplace.

Despite the machine being released in 1994, it took a few years for take-up to reach a point where it featured on hit records. It was not until the late 1990s that commercial hits were being produced on the RADAR, in both the UK and the United States. The reason for this is due to the general 1990s preference for new technological integration into existing workplaces as opposed to the full replacing of technological precursors. For example, Dave Fridmann of Tarbox Road Studios in New York integrated an Otari RADAR II (1999) into his studio alongside an ADAT system, Pro Tools and a much older Otari analogue tape recorder. Colin Fairly of Helioscentric Studios, England, also integrated an Otari into an established workplace: 'The Otari RADAR 24-track hard disk system, I must say, sounds extremely good, considering! We have Pro Tools and all sorts of synthesizer goodies. The Pet Shop Boys are regulars in this room.'[24] In the late 1990s, Dino Elefante, owner of Sound Kitchen Studios in Nashville, blended the RADAR with technological precursors for reasons of both technological choice and cost effectiveness, as he explained: 'I like to look for deals … we never sell anything or trade up. We have the Otari RADAR system, which means I can offer clients 48-track digital recording for $1000 a day or less.'[25]

The RADAR was also embraced by established musicians keen to take control of their recording processes. Guitarist Dimebag Darrell of US band Pantera explained the process of recording their final album *Reinventing the Steel* (2000): 'We did it on a 48-track Otari Radar hard disk recorder. My dad turned me on to the RADAR. He said that we could do anything we wanted with it. It's a lot easier than rolling the old tape and splicing things together. You can do all of that inside the box.'[26] Andy Partridge and Colin Moulding of 1980s band XTC also integrated an Otari RADAR as the central recording device of Moulding's late 1990s home studio.[27]

It is important to note that the RADAR was often chosen as a recording device because of what it was *not*. Whilst the RADAR utilized hard-disk recording, it was not a computer and neither looked nor operated in the same way.[28] However, recordist Mark Howard (Bob Dylan, REM, U2) expressed similar sentiments regarding the RADAR's functionality:

> I get frustrated with the whole mousing around routine. Then you've got this guy in front of the screen and you're like, 'Okay, you can do this and blah blah.' I'm not sure if it's a loss of control thing, or you're waiting on somebody, or it's like, 'Okay, here we go, we're gonna record, and sorry we gotta reboot.' It takes the wind out of you and I've been put in that spot. It's [Otari RADAR] damn reliable and I can do everything Pro Tools can do if not faster, and I think it sounds better.[29]

The RADAR featured most of the functionality of Pro Tools, yet looked and operated in a similar way to an analogue tape machine. The technological learning curve from analogue and digital tape machine operation to the Otari RADAR was less than the move from tape recorders to computer-based DAWs such as Pro Tools. Like the ADAT, the RADAR empowered both musicians and semi-professional recordists, particularly those operating outside the commercial mainstream. For example, the RADAR was used to record independent artists' records in the late 1990s, including those by Youssou n'Dour (*La Cour des Grands*, 1998) and Enrique Iglesias' *Be With You* (2000). Jim Spencer recorded UK indie band The Charlatans' sixth studio record *Us and Us Only* (1999) on a RADAR and the system was also employed on The 2 Live

Crew feat KC *2 Live Party* (1998). This illustrates the RADAR's implementation across a particularly diverse range of artists, genres and styles in mid-to-late 1990s record production. The RADAR can, therefore, be seen as an empowering, accessible device that symbolized technological democratization. In fact, the RADAR was rarely used on big budget, major label commercial recording sessions since the high-end analogue and digital tape machines were still in widespread use – an exception being the recording of U2's 'The Sweetest Thing' (1999) at Westland Studios, Dublin.

A key record illustrating the functionality of the RADAR is UK soul artist Gabrielle's 'Rise' (2000) taken from the album of the same name. This project-studio-produced hit was led by Massive Attack producer Johnny Dollar and assisted by Simon Palmskin, as he pointed out:

> I'm a great believer in not making music in studios. We did a lot of the work for 'Rise' in my back room at home, where I've only got a Mackie desk, one of the old 16-bit RADAR machines, an Akai MPC60 and S3200, and a couple of bits of outboard.[30]

In 2000, much of the technology that Dollar describes was dated and certainly the tools of project and semi-professional workplaces and/or musicians. This keen effort *not* to create a recording using the standard tools or workplace situates Dollar as an outlier in late 1990s record production; this aspect of recordist working practices is discussed later in Chapters 4 through 6.

This modern R&B song focuses around a drum loop with accompanying bass and string lines and gospel-style choir backing vocal segments. In the style of Dollar's late 1990s trip-hop group, the constructed drum loop features audible edits and results in a far from smooth rhythmic progression with audible start and end points. Yet the RADAR's sophisticated editing capability enabled the recordists to apply the lo-fidelity, 'cut and paste' aesthetics prevalent in trip-hop genre to Gabrielle's R&B hit. Dollar described how the functionality of the RADAR enabled him to construct the rhythmic elements:

> Later on, in order to add some variation to the loop, we played with the attack time of the envelope at the beginning of the sample as we finally laid it down to tracks on the Otari RADAR. This allowed us to change how hard the kick drum at the beginning of the sample sounded throughout the track – at the beginning of the song it's really hard, but it softens off elsewhere, which helps provide some motion.[31]

This detailed editing capability is precisely what set the RADAR out from the ADAT. Like the sampler, the functionality of the RADAR to alter the envelope of sounds and construct loops within the machine blurred the lines between composition and recording device. This is also illustrated in perhaps the best-known application of the RADAR to a commercial recording: Blondie's 'Maria' (1999), taken from the album *No Exit* (1999). This recording was completed at the home studio of Blondie guitarist Chris

Stein and produced by classical and contemporary recordist Craig Leon – Blondie's original recordist on *Blondie* (1976), as well as Ramones' *Ramones* (1976) and Richard Hell and the Voidoids' *Blank Generation* (1977). With *No Exit*, Stein recalled attempting to recreate the analogue aesthetics of 1970s Blondie without the temporal and financial constraints of a professional recording studio, as he stated:

> Chris's basement was an unusual choice ... but it worked very well because it gave us the freedom to experiment. We weren't on a shoe-string budget – far from it. Basically the budget was whatever it took to make the record. But when you are paying £1,000 a day for a top studio you do become very aware of the clock ticking, and this in itself can be a bar to creativity.[32]

A significant challenge presented to both musicians and recordists was constructing a record that would fit sonically with the band's then 25-year-old back catalogue whilst at the same time slot into a contemporary music landscape. Stein and Leon 'bridged' both this era and sonic aesthetic gap by placing the RADAR at the centre of their recording workflow, as Leon went on to say:

> The best thing about RADAR is that it's a technological device that doesn't sound digital. To me this is important, because I love the old analogue sounds and would never want to work exclusively in the digital domain. I certainly wouldn't want to do drums digitally, because I don't think digital can provide the right depth and clarity at the top end. But we used RADAR for pretty much everything else.[33]

This reference to 'old analogue' sounds and the aesthetically 'analogue' functionality of the RADAR – as previously described by Howard and later by Street – is another good example of the RADAR as a technological 'bridge', between both historical eras of sound recording and production technology and the mechanical/computational gap between tape and DAWs. However, whilst Leon preferred the sonic character of drums recorded in the analogue domain, the editing capability of the RADAR was employed to manipulate the live, acoustic recordings, as he stated, 'We used Electric Lady to record bass, drums and two guitars. We ended up mutating everything we recorded there, including the drums, which I put back into the RADAR so I could move them around.'[34]

Whilst 'Maria' is the sound of a band performing live and retaining analogue aesthetics, the record itself was constructed entirely in the digital domain. In fact, in order to create a quantized, DAW-produced 'feel' to the track, its composition began as MIDI tracks which the band later played live to, like an elaborate click track. So, whilst the components of 'Maria' began as synthesized loops, they were eventually replaced by live instrumentation, as Leon suggested:

> We didn't use any sequencers on the actual record – it was all done live. We put everything we did on the RADAR, and at the end of each day I'd go through it and see what we wanted to keep. After about a month we had worked up about 25

ideas, some of which were very much like the original demos and some that had mutated into completely different songs.³⁵

The application of the RADAR to Blondie's recording process assisted a long-established band, whose recording experience was predominately in the analogue domain, in creating a then current, modern record.

Apple and Pro Tools

Apple computers have remained the platform of choice for many recordists since the mid-1980s, mainly due to their stable operating systems and software compatibility. Early Apple computers were released as far back as the late 1970s, but it was the introduction of both the Macintosh and the Apple II in 1984 that cemented Apple's position in the computer market, as Negroponte explained in *Being Digital*:

> The Macintosh was a major step forward in the marketplace and, by comparison, almost nothing has happened since. It took all the other computer companies more than five years to copy Apple and, in some cases, they have done so with inferior results, even today.³⁶

Negroponte quite rightly cites Apple's 1984 Macintosh as a major step forward and the introduction of the Macintosh had major implications for the recording industry. Indeed, by 1987, Apple's Macintosh II was released – a groundbreaking design featuring an optional 20 MB or 40 MB hard-disk storage system and 16 MHz processor. The colour capabilities and stable operating system (from 1984 to 1987, this was Mac Operating System versions one through four) positioned the Macintosh as a desirable choice for audio industry personnel looking to integrate computer-based production software into their studios. Somewhat coincidentally, in 1984, US manufacturer Digidesign began producing early versions of their software packages that have since become almost compulsory tools for all recording and production workplaces, from the professional industry down to home studio set-ups. Originally entitled 'Digidrums', the company released its Sound Designer software in 1989, widely regarded as the first audio editing software for the Macintosh. The company furthered this concept in 1989 by releasing Sound Tools, an early version of the Pro Tools software that proliferated through the 1990s. This embryonic version of the now ubiquitous DAW would go on to revolutionize the recording industry with its sophisticated audio and MIDI recording and editing capability as it set itself apart from MIDI-based sequencing packages such as Pro-16, Pro-24 and Creator with four tracks of audio recording and editing capability. A hardware–software package that could be installed on and run from a Macintosh computer, Pro Tools v1 was based around two Motorola DSP cards, a rack-mountable hardware interface with playback of up to four simultaneous signals and a software package featuring an editing window whereby audio track waveforms were represented visually and could be manipulated with a number of editing 'tools'. This real-time, non-destructive audio editor enabled a level of micro waveform editing never seen before in the recording industry and was quickly hailed as another revolution. However, with this seemingly overnight change came a new set of challenges for those required to operate and maintain developing DAWs. The Pro Tools precursor Sound Designer was installed in Abbey Road Studios almost as soon as it was available. Former Abbey Road maintenance engineer Melvyn Toms recalls the consequences in the studio's technical department, as he states:

> We're all so computer literate now, but at that point in time, it was a means to an end. If you take a classical music editor, he has just about gotten over the shock of throwing away his scissors and sellotape when he's using this hardware thing that controls these clunky boxes. It was so slow and tedious you wouldn't believe it. Now, we're asking them to throw away these systems and sit in front of a workstation. These guys had an enormous understanding of music and repertoire, they could liaise with record producers, they could interpret a score – but a computer? I found I wasn't able to access the information because there was no Internet and I didn't have the contacts with the right sort of people to help me sort out some of the more buried problems of computers and systems.[37]

Toms illustrates the sudden move from analogue tape towards the integration of digital tape machines and then to computer-based workstations. Building on his previous observation that the absence of digital audio analysers led to scepticism amongst personnel, this statement substantiates how the introduction of computers resulted in some engineers being 'unable to cope'. Indeed, former AIR studio manager Malcolm Atkin substantiates these points that, by the late 1980s and into the early 1990s, digital audio files began to present compatibility issues from system to system:

> We then got to a situation where the clients were using [Pro Tools] at home and they were coming in with Pro Tools files. In the early days, every time a Pro Tools system came through the door, it wasn't compatible with the files they'd brought with them. It was a nightmare.[38]

By 1992, more than 3,000 Pro Tools v1 systems had been installed around the world. Yet whilst take-up in the professional industry was quick, it was not until much later in the decade – and towards v5 – that Pro Tools was used to create chart hits. This was less due to the software's capability and more down to computer processing power and RAM; whilst Pro Tools was a relatively affordable software package, the computers and hard-disk space required to run it adequately were still extremely expensive, and it took a number of years until the necessary computer specifications were affordable enough to run it well. As noted by Greg Milner,[39] the first number 1 record to be recorded, edited and mixed entirely within Pro Tools was Ricky Martin's global hit 'Livin' La Vida Loca' (1999), but there were a multitude of artists and recordists who grasped the compositional and production capability of Pro Tools into the late 1990s.

By 1997, Digidesign had released Pro Tools v4, supporting 24-bit audio, 24 tracks of audio recording capability and a new set of 'AudioSuite' plug-ins. The software package could also support MIDI tracks and was often synchronized to analogue tape machines. A former analogue loyalist, Wisconsin-based recordist Butch Vig was an early Pro Tools convert. Having set up Smart Studios in Madison in 1983, Vig built a reputation for 'turn(ing) your noisy garage band into something the whole world would love'.[40] By the early 1990s, Vig's production credits included Sonic Youth's *Dirty* (1990), Nirvana's *Nevermind* (1991), L7's *Bricks Are Heavy* (1992) and Smashing Pumpkins' *Gish* (1991), all either independent or formerly independent recording artists who came to represent early 1990s grunge genre. During the 1990s, Smart Studios was an almost entirely analogue recording facility, housing a Studer A827 analogue recorder, as well as a Trident ADC mixing console (1997); however, by the late 1990s, Vig had incorporated a Sony 3348 DASH machine into the workflow. He explained Smart Studios' steady move away from analogue equipment and towards computer-based recording: 'Over a period of time, we went to a more sophisticated eight-track to a sixteen-track to a 24 to a 48, to now a full-on Pro Tools System. It was a slow evolution.'[41]

By the late 1990s, Vig had moved away from recording and production to focus on his own synth-rock band, Garbage. In the recording of their second album, *Version 2.0* (1998), Vig embraced digital technology in order to divert from the guitar-based, live performance music he had been associated with. Vig's scepticism is indicative of a common feeling amongst recordists of the era and will be discussed at length in Chapter 6. However, he described being converted to Pro Tools once he was confident of the system's stability:

> Once you get into Pro Tools ... there's no coming back. I dove into it to record *Version 2.0*, and I think I was skeptical because I was such an analog freak when I first started out. I was afraid it would sound crunchy, not transparent enough, and the first [versions of Pro Tools] did sound that way, but the 24-bit system is very transparent.[42]

Pro Tools editing is particularly evident throughout 'I Think I'm Paranoid' (1998), the second single from *Version 2.0*. The percussion loops are reversed and placed throughout the track – during the introduction (0.00–0.08) and bridges (0.20–0.25), and time stretching is audible on key vocal sections, particularly during the bridges at 0.20 and 1.24; this effect is made into a particularly notable feature during the coda from 2.53. Starting at 2.06, the middle break can be conceived as a Pro Tools showcase, featuring multiple sampled percussion and loops flying around the stereo field, as well as heavily processed vocal snippets treated with band-pass filters and other effects. At 2.24, the entire mix is slowed to a halt, rather like a vinyl record that has been manually stopped. Vig stated:

> We recorded most of the tracks into Pro Tools, then we would edit or process or whatever we ended up doing, which we do actually a lot, and then when it came time to mix the rhythm tracks, stuff was all transferred to the Studers[43]

Such was the presence of Pro Tools record construction in Butch Vig's Garbage production that by late 1998 he was advertising the system. In a 1998 Digidesign advertisement, Vig's picture was placed above the caption: 'Pro Tools Takes Our Music into the Next Dimension'.[44]

By 1999, Digidesign proclaimed that 'More hit records are produced with Pro Tools than all other Digital Audio Workstations combined'.[45] Yet, until the turn of the millennium, DAW-recorded hit records were still in the minority when compared to those recorded to analogue or digital tape. The updated Pro Tools v5 (1999) was the most stable system yet and resulted in increased take-up, particularly in the US industry. One such individual to embrace the new system was US songwriter-producer David Frank, a classically trained pianist, Berklee College graduate, former member of synth-pop duo The System and lead synthesist on multiple 1980s hits, including Chaka Khan's 'I Feel for You' (1984), Phil Collins's 'Sussudio' (1985) and Steve Winwood's 'Higher Love' (1986). Having installed Pro Tools in his Canyon Reverb home studio in Los Angeles, Frank synergized the MIDI capabilities of EMagic's Logic DAW with the audio-tracking functionality and hardware interface of Pro Tools to create an almost entirely digital recording set-up. It was on this system that Frank produced one of the decade's most successful hit records, Christina Aguilera's 'Genie in a Bottle' (1999). A groove-oriented, R&B-influenced pop track, 'Genie in a Bottle' features little to no live performances aside from the lead vocal. Built on multiple rhythmic loops and melodic synthesis lines, the track is a glossy, heavily processed showcase of DAW functionality. Multiple programmed lines are seamlessly integrated into a cohesive backing track to which Aguilera performed her vocal and backing vocal parts. Frank pointed out:

> The whole song is really just an eight-bar looped sequence containing a number of different parts. Obviously there's an intro and a couple of little stops, but the only other way we introduced variation in the backing was by switching parts on and off throughout the song.[46]

The whole digital aesthetic of 'Genie in a Bottle' was evident throughout, featuring a multitude of micro-processing techniques, such as tightly edited samples, perfectly constructed loops and short effects bursts. Such intricate programming could only have been achieved on a DAW and set a new precedent in terms of the possibilities of fully digital, DAW record construction for twenty-first-century popular music. Frank recognized the final mix stage of 'Genie in a Bottle' as significant in determining the overall sound of the track:

> We put everything to analog tape and did a mix. But after a week or so we weren't really happy with the mix. We had gotten really used to hearing the vocals coming directly out of Pro Tools. There's a certain edge that you get with digital that you don't with analog. We couldn't get the snare and kick sounds we wanted with the analog tape; analog warmed it up too much. So we just mixed directly from Pro Tools.[47]

At the turn of the millennium, 'Genie in a Bottle' perhaps signified the future of DAW-based, modern pop recording techniques. However, the end of the 1990s also saw another technological turning point in terms of the sonically discernible foregrounding of effects processors. The use of plug-ins – small pieces of DAW-compatible software that could be inserted into software mixer channels – proliferated in the late 1990s as DAW functionality increased, the systems became more stable and computer processing power enabled greater simultaneous operation of both software DAW and plug-ins. Released by US manufacturer Antares in 1997, the 'Autotune' plug-in was one such technology that quickly became a signature motif through R&B, pop and hip-hop records at the turn of the millennium. A small pitch-shifting tool designed to correct micro pitching issues in vocals and instruments, the plug-in featured a basic pitch graph editor enabling the user to manipulate individual notes to a predetermined degree of pitch correction. Whilst designed to be a discreet technology to be applied to odd inconsistencies in larger vocal and instrument performances, the Autotune's 'automatic mode' rate could be set to pull the note towards a target pitch at a predefined speed. When this rate was increased, the resulting signal would 'lock' to the target pitch and create a dehumanized, vocoder-like effect. This was used to groundbreaking effect in Cher's 'Believe' (1997). The Autotune can be heard throughout the track, particularly noticeable on 'can't break through' (0.36–0.38) and on the words 'sad' (0.44) and 'time' (0.48). London recordists Mark Taylor and Brian Rawling, who recorded the track at Dreamhouse Studios in Surrey, UK, originally attributed the distinctive vocal effects to a Korg Vocoder in an attempt to keep their production motif 'a trade secret'[48] until eventually revealing it as the Antares Autotune. In fact, the distinct sound of the vocals led to the Autotune being called 'the Cher effect'[49] for some time before the Antares proliferated into the commercial recording mainstream. However, despite ongoing controversy, the Antares Autotune soon became the 'must-have' plug-in for recordists and enthusiasts working in pop music production. The application of the Autotune effect, not as it were originally intended, but as a prominent, foregrounded vocal effect, proliferated long into the 2000s and became a signature motif on many hit albums of the early twenty-first century, including Mirwais' *Production* (2000), Akon's *Trouble* (2004) and later on used prolifically by US rappers T-Pain, on his albums *Epiphany* (2007) and *Thr33 Ringz* (2008), and Kanye West on his album *808s and Heartbreak* (2008).

These last few sections have considered some of the key, then cutting-edge technologies used in 1990s commercial record production. However, whilst these new digital recording systems had a transformative effect on the production of popular music, they certainly did not render technological precursors obsolete. In fact, analogue tape recorders continued as one of the recording mediums of choice well into the new millennium.

Analogue recording, technological iconicity and the 'vintage'

At this stage, it is important to acknowledge – and in doing so, begin to theorize on - the use of technological precursors in the kinds of contemporary commercial record production dealt with in this book. This is a particularly interesting yet understudied area of record production discourse that I hope will be further illuminated through the recordist discussions and analyses later on. Throughout this chapter, references to the use of technologies considered 'vintage' (such as Ballard's use of the 1954 AKG C12) and technological precursors (such as Dollar's use of the AKAI MPC60) feature regularly in the context of both workplace and recordists' uses of then current digital recording systems. As featured in my previous work,[50] I have focused on applications of such technologies to contemporary recording workflows. Not only is this in itself a critique of determinism (otherwise, why would recordists and workplaces choose to look 'backwards' when making technological choices?), but it also points to a kind of iconification of recording technologies. As discussed in my previous work,[51] some past recording technologies are lauded, iconicized and routinely applied to contemporary recording sessions, whilst others fall by the proverbial wayside and are considered obsolete and/or forgotten. Additionally, by the 1990s, technologies that were by then considered 'vintage' were routinely applied to commercial recording sessions.

Until the late 1970s and the advent of digital recording, professional recording studios worked solely within the analogue domain. Upgrades usually took place as analogue multitrack capabilities increased, particularly from 4-track to 8-track and from 8-track to 16-track in the 1950s, 1960s and 1970s, respectively. The introduction of digital recording equipment in the late 1970s was pivotal. Almost overnight, high-end sound recording technology transformed and the systems used until that point were considered redundant. This sudden change was epitomized in Abbey Road Studios' 'Sale of the Century'. On 15–16 October 1980, the studio held a sale of its redundant recording equipment. As Don Weller remarked in a 1980 article in *Billboard*:

> LONDON – Buyers from all over the world are expected for the recording equipment 'Sale of the Century', taking place Oct 15–16 in EMI's famous Abbey Road Studios. Centrepiece of the sale is the 4-track, Studer 337, on which 'Sergeant Pepper' was recorded, alongside a Mellotron with many of The Beatles original tapes intact. Aside from such memorabilia, the main sales covers multi-tracks, mixing desks, monitors, mikes, stands and screens, test equipment, disc cutting and tape duplication equipment, reverbs, noise reduction, delays, flangers and much more, along with a jumble sale of other oddments. It's a case of off the old and on with the new at Abbey Road, where a 16-channel digital mixer developed and manufactured at the Thorn EMI Central Research Laboratories in Hayes has just been installed for operational evaluation.[52]

The advertisement is significant for a number of reasons. First, the 4-track recorder and Mellotron, as used by the Beatles, are described not as working, useable pieces of equipment but as 'memorabilia', implying that the systems are collectors' items of historical value. Additionally, this also illustrates an early reference to vintage equipment as being associated with memorable artists or events, the very presence of these systems invoking the aura of canonized artists and their recordings. The 4-tracks were not being sold on their use value, but on the basis that they were associated with the Beatles. Secondly, the statement 'off the old and on with the new' is indicative of the tech-utopian culture at the time. As has been recognized by many scholars,[53] the influx of digital sound recording and music technologies into the industry during the 1980s had a divisive effect, with some recordists welcoming new digital recording devices and others holding more sceptical views; this is discussed further later on.

The BBC Redundant Plant (as it was officially titled) was based in Power Road, Chiswick, specializing in the resale of its antiquated sound recording, broadcasting and television equipment to specialist recording and broadcasting facilities, as well as the general public. The plant itself was instrumental in supplying outdated systems to the BBC's own Radiophonic Workshop, as former manager Brian Hodgson stated:

> In the very beginning, Desmond [Briscoe] had been given £2000 and the key to 'redundant plant' [the BBC's junk pile] and that was it! The place kept going for years on what we called 'fag-ends and lollipops'. 'Fag-ends' were the bits of unwanted rubbish that other departments had thrown away; 'lollipops' were the much rarer treats that were occasionally sent down to keep Desmond [Briscoe] quiet.[54]

The BBC Redundant Plant was a significant retailer of vintage technologies and precursors, until it ceased to exist in April 1996. Arguably, retailers like Vintage King, Pro Audio Europe and eBay filled the leftover void, although none operate on the same scale. The BBC Redundant Store and Abbey Road's Sale of the Century were instrumental in the resale of perhaps the first 'batch' of vintage technologies, particularly once 16-track analogue tape recording was superseded. Indeed, both outlets served as an important predecessor to the vintage market today. However, both outlets reinforced the perception that vintage sound recording equipment was either redundant, implying loss of meaning or function, or for collectors' interests only. Any ongoing use value of the second-hand equipment was largely ignored.

Technological development in sound recording was also recognized in the 1980s by the TEC foundation, an association originally founded by *Mix* magazine, then incorporated into NAMM late into the 2000s.[55] Each year, the TEC foundation nominates and then 'inducts' individuals – usually recordists, workplace owners and technical standards inventors – and technologies deemed to have made outstanding contributions to the audio industry into its so-called 'Hall of Fame'. This acknowledgement of the impact of technology and process can be considered a kind of canonization 'mirroring' musician and composer canons. Whilst the 'induction' of recordists into the NAMM 'Hall of Fame' began in 1985, it was not until 2004 that the organization bestowed the honour on technologies. Amongst the first set of inductees were the AKG C12 microphone, the SSL 4000 mixing console, the NED Synclavier, the ADAT and Digidesign's Pro Tools. This honouring process reinforces a technology canon that, by the 1990s, was already partly established and in recent years has contributed to the separation of past technologies considered obsolete and those deemed worthy of lasting value.

This lauding of past technologies was evident in the 1980s recording workplace: a result of both technological canonization of past devices and the application of analogue and past technologies as a political statement against digital audio. U2's multi-platinum selling album *The Joshua Tree* (1987) utilized both vintage and technological precursors – including the Neve – as well as live, 'performance capture'-oriented techniques. As Daniel Lanois pointed out: 'I cannot think of any other artist of the late 1980s that would have required – or settled for – this method of recording and production. Yet it suited *The Joshua Tree* perfectly.'[56]

Another example lies in the recording of Talk Talk's *Spirit of Eden* (1987) album. Engineer Phill Brown deliberately used what he referred to as 'relatively old fashioned equipment where possible'[57] and stated: 'We approached the album as if it was night time in 1967. I used no Dolby noise reduction, and we confined ourselves to equipment and microphones that were around prior to 1967.'[58] The album has a particularly ambient, live feel with distant, heavily reverberant, processed vocal tracks and an overall analogue aesthetic, entirely indicative of analogue recording and 'performance capture' techniques.

So far, this book has framed sound recording technologies in a sequential, chronological trajectory, situating multiple modern records in their then current technological contexts. It is important to note that many commercial recordings of the 1980s and 1990s were made on technological precursors and on analogue systems. Indeed, one of the most commonly applied recording technologies to commercial music production sessions throughout the 1980s and 1990s was not a digital recorder at all, but the Studer A800 24-track, microprocessor-controlled analogue tape recorder. Released in 1978, this machine soon infiltrated professional recording workplaces across Europe and the United States and was used as the main multitrack machine to record hundreds, if not thousands, of hit records long into the 2000s. It is important to note that analogue machines were often employed on recording sessions as a deliberate, political statement against digital recorders.[59]

Installed in The Hit Factory, Puff Daddy's own Daddy's House Studios and Music Palace in New York, as well as the Death Row studios in Los Angeles, the A800 was the recorder of choice for hundreds of commercial R&B, hip-hop and neo-soul records of the 1990s, including Dr Dre's 'Nuthin' but a "G" Thang' (1993), Busta Rhymes's 'Woo-hah! Got You All in Check' (1996) and Puff Daddy and Faith Evans's 'I'll Be Missin' You' (1997). Almost twenty years after its release and in a technological landscape dominated by digital devices for fifteen years, the A800 flourished and continues to be referred to as the 'gold standard', 'legendary' or the 'pinnacle' of multitrack sound recording fidelity.[60] The machine was also a popular choice for recording grunge and 'alternative' rock musics throughout the 1990s. Dave Jerden recorded Alice in Chains' debut album *Facelift* (1990) to an A800 at London Bridge Studios in 1990. Rob Cavallo recorded Green Day's *Dookie* (1994) to an A800 at Fantasy Studios in California. As will be illustrated later on, the application of technological precursors to contemporary recording sessions did not – and does not – occur in a vacuum, neither can it be attributed to nostalgia alone; a series of often complex decisions and critical reasoning, often based on perceived sonic aesthetics, informs such choices. Certainly, the combination of analogue recording with vintage technologies contributed to the sonic separation of grunge and alternative musics out from the commercial mainstream. One particularly innovative use of this winning combination was recordist Sylvia Massy's application of the Studer A800 and 1972 Neve 8068 console – considered vintage by the mid-1990s – to multiple US alternative artists of the 1990s. In recording Tool's *Undertow* (1993) at Sound City Studios, Los Angeles, Massy's workflow included vintage Neumann microphones, often used as ambient pairs, through the studio's vintage Neve 8068 console into Studer A800 and A827 tape recorders. She also applied 1968 Urei 1176 and 1178 compressors and a 1959 Fairchild 670 limiter; the latter device is one of the most revered and iconicized audio processors in recording history. Long into the twenty-first century, the position of the Fairchild 660 limiter has only been elevated further, as demand for the device continues to increase simultaneously to the declining supply of operational machines.[61] At the time of going to press, the Fairchild 660 limiter retailed for $42,000 in the second-hand market.[62] Largely a result of its use in Abbey Road Studios throughout the 1960s and most famously applied to most of the Beatles recording sessions, the Fairchild 660 has been referred to as 'the holy grail',[63] 'the gold standard'[64] and 'highly prized'[65] and is renowned for 'colouring' instruments with a 'soft distortion' and 'percussive' tone. The application of such a device to recording sessions is, therefore, loaded with implication: historical, cultural, technological, musical and sonic meanings are imbued into recordings with every application of the device and with it, a kind of sonic authentication. In recording System of a Down's *System of a Down* (1998), again at Sound City Studios, Massy integrated further vintage technologies into her workflow, incorporating a barely operational broadcast compressor into the session:

> The 'Army Man' is a crusty old Western Electric frankenstein broadcast tube compressor I dragged out of an old radio guy's garage in Pasadena around 20 years ago. It has exposed wiring, which I have not covered up, making it extremely dangerous ... I have not done any maintenance to make this ancient compressor work properly. In fact, I don't want it to work properly because it makes anything you run through sound furry and explosive. For example, I'll route a mono drum room mic through it for extreme compression. Doing this makes the drums feel exciting without accentuating the high end on the cymbals. During a session, Serge from SOAD stuck a little toy army man in it, thus the nickname 'Army Man' was born.[66]

Massy's 'Army Man' is a Western Electric RA-1217 limiting amplifier, built in 1948 and used primarily in the radio and telecommunications industry. This intentional application of a then unique device to a recording session 50 years after its construction – and particularly in the barely functional state it was in – demonstrates Massy's intention to apply unique sonic textures to her productions. In doing so, once again she created one of the most sonically identifiable records of the 1990s. On 'Sugar' (1998), for example, the guitars – as well as the entire mix – are subject to the 'extreme compression' Massy describes, featuring the noisy, 'furry' and unique tonality of the RA-1217. On 'Know' (1998), this is audible throughout, but particularly noticeable on the introduction where a noisy hum is exposed against the drum fills until the guitar finally enters at 0.06. The same noise is also heard during the instrumental break between 1.42 and 1.45. The sound of a unique, antique processor here is imbued into the entire recording and, in the context of its use in an entirely analogue signal chain, created a distinct sonic signature for System of a Down and separated their music out from other so-called 'nu-metal' acts of the late 1990s.

Massy was one of the few recordists dedicated to the analogue domain and vintage technologies by the late 1990s. In a landscape dominated by digital recording and processing, such precursors, vintage and antique technologies were almost always deliberately employed to sessions as sonic differentiators – a means of creating unique tones in an increasingly homogenous recording technology industry. Such demand for unique and original sounds can be traced back to at least the 1960s but, by the 1990s, recordists had at their disposal a far greater palette of technologies with which to work.

Summary

If, as Taylor suggested, 'the advent of digital technologies in the early 1980s marked the biggest shift in Western music since the advent of musical notation',[67] the proliferation of digital recording in the 1990s marked a further move away from 'performed' musics and towards entirely new, digitally constructed forms. This shift is recognizable not only in the resulting music but in the evident changes to recording workplace, increasingly blurred conflations of recordist, composer and musician roles, and the foregrounding of technological intervention. What is significant about 1990s recording technology is the obvious alignment of particular devices to aesthetic musical directions and genres. Patterns exist between the choice of recording technology and musical elements, style and, therefore, such technologies become assimilated into the relative production toolbox. The ADAT and RADAR were ultimately responsible for a technological shift away from the professional workplace and towards project studio set-ups; whilst the house and hip-hop hits of the late 1980s could be attributed to underground and 'alternative' music lucky breaks into the commercial mainstream, by the late 1990s, bedroom and project studio hit records were commonplace. The ADAT and RADAR did, however, provide recordists with an important 'bridge' between analogue recorders of the 1970s and 1980s and the DAWs of the late 1990s and into the 2000s. As will be illustrated throughout the proceeding chapters, some recordists found the digital recording landscape easier to grasp than others, and there is a sense of 'transition' in those who worked with the ADAT and/or the RADAR. Important to note is the pattern of cheaper technologies present in hip-hop and dance musics; the AKAI MPC, Roland 808 and 909 machines and budget digital recorders became sonic identifiers in much the same way as electric guitars are traditionally aligned to rock music; albums, such as Kanye West's *808s and Heartbreak* (2008), continued to foreground the device long into the 2000s. By the 1990s, the hard utopianism so prevalent in the 1980s had begun to wear off. Hybrid workflows, the integration of new technologies into older style workplaces and the inability of any digital recorder to surpass the iconicity of the Studer tape recorder kept the domination of DAWs at bay until into the 2000s. Additionally, in an increasingly digital recording landscape, analogue, vintage and technological precursors were applied as important sonic differentiators – a relatively straightforward means of separating underground and alternative musics out from the commercial mainstream. Such uses of precursors – particularly when combined with unorthodox techniques – led to some of the most successful music of the era. It is, however, important to assert that such technological application does not occur in a vacuum. Behind every choice and application of recording and production technology to a musical instrument lies a decision – a conscious choice on the part of the recordist to apply a particular sonic trope to a piece of music. These decisions are often complex and come loaded with historical, cultural and technological meanings.

4

Maverick Methods:
Tech-Processual Unorthodoxies in Contemporary Record Production

In 1982, British post-punk band Siouxsie and the Banshees released their fifth studio album *A Kiss in the Dreamhouse* to critical acclaim. In their authorized biography, singer Siouxsie Sioux described recordist Mike Hedges as 'like a big kid, and a great ringmaster for practical jokes',[1] as she described some of his typical recording processes:

> 'Playground' was an apt name for the studios because that was exactly how he [Mike Hedges] treated it. He'd try anything. I remember him once putting a microphone with a Durex (condom) stretched over it in a bucket of water to see what it sounded like.[2]

These techniques, those that epitomize *maverick methods*, are the ones that musicians – and, indeed, readers of post-punk biography – remember, that stick out above the mundanity of common studio practices. Techniques such as the one Sioux describes are nowhere to be found in engineering handbooks, education curricula or manufacturer user guides. Hedges' microphone technique is indicative of what some scholars and recordists[3] have referred to as 'rule breaking' – that being an isolated tech-processual incident or, indeed, an entire methodology (and everything in between) that is not indicative of established audio engineering or music production 'best practice'. This is by no means anything new nor exclusive to 1980s and 1990s recording practice. In fact, sound recording history is full of examples of new recording techniques stemming from unorthodox uses of technology and practice. In saying that, tech-processual unorthodoxies were more prevalent in contemporary recording (1980s onwards), largely due to a greater pool of available technologies and techniques. This chapter, therefore, deals with the idea of music recording and production 'standards', challenges to such convention and the mythologization of process. Specifically, the chapter poses the following questions and seeks to unravel some of the processual issues in 1980s and 1990s popular music recording with examples: When applied to technological and/or processual practice, what does 'industry standard' mean, and how are such practices articulated and disseminated? How has a historical continuum of recording practice reinforced 'standard practice' and ideas of 'established' techniques? How and in what ways are recording techniques 'mythologized'? Which techniques can be considered 'maverick', and how do these techniques align – or not – with the aforementioned notion of 'standards'? How and why do recordists defy, resist, 'push the boundaries' or 'break the rules' of such 'standard' modes of practice?

Mike Hedges's Siouxsie and the Banshees recording is indicative of a wider issue in music production and how tech-processual practices are represented in historiography – and this is something of a dichotomy. Standardized, 'established' practices – what is taught both theoretically and vocationally, disseminated via textbook and manufacturer guidelines – present us with 'benchmark' processes. On the other hand, the recordists most documented, revered and canonized in popular music history are those who have *not* conformed to such 'standards': those who have seemingly pushed technological boundaries, defied processual convention and created whole new ways of working as a result. That may be because standard practices are simply not as interesting: submerging condom-enrobed microphones in buckets of water is far more innovative, entertaining and memorable than a 'how to' description of simply placing the microphone on its stand with a pop shield and singing through it. Additionally, for every boundary-pushing tech-processual incident occurring in a recording session, there are perhaps many more that conform to the 'standard' or mundane, so again, it is important to situate these events in the wider context and acknowledge that in many recording sessions, conflations of standard practices – and challenges to those practices – occur. However, as discussed in this chapter, the prevalence of such tech-processual 'boundary pushing' is such that it warrants further investigation and elucidation.

Historical conventions and 'standards'

The term 'industry standard' has been – and still is – often used to define current technological use and work(ing) practice(s) amongst communities of recordists. Of course, recordists, workplace and musical aesthetics largely inform the terminology; 'industry standard' is dependent on multiple variables, is interpreted differently among recordists and can change and develop over time. Martland[4] uses the term 'industry standard' to describe the proliferation of disc formats at the turn of the twentieth century. Rumsey described the MIDI protocol as an 'industry standard' interface during the 1980s.[5] Hitchins applies the same term to describe the use of Pro Tools in the recording industry at the end of the 1990s.[6] 'Industry standard', therefore, is a synchronic terminology adopted to describe the dominant technology, process and/or format at a particular point in time. It is, however, a problematic term due to its lack of specificity: Which industry are we talking about and where? The Jamaican recording industry in the 1970s? Or the European classical music recording industry in the 1950s? Even if we flipped these questions on their heads and, instead, asked, 'What was "industry standard" recording process in 1986?' the answer would still depend on locality, workplace, musical aesthetics and the recordist. 'Industry standard' was used in reference to micro aspects of technological specifications, for example, the 'standard' MIDI protocol. Yet, the term also referred to macro aspects of recording practice, which varied widely depending on the genre, workplace and the recordist. So, as with the so-called 'analogue vs. digital debate', we have yet another largely indefinable and, to that end, *unhelpful* terminology that is all too often used as a definite term with an assumed (set of) understanding(s).

This book deals with UK and US commercial music recording and production in the 1980s and 1990s, which is quite a narrow frame from the outset. Even when confined to these parameters, 'industry standard' is difficult to pin down. For example, in the 1980s, 'Neve' and 'SSL' consoles were 'industry standard' desks in elite, large-scale recording studios, primarily in the United States, UK and Europe. Whereas an Atari ST linked in with other MIDI devices would have been deemed 'standard' for home and project studio-based dance music programming by the end of the decade, it was not a technology normally present in a high-end workplace. These are just two examples of how such a flexible terminology is interpreted depending on musical aesthetics and workplace.

Historically, developments in sound recording have been driven by a single, driving force: the quest for 'high fidelity' or 'hi-fidelity'.[7] This term originated in radio broadcasting through the 1930s[8] and was used in the recording industry to describe quality of recorded sound by the 1950s. Indeed, Greg Milner's 'Perfecting Sound Forever' focuses entirely on the drive for audio 'perfection' through the ages. From the acoustic considerations of the recording workplace to the quality of instruments, musical performances and sound recording technology to the mix and mastering processes, the quest for sonic perfection, to reproduce sound, music, *performances* precisely as was originally intended, has been the central premise of the recordist's role. The term 'high fidelity' can be traced back to the 1930s, as Schmidt Horning points out: 'Improvements in the frequency response of records, increasingly referred to as "high fidelity", not only boosted record sales but also created demand for better home reproducing equipment.'[9]

Whilst this book is concerned with 1980s and 1990s popular music recording and production, it is worth framing this era's 'standards' in a brief historical context. Due to demand for increasingly sophisticated classical music recordings, by the 1930s, the focus on sound quality shifted away from the formats and playback devices to the recording environment and equipment. After a dormant wartime period, a number of 'recording engineers, inventors, musicians, equipment manufacturers [and] audio specialists'[10] held the first meeting of the Audio Engineering Society in 1948 at RCA-Victor Studios in New York to promote research and development in audio recording with one key purpose: to improve the quality of recorded sound.

Walking and Talking is a short 1930s film from the EMI archives with Alan Blumlein and other EMI engineers demonstrating 'binaural recording' or what we have come to know as 'stereo'.[11] Blumlein and his white-lab-coated EMI colleagues represent a post-Edison period of intense scientific audio development: improvements to microphones, research into microphone techniques and positioning, followed by US audio engineer John Mullin's developments in magnetic tape recording after he returned to the United States from Europe at the end of the Second World War.[12] Mullin furthered the German 'Magnetophon' tape machine into two prototypes. These were adopted by Ampex,[13] which then triggered widespread production of tape machines by the UK and US audio industries, which were keen to apply the advanced technological development – and dramatically improved sound – to recorded music.

The drive to improve audio recording and sound reproduction technology was furthered into the 1960s with Ray Dolby's pioneering noise reduction system in professional recording studios by 1966. Increased hi-fidelity sound recording was largely driven by research into recording and microphones,[14] groove recording and records,[15] as well as magnetic tape technology.[16] AES provided the ideal forum in which research into acoustics, magnetic tape recording potential and microphone construction could be discussed and disseminated; the forum is the world's leading organization on all aspects of audio recording and production to this day. Analogue tape recording moved through 2-, 4-, 8-, 16- and 24-track capability by the 1970s, with Sony/Phillips pioneering both digital audio and MIDI into the 1980s.

So, often in the professional sound recording industries, 'industry standard' assumed the most cutting-edge, hi-fidelity recording equipment available to professional recording houses at that point in time. Not until the late 1970s did technologies aimed at an emergent musician's market separate the professional from the amateur, the recordist from the recording-enthused musician.

The audio industry's quest for sonic excellence has, however, had less than a smooth trajectory, particularly surrounding reception formats. Public adoption of increasingly hi-fidelity audio rarely kept pace with industry development, and there are many examples of 'tipping points' in the adoption of recorded formats whereby a flawed, lo-fidelity format is embraced due to its convenience. The stereo-8 cartridges in the 1960s and 1970s, Mini-Disc at the turn of the 1990s and, more recently, the widespread adoption of the reductive mp3 format suggest audiences have never fully embraced the audio industry's love of hi-fidelity sound.

Sony and Phillips' introduction of the CD as a consumer format culminated in pressures on the professional recording industry to record, mix and master with the signal being kept in the digital domain for the entire chain. The US industry organization SPARS (Society of Professional Audio Recording Services) developed a code for identifying which parts of the CD had been recorded, mixed and mastered in the analogue or digital domain. The code was stamped on the reverse side of the CD in a three-letter format. As discussed earlier, this was indicative of much tech-utopian feeling in the recording industry throughout the 1980s.

Sound engineering protocol – as defined by scientific research and technology manufacturers – is documented in multiple ways: publications and standards released by AES and in recent times, by Germany's Fraunhofer institute; technology user manuals; audio engineering conferences; sound science books;[17] science-based audio engineering pedagogy; the music technology and audio industry press;[18] the online discussion fora of audio equipment and software manufacturers.[19] These reinforce a conservative, 'rules-based' recording methodology, largely devoid of individuality, creative interpretation or artistic appropriation. This continual, science-driven reinforcement forms a pantheon of both technologies and processes deemed 'standards'.

In saying that, common processual aesthetics permeate the sounds of 1980s records and, therefore, point towards patterns of 'standardized' practices, as depicted in Table 4.1 below. Evidence of large-scale console mixes featuring layers of multitracking,

Table 4.1 Music recording technologies deemed 'standard': 1970s–1990s

1970s	1980s	1990s
8-track analogue recording	24-track digital recording (DASH)	ADAT
16- to 24-track analogue recording	MIDI	OTARI Radar hard disk recorder
16- to 24-track consoles	Large-format analogue consoles (SSL and Neve)	Pro Tools
Sony PCM-1600	Studer A-800	Studer A-800

not previously heard during the 1970s, is particularly notable on Michael Jackson's *Thriller* (1982), Madonna's *Like a Virgin* (1984) and many other large-budget, major label recordings of the early 1980s. Commercial pop music towards the late 1980s lost much of the analogue 'warmth' of the 1970s and began to sound louder, heavier in high-frequency content (suggesting applications of EQ had become more prevalent and, therefore, noticeable) and underpinned by programmed drum machines as opposed to live drummers. The single output of SAW including Dead or Alive's 'You Spin Me Round' (1984), Kylie Minogue's 'I Should Be So Lucky' (1987) and Mel and Kim's 'Respectable' (1987) all featured SAW's signature high-frequency dominant sound; the 'bottom-end roll-off' and 'top-end sparkle' are signature motifs of the production trio. Such EQ aesthetics are heard across commercial popular music of the era. The Nicky Graham-produced *Push* (1988) by UK boy band Bros also featured accentuated high frequencies across the vocals in particular. Pop, dance and hip-hop music became increasingly tempo-bound due to the nature of the technology used to create it. MIDI devices, drum machines and MIDI sequencers in particular operated to tempo maps in bpm, resulting in quantized rhythm patterns and 'fixed' grooves.

Many of these aesthetics are bound up in the technologies used to create them. For example, we can hear programmed patches from the Emulator II on records such as Kraftwerk's *Electric Café* (1986) and Depeche Mode's *Violator* (1990); the Emulator II was also used to create feature synth motifs, as can be heard on Mister Mister's 'Broken Wings' (1985). 'Construction' approaches to recording were more apparent than ever, with albums featuring heavy composite sample editing and 'collage' techniques particularly notable in hip-hop and dance music genres. As discussed earlier, Public Enemy's *It Takes a Nation of Millions ...* (1988), De La Soul's *3 Feet High and Rising* (1989) and Beastie Boys' *Pauls Boutique* (1989) are three notable records realized through significant sample collage, editing and programming processes. Such practice could also be heard in sample-sequencing compositions in early house genre: M/A/R/R/S' 'Pump Up the Volume' (1987) was a significant landmark in such sample-constructed house music due to the large number of samples present in the track. These aforementioned records were made using practices well established in the avant-garde, and to a lesser extent in commercial popular music,[20] but by the late 1980s had become 'standard' practices amongst hip-hop and dance music artists. Technology-driven 'construction' approaches that featured little to no evidence of live recording had become normalized, conspicuous and ubiquitous.

The 1990s signified a 'break out' period in terms of commercial recording and production practice. As demonstrated by many recordists in late 1980s hip-hop and dance music production, it was possible to achieve successful productions without the need for high-end studio equipment, recordists or techniques. To that end, contrasts exist amongst 1990s working practices in parallel to the 'technological mash-up' as described earlier. On the one hand, such variation in recording practice points to an absence of 'standard' practices, perhaps for the first time in sound recording history. On the other, 'standard' recording practices became more niche and aligned with genre and aesthetic intention like never before; furthermore, a marked return to 'standards' of prior eras became evident. Professional studio recording techniques, featuring the blending of live and programmed instruments via large-scale consoles were still very much in existence, with Neve and SSL mixing still popular amongst many recordists. A significant 1990s demarcation lies in the prevalence of hard-disk-based multitrack recording, particularly on the Otari RADAR. The Spice Girls' debut album *Spice* (1996) can be thought of as a continuum of the sonic aesthetics present in SAW's 1980s production methods; the presence of high-frequency EQ, particularly on the vocals is notable, as is the presence of sequenced backing tracks and minimal live performance.

Challenges, unorthodoxies, binaries and the mythologization of technique

In *The Poetics of Rock*, Albin Zak recognized the lack of acknowledgement recordists often give to the technical aspects of their practice:

> Although record making is extremely technical, comments on the nature of its process and criteria – even by those responsible for its most technical aspects – routinely de-emphasise theoretical principles or justifications.[21]

Zak is quite right; recordists often 'play down' their technical knowledge and the application of it to recording sessions, preferring to focus on interactions with musicians, attitudes towards technology or processual techniques.[22] This serves as an essential caveat to what I am about to say: it is this very withholding of the mundane, accumulated technical expertise that is so essential to recordists' work, yet simultaneously so unremarkable. To that end, it is quite possible that plenty of 'standard' practices exist within most commercial recording sessions, it is simply that they are not exciting enough to report on; let the textbook 'how-to's' take care of that. In that case, it is quite possible that these 'unorthodoxies' and challenges to standard practices are more prevalent simply because they are more reported; they are more reported because they are more exciting and because of what they do *not* represent and therefore serve as welcome breaks to the norms of tech-processual practice.

Whilst this book focuses on contemporary recordists and techniques, it is worth considering historical conventions and examples when thinking about how – and what and when – recording techniques came to be considered 'unorthodox'. Let's consider the work of 1960s London recordist Joe Meek. Along with George Martin, Phil Spector and Brian Wilson, Joe Meek's place in popular music history is that of a sonic pioneer: a maverick producer revered for his boundary-pushing recording techniques and technological innovation.[23] Many of today's recording and production standards, for example, the 'home studio', the application of spring reverbs to vocal performances, 'over compression' and the 'crushing' of overall dynamic range have been attributed to Meek and his company RGM Sound in the early 1960s. In contemporary recording, such popular production aesthetics are taken for granted: had Meek not sent audio signals through a broken fan heater or exploited tape saturation[24] we may not have had distortion as a creative effect, the ducking, pumping and breath-like compression techniques now ubiquitous in dance music or even the so-called 'loudness war'. The portrayal of recordists on film has been recognized as problematic,[25] but an important central theme runs through the 2008 Joe Meek biopic *Telstar*, despite the problematic portrayal of the recordist. Here is a recordist who 'broke the rules', whose tools and techniques baffled the musicians and associates he worked with, who painted sonic pictures in his mind and worked with whatever means he could to realize them. However, at this point in history – as Clem Cattini (played by James Corden) conveys to Meek in *Telstar* – such operational practice was considered madness.[26] Apparently, ludicrous techniques, such as Meek's bathroom echo chamber and the mic'ing up of the toilet bowl, were considered more a product of flawed, eccentric character than sound engineering prowess, but that is not to say there was no method in the madness; Meek's recordings are revered and canonized as some of the most innovative of the 1960s.

Binaries

In 2009, I interviewed Van Morisson's recordist Mick Glossop about creative practice in recording techniques. Glossop spoke of Joe Meek's work as signifying a marked shift in popular music production away from so-called 'industry standard', 'performance-capture' approaches and towards the technology-centric 'construction' of 'records'. He said of the early 1960s:

> Industry standard techniques were in existence, but Joe Meek wanted something else and he was the start of using the studio as a creative tool where the idea is not to make a faithful reproduction, but to create a recording that has its own qualities – in the same way that there's a difference between a movie and a stage theatre production.[27]

This movie–theatre binary analogy illustrates the diametric between stories constructed from multiple performance takes and those that are performed and 'captured' continually. These are two discernible dimensions of recording practice and the parallels are obvious, but there is more to be extrapolated from this recognition of 'performance capture' and 'construct'. At one point in history, then, 'constructing' records from multiple, engineered sound sources as opposed to capturing a performance was considered alternative. Mad, even. As the decades wore on, such practice was assimilated into the pantheon of techniques and, therefore, became 'standard' practices.

Meek's challenge to then standard engineering practices is also a good example of the 'perfection–imperfection' binary Hamilton discusses in *The Art of Recording and Aesthetics of Perfection*: 'A perfectionist aesthetic of recording aims to screen out allegedly contingent imperfections of live performance.'[28] Hamilton went on to explain imperfectionist recording as 'purist, in wanting to maintain the diachronic and synchronic integrity of the performance, which perfectionist recording creatively subverts'.[29] However, Hamilton's assertions also make assumptions as to the recordists' intention. For some recordists, such as Steve Albini and specifically his work on Pixies' *Surfer Rosa* (1988), the intention of capturing an artist with all the performance nuances intact is a 'perfectionist' approach, that being to extrapolate the best possible performance from the artist without the need for excessive technological intervention. On the other hand, 'constructed' recordings may be intentionally 'imperfectionist'. In Chapter 7, Madonna's 'Ray of Light' is an analytical case study. Recordist William Orbit constructed the record from multiple performance takes, sampled synthesis and programmed loops, yet Madonna's mantra for Orbit's recording process was 'Don't gild the lily'. In this case, the perfectionist–imperfectionist binary does not comfortably align with 'performance capture' and 'construction' approaches to recording, as much is dependent on the recordist's intention. Joe Meek's 'perfectionist' approach was strongly aligned to his imagining of a particular sonic soundscape. Hamilton does, however, recognize that 'for one person's technical shortcoming is another's aesthetic decision'.[30] In other words, 'mistakes' can be intentional.

The mythologization of technique

Scholars have recognized early 1960s popular music recordists as representational of a 'turning point' away from the 'performance capture' approaches employed by classical music engineers of the early twentieth century and towards creative, interpretive methodologies whereby the impact of studio techniques is sonically discernible on the recording, as Jamie Sexton suggested:

> Avant-garde techniques were increasingly smuggled into pop productions, leading to more complex recording techniques and the rise of the producer as a creative figure (as opposed to a functional engineer): George Martin, Joe Meek, Phil Spector and Brian Wilson all gained reputations as sonic alchemists, capable of using the studio in a creative and constructive manner.[31]

Sexton makes two significant points here: first, that popular music recordists in the 1960s used techniques already well established in the avant-garde and, second, the mention of 'alchemist' to describe perception(s) of their influence. As recording techniques reached this 'fork in the road', the creative appropriation of technologies and process in record 'construction' became less understood. No longer were engineers simply capturing a performance. Surely, then, the canonization of 1960s recordists is, to an extent, based on the mythologization of both the recordists' role and their working practices. Let's examine this concept further. 'Studio magic'[32] is often used as an umbrella term for seemingly 'indescribable' creative recording techniques. Similarly, terms such as 'wizardry',[33] 'alchemy'[34] and 'trickery'[35] are ascribed to recording techniques and the goings-on in a recording studio; these are broad, non-technical terms evoking mystery, conjury and implying the intervention of inexplicable forces on the recording process. Taken literally, this is of course not the case; supernatural forces are not at play inside the recording workplace. The idea that *what recordists do* 'behind the closed doors' of their workplace is somehow attributable to supernatural forces is, however, a result of a range of factors. First, the historical role of the recordist – and their work – is one that is concealed[36] and, unlike the performer's role, takes place away from the public arena. As pointed out in the Introduction, until the very recent advent of recordist biographies and documentary films, which have slowly revealed the nature of recording processes, the internal operations of recording workplaces have remained hidden from view. In an extreme example, the German group Kraftwerk operated from their own studio: 'Kling Klang' in Düsseldorf. Operations within Kling Klang were – and remain – notoriously secretive. Within this 'Willy Wonka' style factory, the group operate with all visitors and mail consistently turned away from the premises.[37] Secondly, the historical situation of sound recording technologies in the space of the elite recording studio confined operational understanding to a select few, highly skilled technicians. Until the late 1980s, high-end analogue tape recorders, large-format mixing consoles and digital effects processors, such as those made by AMS, were, until recently, tools of an elite guild,[38] thus rendering sound recording the discipline of an exclusive minority. Thirdly, and related to the second reason, such ideas are due to tensions surrounding the acquisition and preservation of technical knowledge. Historically, the dissemination of sound recording knowledge has been confined to the workplace. 'Senior' engineers would impart skill sets to 'juniors'; the process of 'earning one's stripes' through endless tea making and cable tying before advancing through the studio 'ranks' is a well-documented discourse in recordists' biographies and in the education arena. With regard to the latter, until recently, specialist sound recording education has also been confined to an elite set of universities. In 1946, the Second Viennese School composer Arnold Schoenberg wrote a letter to Robert Hutchins, then chancellor of the University of Chicago.[39] In it, he outlined a rationale behind the education of 'soundmen' to 'be trained in music, acoustics, physics, mechanics and related fields to a degree enabling them to control and improve the sonority of recordings, radio broadcasting and sound film'.[40] Later, the concept of Schoenberg's 'Tonmeister' was explored by John Borwick in a 1973 paper for AES.[41] In the twenty-first century, there are just ten institutions running 'Tonmeister' degrees in the world[42] and whilst we have witnessed the global proliferation of music technology courses in further and higher education in the last twenty-five or so years, such training was, until then, guarded by a small minority of elite institutions and recording houses. With skill sets confined to such a small circle of privileged, male individuals (and I am certain this goes a long way to explain the lack of women in the recording industry, noting Schoenberg's reference to 'soundmen'), it is no wonder that for the majority of individuals – to include musicians and music industry personnel – sound recording and music production is something of a 'black art'. Mick Glossop suggested:

> Engineers were these conjurers and it was very exclusive, but then that all started to merge with musicians. The engineer lost that mythical role of being this special guy with the pointed hat and the magic wand.[43]

Glossop recognizes the mythology surrounding engineers and their ability to interact with technologies in the way Sexton previously described as 'sonic alchemy'.[44] Also cited is the 'exclusivity' surrounding the role of the engineer, which provides further evidence of an elite industry closely guarding its 'secrets'. However, the demystification of the engineer's role alongside the advent of new technologies, new consumers and the audio technology press is no coincidence. Undoubtedly, the rise of new consumers, the widespread dissemination of digital technologies, as well as a (largely perceived) democratization of recording and production *skill sets* in the 1980s and beyond, contributed to the demythologization of the recording engineer.

Meek's practices were sonically conspicuous by the absence of conformity to established methods. How, then, have such nonconformist approaches manifested in modern records?

Rule breaking

By using the term 'rule breaking', what we're really talking about is deviance: deliberate straying from established norms and practices that exist in niche communities of practice[45] as well as in wider society. To that end, the works of prominent sociologists, particularly Merton[46] and Becker,[47] are useful in helping us understand recordists who deliberately 'go against the grain'. For example, Becker understood outsiders to break rules constructed by established groups. If we consider the realm of recording and production knowledge – as accumulated in both technical and scientific communities and amongst practitioners working in the music recording industries – we notice that many revered recordists were, indeed, outsiders. That is, their working practices differed from the established rules of their peers. Specifically related to music, Simon Frith suggested the avant-garde in popular music offers 'musicians and listeners the pleasures of rule breaking'.[48] This is a pertinent observation as it is those recordists who brought techniques well established in the avant-garde into the popular and rock music recording process that are arguably the most revered. Lucy Green suggested that deviance from established *musical* practices is often turned 'ironically … into an assertion of … real, closely guarded, musical superiority'.[49] Matthew Bannister went further to describe Brian Eno's 'codified and formalized' rule breaking as an assertion of superior creativity.[50]

Table 4.2 A breakdown of tech-processual unorthodoxies in contemporary record production, 1980s and 1990s

Faults and Flaws	Processes	Anachronisms
Noise/distortion	Tape recorder manipulation	Early electronic instruments (1980s and 1990s)
Tape hiss	Overspill	1970s consoles
Wow and flutter	Nonconformist microphone techniques	Early digital devices (1990s)
Vinyl crackle	Console manipulation	Early MIDI systems/analogue drum machines (1990s)

All these describe *musical* rule breaking, of which there is a long tradition in both composition and performance dating back centuries. But what of rule breaking in sound recording practice?

In his 2005 Art of Record Production paper, Andy Keep described technological unorthdoxies as 'creative abuse' that being 'the deliberate use of a piece of equipment beyond the manufacturers recommendations to look for unexpected timbres and behaviours through faults, flaws, or processing errors'.[51] An example of this manifests in the 2001 Line 6 'Echo Farm', a DAW plug-in featuring multiple time-based processing parameters. A control on the plug-in, labelled 'wow and flutter', illuminates how once-unwanted equipment flaws – in this instance, an undesirable effect caused by speed irregularities on analogue tape recorders – has, over time, become a desired effect in contemporary music production. But long before manufacturers began creating features from technological flaws, recordists figured out ways of (mis)appropriating technology – or, indeed, creating features from so-called 'flaws' – in order to create new sounds.

Three distinct areas of what I have termed tech-processual unorthodoxies are evident in contemporary record production: first, as Keep described, unorthodox uses of technology and the apparent 'embracing' of faults and flaws, which is at odds with the historical quest for sonic hi-fidelity; second, the intentional unorthodox processual application of microphones, appropriation of mixing console features and other recording devices (such as that described by Siouxsie Sioux); and, third, the foregrounding of what I call 'technological anachronisms', those being sound recording or music technology devices belonging to past eras or, indeed, alternate tech-processual settings. These are outlined above in Table 4.2.

Producer Mick Glossop echoed both Green and Bannister when he linked deviance from standard techniques with creativity:

> The notion that you can abuse – well perhaps not abuse – but certainly start to use microphones and other recording equipment in more unconventional ways to be more creative – that started to bring about this completely new language of

recording. But as time goes on, new ideas become assimilated into the existing vocabulary of techniques that get used. And they're regarded – not as correct – but certainly as legitimate ways to record things. But then there are always newer people coming up with new ways to record things, which older people regard as wrong or not industry standard.[52]

Glossop also conflates unconventional creative recording practice with the 'new', suggesting that younger, creative and 'boundary-pushing' recordists are those whose methods are more likely to be considered unorthodox; older recordists are more likely to adhere to conventions and, indeed, 'industry standards'.

Keep and others have focused on the interaction(s) between recordist/user and the sound recording system. However, less common are studies into tech-processual unorthodoxies and their resulting, sonically discernible aesthetics in popular music recordings. The next few sections detail how such tech-processual unorthodoxies manifested in commercial records.

Processes

Sexton and others recognized the assimilation of avant-garde recording techniques into popular music recording and production, and many of these techniques manifested in the particularly influential tech-processual practices of recordists including Brian Eno and Trent Reznor.[53] Eno's techniques are realized in – and considered through – his solo production work, particularly *Music for Airports* (1978) and *My Life in the Bush of Ghosts* (1981). Yet the ways in which Eno's techniques manifest in his commercial work are less discussed. His 1987 production of U2's *The Joshua Tree* is one such example. Let's consider the recording of 'Where the Streets Have No Name', which Eno himself referred to as a 'nightmare of screwdriver work'.[54] Indeed, the recording of this particular track was so problematic that Eno admitted to attempting to 'stage an accident'[55] to wipe the tape so the recording could start again. In this track, the recorded performance has taken place before all musicians were comfortable with the arrangement. Additionally, a click track has not been used, which explains the natural deviations in tempo throughout. Mix engineer Steve Lillywhite described the difficulties in mixing the track due to large amounts of overspill present on each instrument track – a common result of a traditional, live recording whereby all musicians are recorded simultaneously in the same room. The previously mentioned 'perfection–imperfection' binary is elucidated here: drum discrepancies are kept (2.17) as well as a vocal performance that becomes increasingly lethargic and speech-like towards the end of the track (4.15). This is not to suggest the absence of technological intervention. In fact, the beginning of 'Where the Streets Have No Name' features an introduction entirely constructed from mixing console manipulation. At nearly a minute in length, we hear a distant, reverberant organ slowly increasing in volume; the organ becomes increasingly 'full' and present. This has been achieved by sending the organ to a reverb, with the original organ channel fader pulled down and reverb return on the console audible. As the reverb return increases in volume, the original organ channel recording is faded in, thus creating a sense of 'approach'. Such tactics were often used by Jamaican dub producers in the 1970s: a niche technique that slowly made its way into the commercial mainstream.[56] On the one hand, none of these recording aesthetics are unusual: we have a traditional, performance-capture approach of a live, four-piece band playing what they felt was an unfinished track. On the other, let's now position 'Where the Streets Have No Name' in the context of other rock music of the era: Whitesnake's *Whitesnake* (1987), Guns n' Roses' *Appetite for Destruction* (1987) and Bon Jovi's *New Jersey* (1988). Particularly, Mike Stone and Keith Olsen's slick production on *Whitesnake* as well as Mutt Lange's groundbreaking SSL-constructed *Hysteria* were released in the same year and are sonically and aesthetically opposite to *The Joshua Tree*. Of course, the musical, lyrical and performance differences are apparent, but Eno and Lanois' tech-processual practice is so stylistically and aesthetically removed from the era in which it was created that it is conspicuous by the absence of then cutting-edge technologies that were, at that point in time, ubiquitous in the elite recording industry.

The presence of experimental techniques perhaps more associated with the avant-garde was evident long into the 1990s. Take Nine Inch Nails' 1999 double album *The Fragile*. Songwriter-recordist Trent Reznor and recordist Alan Moulder created *The Fragile* using then cutting-edge equipment, including two Apple iMac computers running eMagic's Logic Digital Audio Workstation.[57] Much of the record was constructed from sampled snippets of short drum, guitar and piano performances; evidence of sequencing, looping and programming is apparent throughout the record. However, the sonic aesthetics of *The Fragile* exhibit a range of techniques and demonstrate a continuum of avant-garde practices in the commercial mainstream. Alan Moulder described realizing the musical potential of everything and anything they could amass from around the studio, with emphasis on creating sonically distinctive percussive loops:

> We had a shopping trip to a percussion store and ... just amassed as much junk as we could from around the studio: various sized boxes, empty water bottles and so on. I set Trent up in a small area of one of the live rooms, surrounded by all of this junk, so that he could use different mallets to hit things and make them resonate without having to worry too much about how they would sound.[58]

This experimental technique is heard in the percussive loop introduction of 'Into the Void'. Here, we hear ambient recorded loops of the various percussion 'junk' Moulder describes. The first is a tinny, resonant, glockenspiel-like three-note loop; the second a more experimental, six-note phrase overlaid on the first loop. This ambient, acoustic introduction is consolidated with the addition of the cello, playing underpinning chords at 0.15, joined by a heavily chorused electric guitar riff at 0.30. The result is an acoustic, experimental, quite minimalist introduction, until the programmed kick drum enters at 0.46; this pulls the track in an altogether different sonic direction. The strong avant-garde references in the first bars create a sonic picture that is then destroyed and recreated using alternate, then current sounds and process.

Moulder went on to describe further unorthodox techniques. Drum loops were created by recording signals from ambient microphones positioned in Reznor's studio live room, where an acoustic drum kit would be played along to a programmed loop sent through the PA system in a variation on an echo chamber.[59] Furthermore, the microphones were positioned to capture the drums as well as resonance from multiple acoustic guitars present in the room. Overall, *The Fragile* is a good example of a record constructed from multiple recording techniques, traditional and current, orthodox and challenging.

Faults and flaws

In *Living Electronic Music*, Simon Emmerson stated:

> Distortion, tape hiss, vinyl surface noise, low bit rates – all in their time were considered transitional to something 'better'. But they are also 'the grain of the system', a signifier (a signature) of its idiosyncrasy and character, but also its 'time stamp' (its *timbre*). Such noise is identified with the limits of systems (both analogue and early digital).[60]

In the late 1990s and through the turn of millennium, the apparent 'embracing' of equipment flaws and lo-fidelity aesthetics of early sound recording began to (re)emerge in the sound of commercial music releases. Massive Attack's *Mezzanine* (1998), Portishead's *Dummy* (1994) and Tricky's *Maxinquaye* (1995) are some of the successful 'trip-hop' records featuring such aesthetics. A good example of foregrounding equipment faults and flaws, not simply for nostalgic effect, lies in Eminem's 1999 single 'Stan', from *The Marshall Mathers LP*. The song begins with a prominent, programmed kick drum and bass guitar rhythm with an acoustic guitar against a backdrop of torrential rain. We also hear prominent vinyl crackle, attached to a sample of Dido's 'Thank You' (1999), which has been treated with a band-pass filter. Such prominent production aesthetics are not simply for nostalgic effect. And we are not simply listening to 'Stan' the record: we are situated in a room with 'Stan' the protagonist who, in turn, is listening to Dido's 'Thank You': on vinyl, played back on a lo-fidelity system (indicated by the application of band-pass filtering) in a small room where outside it is raining. Allan Moore uses 'embodied meaning'[61] to describe, amongst other interpretations, a musical motif elucidating a lyrical reference. In 'Stan' the presence of vinyl crackle – a past, technological aesthetic – is there to situate the listener in the place of the protagonist. On the one hand, this is nothing new. On the other hand, considerable technological intervention and sonic construction are evident in 'Stan', used to create a distinctive sonic realm for the protagonist. Such aesthetics are used to evoke a past format and reception device as opposed to being applied simply as part of the production process: 'Stan' still features the upfront vocal, programmed drums and bass consistent with rap music of the era.

An example of faults and flaws embedded into the production process is found in Red Hot Chilli Peppers' 2000 album *Californication* recorded by Jim Scott and produced by Rick Rubin. The recording of this album exemplifies a traditional, 'performance-oriented' approach with all musicians recorded simultaneously. Drums were placed on a raised platform in the centre of Ocean Way's live room; vocalist Anthony Keidis sang in a small vocal booth and Flea and John Frusciante's amplifiers were isolated from the other instruments. The members of the band were no more than 10 feet away from each other at any one time during the recording. The album was recorded to an Ampex 24-track analogue tape machine via a 1970s Neve 8038 desk, then tracked to Pro Tools where minimal editing and 'comping' took place.[62] No Dolby noise reduction was used in the recording as both the band and the producer wanted to keep the 'hiss' and retain an 'analogue' aesthetic. The intentional inclusion of such lo-fidelity aesthetics manifests in two sonically discernible noise types on the album: the recording features audible 'hiss' from the analogue tape and lack of noise reduction – unusual for a record made at the turn of the millennium. Evidently, a blend of technological anachronisms and the prominence of apparent flaws have resulted in a record unusually performance-centric for its time. However, *Californication* also features significant dynamic range reduction, constant static noise throughout and notable low frequency absence, leading some in the industry to conclude the album was a casualty of the loudness war.[63] These aesthetics are at odds with each other: the deliberate referencing of past technological limitations is married with a controversial 'brick wall limiting' technique. Additionally, the record is a good example of tech-processual hybridity at the turn of the millennium.

Anachronisms

The 1990s was a complex time for sound recording and music technologies as 1980s MIDI and early digital recording systems became antiquated and the commercial recording industry embraced computer-based DAWs. This led to a kind of technological mash-up in contemporary music production; tech-processual practice was certainly in a state of flux. The use of technological precursors was evident amongst 1990s artists; in a time of proliferating digital recording, such vintage technologies acted as important sonic differentiators, particularly in rock music, but across emergent genre hybrids including big beat and trip hop. At the turn of the millennium, records featuring technologies more at home in the 1960s were quite prevalent: Soundgarden's use of the Leslie Loudspeaker cabinet in 'Black Hole Sun' (*Superunknown*, 1994), Radiohead's prominent use of the Ondes Martenot in 'The National Anthem' (*Kid A*, 2000) and Eels' Mellotron-centric composition 'Souljacker Part 2' (*Souljacker*, 2001) are three examples of contemporary records featuring music technologies associated to an altogether different era of popular music record production. Applications of technological precursors manifested in both big beat and trip-hop genres too. Detailed analysis of Fatboy Slim's 'Praise You' (1997) features later on, but plenty of early drum machines, analogue synthesizers, 1980s sampling devices and early MIDI systems are sonically discernible throughout Chemical Brothers' *Surrender* (1999)[64] and Moby's *Play* (1999).[65] The use of analogue tape loops, 'vintage' mixing consoles and lo-fidelity recording aesthetics such as vinyl crackle was a prominent feature in the trip-hop genre, emerging from Bristol in the mid-1990s.

One example of how technological anachronisms manifested in commercial music can be found in UK big beat act The Prodigy. Throughout the 1990s, many dance music producers were working on computer-based audio and MIDI sequencers, such as eMagic's Logic and Steinberg's Cubase. Prodigy songwriter-recordist Liam Howlett, however, preferred to programme on his 1989 12-bit Roland W-30 hardware synthesizer[66] and manipulate analogue tape to achieve a unique signature sound. The Prodigy's *The Fat of Land* (1997) was one of the most commercially successful records of the decade and its overarching sonic character was in no small part due to the then antiquated technology used to create it, as Howlett described with reference to the single 'Firestarter':

> For 'Firestarter', we did the old trick of recording it onto tape, turning the tape over and getting all the reverse reverb effects. I love that effect. I've never found a processor that can produce the same effect.[67]

This short, full reverb can be heard immediately preceding vocals throughout Firestarter's verses. The track does, however, feature many techniques common throughout 1990s practice; samples, for example, feature throughout. In this case, the 'hey' repeats are taken from The Art of Noise's 'Close (To The Edit)' (*Who's Afraid of the Art of Noise* 1984) and the guitar motif from The Breeders' 'S.O.S' (*Last Splash*, 1993). The Art of Noise (of which Trever Horn was a member) were in themselves pioneers of sampling utilizing early digital synthesis, so in sampling from this record, Howlett contributes to a continuum of sampling practice, referencing an early, groundbreaking example.

Another example manifests in an altogether different recording: that of D'Angelo's critically acclaimed neo-soul album *Voodoo* (2000). Recorded and mixed by Russell Elevado at Jimi Hendrix's Electric Lady Studios in New York, Voodoo was recorded '85%'[68] live to 2″ analogue tape via a 1970s Neve 8078 console. Elevado, a recordist trained at Arthur Baker's Shakedown Studios, had become disillusioned with technological change during the 1990s and admitted to being 'about to quit'[69] due to the proliferation of computer-based recording and programming. In agreeing to record and mix *Voodoo*, Elevado committed to working with equipment 'made before 1975'[70] and intentionally returned to a traditional, live performance-led recording method, as used in the 1970s. Tape manipulation was undertaken for creative effects (similar to that Howlett employed on 'Firestarter') noticeable throughout the record, but particularly on the track 'The Root' (2000). Between 2.31 and 2.38, we hear a tape flanging effect, caused by summing two vocal tracks (in this instance, it is only the vocal and not the entire track that has been flanged) played simultaneously on two separate tape machines, with slight pressure manually applied to one tape reel as it plays back, thus causing phase inconsistencies. Further, tape manipulation is present between 3.14 and 4.15 where a guitar solo recording is played backwards, as Elevado stated, 'Originally it was a straight guitar solo, then we just flipped the tape and played it backwards and it was like, "Yes, that's it"!'[71] A loud burst of noisy hiss is also present between 4.03 and 4.09. Whilst these aesthetics are true to the limitations of the equipment used on records by Elevado's 1970s reference artists, the sound of *Voodoo* was particularly notable for the absence of conformity to then standard practices, common amongst contemporary, commercial US R&B production of the time.

Summary

Evidently, it is those recordists who have *not* conformed to formulaic principles of audio engineering that are the most revered in popular music historiography, and this has much to do with their nonconformist approach to recording. *Maverick methods* were clearly evident throughout 1980s and 1990s recording and production practice. In the 1980s, changing practices were strongly linked to technological development, and the increase in multitrack and post-production options enabled recordists to work with a larger sonic canvas from the outset. Established, performance-capture-based approaches to recording were still commonplace, although new technology-driven, 'construction' approaches were also established by the middle of the decade. Standards were strongly aligned to aesthetic intention; Brian Eno would not have used the same tech-processual practices as Tim Simenon and vice versa, due in part to the underlying musical intention being so vastly different. Musically aligned processes were also evident throughout the 1990s, although applications of technological precursors to recording processes were evident, particularly due to low-fi aesthetics being key sonic signatures of some commercial musics. To that end, maverick recording processes in the 1980s can be seen as a result of increased options, larger technological toolboxes and the prevalence of digital synthesis. In the 1990s, such options were ubiquitous and increasing all the time; *maverick methods* were more a result of the state of technological and workplace flux.

It is unsurprising that until the 1980s, workplace recording practices were subject to speculation. Both elite recording houses and the technological means used to create records were concealed, guarded and unrelatable to the music-consuming public, as well as many musicians with no access to recording equipment. The widespread dissemination of cheaper music technologies in the 1980s increased accessibility, placing devices into the hands of musicians and DJs, but there is no evidence that any democratization of traditional recording *skill sets* took place. In fact, such practices were still confined to elite recording houses throughout the 1990s.

Historically, those who have consistently 'broken the rules' of what is possible in sound recording and production appear to be linked with heightened creativity and sonically discernible recordings. Recordists who perceived their then cutting-edge tools as creatively limiting and requiring modification, those who employed technological anachronisms as sonic differentiators and those who embraced the faults and flaws of technological precursors and incorporated them into the process all contributed to a set of canonized techniques and processes. Historically, such *maverick methods* are considered equal to that of many revered musicians: the induction of Berry Gordy Jr, Sam Phillips, Phil Spector and Tom Dowd – along with artist-producer Frank Zappa – to Cleveland's Rock and Roll Hall of Fame and Museum are indeed testament to this.

This underlies tensions existing between scientific-based principles of audio engineering, the technological development stemming from the discipline on the one hand and the artistic appropriation, (mis)interpretation and individualized working practice on the other. The result of all this is two conflicting histories of sound and music recording: one detailing the science of sound and technology, the principles, the protocol, the research driving technological change; and the other commending and canonizing those who worked against it, their artistic innovation, their 'creative abuses', their unorthodoxies. Their *maverick methods*.

5

Sound Recordists in Flux: The Diversification of the Recording and Production Role

Having dealt with sound technologies through the 1980s and 1990s, as well as discerned between historical, 'standard' and unorthodox implementations of such technologies, this chapter turns the spotlight onto recordists and their role in popular music record production. The discussion first situates the discourse in a historical context before focusing on key individuals whose working practices significantly impacted the sound of popular music during the 1980s and 1990s. This is not an exhaustive list; I am certain that many more recordists and recordist teams featured heavily in shaping the sounds of popular music during these decades. However, the examples featured in this chapter are intended to bring new, modern recordist discourse to the fore. It is not my intention to establish a new or modern 'recordist canon', rather to illuminate the ways in which contemporary recordists have impacted the sound of popular music and to shift the discourse away from the 1950s and 1960s. I am, however, by no means the first person to have recognized this influence. For example, in 1995 Michael Chanan recognized, 'Musical power is now in the hands of the technologically aware, of the producer, sound engineer, mixer and remixer.'[1] In *Pop Music, Technology and Creativity*, Timothy Warner suggested, 'A fundamental aspect of the relationship between technology and pop music is embodied in the record producer, who oversees the production process in the recording studio.'[2] The ways in which recordists 'oversee' the production process have changed over time. According to Kehew and Ryan,[3] the Beatles were the first artists to be allowed into the control room at Abbey Road's renowned Studio 2; until then, a studio hierarchy existed where the status of recordists was higher than that of artists. As artists became more 'production aware', their influence permeated the production as well as the performance process; Pink Floyd and their work in the 1970s is a good example of this. Specifically, this chapter focuses on the role of recordists. Since the 1960s, recordists were – and still are – often selected by musicians, managers and A&R representatives on the basis of their production style or 'sonic signature', which has sometimes resulted in 'brand' recordists – for example, Phil Spector's unique 'Wall of Sound', John Loder's strong alignment with underground, 'alternative' or non-mainstream musics and Absolute's affiliation to young, commercial pop stars in the 1990s. Here, the character of modern records is discussed with a focus on the recordists and their 'sonic imprint'. Organized loosely by era, recordists working both within and outside the commercial mainstream are discussed. This chapter also focuses on some key questions, namely: What is the role of the recordist? Which recordists worked on commercial popular music recordings during the 1980s and 1990s, and why were their practices important? How did the recording and production role changed during the 1980s and 1990s?

It is no coincidence that the *presence* of the recordist in the studio recording process has 'leaked' onto the final recording, not simply by means of the sonic imprint but also by way of the verbal interactions between performer and recordist. For example, at the end of The Smiths' 'I Started Something I Couldn't Finish' (1987), Morrissey is heard asking recordist Stephen Street, 'Is that alright, Stephen?'.[4] On Eminem's 2000 single 'The Way I Am', he is heard during the intro saying, 'Dre, just let it run ... ',[5] as he communicates with producer Dr Dre. At the end of his hit single '99 Problems' (2003), Jay-Z is heard saying, 'You're crazy for this one, Rick. It's your boy',[6] to producer Rick Rubin. These are just a few examples and I am sure there are many more, but these interactions demonstrate the integral role of the recordist in the making of the recording: the artist has deemed the recordist's influence so valuable that they are willing to allow their presence to be forever ingrained on the text both sonically and verbally. These examples serve as important acknowledgements to the influence of the (usually behind the scenes) technician; however, this is a very recent development – the recordists' role has, until recently, been one that is concealed.

Historical context of the recording and production role

In his book *The Recording Angel*, Evan Eisenberg identifies three generations of classical producer in Fred Gaisberg, Walter Legge and John Culshaw. Eisenberg highlights the changing role of the producer: Gaisberg the businessman and engineer; Legge the perfectionist; and Culshaw the record-maker.[7] In using these conflations, Eisenberg acknowledges the complexity of the producer's role from its inception, highlighting the absence of clear responsibilities attached to the producer's role. At the turn of the twentieth century, Fred Gaisberg was one of the earliest, prolific sound recordists, producing hundreds of recordings for The Gramophone Company, including the famous Milan recording of opera singer Caruso.[8] A pianist and technician, Gaisberg later described having to deal with artist 'Gramo-fright'[9] on a regular basis, his role not confined to recording but extending to the strategic dealing with artist nerves. Walter Legge, an engineer working as Gaisberg's assistant at HMV by the 1920s, significantly expanded the company's repertoire to include singers such as Maria Callas. John Culshaw, one of Decca's most prolific engineers through the 1940s and 1950s, was a pioneer of creative recording techniques, including the now-ubiquitous 'Decca tree' orchestral microphone technique. In the first half of the twentieth century, the differences between these recordists may have appeared negligible. We can reflect upon their influence and understand the nuances present in their role. To that end, the role of the 'producer' has never been clear cut; each enters their profession bringing different skill sets, intentions and vision. Mike Howlett describes the producer:

Producers come in from generally 2 broad halves. One of them is as an engineer who moves onto directing the project and the other is the musician side, usually the arranger producer. There are lots of variations on it, but a lot of producers are simply the project managers with a sense of humour.[10]

Howlett's observation of the requirement for humour may seem anecdotal, but there is much evidence to support the often eccentric and charismatic personalities of many producers, especially throughout the 1970s. Such understudied luminaries as Gus Dudgeon, Roy Thomas Baker and Tony Visconti brought a flamboyant, often extraordinary presence to their recording sessions that mirrored the often eccentric personalities of their artists: Elton John, Queen and David Bowie, respectively.

The recording engineer's role was somewhat different. Predominantly technical, the role required a high degree of system operation skills. The engineer was often a background figure,[11] wholly responsible for the smooth running of equipment and recording session. The producer, however, was someone employed by a record company – on a permanent basis in the early twentieth century – to oversee the entire recording, organize the recording session and, ultimately, to extrapolate the best possible performance from the musicians. These chasmic differences between the roles of musician, engineer and producer remained, arguably, until the late 1960s, by which time evidence of a coalescence of roles was beginning to emerge.

The tape-op

As well as the engineer and the producer, one important yet supporting studio role common throughout the 1960s and 1970s was the tape operator, or 'tape-op' for short. In a studio session, it would be the tape-op's responsibility to set up the tape machine, operate it, punch in overdubs and write up the box labels.[12] In elite studios, this was a common beginner's role, with many producers and engineers starting off in a 'tape-op' capacity, such as producer John Leckie, who worked as a tape-op at Abbey Road at the turn of the 1970s. Such was the significance of the role that a US audio magazine is named after it. A typical example of studio layout and personnel hierarchy necessitating a tape operator is found in operations in London's Marquee Studios. In 1973, recordist Phil Harding took on his first role as a tape operator, working on sessions with recording engineer Phil Dunne and producer Gus Dudgeon, who referred to his assistants as 'tape jockeys':

> When I started in 1973, the assistants used to be in a different room to the control room. Between the tape room and the control room was a well, a tiny courtyard, like many city buildings, there was a gap in the middle and you weren't allowed to build across that.[13]

Additionally, the tape-op's role was seen as ancillary: 'When I started as a tape-op in the 1970s, the engineer was this wizard!',[14] stated Mick Glossop in reference to his early 'tape-op' role. One of the main reasons a professional studio session necessitated a tape-op was due to the size of large-scale mixing consoles. Often, a recording engineer and producer would monitor performances from the control room, with the musicians positioned 'the other side of the glass' performing on the studio floor. During the 1970s, large-scale mixing consoles were often a 'split' design that being the recording input and tape return monitoring channels were 'split' across the desk. Due to the large size of the console, it would be physically difficult for a recording engineer to monitor input channels and operate the tape machine simultaneously, thus necessitating a tape operator. In the early-to-mid-1970s, both MCI and Harrison manufacturers developed the MCI JH-400 'in-line' mixing console,[15] whereby the channel input and the tape return were incorporated into the same channel strip. This development resulted in a substantial reduction in console scale – a 24-channel desk almost halved in size. At first, 'in-line' consoles were installed only in the top studios. For example, the 32-channel 'in-line' Cadac installed in Wessex Studios in 1976 featured such configuration. However, by the turn of the 1980s, 'in-line' consoles were widespread – their technology having been replicated by other manufacturers such as Neve and SSL – and therefore, the recording engineer was able to operate console and desk more easily. A further shift occurred in the early 1980s once the use of 'in-line' and automated consoles proliferated, and again later into the decade with the advent of computer-based recording, as Chris Sheldon points out:

> Tape-ops, their traditional role as auto-locator and punching in and out on analogue tape machines, kind of went by the window. They then became computer operators and were expected to know how to use samplers, then later on Pro Tools.[16]

Interestingly, Sheldon conflates the decline of the tape-op with the rise of the programmer, suggesting that many tape-ops redefined their role in line with technological change. The decline of the 'tape-op', therefore, did not occur simultaneously to a decline in the use of analogue tape. Moreover, developments in other music and recording technologies required technical assistants to diversify their skill sets to a changing technological landscape.

Recordists and the diversification of skill sets in the 1980s

Both scholars and practitioners alike have acknowledged the complexity of the recording and production role during the 1980s. Undoubtedly, emergent technologies had a remarkable effect: traditional roles of producer, engineer, tape-op and musician merged with computer programming, DJ and performance roles in an unprecedented way and this in no small way down to the technological acceleration, as Phil Harding pointed out:

> The mid-1980s onwards saw engineers having to transform themselves into doing more than just recording and mixing. If they didn't really understand the

technology, they had to grasp it pretty quickly because you got to the point where producers and bands expected an engineer to be able to program a Linn drum machine or a Linn 9000 or Cubase. If you turned up to a session and the engineer can't do that, well ... So that was the start of engineers having to diversify their technical ability as a skill base that was expected and taken for granted, even though you wouldn't necessarily get paid any more, especially if you ran your own studio.[17]

This diversification of skills illustrates the sudden demand placed on engineers in the 1980s to become something *more*. Whilst this demand on skills acquisition followed a natural trajectory through the 1970s as increased tape recording capacity proliferated, in the 1980s the acquisition of both digital hardware and computer-based skills became a necessity for many engineers in order to keep up with technological change that was occurring at an unprecedented rate. Mike Howlett pointed out a simultaneous, marked shift in power divisions amongst studio personnel:

Programmers, especially toward the end of the 1980s became much more powerful. In a way, it depended on the kind of producer you were, but producer programmers became a new phenomenon who would combine the job.[18]

This 'power shift' that Howlett describes is particularly significant, as it marks an altogether *new* role in the production process. The abilities of a computer programmer, who could operate the complex parameters of MIDI sequencers and samplers, were in high demand, rendering the role of the traditional engineer to a more narrow, specialist field. Stephen Hague is a good example of this producer–programmer conflation at the turn of the 1980s. Having begun his career programming and performing analogue synthesizers for producers such as Lenny Woranker and Richard Perry,[19] as well as performing with his own group, Jules and the Polar Bears, Hague set up his own recording studio and began producing artists whose music centred on analogue and digital synthesis. As a prolific keyboard player, Hague was one of the first UK programmer/producers to wholly embrace digital recording and as such pioneered much of the resulting 'synth-pop' of the decade including OMD's *Crush* (1985) and Pet Shop Boys' *Please* (1986). An example of Hague's production/programming conflation manifests in New Order's 1987 single 'True Faith' (1987), whereby Hague recorded to two synchronized Sony DASH 3324 machines via an early version of MOTU's performer on a Macintosh SE. New Order and Stephen Hague completed much of the initial synthesizer programming on a Yamaha QX1 hardware sequencer and Emulator II. Very little 'live' recording featured on this record aside from the lead vocal and a live hi-hat cymbal; Hague's production role was to programme, synchronize and sequence as oppose to capture, record and mix. In his 2000 book *Electronic Media and Culture*, Simon Emmerson recognized this shift: 'we have seen the possibility of a music of technology with the clear imprint of the human WILL rather than the human PRESENCE.'[20] What Emmerson notes is the increasingly dehumanized sonic canvas of popular music recordings featuring limited live performances and, instead, layers of programmed instrumentation resulting from largely digital music production processes.

The 'artist-producer'

In this section I want to make a clear distinction between an 'artist-producer' and a 'production-aware artist', as in the past, these two roles have been conflated. In his book *The Producer as Composer*, Moorefield argues the recording studio became the musical instrument of the producer. He cited Pink Floyd as one group who immersed themselves in the entire production process when recording *Dark Side of the Moon*.[21] Rather than artist-producers, I would suggest Pink Floyd were classic examples of the 1970s *production-aware* artist. Like the Beatles before them, Pink Floyd knew the potential of studio technology on their sound and by the early 1970s had demonstrated this awareness, but Alan Parsons and Chris Thomas were still credited for engineering and mixing, respectively. There is, however, evidence of entirely self-produced artists or artist-producers before the 1970s. Frank Zappa was one artist who, in the mid-1960s, took over his friend Buff's Pal studios, renamed it 'Studio Z' and continued to co-engineer and co-produce his material from there, as Michie wrote in *Mix*:

> This aberrant device-centric behavior, a theme that recurs frequently in Zappa's lyrics, was made possible in part by the fact that Pal contained the world's only staggered head, 5-track, half-inch tape recorder, constructed by Buff at a time when mono was the industry standard.[22]

This not only suggests the presence of an artist-producer but an artist aligning himself with an engineer and studio owner at the forefront of technological development. Another example of the artist-producer is the German electronic group Kraftwerk, which operated and self-produced from their own studio in Düsseldorf, named Kling Klang. These examples – all from the 1970s – illustrate the increasing role of the musician in tech-processual practices and a move towards a more production-aware artist. However, it is important to note these examples as exceptions as opposed to the rule, and it was not until the 1980s that the artist-producer had fully evolved.

Trevor Horn is one example of the artist-producer at the turn of the 1980s. With The Buggles, Horn took on the role of producer as well as musician and performer, which culminated in a particular, sonically discernible identity due to the obvious influence of recording technology on the resulting recordings. The beginning of the 1980s saw a marked progression in mainstream popular music with synthesizers becoming ever more prevalent. This 'synth-pop' genre thrived on the emerging digital synthesis, Fairlight CMI and Synclavier technologies to such a degree that the beginnings of 'programmers as performers' became increasingly evident. Indeed, Gary Numan (Tubeway Army) and Dave Stewart of The Eurythmics became renowned as artist-producers and pioneers of the 'synth-pop' genre, with tracks such as 'Are Friends Electric' (1979) and 'Sweet Dreams (Are Made of This)' (1983), respectively. These examples illustrate the manifestation of the artist-producer through synthesis and early digital technologies at the turn of the 1980s, and in all these examples the artist is also credited as producer.

This artist-producer role manifested itself in other ways too, becoming increasingly evident through emerging dance and hip-hop genres. In the United States, hip-hop developed as the newest underground style, accompanied by – and arising from – its own street culture. The DJ was central to this emergent genre, with early releases, including The Sugarhill Gang's 'Rappers Delight' (1979) and Grandmaster Flash and the Furious Five's 'The Message' (1982), featuring DJs as performers, as well as containing lyrics about DJs in their songs. One of the first hip-hop DJs to be fully presented as a performer was the late Jam Master Jay from Run DMC. He was no background figure, and the group's performances, music videos and live appearances focused just as much on Jay as the Reverend Run and DMC. The DJ as performer was a common sight through 1980s hip-hop: Spinderella from Salt N' Pepa was central to albums including *Hot, Cool and Vicious* (1986) and *A Salt With a Deadly Pepa* (1988); Terminator-X from Public Enemy played a key part in albums including *Yo! Bum Rush the Show* (1987) and *Fear of a Black Planet* (1990); and Prince Paul, De La Soul's producer, is featured prominently on albums including *3 Feet High and Rising* (1989) and *De La Soul Is Dead* (1991). These DJ producers blurred the lines between performance, composition, 'replay' and production and were all high-profile members of successful hip-hop groups, as Beadle points out in *Will Pop Eat Itself?*:

> The development of DJs as artists in their own right was inextricably bound up with the rise of Rap. Indeed, as the 'producer-as-artist' increased his profile in the late 1980s, the concept of the DJ-producer became more and more common.[23]

Beadle is right in that hip-hop contributed to the rise of the DJ, and whilst hip-hop was full of DJ-performers, DJ-producers in the genre were scarce and, as in rock music, producers were still 'behind the scenes' personnel: producers Herbie Luv Bug (Salt N' Pepa), Rick Rubin and Russell Simmons (Run DMC) and Prince Paul (De La Soul) did not regularly perform with their artists. However, hip-hop was not the only genre contributing to the rise of the DJ; the DJ-producer that Beadle identified in 1993 could be found in abundance within another genre of music.

In the early 1980s, a 'Hi-NRG' style of minimalist disco music emerged in the United States. Finding its way to the primarily gay-oriented New York club scene, it was picked up on by DJs in the UK. Initially, the music remained underground, but aggressive promotional tactics, coupled with a word of mouth 'buzz', enabled DJs such as Ian Levine from the London club 'Heaven' to draw in big crowds of clubbers (Brewster & Broughton, 1999). But Ian Levine was not the only DJ trying to capitalize on this growing music scene. DJ turned producer Pete Waterman signed two other producers to his PWL company in 1984: Mike Stock and Matt Aitken. Having had relative success with Hazel Dean's 'Whatever I Do (Wherever I Go)' (1984), as well as a Eurovision entry, they were on the lookout for bigger and better things. They found this in the goth-Hi NRG crossover act Dead or Alive and after a few attempts with their first single, 'You Spin me Round (Like a Record)' (1984), the track went to number one in the UK charts in 1985. So, whilst hip-hop saw the rise of the DJ-performer, dance music saw the rise of the DJ-producer. SAW became pop record producers shortly after the Dead or Alive single, but that left a hole in the dance scene that would only go on to be filled by many others: Bill Drummond and Jimmy Caughty from The KLF, who pioneered alternative dance and situationist art-inspired sample collage techniques through albums such as *1987 (What the Fuck Is Going On?)* (1987) and *The White Room* (1991); Coldcut, particularly with their album *What's That Noise* (1989); Tim Simenon from Bomb the Bass; A Guy Called Gerald; and Liam Howlett from The Prodigy are all good examples of the late 1980s DJ-producer. Others have observed the rise of this type of producer. In *Good Vibrations*, Cunningham makes similar observations:

> In no small way, new technology has aided the rise of DJ-producers, who have been able to produce fresh-sounding remixes for club audiences … among these remix producers are Paul Oakenfold and ex-Housemartin Norman Cook[24]

Cunningham is right where he discusses the rise of DJ-producers. Additionally, the DJ-performers and DJ-producers, identified as emerging and existing in the late 1980s, manifested in a much bigger *tour de force* by the early 1990s. Indeed, Norman Cook – aka Fatboy Slim – and Paul Oakenfold are two prime candidates for what has been termed the *Superstar DJ*,[25] and the early 1990s was the beginning of an almost decade-long reign for this producer type. These superstar DJs were not just performers or producers of their music; they encompassed all aspects of musical and production practice, previously confined to multiple individual roles. From remixing contracts to headlining 'superclub' nights as DJs and from sequencing and arranging dance tracks to performing 'live' and self-promoting, this kind of producer existed across underground dance genres and eventually into mainstream popular music. The late 1990s culminated in some of the biggest commercial successes for 'superstar DJs'. For example, US electronic musician and DJ-producer Moby created one of the most successful records of the decade with *Play* (1999). The Chemical Brothers' 1999 track 'Hey Girl, Hey Boy' that celebrated and epitomized the, by then iconic, status of the 'Superstar DJ' was taken from another multi-platinum selling record, *Surrender* (1999). The late 1990s was the 'golden age' of the DJ-producer: a natural culmination of the manifestation of the DJ role in early hip-hop and dance music over the previous twenty years.

Many of the DJ-producers and superstar DJs of the late 1980s and early 1990s had side projects in remixing. The rise of the 12″ single in the 1980s, coupled with advanced audio sequencing and editing platforms such as MOTU's Performer and Digidesign's Soundtools in the early 1990s as well as the emergence of club culture, resulted in an unprecedented demand for the extended remix. By the mid-1990s it was not uncommon to see that a successful single was in fact a remix and not the original version: Norman Cook's reworking of Cornershop's hit 'Brimful of Asha' (1997) is a good example of a light acoustic track given a technological overhaul by a prominent DJ-producer/remix engineer. Paul Oakenfold's 'Perfecto' remix of U2's 'Lemon' (1993) is another good example of a then current, prominent DJ reworking a rock track into an altogether different style to appeal to a dance music audience. Undoubtedly, technological change played a large part in sending the DJ to this new 'superstar' level. As Beadle points out in *Will Pop Eat Itself?*:

By 1987, a producer credit could help to sell a record, particularly a twelve-inch remix. The words 'Shep Pettibone remix' or 'Julian Mendelsohn remix' ... meant something to the purchaser. Very few producers of the 1960s and 1970s could make that claim.[26]

Thus far, different types of DJ in existence in the late 1980s and early 1990s have been identified, but there were other roles emerging at the same time, which were possibly more influenced by technological change than the DJ.

Recordists, 'multitasking' and the indefinable role

In *Sample and Hold: Pop Music in the Digital Age of Reproduction*, Andrew Goodwin suggested, 'as electronic technology has become naturalised, audiences have become habituated to seeing pop performers as technicians, computer programmers, DJ's or studio engineers'.[27]

By *naturalized*, Goodwin suggested that the aural perception of prefabricated sounds within both analogue and digital musical equipment has become just as familiar as the sounds from traditional instruments. However, the important point here is that in 1990, Goodwin recognized the changing roles of programmers and engineers and this was undoubtedly the case. In the mid-1980s, a prominent discourse was that programmed or computerized, synthesized music was not 'real'. This quite negative line was reinforced by campaigns by the Musicians' Union with their 'Keep Music Live' campaign. Whilst this campaign has been in place since 1965, it became more prominent during the 1980s with the advent of synthesized and pre-recorded samples being integrated into live performance shows. Similar thoughts permeated general discourses in the mainstream media. Programmed sounds were considered 'fake' and users considered lacking in musical ability or 'talent'. In 1986, keen to counter such claims, Pet Shop Boys took to then ubiquitous television show, *The Old Grey Whistle Test*, to perform the track 'Opportunities (Let's Make Lots of Money)' (1986) from their co-produced album *Please* (1986). The performance is significant for a number of reasons: Neil Tennant and Chris Lowe perform against a backdrop 'wall' of Fairlight CMI screens, running fixed screenshots of programmed sequences on the 'Page R'. Lowe also has a further two Fairlight CMI machines to his left, presumably running the backing rhythm. Tennant sings the track live whilst simultaneously playing an Emulator II and another unidentified keyboard to his right, whilst Lowe performs on the Yamaha DX7 and Technics PX1. The point is that this performance was a strong rebuttal against accusations that electronic music could not be performed live. Tennant and Lowe concentrate hard as they move between synthesizers, dropping in contrasting phrases and melodies on alternate patch settings. Here, we see a musician duo performing their music live using then non-traditional, entirely synthesis-based instrumentation. The pop performer as computer programmer, synthesist and technician had, indeed, been naturalized.

This conflation of computer-based performance would only proliferate into the 1990s. Stephen Street cites the advent of Pro Tools as the cementing of the programmer's role during the mid-1990s:

> There was a time when Pro Tools first came out that the producer wouldn't go near it – he'd have a Pro Tools programmer. That would often be people who were great at programming Synclaviers for instance and Fairlights and so on, they would be the techy-minded people who would do that kind of thing. Of course now, you have to be a 'jack of all trades'. So really, the boundaries have been blurred to the point where to do engineering and production, you've got to be pretty adept at being a computer programmer now. Everything is computer based.[28]

Street suggests that the role of the computer programmer was a natural continuum from the programmers of early Synclaviers and Fairlights. By using the term 'techy-minded', he clearly believes programmers are different to producers. However, he has also recognized how the role has further morphed in that the demand in the contemporary climate is for the 'jack of all trades': the all-encompassing 'producer-engineer-programmer' who can do everything. Phil Harding has also pointed out the difference between production roles in the 1960s and 1970s compared to the contemporary era:

> everyone had to learn to multi-task. Once, you had producer, engineer, musician in the 1960s and 1970s, now you've got a producer who is also an engineer and a musician and an engineer who is also a producer and a musician and a musician who is also a producer and engineer. Certainly on the studio side, everyone has had to learn to do everything, which is no bad thing because if you pick up regular work, you're always going to end up doing what you are hopefully best at.[29]

Harding has cited the shift towards today's all-encompassing producer as a positive move, but so-called 'jack-of-all-trades' producers have always been present in popular music production. In *Repeated Takes*, Michael Chanan suggested:

> in every period, several different levels of activity co-exist and with them, various different types of producer: the entrepreneurial, the corporate and the independent, the jack-of-all-trades and, last to emerge, the artistic.[30]

This acknowledgement of producer 'types' and the variety present in their skill sets is why the specificities of the role are so difficult to pin down. And whilst 'jacks-of-all-trades' or 'multitasking' producers existed in the 1980s – Mute Records' Daniel Miller is one example of a musician-turned-'producer'-turned-entrepreneur – it is difficult to elucidate an example 'producer' who did *not* possess other skills besides 'project management': either musical, business or technical, as Harding describes. To that end, the term 'producer' to describe a 'project manager' of a recording session is problematic: if it is not possible to define a precise skill set or role description and if so much variation exists within the skill sets of individual 'producers', then the role becomes difficult to define or categorize.

There are historical examples preceding the era covered in this book. These examples demonstrate multiskilled individuals existed in the recording industry long before the more foregrounded role conflations in the 1980s and 1990s. For example, Sam Phillips was a studio manager, technical operator of analogue tape machines, recordist, record label manager and A&R manager of his 'Sun' record company.[31] Berry Gordy of Tamla Motown could also be considered a 'jack-of-all-trades', as he took on executive, business, talent scouting and production duties.[32] Perhaps the proliferation of digital music technologies by the 1990s resulted in a new 'jack-of-all-trades' type, mirroring the 'one-man band' Phillips and Gordy examples of the 1950s and 1960s, respectively? Two issues emerge that require further exploration: firstly, the presence of 'auteurs' in contemporary record production through the 1980s and 1990s and, secondly, the fragmentation of 'team-based' production as a result of workplace and technological flux. But there are others who have witnessed first-hand the implications of working alone as opposed to working as a part of a team. In Chapter 1, the rate at which recording studios began to diminish in both prevalence and size was illustrated, in the discussion surrounding the shift away from the recording studio per se towards a smaller, compact recording and production workplace.

Auteurism

Whilst it is widely recognized that the Cahiers du Cinéma encouraged widespread discourse on the subject, early references to auteurism were evident some time before. Indeed, Watson suggested that 'the central role of the journal in propagating and disseminating that thesis cannot be underestimated'.[33]

One key concept derived from film theory is 'auteurism' – that a producer's role is akin to that of a film director. Early studies, such as Charlie Gillett's paper on 'The Producer as Artist',[34] as well as later works including Evan Eisenberg's *Recording Angel*[35] both consider the 'music producer as auteur'. For example, Gillet stated in his 1977 work: 'In much the same way that, in films, the film is the work of the director, and the star simply does what he is told by the director, so in music.'[36] In the late 1970s, the role of 'producer' may have been easier to ascertain, but auteur theory is problematic due to the largely collaborative nature of recording and production. Additionally, the presence of business and economic personnel – managers, A&R executives, distributors – in the life cycle of a record dictates that artists (and indeed recordists) have varying degrees of creative control. Later on, auteur theory evolved into less a direct correlation to film roles and more – as Paul Watson explained – 'a critical strategy for sorting the artistic wheat from the generic chaff'.[37]

Zak has acknowledged the problem with the producer as auteur because often the artist, producer and engineer work as a collaborative team towards the creative vision of the record:

> For whether they begin as performers, song writers, arrangers, engineers or producers, all are working on the same thing, the record. With that as the central

focus, what Dickenson calls 'the process itself … the life of the event' becomes paramount, and anyone with the ability to foster it in some way may rightly claim the title of 'producer'.[38]

Auteur theory as applied to the producer may have held more relevance in pre-1960s record production. In his book *The Recording Angel*, Eisenberg writes:

> But for the most part the small army of engineers, studio musicians and assistant producers that takes part in a typical recording is simply ignored. In charge of this small army is the producer, who is the counterpart of the film director.[39]

Eisenberg has made a clear link between the producer and film director in an example of classic 'auteur' theory. However, it is difficult to make these comparisons without detailing the complexities of the role. In the 1950s and 1960s, the era that Eisenberg refers to in his discussion of Culshaw and Legge, the producer as auteur may have held some significance. There were substantially fewer record producers in those days than there are now. There were no such things as home studios, and artists who were involved in all aspects of the performance, recording and production were extremely rare, if not, non-existent. Not only that, but Culshaw and Legge were not working with artists per se, those with an original set of creative musical ideas, but classical musicians playing from written notation. Zak quite rightly critiques this notion in his book *The Poetics of Rock*, where he highlights the problem in applying the auteur theory to the producer 'types' of today:

> But the idea that a producer should be such an auteur – imposing his or her own sound and vision on diverse projects – is controversial, as is the 'artist/record producer' conflation (unless, of course, the producer is also the featured performer).[40]

Whilst Eisenberg may be right in that early record producers displayed auteur-like traits, this is a problematic theory in post-1960s record production. The idea of a film director as auteur was criticized by many twentieth-century scholars as being too biased towards the creative vision of the director. Film-making, it was argued, is a collaborative process, and therefore it is problematic to suggest the vision of the director is any more or less important than the actors, cinematographers, screenplay writers or even the film producers.[41] This is a simple critique that can also be applied to the producer in a music context; it simply does not allow for the creative vision of the artist, the direction of the song or source material as intended by the performer, the engineer or assistants. Also, it fails to acknowledge the A&R department of the record company who – up until recent times – were ultimately responsible for making the initial discovery of 'talent' and the subsequent marketing of the end product.

Without suggesting that auteur theory is *entirely* irrelevant when applied to the producer, the point – in that the producer has creative directorship – has been largely overlooked. If the auteur is one that *directs* (the quintessential role being the directorship of the creative vision) then the *true* producer as auteur must surely have control over all factors that contribute to that creative vision. From artist and repertoire to songwriting, from recording and production to release and distribution, true auteurs are in the minority and have rarely been acknowledged in the course of academic discourse. Perhaps then, examples of 'auteurist' production *can* be found in 1980s production. SAW is one example of a three-individual production team overseeing a record label, A&R duties, writing, arranging, recording and production duties under the 'PWL' banner between 1985 and 1992. In this instance, the artist had less influence over the creative direction of the music: SAW developed a formula using technologies described earlier and then 'interchanged' artists into their production template. The focus of auteur theory is on the individual as opposed to a team, but in this instance, the inextricable nature of SAW in their songwriting, production practice and commercial release has often led to them being considered 'as one' and rarely discussed as individuals. The entire creative vision was realized by the production team with little to no artist intervention beyond the vocal performance. However, even in this outlier example, SAW still collaborated with a team of recording and mix engineers, including Karen Hewitt, Phil Harding and Ian Curnow. In fact, the team at SAW was large; various business associates and assistants worked at PWL[42] and regardless of their collective power, they still required their performers to 'front' their records in the media.

In an altogether different example, Daniel Miller, a Kraftwerk and Can-inspired film editor and keyboard player, founded the Mute record label in 1978 when he self-released the track 'T.V.O.D' under group moniker 'The Normal'.[43] Miller went on to sign Depeche Mode, Yazoo and Erasure, yet during this era, he was often credited as a co-producer along with the artist. Whilst he was responsible for the record label and business aspects of running it, there is still evidence of collaboration between himself and his artists.

Mike Howlett, who, in his 2009 PhD thesis, argued for 'the record producer as nexus', dealt with the producer as part of a collaborative team. He maintains that in *all* circumstances, the role of the producer is one of nexus between the creative inspiration of the artist, the technology in the studio and the commercial intentions of the record company. Howlett's contextualization is in his own experience as record producer:

> Since not all producers share the same balance of these skills and qualities (musical, technical and interpersonal), I have posited the constant role as that of a *nexus*. Sometimes the decision for a particular choice is made by the engineer, sometimes by the artist (and often enough the decision is a collective agreement), but in every case the act of choosing is definitive – it has a specific and identifiable effect on the recorded work – and in that act is the role of the producer as nexus.[44]

The idea of producer as nexus is in many instances more robust than auteur theory, specifically because it acknowledges the recording and production process as a collaborative one and one that features and accounts for a range of both technical and non-technical skills.

Most scholars in the field have preferred to use the 'artist-producer' conflation when discussing the merging of roles. In *Pop Music, Technology and Creativity*, Warner suggests:

> The strong link between pop music and an ever-developing technology ensures a continually evolving 'sound' in pop, while the presence of an often more extensive team behind the production of a pop record undermines the notion of a single artist/creator and hints at the range of procedures involved in the production process.[45]

Not only is Warner suggesting a complex, extensive range of roles involved in the production of popular music, but he also stresses the *importance* of the production by suggesting that the presence of a team *undermines* the notion of a single artist.

From label to freelance, team to individual

In his 2009 article 'The Software Slump', Andrew Leyshon noted 'falling recording budgets, declining demand for studio space-time, deteriorating employment conditions, continuing erosion of barriers to entry, runaway production and, increasingly, studio closures', citing the proliferation of software and home production as having a negative impact on the UK's recording sector.[46] This situation did not, however, occur overnight; the so-called decline of the recording sector can, arguably, be traced back to the 1970s when standalone, commercial recording houses with no affiliation to a record company (unlike EMI, Decca and Pye in the 1960s) began to emerge.[47] This enabled producers to work as freelancers without being tied to an individual label. Label loyalties, as described in the early chapters of Glyn Johns' autobiography,[48] no more existed, and producers could hop between studios, artists and records freely. By the late 1970s, such producers were building their own studios and, therefore, becoming direct competitors with the studios that had originally hired and trained them. Gus Dudgeon's 1977 custom construction of 'The Mill' studios in Berkshire is a good example of this. By the 1980s, another layer of competition arose as a direct result of technological change. The advent of much of the equipment described in Chapter 2 – Atari ST computers, budget samplers, MIDI equipment, synthesizers – enabled musicians, DJs and programmers to house music production equipment in their homes or even in a room. Subsequently, and as described earlier, plenty of popular chart music of the late 1980s was made in small home and project studios not in elite recording studios. As outlined in my 2012 article 'Revisiting the Double Production Industry',[49] the late 1980s also saw the proliferation of music technology magazines aimed not at elite industry recording personnel but at musicians, DJs and programmers keen to maximize the potential of budget, digital technologies. Paul Théberge suggested that 'without the simultaneous growth of the musicians' magazine industry, it is unlikely that [digital music technology] would have achieved anywhere near the magnitude that it has today'.[50] So, the move away from label-centred production to freelance is the result of a combination of factors: the increasing profile of the producer in the 1970s, the advent of programmable music technologies in the 1980s and the growth of the music technology press that recognized this growing market of technology consumers and provided an accompanying discourse and community. This advancement towards singular working practice continued through the 1990s but resulted in many producers feeling isolated and lonely. Examples of the producer's changing workspace can be found in Chris Sheldon and Stephen Street, both of whom worked regularly at Townhouse Studios in the 1990s before moving into their own facilities. Chris Sheldon moved from being employed predominantly at Townhouse Studios to owning, managing and producing in a small space on an industrial estate in Crouch End, London, by the late 1990s:

> The camaraderie as well. At the Townhouse, we'd all pile in around supper time and I'd be talking to people like Stephen Street about what he's doing, or another band. I loved that and I really miss that and it won't happen again.[51]

Sheldon mentions Street in particular, who also worked prolifically at Townhouse and the now defunct Olympic Studios. Street has also found himself in recent times having to operate in a more singular fashion. I read Sheldon's comments to Street and he responded, recalling the atmosphere at Townhouse Studios in the 1990s:

> I totally agree. I used Townhouse a lot because I loved it. It had a vibe and it felt like things were happening there. You'd walk in there, and obviously Chris (Sheldon) would be there and Chris Thomas would be working there with Pulp or whoever, and I'd be there with Blur perhaps and it was great.[52]

What these comments illustrate is how the producer's role has become more individualistic. Not only that, but the producer now finds himself working in smaller, project-style studios not dissimilar to the home and project studios of the late 1980s. The changes in workplace and technology have compounded in such a way as to isolate the producer from collaborators, thus eliminating social aspects of traditionalist recording practice. This notion of isolation has been touched upon by Théberge, but in the context of the home studio environment:

> Often ignored in this scenario of the home studio is the manner in which the domestic space has been transformed into a production environment. It seems to me that there is something else quite striking about this particular manifestation of contemporary music-making that is very different from previous uses of music technology in the home; that is, the degree to which the home studio is an isolated form of activity, separate from family life in almost every way.[53]

Whilst Théberge is talking specifically about home studios and their effect on domesticity, we now find the producer, whose previous realm was the high-end professional recording studio, operating in similar home-studio-sized workplaces. Clearly, Sheldon and Street have recognized the isolating nature of having been moved away from high-end recording studios that were collaborative workspaces by nature and into the realm of a workplace and practice where their input alone is all that's required.

By the 1990s, the role of the producer had changed dramatically. From being a 'project manager with a sense of humour', as Howlett described, to a 'jack of all trades' as Street acknowledged, the producer evolved into a single, freelance operator. In many cases, producers now work from self-contained facilities and, in other instances, they move freely from project to project and from studio to studio. In fact, the only studio that remains partially attached to a record label in the UK is EMI's Abbey Road.

The enthusiast

London's 1990 MIDI Music Show was explicitly marketed towards 'enthusiasts'.[54] This reference to such a demographic is one of the earliest so far discovered, suggesting that this new type of audio and music technology consumer emerged during the late 1980s. However, it was not just trade shows that targeted this new group. Interestingly, the back cover of David Mellor's book *How to Set up a Home Recording Studio* has a list of bullet points relating to its contents. The first reads, 'For musicians, recording enthusiasts and students'.[55] By 1994, entire texts were aimed at this demographic, including Michael Talbot-Smith's *Audio Recording and Reproduction for Audio Enthusiasts*.[56]

This suggests that by the mid-1990s, the 'enthusiast' group was not just considered alongside others, such as musicians and students, but was a whole, established demographic that could be targeted directly. Terms such as Toffler's 1980 futurist 'Prosumer'[57] and Axel Bruns's later 'Produser'[58] became more prevalent in the audio industry as this consumer group increased. Indeed, the presence of the 'enthusiast' around 1990 was that widespread that it became an entirely new, totally identifiable recording and production role. With the amateur musician opting for the portability of 4-track tape recording and the professional opting for a more high-specification project studio, the 'home studio' became the domain of the ultimate gadget-consuming hobbyist: the recording and production enthusiast. It is, however, important to note that there is no evidence of this identifiable, technology consumer demographic competing directly with established producers, musicians, DJ-producers or programmers. Whilst such consumers may have appeared threatening to the professional industry towards the late 1980s and through the 1990s,[59] this has more to do with discourses of empowerment used to market budget technologies than any direct threat to established, professional skill sets.

The underground and a 'sonic continuum'

So far, I have considered recordists working within the confines of the commercial mainstream. However, that is not to say that recordists working outside, beyond and on the fringes of the commercial mainstream have not contributed to the sound of modern records. In the late 1970s, London-based advertising jingle producer John

Loder bought an 8-track analogue tape recorder following a request from the newly formed anarchist punk band Crass to record their demo. Upon integrating his new multitrack in the outside garage of his Wood Green home, Southern Studios was formed. Loder's production on Crass' album *The Feeding of the Five Thousand* (1978) is particularly notable. In 'Do They Owe Us a Living?' (1979), for example, the absence of any editing, ambience or time-based effects processing results in a particularly abrasive, 'upfront' and 'raw', unrefined sound. As a punk record, the sonic character of *Feeding* ... is a stark contrast to the large-scale mixing console, multitracked guitar construction in the Sex Pistols' Chris Thomas and Bill Price-produced *Never Mind the Bollocks* ... (1977).[60] Featuring all the hallmarks of 'classic rock' record production, Sex Pistols' debut album was largely received in the commercial mainstream as quintessentially 'punk'. Yet John Loder was an early adoptee of 'do it yourself' or 'DIY' recording aesthetics.

After recording *Feeding*... in October 1978, John Loder became the go-to alternative recordist for a generation of alternative and independent musicians. The names 'Southern' and 'Loder' soon caught on, not just amongst UK scenes but also throughout *global* underground culture. Loder went on to produce all of Crass' follow-up albums during the early 1980s. By that time, Loder's sonic signature was well established and, as Crass founder Penny Rimbaud pointed out, 'Crass Records became the label that every aspiring punk band looked to, Southern Studios their destination, and John their engineer of choice.'[61] By the mid-1980s, Loder's studio, DIY recording techniques and newly-formed record label Southern Records had become a hub of alternative music culture, with many affiliated record labels, Dischord and Touch and Go in particular, sending artists to be recorded there. Southern Studios became synonymous with authentic independent artists and classic recordings: Ministry's *The Land of Rape and Honey* (1988), The Jesus and Mary Chain's *Psychocandy* (1985) and Therapy?'s *Pleasure Death* (1992) are just three notable albums recorded in their entirety or in part at Southern Studios. Harvey Birrell, Loder's former assistant, continued to operate Southern Studios until its eventual closure in 2012.[62]

It is important to note what can be construed as a *continuum* of Loder's sonic signature. Chicago-based noise-core band Big Black's *Songs About Fucking* (1987) album is significant in that sense. Featuring the same rawness and 'under mixed' vocal production so central to Crass records,[63] 'Side 1' of *Songs About Fucking* features Loder's sonic signature in its abrasive, distorted guitars, high mid-range fuzz and 'buried' vocal mix. This record was a turning point in the career of the band's frontman, Steve Albini, who went on to record Side 2 of *Songs* ... along with many more records including Pixies' *Surfa Rosa* (1988), PJ Harvey's *Rid of Me* (1993) and Nirvana's *In Utero* (1994). Furthermore, Therapy?'s *Pleasure Death* (1992), produced entirely by Loder's assistant Harvey Birrell, features similar 'buried' vocals, 'enveloping' guitars and prominent drums – arguably a more refined, 'produced' version of Loder's style suitable for the commercial mainstream. Loder, Albini and Birrell's 1970s–1990s alternative recording aesthetics are now central to a kind of 'under production' present across independently produced music that places performances to the very foreground and minimizes the discernible presence of recording technology. As such, it is unsurprising that such aesthetics are considered barometers of musical 'authenticity', despite the problematic nature of the term in popular music studies.

Summary

This chapter has highlighted how the role of the recordist has changed along with technology, the sonic continuums of musical genre – both in the commercial mainstream and in 'underground' musics – and issues of workplace flux. The role of the tape operator declined almost simultaneously to the advent and proliferation of 'in-line' mixing consoles and demand for computer, sampling and synthesis skills. Whilst this role lost relevance into the 1980s, the 'role' of the recordist diversified with the blurring of DJ, performer, musician and producer roles.

Whilst true 'auteurs' are a minority, the application of the term to describe what it is a producer *does* is deeply problematic. In fact, the term 'producer' is, in itself, one that is convoluted, means different things to different individuals and is interpreted differently depending on era in music history, genre or musical situation. Thus the term 'producer' is difficult to define, apply or categorize; it is a highly individualistic role that can be undertaken from different angles. Historically, the origin of the producer has been in songwriting, arranging, musicianship, engineering, management and in A&R, yet the term is harder to define than ever before due to the multitask nature of the job. Indeed, I make no attempt to offer such a definition here. So-called 'jacks of all trades', whilst prominent towards the end of the 1980s and through the 1990s, have always been prevalent in the recording industry. Recordists have often multitasked or gained their role by possessing a skill set made up of various technical and/or musical and/or business skills, as many scholars have noted. As Théberge has suggested – and as illustrated with multiple examples in this chapter – the role of the recordist simultaneously diversified and became more isolated through the 1980s and 1990s. It would be wrong to suggest this was due to technology alone. The shifts in workplace, a changing recording industry economy and the rise of computer-based software programming skill sets, all contributed to changes in the recording and production role, to the point where by the late 1990s, the naturalization of musicians performing with computers was fully realized. Ultimately, the recordist 'types' evident are based on demands of musicians, performers, managers and music industry executives who use their services. Therefore, whilst musical aesthetics and direction, genre and style nuances, as well as sound recording and production technology, have largely informed the changing role of the recordist, such influences have varied in impact on the recordists' role in different points in history.

6

Sound Minds: Mapping Recordists' Attitudes

In *Good Vibrations*, Mark Cunningham stated:

> Sound effects, which had taken the previous generation of artists many weeks, even months, to perfect through antiquated methods were 'stolen', fed into samplers and applied to mostly unrelated new records. 'Revolutionary!' was the cry from one side of the industry. 'Sacrilege!' countered the opponents.[1]

Cunningham's observation of an attitudinal divide amongst members of the recording industry in the 1980s pertains only to their responses to samplers. However, this separation was indicative of a broader antithesis: 'traditionalist' recordists, often whose experiential expertise derived from 1960s and 1970s recording practice, and 'technophiliac' recordists, often younger and embracing new technologies. Such polar recordist 'types' have been acknowledged by Brock-Nannestad,[2] Durant[3] and Bennett,[4] but the dichotomy manifests in wider philosophical discourses of technological determinism and pessimism, such as Steven Jones' *Against Technology*,[5] Andrew Feenberg's *Questioning Technology*[6] and Tyler Veak's critical response, *Democratizing Technology*.[7] In this chapter, the ways in which recordists' standpoints, such as those described by Cunningham and many more, influence their tech-processual practice are explored. Such polar recordist 'types' have been affiliated with the flawed, yet prevalent 'analogue vs. digital debate', as addressed in the introduction. I am not denying the existence of such a debate, but the idea is unhelpful and results in a reductive discourse that fails to analyse the complexity of either sonic domain or the prevalence of hybridity in both technological application and processual technique. In saying that, multiple scholars deem this oppositional framework worthy of contextual focus: Barlindhaug's *Analogue Sound in the Age of Digital Tools*[8] and Berk's *Analogue Fetishes and Digital Futures*[9] are just two examples. Many analogue sound and music technologies – tape recorders, Roland 808 and 909 machines, analogue mixing consoles – are now considered 'vintage' systems, or at least technological precursors, since the turn of the millennium.

Despite the flawed 'analogue vs. digital debate', the aforementioned recordist 'types' *loosely* affiliate with one or the other sonic domain: 'traditionalist' recordists working in a 'performance capture', 'music first', often 'analogue' paradigm and 'technophiliac' recordists preferring technology-driven recording techniques using significant multitracking, post-production processing and other 'construction'-based techniques. Indeed, 'traditionalists' and 'technophiliacs' are useful labels, but it is vital to acknowledge the mass of grey area, the flexibility in these paradigms and the 'shifting' of recordist attitudes over time and circumstances such as artist's aesthetic intention, workplace technology availability and temporal and budget constraints. In other words, whilst 'traditionalists' and 'technophiliacs' exist – and certainly have done throughout the era of focus in this book – recordists exhibit far more complex and, indeed, flexible tech-processual standpoints than that apparent on the surface.

The impact of new sound recording and music technologies from the late 1970s had a remarkable effect upon the overall sound of popular music recordings. However, this does not explain why some recordists chose to adopt new technologies, whilst others put up varying degrees of resistance in this era of significant technological change. Why did some recordists stick with the 'tried and tested' methods and technologies of old?

A good range of ethnographic work has already been carried out on sound recordists and their working practices, and such sources have been extensively examined and cited here. Interview collections are particularly useful resources in ascertaining the technological and processual preferences of sound recordists. Anthologies such as Buskin's *Inside Tracks*,[10] Simons' *Studio Stories*[11] and Massey's *Behind the Glass Volumes I and II*[12] are helpful points of reference, as are recordist interviews carried out with journalists in *Sound on Sound, Mix* and other music-related periodicals. The *Journal on the Art of Record Production* has also published several high-profile recordist interviews, including Richard James Burgess' interviews with Wendy Page[13] and Linda Perry.[14]

The attitudes of recordists and their standpoint(s) towards their interactions with artists, technologies and workplaces are vital, yet rarely acknowledged, aspects of the recording and production process. Such attitudes affect technology choices, processual techniques, as well as overall aesthetic intentions. Indeed, recordists are often sought *precisely* for their aesthetic preferences and/or creative directions; a crucial understanding or 'match' between the stylistic attributes of artist and recordist is regularly sought by both parties and considered an important part of establishing a cohesive and shared direction.[15]

So, with that in mind, this chapter cross-references existing interview material with further ethnographic work conducted exclusively for this book.

It must be stated that relying on interview material alone is problematic. Albin Zak rightly recognized the difficulties in dealing with oral histories, as he stated in his issue 2 editorial for the *Journal on the Art of Record Production*: 'the oral accounts of practitioners, though problematic, are among our most useful resources. If, for example, we are to engage the entire musical surface, it is helpful to know what kinds of concerns were paramount to those who made it.'[16] Problematic for a number of reasons: subjects often talk with the benefit of hindsight, which may or may not impact on the account of events; the passage of time can cloud the accuracy of memories, judgements and reasoning, which can – in some instances – dilute testimonies or, on the other hand, cause particular events to be exaggerated or their significance played down. Furthermore, recordists have been known to deliberately withhold significant aspects of a recording process when being interviewed, for reasons of loyalty to other individuals involved, to keep their techniques a secret or to conceal conflicts or other issues affecting the recording session. For example, this is evident in Mark Taylor and

Brian Rawling's decision to attribute the vocal processing on Cher's 'Believe' (1998) to a vocoder and to keep their use of the Antares Autotune a secret.[17] Regardless, Zak is right in that it is helpful to understand the concerns of recordists in the record-making process. I would go further and argue that recordists' attitudes and standpoints towards their technological and processual practice(s) are so significant that they impact on the aesthetic direction of the recording session and, thus, what is eventually heard. Therefore, in engaging and understanding the wider 'musical surface',[18] we must not only 'pay some attention to the man behind the curtain'[19] but draw attention to their agency in the recording process and the intricacies of his or her technological and processual views. Additionally, many of the notable standpoints addressed in this chapter are shared and, therefore, corroborated by multiple recordists.

In the case of this study, care has been taken when questioning, recording and analysing recordists' testimonies of their working practices. Like musicians, recordists are passionate, often emotive individuals who care deeply about their art. The main difficulty encountered with this research was separating out explicit reference to tech-processual practice from mere opinion and emotion. Yet upon close analysis, distinct attitudinal patterns emerge between multiple and, in most cases, unconnected recordists. Such consistencies are teased out from the bulk of the interview material and discussed as key, clearly identifiable thematics.

After extensive ethnographic work carried out specifically for this project, attitudes of utopianism and pessimism certainly became clear, seemingly substantiating prior work, but the bigger picture is more complex. I am by no means suggesting these attitudes are the *only* ones expressed by recordists nor are these attitudes expressed exclusively or without overlap. Through the process of extracting relevant material, patterns are evident, and distinct correlations can be drawn between recordist attitudes and their tech-processual practices.

A diagrammatical representation of recordist attitudes is presented in matrix form in Figure 6.1. Here, recordist attitudes are plotted against the broad positive–negative and traditionalist–technophiliac axes – well-established, recognized attitudes already identified by Cunningham[20] and Bennett,[21] amongst others. It must be noted that whilst some recordists express one explicit viewpoint, others voice multifaceted and even contradictory perspectives, hence the acknowledgement of 'grey area'. Within this attitudinal matrix lies unexplored territory: In what ways do recordists express such attitudes, and how do these standpoints manifest in their tech-processual practice? Rebellion, utilitarianism, nonchalance, Luddite, risk aversion, scepticism, option anxiety and even ignorance were found to be prevalent amongst the attitudes of many contemporary recordists. These findings present a detailed reasoning behind the tech-processual choices made by recordists and are particularly helpful in explaining the use of technological precursors or 'vintage' systems in contemporary record production. This is important, because until now, such choices may have been attributed to nostalgia or sentimentalism.[22] The main objective in this chapter is to highlight the effect of recordist attitudes on their technological and processual techniques that are not only an important reason behind artist, management and A&R hiring choices but can 'steer' the sound of a record. Let's break down the attitudinal matrix in Figure 6.1 in more detail.

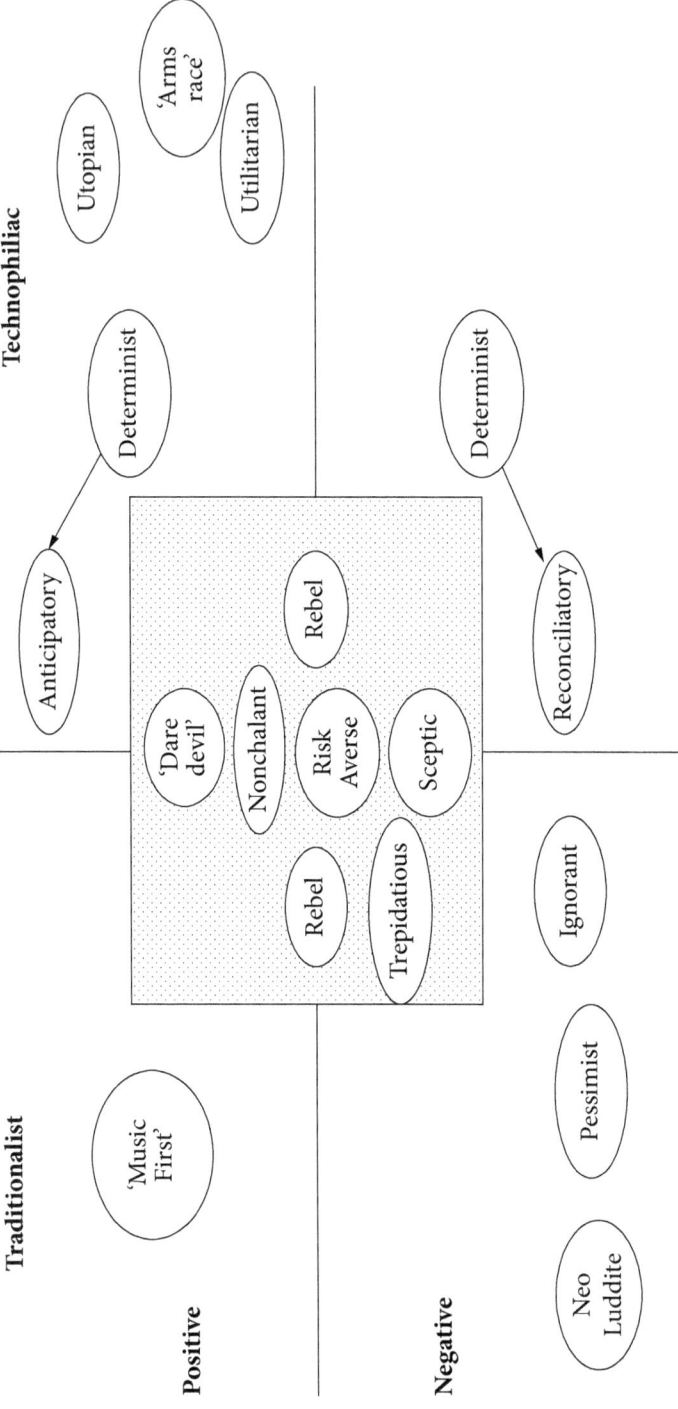

Figure 6.1 Attitudinal matrix depicting tech-processual standpoints of sound recordists in the 1980s and 1990s.

Music first

The late Phil Ramone gave the keynote interview with Maureen Drony at the 2008 *Art of Record Production* conference. Afterwards, he launched his book *Making Records*,[23] a highly anticipated account of his recording career, including producing albums for artists such as Billy Joel (*Innocent Man* (1983) and *The Nylon Curtain* (1982)) and Frank Sinatra (*Duets* (1993) and *Duets II* (1994)). I asked him to sign the book; in it, he wrote:

Dear Sam,
Music first.
Phil Ramone.

At the time, I was studying for my doctorate and whilst I had skeleton ideas surrounding my main thesis, it was not in any way structured or formed. Without even reading the book, Ramone's comment encapsulated a mission: an overarching vision that he felt compelled to pass on to others. I am certainly not the lone recipient of this advice: 'As I've told my students, the mantra that should guide every songwriter, singer, musician and producer who cares about what they do is, "music first"'.[24] If such a 'mantra' can guide the entirety of a recordists' successful career, then it must infiltrate each recording, musical interaction and production aesthetic, therefore influencing the aesthetic direction of the record. Ramone is not alone. This 'music first' mantra is prevalent amongst recordists of all genres, eras and levels of success. George Duke, musician and producer of various soul and R&B, suggested, 'Whether you're talking about samples or live musicians, you've got to start with something that's good.'[25] Rick Rubin, producer of Jay-Z's *The Blueprint* (2001), Beastie Boys' *Licensed to Ill* (1986) and Slayer's *Reign in Blood* (1986), amongst many others, goes further in suggesting that the 'music first' directive is the responsibility of the producer as much as it is of the songwriter: 'I think the most important thing a producer can do is spend time getting the songs into shape before recording. The material is so much more important than the sounds.'[26]

Recordists also express such 'music first' attitudes in the context of acoustic and electronic and 'synthesized' or 'programmed' musical instruments. For example, George Martin suggested: 'I think the sound of a natural instrument is best. One of the dangers of all this technology and eternal synthesised sound and programming and mechanics is that it is making music a bit sterile.'[27] The preference for acoustic and electric instruments 'spills over' into wider sound recording and music technologies. As discussed earlier, the advent of computer-based DAWs and the sophisticated editing and manipulation tools therein only exaggerated an existing divide between 'traditionalist' and 'technophiliac' producers. Consider the standpoint of Stevie Wonder and (artist) producer Walter Afanasieff: 'Sure you can go and "Pro Tool" anything to death, but if you don't have a good song and a good performance from the beginning, you're going to get into trouble.'[28]

This idea that the more 'synthesized' or technologically inclined the production, the less 'performance-centric' the result is one shared by many recordists. This suggests that recordists are acutely aware of the 'dehumanizing' effects of certain sound recording and music technologies. For example, Johnny Cash, Jay-Z and Red Hot Chili Peppers' recordist Rick Rubin commented, 'I hate technically slick records that have no sense of emotion.'[29] To that end, recordists with a strong 'music first' standpoint tend to place more importance on the *personnel* involved in the recording *process* than on the sound recording technology. This view is shared by many recordists, particularly those working in R&B and hip-hop genres. For example, Eminem and Snoop Dogg recordist Dr Dre commented, 'The equipment is important, but, to be honest, I'm still working on the same board I've worked on since 1990. The important part is who's pushing the buttons.'[30] So, technology alone is no match for knowledge and experiential expertise. Robbie Adams (recordist for U2, Smashing Pumpkins, Leonard Cohen) agrees: 'Mixing, like music, is a very personal thing. It's the people that are important, and the machines and the quality of them is very secondary.'[31] 'Music first' recordists shift the focus of their work away from the technology and towards the people, musical and creative ideas that result in a popular music recording. Early popular music recordists such as the late Les Paul expressed such views long into their career, 'What kind of gear do I have in there? [Paul's own studio] It doesn't matter. Because it's not the gear that makes the talent.'[32] And later pop recordists such as Will Mowatt suggested: 'In terms of the creative process, what comes first is the idea. That spark which sets the whole thing on its way. Technology – hardware and software – is just one piece of the puzzle.'[33]

One of the UK's most successful recordists, Hugh Padgham, was at the height of his career in the 1980s. Credited on albums such as The Police's *Synchronicity* (1983) and *Ghost in the Machine* (1981), as well as Genesis' *Genesis* (1983) and Phil Collins's *Face Value* (1981), Padgham has often voiced a 'music first' approach to recording, but his views have morphed with other standpoints:

> Now, some producers and engineers would absolutely love the idea of being able to sit in front of their Macintosh and go crazy and change it all. For them, that sort of electronic manipulation would be very satisfying to do. I, however, can't tolerate that kind of thing.[34]

Here we have a 'music first' standpoint contextualized within a tech-processual paradigm that Padgham *does not* subscribe to. Padgham's reference to computer-based production capabilities points to an altogether different standpoint existing amongst his contemporaries.

Utopianism

Tech-processual idealism certainly manifested in recordist standpoints during the advent of the digital recording age from the late 1970s. Indeed, the attitude is still prevalent today, with many recordists championing new and improved technologies, signing technology endorsement deals and working directly with equipment manufacturers, such as Butch Vig's work with Digidesign as described earlier.

Whilst tech-utopianism was also expressed by many engineers and producers working throughout the 1980s and 1990s, I found 'hard utopianists' to be scarce: that is, recordists believing that the advent of new, predominantly digital recording equipment would make for perfect sound recordings. Rather, an *impression* of utopian beliefs was present amongst some recording engineers and producers – an attitude towards technology that goes beyond that of tech-determinism and into the realm of tech-utopian ideology. The marriage of tech-utopianism and competitiveness/ambition was also highly prevalent amongst recordists working through the 1980s and 1990s. One such figure was Culture Club and Human League recordist Steve Levine, former chair of the UK's Music Producers Guild, who said of digital tape recording:

> People make such a big deal about working with digital tape machines. People who slag off this technology have nowhere near the experience of it that I have. Probably, they haven't even seen a digital tape machine![35]

In a 2009 interview, Levine pointed to age as a determining factor in the 'traditionalist'/'technophiliac' split:

> The one advantage I had was that I was young enough at the time to embrace the new technology like it was the greatest thing ever, but I didn't have any baggage. I didn't have any 70's baggage.[36]

By '70s baggage', Levine implies that young recordists at the turn of the 1980s were able to embrace new tech-processual methodologies easily having not experienced years of analogue recording practices. Age may be a factor in the expression of tech-utopian views, but it is argued here that peer pressure and the use of technology-driven recording and production methodologies had a greater bearing on the expression of tech-utopian ideals. For example, Mike Howlett (Flock of Seagulls' *Flock of Seagulls* (1982), Martha and the Muffins' *Metro Music* (1980)) worked through the 1970s as a recordist and musician, yet embraced the digital recording age: 'I absolutely loved all this stuff and I was always "let's do it, let's use it" instead of waiting for someone else to find out about it.'[37] He went on to say about the advent of MIDI: 'I loved them. [MIDI technologies] I was working in Los Angeles in 1983 when somebody bought 2 [Yamaha] DX-7's [synthesisers] into the studio and we hooked it up and stuck the 5-pin DIN plug together and thought, "Wow, look! I can play this and it'll do that!"'[38] The manipulability and flexible nature of MIDI technologies appealed to many recordists of the era, as pointed out by scholars such as Théberge[39] and Durant[40].

Trevor Horn, arguably at the very forefront of modern recording and production from the late 1970s and throughout the 1980s, was another producer who often expressed tech-utopian ideals:

> So when digital came along, it was like manna from heaven for me. It was wonderful because it meant you could do all kinds of things without losing quality. And I felt the quality of even the earliest digital machines was fine – it just took people a long time to get used to the sound.[41]

Horn acknowledges an important point: the notion that time played a large factor in the adoption of digital technologies manifested in multiple attitudes. For some, the assimilation of digital technologies into the recording workplace was a slow process. 'Get [ting] used to the sound'[42] and also synchronization and integration issues were two time-based factors. For some recordists, the adoption of digital technologies was a quick one and updates could not come soon enough. Take the production house PWL at Borough Studios, the workplace of British production trio SAW. In his 2004 book *The Hit Factory*, Mike Stock expressed a hard utopianist, borderline utilitarian viewpoint when discussing music technologies in the 1980s:

> It was the era when producers moved rapidly from using acoustic pianos, acoustic guitars and drums to synthesizers, drum machines and samples. It wasn't always an easy transition, although the new technology gave us the means to create perfect sounds and instant hits.[43]

This view was corroborated by SAW recordist Phil Harding, as he stated:

> It always fascinated me – and I suppose this is the way with any programmer, musician or a production team – you come up with an armoury of stock sounds. So you say, 'I'm going to use that drum sample, program it on here, but that's the sound I'm going to use. I'm going to use one of four basses and I'm going to use one of these four Roland pad sounds. And that becomes your sound.' That was why everything was so quick at PWL and that was why everything sounded so similar.[44]

The standpoints of SAW recordists represent a 'polar' viewpoint to that expressed by Ramone, Padgham, Rubin and others. Here is a clear utilitarian ideology underpinning the 'factory' output of the UK's then most commercially successful production house. Stock acknowledges a sense of 'transition', but as Pete Waterman pointed out, the production trio began in an era where digital technologies were already established:

> We were very technology minded and even today we probably have more equipment at PWL than any other studio in the UK. If there's something new, I want to hear it. In 1984, we were at the forefront of a new wave of technical producers and we were throwing away all the shackles, which had been put on producers in the past. We didn't want drummers and would never entertain the thought of having a real, live drummer in our studio.[45]

Waterman clearly embraced the 'dehumanizing' effects of programmed, synthesized sounds as opposed to musicians and traditional acoustic instruments. SAW pushed 'performance' boundaries with programming-heavy composition and also blurred the lines between composition and production. Phil Harding, SAW's mix engineer, described technology at the PWL recording house at the end of the 1980s and going into the 1990s:

> I'd say in the 1980s, we were always hungry to move forward. SAW made the Linn 9000 last right up to the first Cubase on Atari ST, which was quite amazing. I'd say that somewhere in the late 1980s, we were all desperate to move on. Technology

wasn't moving fast enough for those of us that could see the future of it all being in one box.⁴⁶

SAW were indicative of 'technophiliac' recordists working in an industry that, in their view, was technologically slow. As Mike Howlett stated: 'I almost felt they (technologies) were going too slowly. You work out how to deal with stuff that's clunky and annoying and then MIDI came along from a sequencing point of view and you were thinking "thank Christ for that!"⁴⁷

Competitiveness and ambition: The technological arms race

It is unsurprising, then, that a kind of 'technological arms race' manifested amongst the 'technophiliac' recordists of the era. During the 1980s, technologies such as the Fairlight CMI and Sony DASH recorder were prohibitively expensive and as such exclusive technologies in the hands of an elite few. These recordists – SAW, Trevor Horn, Steve Levine and others – jostled for technological ownership at the same time as they did chart positions, as Howlett pointed out:

> there was a bit of a race going on too, a new keyboard would come out. The classic one was the Roland D-50 and it had this fantastic sound. Enya's 'Orinco Flow', that's the D-50 and they did it first and it kind of meant that no one else could really use that sound any more because they got it first. There always used to be this race with new keyboards coming out and you'd go through all the sounds and think, 'that's a good one, we'd better record it before anyone else does!'⁴⁸

Phil Harding corroborated this, suggesting Pete Waterman regularly 'competed' with Trevor Horn:

> As soon as they had something, especially if there was some sounds that were in the charts, Waterman would come in and say, 'listen to this, we've got to have this. Where's that sound come from?' He'd look at the engineers and keyboard players and say, 'Where's that sound come from? Why haven't we got it?' It was like, 'He's got a Fairlight', so he [Waterman] said, 'Well, I'd better have one of them, then.' So £30,000 or £40,000 later from Sycho [equipment retailer] we had a Fairlight system that Mike [Stock] and Matt [Aitken] couldn't work.⁴⁹

It is important to note that 'technophiliac' recordists were more caught up in the utopian ideology behind the so-called 'technological arms race'. Whilst analogue equipment – particularly the ongoing development and proliferation of large-scale mixing consoles during the 1980s – was still very much a part of recording workplaces, this 'technological arms race' was more concerned with new digital technologies. The costs associated with such equipment were largely due to the integration of computer microprocessors and storage. Floppy disks could store a limited number of sounds, so the acquisition and ownership of computer memory became a key factor. The more the technology relied upon microprocessors or the larger the on-board storage capabilities, the more expensive the technology. Stephen Street recognized the technological arms race as being confined to 'technophiliac' recordists: 'People who worked on more synthesised music and more keyboard type things, they were more stuck in the race and trying to keep up with things.'[50] This 'arms race' discourse also manifested in the 1980s emergent music technology press.[51] Compounding feelings in the audio industry, there was an evident group of recordists who fixated on new, high-end digital technologies.

Pessimism

Whilst many recordists during the 1980s and 1990s embraced the technological acceleration and incorporated these new machines into their working practices, others did not. Technological pessimism was rife in the audio industry during the 1980s and 1990s as recordists came to terms with operating new digital technologies and computer-based equipment. Technological pessimism was freely expressed in a number of ways, perhaps none more so than by US recordist Steve Albini: 'The future belongs to analogue loyalists. Fuck digital' was an example of this bold standpoint, written inside the sleeve notes to *Songs About Fucking* (1987) by Big Black – Albini's rock band. Later, in a 2004 lecture given to the Middle Tennessee Students Union, Albini 'lamented the age of over-production in the 1980s'.[52] This is representative of a wider discourse of 'overproduction' or 'overproduced' music during the 1980s.[53] Noting the technology-driven 'construction' approach of many recordists of the era, the term 'overproduction' or 'overproduced' referred to a sense of production *beyond* what was deemed necessary. To that end, the sonically discernible evidence of tech-processual factors upon the final sound recording is enhanced, prominent and obvious. Arguably, the recordist has positioned himself in the performance space.

Rick Rubin's 'hate' of 'technically slick' records mentioned previously is a good example of resistance to technology-driven record production and its concomitant technological aesthetics. This attitude could be construed as technological pessimism: a hard scepticism towards the modern, 'cutting edge' equipment that had the potential to completely change working practices. Rubin was a young producer by the mid-1980s when working on multi-platinum selling records by Run DMC and the Beastie Boys, yet this standpoint was perhaps more understandably taken by older producers – perhaps the ones who may have carried '70s baggage' as suggested earlier by Steve Levine, including George Martin:

> I think its (technology) making music boring. You hear the same sounds over and over again. Maybe I'm old fashioned, but I think the sound of a natural instrument is best. One of the dangers of all this technology and eternal synthesised sound and programming and mechanics is that it is making music a bit sterile. These are wonderful tools if you use them properly, but if you use them to the detriment of real sounds, you get down a cul-de-sac of boring repetitions.[54]

What Martin referred to here is the advent of prefabricated sounds that would often be integral to MIDI synthesizers used in repetitive, sequenced lines often programmed on digital systems such as the Fairlight, Synclavier or Atari. Martin suggests there was a subsequent negative repercussion on music, in that the consequence of using technologies to the detriment of 'real sounds' resulted in music sounding sterile. He acknowledges that the technologies are 'wonderful' if used properly, but makes little demarcation between proper or improper use. However, what he does acknowledge is a difference between the use of real and prefabricated sounds as being 'dangerous' – something that Neil Postman also cited as a key theme of technological pessimism in his key work *Technopoly*.[55] This idea that modern technologies posed a threat to recording and production aesthetics or 'the way things were' was an opinion common to traditionalist record producers. For example, AC/DC and Bob Marley recordist Tony Platt suggested:

> The advent of digital recording and the advent of CD was really a matter of just coming to terms with another set of technology and I got very frustrated with people taking the view that this was the answer to everybody's prayers and all of the problems we experienced with analogue would be solved in one go ... it was a lie. And nobody should have fallen for it.[56]

These viewpoints are, however, problematic since they do not articulate the fundamental *problems* with new digital technologies. Thus, they are good examples of technological pessimism: resistance to new technologies with little context. Such views were also expressed towards particular devices or systems. For example, in 2007, hip-hop recordist Dr Dre described his venture into Digidesign's Pro Tools DAW: 'I tried to record into Pro Tools and got one of the best Pro Tools operators down to record the music, and it's just not me. It wasn't good.'[57] Again, no explanation behind this decisive experience, simply that 'it wasn't good.'

Scepticism

More prevalent amongst 1980s and 1990s recordists was a softer form of tech-processual resistance. Scepticism surrounding new technologies was perhaps more common than hard pessimism. Let's consider this quote by Foo Fighters and Pixies recordist Chris Sheldon:

> I was definitely somebody who was wary of new technology, mainly because I didn't know how to use the bloody stuff. I was never one to jump in and go, 'this is it! I've seen the future!' I'm not that technically minded. I choose not to be. All this stuff is a means to an end. Rather than, 'I love this stuff; it's all so brilliant, oh and lets record some music as well!' So I was always somewhat sceptical about it.[58]

Here, we see a much more reasoned approach as to why these new technologies presented such a challenge. Sheldon suggests the learning curve associated with new systems: 'I didn't know how to use the bloody stuff'[59] was a key issue in adopting new technologies. This is just one example of a reasoned sceptic; other recordists have specified their concerns with new technologies more directly. So what were the main reasons behind recordists' scepticism during the 1980s and 1990s? Two key reasons become clear: new technologies as 'recording session hindrances' and new technologies as 'creators of option anxiety'.

New digital technologies as session hindrances

Integrating new systems to existing workplace set-ups involved synchronization and, in many cases, the conflation of technologies from analogue and digital sonic domains. Sometimes, new technologies were chosen on the basis of their operational similarity to previous analogue systems. For example, Stephen Street describes his choice of the Otari RADAR hard disk recording device for much of his 1990s 'Britpop' genre productions:

> I'm not into computers and fiddling about with a mouse because I think that kind of technology can get in the way of the artist/producer relationship. But with RADAR (Otari HD Recorder), the remote sits on the desk and looks and feels like a tape machine, so people don't even think about it – it's just there recording whatever you are doing with the band.[60]

Street implies that a computer could detract from the all-important artist–recordist relationship in a workplace environment. Even utopianist recordists admitted to a sense of 'intrusion' of technology on the 'flow' of recording sessions. Consider Steve Levine's description of the Simmonds SDS and SDX synthesizer drum machine systems:

> The Simmonds [SDS series] gave way to the SDX, which was also painful to use, mainly because the technology was being pushed to such a degree … when it worked, you were like, 'Oh my God, this is fantastic!' but more often than not it didn't and I had a lot of down time.[61]

Mick Glossop recognized the challenges associated with some of the first automated mixing consoles. Whilst these were analogue devices, their automation sections were often computer-driven, with mixes having to be saved to floppy disks. Glossop recalled: 'I still remember the first mixes I did, where the computer would crash and it would delete the directory on the floppy disk as well. So you didn't just reboot, you lost all your mixes. You'd be 10 hours into a mix and you'd lose the whole thing.'[62] The impact of such interruptions had both time and budget consequences, but other recordists describe the impact on creative and artistic flow. As Phil Ramone pointed out in *Making Records*, 'Interrupting the flow of the session to say, "Excuse me – we've got to fix a microphone," or "Sorry, the board hiccupped" is like blocking the path of a marathon runner in the last quarter-mile of a race.'[63]

Chris Sheldon described entire days lost with the installation of new technologies: 'Basically, when people walked in with this technology, you knew the day was over trying to get these things to work. There was no constructive recording done!'[64] These remarks suggest that many recordists attempted to work with new systems, to integrate new technologies into their workflow, but were deterred by difficulties encountered with session workflow. Steve Albini corroborates this justification:

> I simply don't have time to allow the equipment to interfere. Up until now, working with those technologies has always been slower, more cumbersome and more frustrating and so I've refused to do it. I disagree with the mythological conventions of digital recording and I find them to be intrusive.[65]

By 'mythological conventions', Albini refers to the utopian discourse surrounding then new – and current – digital recording and music technologies. As described earlier, the notion that new technologies were faster, easier to use, more convenient and cheaper was the opposite to the realities faced by some recordists. These negative, day-to-day encounters with new technologies were one of the underlying reasons for scepticism amongst recordists of the era.

Limitations – option anxiety

New technologies as session hindrances were just one factor influencing a sceptic viewpoint. Part of the utopian dialect surrounding new, predominantly digital systems was their flexibility, their capacity for creative exploration and the seemingly endless options associated with their use. For example, up until the late 1970s, a succession of 8-track, then 16-track, and then 24-track analogue tapes were the only means of multitracking. Of course, tape machines were sometimes locked and synchronized together to create more tracks or techniques such as 'bouncing' or 'fattening'– the process of combining pre-recorded tracks in order to free up tracks on multitrack recorders – were used to create more options in the recording session. However, with the advent of MIDI-compatible technologies, an almost endless set of parameters were presented to the user – an apparently limitless amount of potential options and freedom. Again, the aesthetics of 'options' and 'freedom' permeated manufacturer and industry discourse, compounding the utopian view that new technologies could only be a good thing.[66] However, many recordists of the era found that the reality of working within an endless set of parameters was in fact detrimental to their working practices. Subsequently, the issue of 'option anxiety' informed technological scepticism perhaps more so than any other factor. Consider recordist Martyn Ware's point: 'It's difficult to appreciate it when you are in the middle of a recording, but the more restricted you are, the more creative you have to be and the more you are focussed on the job in hand.'[67] Ware's observation is just that and he makes no reference to how options have impacted on his sessions. However, other recordists certainly attribute limiting their recording parameters as a way of ensuring effective workflows. As William Orbit suggested: 'Really, I've been working towards leaving aside the technicalities for a number of years. Getting more and more simple. Creating mixes with less and less inputs on the desk.'[68]

The deliberate setting of a restrictive working framework points towards a sense of control the recordist needs to feel over the technologies they work with, which is precisely what Strawn referred to in his AES address.[69] Consider this point of view from UK recordist Flood (Mark Ellis): he explicitly refers to a master–slave relationship between recordist and technology.

> I am an advocate for technology as long as its something that's used rather than something that somebody is used by. It's very easy to become a slave to technology and do something over and over again. Even though you have the ability to try a lot of options with a computer, that doesn't mean that it will be done any better or quicker.[70]

Later in the 1990s, Flood went on to specify the difference between 'options' on analogue tape machines and with MIDI systems: 'Digital recording is a bit like MIDI, it's way too fluid. You can all too easily chop and change things, and you have potential options all the time. Whereas when working with analogue tape, you commit yourself to some degree when you record something.'[71] The decisiveness involved with analogue tape recording is significant in determining why some recordists felt sceptical about working with MIDI or other new digital technologies. Seemingly unaware of this common standpoint, Michael Bradford, producer for Anita Baker's *Rhythm of Love* (1994) and New Radicals' *Maybe You've Been Brainwashed Too* (1998), ascribed his own views surrounding 'options' as 'radical':

> I don't believe in options. I'm radical that way. I don't like options because they just mean you take more time. I've been in this business 20 years and when I started out, you didn't have nearly as many tracks to work with as you have now and you had to make decisions – you had to say – this is what I want it to sound like ... it just takes too long. I'd rather make a decision up front.[72]

Bradford describes the impact of technological option on the temporal aspects of recording sessions. Stevie Wonder, Mariah Carey and Celine Dion recordist Walter Afanasieff's view is more generic, as he suggests:

> We have so much freedom, so much room for error, that at the end of the day its not about aesthetics, its that we didn't do it right – we went too far, we did too much. There are times when I wish I had the same circumstances George (Martin) had during Sgt. Pepper. I wish that singers didn't come into the room and say 'I want to do 12 more tracks, I'm not happy with this.'[73]

Afanasieff appears to conflate increased multitracking capabilities with a perceived loss of power; committing performances to tape because of temporal or technological constraints puts a great deal of control in the hands of the recordist. As performers have become more aware of multitracking capabilities, more options are presented to them in a recording session. For some recordists, such freedom might be seen as a positive, as Will Mowatt suggested, but for others, it results in a frustrating – not to mention hindered – recording experience.

Nostalgia

At the beginning of this chapter, I suggested that scholarly discourse has already noted two distinct 'camps' of recordists: the 'traditionalists' on the one hand and the 'technophiliacs' on the other. There might be a third, as scholars such as Timothy Taylor[74] and David Toop[75] have recognized what they perceive to be nostalgia amongst certain musicians and recordists. This is an interesting observation – and a contested point in academic studies. I am not suggesting that nostalgia does not – or *did not* – exist amongst recordists. Indeed, hints of nostalgia come through in recordist interviews, such as the point made previously by Walter Afanasieff. However, at this stage, I assert that attributing a recordist's tech-processual standpoint to nostalgia alone is deeply problematic. In *Ocean of Sound*, David Toop suggested:

> musics which attempt to make a nostalgic, exaggerated return (to past musics) … can only seem ludicrous at a time when computers think faster, clone replications at will and spread information over vast distances in intricate, often unidentifiable webs.[76]

Whilst Toop refers to musics, as opposed to recordists, the sonic character of 'past musics' is largely achieved through the recording and production process. The problem with Toop's suggestion is that it ignores aesthetic intention and direction of those contributing to the music production process. As pointed out earlier, technological choice is strongly aligned to musical direction. Morton explicitly refers to nostalgia amongst recordists in *Sound Recording*, as he suggests:

> There are important niches in the recording industry where a conservative culture of engineering maintains that high-quality analog sound recorders are better for certain purposes. This aesthetic justification for the use of a particular recording technology echoes the way musicians and recording engineers have for many years used their prerogative in the studio to make crucial technological choices, except that in this instance it is turned on its ear by the fact that they sometimes cling to an older technology instead of embracing the new one … clearly nostalgia and fashion create temporary reversals of the trends.[77]

On the one hand, Morton attributes agency to the recordist, recognizes the importance of recordists' technological choices and realizes that analogue sound recording still has a place in today's industry. However, to attribute the aesthetic justification of analogue technology to nostalgia and fashion alone is difficult to reconcile. It is not clear what Morton refers to when discussing 'trends', but it is important to note that with the advent of the digital age, analogue recording did not simply disappear. On the contrary, analogue recording and the tools and techniques associated with it are used as important sonic differentiators in a music industry that has been dominated by digital recording, processing and formatting for the past thirty years. Furthermore, many recordists view their technologies as 'tools of the trade' and, as previously described, focus more on the source material and/or personnel. For example, recordist Steve Albini suggested: 'I'm not a nostalgic person. I don't have any kind of romantic association with the tools of my trade. I see them all as functional.'[78]

The problem with attributing technological precursor use to nostalgia lies in the breadth of reasoning as to why recordists opt out of using new technologies. There is the aesthetic direction of the music, the artist, management and recordist intention and the availability of technologies in the workplace. Furthermore, recordists often make technological decisions based on the quality; if a precursor is perceived as bringing about better results, what – or where – is the incentive to move on from it? Additionally, nostalgia, which by definition pertains to a 'sentimental longing or wistful affection for a period in the past',[79] is difficult to attribute to younger recordists who were not alive or working during the initial periods of their chosen technology. Steve Albini, for example, began recording in the early 1980s – long after the advent of 4-, 8- and 16-track analogue tape recording. That is not to say that younger recordists still cannot 'long' for a point in time they were not physically living or working in, but it does make it harder for nostalgia as an explanation to stick. Pinch and Trocco recognized nostalgia as being problematic reasoning behind the resurgence in 1960s analogue synthesizer usage at the turn of the millennium, as they argued:

> It is easy to dismiss this analogue revival as a form of nostalgia. Nostalgia is usually taken to be a means whereby present uncertainties and discontents are addressed by drawing on a past era or culture. We get nostalgic only when we are having a problem with the present. Certainly it is easy to romanticise the sixties and to treat an interest in sixties technology as part of a yearning for the values of the peace and love generation and the definitive music it produced. But we think something more interesting is going on. In users' adaptation of and reversion to old technologies we see salient criticisms of how the synthesiser has evolved and expressions of genuine feelings of loss.[80]

Such feelings of loss – whether genuine or not – are indicative of nostalgia, but Pinch and Trocco are quite right in that later analogue synthesizer usage cannot be attributed to nostalgia alone. The build quality, sonic characteristics and aesthetics of 1960s and 1970s analogue synthesizers were far removed from the MIDI synthesizers of the 1980s and the skeoumorphic 'soft synth' plug-ins at the turn of the millennium. In *Analogue Sound in the Age of Digital Tools*, Gaute Barlindhaug recognized that digital appropriations of analogue tools in the early 2000s cannot simply be attributed to nostalgia, as he stated:

> By following this quest for analogue sound, digital technology helps to create an acknowledgement of analogue aesthetics. This must not be seen as merely an act

of nostalgia, but rather as a sense that the context of its use is what really makes a particular technology novel.[81]

Indeed, context is an all-important factor when considering technological precursor use in contemporary recording. But there are other more complex views worth considering.

Risk aversion, neo-Luddism and nonchalance

Risk aversion, a concept dealt with more in economics[82] and psychology[83] than phonomusicology, evidently manifests in recordists' decision making. Few references to the presence of risk aversion in the music industry exist; however, in *Succeeding in Music: Business Chops for Performers and Songwriters*, John Stiernberg discusses the notion of risk around members of the music industry generally:

> Some people thrive on risk; others tolerate and manage it. Some individuals can't handle any level of risk. ... you can enjoy a successful career in music regardless of your tolerance for risk. Simply put, it's ok to be risk-averse.[84]

Indeed, risk tolerance is variable amongst individuals generally,[85] but risk aversion in relation to recording technologies is certainly prevalent amongst recordists. Like others who rely on interactions with tools and technologies in their trade, recordists spend much time trying and testing tools, integrating tools into their workflow and coming to rely upon their (tried and tested) interactions with those tools to deliver results. Such results are not confined to the recordist; they impact on the sound of a recording, the artist, musicians, other management and label personnel and, ultimately, audiences and legacy. There is a lot at stake; changing tools and technologies means changing techniques and methods. If a recordist has produced successful results, not simply measured by commercial success but in the relationships formed with their peers and other individuals in their music industry network, they may be reluctant to change technologies and, by default, change methodology. Let's consider the founding member of UK dance crossover act The Prodigy, Liam Howlett. Howlett's working practice centred around programming and sequencing on a Roland W-30 sampler workstation. Such a method produced a great deal of success with *Experience* (1992) and *Music for the Jilted Generation* (1994). In 1997, when considering using a computer-based sequencer, Howlett stated, 'The thing with Cubase is, I was scared to go on to it. It wasn't because I was against it, I was just scared. I thought it would change the sound and change the way I write music.'[86] As discussed in Chapters 1 and 2, digital technologies went through a number of changes during the 1980s and 1990s, and the move from analogue tape to computer-based systems was not entirely smooth. Howlett is recognized as a dance music recordist, but risk aversion is not confined to any particular genre. Stephen Street explicitly referred to risk aversion as a key factor in remaining with then antiquated technologies in the recording of Blur's *Parklife* (1994), as he suggested:

> I was a C-Lab user, with the old Atari 1040. That's how we did [Blur's] 'Girls & Boys', all the programming on that was an AKAI sampler, Atari sequencer. It was the standard. So, for years and years and years I stuck with C-Lab. I didn't like the other things. Once you got in with one system, I always felt it difficult to adjust to something else. That's why I didn't like Pro Tools when it came out because to me, it was very different to what I was used to with C-Lab. My view was, get what you feel comfortable with and get good at it, rather than trying to change too many things.[87]

The difference between these two recordists is that Howlett's use of technology is intrinsic to both his production and songwriting process. Howlett *fears* a loss of songwriting method, whereas Street cites comfort as the main reason for sticking with his tried and tested methods. Fear of new technologies and the impact they may have on a sonic signature is a pattern amongst recordists and part of an off-shoot of risk aversion, that of trepidation. Some individuals who did not show hard pessimism or even scepticism towards new technologies were, nevertheless, cautious about venturing into new sonic domains. Rodney Jerkins, also known as Darkchild, has produced and remixed multiple hit R&B records throughout the 1990s and into the present day. He is credited as producer on Whitney Houston's *My Love Is Your Love* (1998), Brandy's *Never Say Never* (1998) and Destiny's Child's *The Writing's on the Wall* (1999). He suggested, 'You have to be careful. Sometimes, new technology will make you change what you've been doing that is making you sound incredible. You can try something new and it can screw you up.'[88] Again, Jerkins cites the compromising of his sonic signature as reason to exercise caution in adopting new technologies. Working in an entirely different genre, UK recordist Chris Sheldon conflates a number of factors as informing his trepidation towards Pro Tools at the turn of the millennium:

> I had to learn. I didn't want to take that step and say, 'well, I'm not going to use analogue [tape] any more'. It took me a while to do that. And it wasn't because of any deep-seated, staunch 'analogue forever' approach. I was scared! I knew the analogue stuff worked. I knew I could rely on it. It was around about the late 1990s when I thought, 'I'm going to do this. I'm not going to use tape.' It was nerve wracking! I was nervous about losing information, a hard drive crashing or something. I used to back up like a crazy man! I was nervous about the sound of it, because it sounded different. I never used the DASH system, so I wasn't used to it. I used analogue [tape] until I went to Pro Tools.[89]

Sheldon has conflated a number of quite different issues:

- Recognition that recording industry technology has moved on
- Experientially informed reliability of analogue recording technology
- A perceived unreliability of digital technology
- Lack of experience on digital technological precursors
- Differing sonic character associated with digital technology
- The learning curve associated with Pro Tools

In themselves, these are all quite valid reasons for sticking with a technological precursor, but together they form a convincing and logical approach to dealing with new technologies. Sheldon's views are a good counterpoint to accusations of nostalgia and/or fashion associated with the use of analogue tape. None of his reasoning pertains to any kind of sentimental or sepia-toned affiliation to analogue technologies, and he explicitly states his reasoning was not informed by analogue loyalty. Furthermore, Sheldon's trepidation at jumping from analogue tape straight to Pro Tools is also indicative of not having worked on digital tape recorders, the ADAT or the Otari RADAR, and, therefore, not experiencing such 'bridge' technologies, as discussed earlier. However, whilst Sheldon's views are more complex than simple 'technophobia', that is not to say that such attitudes did not exist. In fact, it was during this late 1990s era that 'technophobia' surrounding new digital technologies was acknowledged; Paul White's book *MIDI for the Technophobe*[90] is a good example of how such feeling could be addressed.

Technological resistance was certainly prevalent amongst the recordists of the era and manifested in neo-Luddite reactions. Whilst not holding such beliefs himself, recordist Tony Platt recognized Luddite standpoints amongst his peers and attributed this to issues surrounding technological integration and operation, as he stated:

> This sort of adversarial aspect of technology definitely started to emerge as technology became more complicated. It's one of the reasons why I see how people have this attitude towards technology now – there were people my age who were Luddites and said, 'I don't want to have anything to do with this technology. It's a load of fucking nonsense.' You can see why because you had to fight the damn stuff to make it work for you.[91]

Dance music artist-recordist Norman Cook admitted to having neo-Luddite views, particularly surrounding DAWs. Cook stuck with MIDI programming on an early version of Cubase on his Atari ST into the new millennium and ignored the developments in digital tape and hard disk recording. However, Cook clearly linked his neo-Luddism back to risk aversion, as he stated:

> Sure, I was tempted to have a look at PC's and hard disk systems but, at the end of the day, I'm a bit of a technophobe. A bit of a luddite. I hate learning how to use new stuff. And then, of course, there's the big worry that getting some new gear and not being able to recreate that same sound you've been used to for the past seven years. It was all too risky.[92]

The resistance of new technologies due to risk aversion and neo-Luddite views are quite logical. However, some recordists operated in what can be described as a technological 'bubble', almost entirely unaware of the unfolding technological development going on in the recording industry. Dance music recordist William Orbit's views can be described as nonchalant; the recordist expressed no pessimism, scepticism or other discernible viewpoint towards new technologies. Instead, he stuck with his Atari ST computer and outboard samplers until the turn of the millennium. During a 1996 interview with *Sound on Sound* magazine, Orbit stated, 'I haven't the faintest idea how to work many of the things I see in your magazine. Things like Wavestation and the Yamaha ProMix – I just haven't got the time to get into them.'[93] What is evident here is a whole range of complex, often interlinked reasoning behind technological choice and processual decision making. Sticking to 'tried and tested' methodologies and technologies has little – if anything – to do with nostalgia, sentimentalism or romantic associations with technologies. A significant reason may well be cost: new technologies are often expensive and if a recordist is happy with their existing technologies, they may not consider the investment in new systems worthwhile. That is not to say that the only reasons behind recordists' maverick methods were either economical or sticking with 'what they know'. Indeed, tools and techniques were – and still are – used for political reasons too.

(Un)conventionality, tech-processual unorthodoxies and rebellion

As I discussed in my 2014 AMS lecture at the Rock Hall Library and Archives, there has, to some extent, always been elements of rebellion amongst record producers and this was particularly apparent in 1990s commercial popular music production. As previously outlined, recording and production practice portrays a set of standards, principles and rules, which have evolved through generations of sound recording history. What is evident in the following examples is that the recordist is rebelling against, or at the very least resisting, what is considered sound engineering and/or recording and production protocol. Whilst I have previously detailed unconventionalities in recording and production, acts of technological rebellion are different. Implementing a piece of technology or processual technique to deliberately and explicitly defy conventionality is not the same as employing a technology or process due to risk aversion, sonic characteristics or an utopianist–pessimist outlook. For example, let's consider recordist William Orbit and his use of the Atari ST on Madonna's *Ray of Light* (1997). At first, there is nothing strange or indeed unorthodox about the application of this technology. However, the record was made in 1997 and by this time, the Atari ST was long out of manufacture and considered out of date, particularly in comparison to new DAWs with improved audio-sequencing capabilities, such as Digidesign's Sound Tools. Orbit commented on a particular *Ray of Light* session:

> I didn't know that [use of an Atari ST] was unusual until about two-thirds of the way through [recording Madonna's *Ray of Light*], when people would comment on it. At one point the thing even caught fire. Really. Smoke coming out of it. It was like, 'What's that smell? Oh. It's burning components.'[94]

Orbit realizes his use of the Atari was 'unusual' only after others point it out. Therefore, his use of a technological anachronism is not deliberate, nor is it due to a standpoint of 'resistance' or indeed rebellion. Orbit employed the Atari on

Ray of Light because that was his tried and tested technology. Tech-processual unorthodoxies also arise about creative experimentation. Again, this cannot be interpreted as an expression of rebellion but curiosity. AC/DC and Bob Marley recordist Tony Platt recalled a session of recording experimentalism with recordist Nigel Green: 'I remember a slightly enhanced night, where we spent [it] strapping 2 mic's together and tried to get them to spin to see if that would have the same effect as a Leslie cabinet.'[95]

The aforementioned examples point towards tech-processual unorthodoxies born out of nonchalance or experimentalism. Notably, some recordists speak directly about their resistance to conventionality: a more defined and distinct standpoint to mere experimentalism or 'individualized' working practices. As U2 recordist Daniel Lanois stated:

> I would always try to integrate unorthodox gear together. For example, I would use a guitar amplifier as a processing device by remiking and then setting up a chain of effects and processing gear.[96]

By explicitly referring to 'unorthodox gear', Lanois is admitting to regularly using techniques and equipment that go against standard engineering practice. He uses the example of a very unusual method of remiking a guitar amplifier so it 'becomes' a processing device. However, whilst Lanois gives a straightforward description of his methods, Flood's expressions are more aggressive and arguably more in keeping with a rebellious attitude, as he stated in *Sound on Sound*:

> What's to stop PJ Harvey sticking a guitar through a VCS3? Nothing. What's to stop Nitzer Ebb going for total rock-out guitars against a full-on analogue sequencer? Nothing. So cross fertilisation and trying different things is important. If you do a remix, what's to stop you shoving a guitar through a ring modulator?[97]

Steve Albini, often expressing technological pessimism in his viewpoints, also implied a rebellious nature during an interview in *Music Producers*: 'I hate compression. Pounding everything with compression is so standard a trick now that records made without it sound distinctive. That's what keeps me in business.'[98]

Albini echoes Rick Rubin's earlier comments about hating 'technically slick' records. Albini is, however, not only setting out his dislike of an industry standard practice but is explicit in his admission to going against it. His argument is particularly convincing, in that 'standard practice' brings about such predictable results that the process of going against it can produce something highly individualistic, which is distinctly recognizable on records such as PJ Harvey's *Rid of Me* (1993). He argues that his own records are more distinctive on the grounds that he regularly goes against standard protocol. Returning to Mick Glossop's quote about 'abuse' in recording techniques (page 85) and his connection between creativity and the unconventional use of technology and methodology, Glossop stated that with time, these unconventional methods feed back into 'standard practice', thus only being considered 'unconventional' for a relatively short period of time. Whilst this could certainly be said of maverick recordists such as George Martin and

Joe Meek, it would be difficult to attribute the same impact to Lanois, Albini and Flood. Even though their working practices go beyond 'unconventionality' and into the realm of rebellion, they do not (yet) have the same pervasive influence on recording culture.

Summary

Many recordists have acknowledged the challenges faced by the technological acceleration of the 1980s: peer pressure, pressure internationally (in the case of UK producers), learning curves, economic and time factors as well as changing roles. They recognize the challenge – in many cases with the benefit of hindsight – of balancing these variables against a complex and fast-changing technological landscape.

Having unpacked the utopianism–pessimism dichotomy existing amongst recordists' attitudes, a far more complex picture emerges. As the technologies described in Chapters 1 and 2 proliferated through the recording workplace, recordists adopted them with varying degrees of positivity and negativity. We know that 'traditionalist' and 'technophiliac' recordists existed during the era, yet new technologies caused a complex and multifaceted set of reactions amongst recordists. It is important to point out that these attitudes did not – and do not – exist in isolation. Moreover, these illuminations need to be viewed in the context of era and with a degree of crossover and fluidity.

The potential use value of mass 'factory style' music production manifested in the prolific output of SAW, whose utopian, utilitarian production values led to their commercial success. On the other hand, Steve Albini's refusal to comply with standardized, digital audio-based tech-processual practice in the 1990s situated him as an outlier, mirroring the non-commercial mainstream artists he worked with. Evidently, the attitudes and standpoints of these recordists impacted on their tech-processual practice, and this is something that I'd suggest needs consideration when discussing the working practices of recordists in future.

7

Analysing Technology and Process in Popular Music Recordings: A Tech-Processual Methodology

Analytical methodology

As set out in the Introduction, the impact of sound and music technologies on popular music recordings cannot be illuminated via musical descriptors alone. In this chapter, I illustrate how the sound recording and production technologies discussed in Chapters 1, 2 and 3, as well as recordist agency, as discussed in Chapters 4, 5 and 6, impact on what we eventually hear. In all the example *modern records* analysed in this chapter, the 'sound of technology', as described in Chapter 2, is clearly evident. All recordings demonstrate technological hybridity employed in a recording session, as set out in Chapter 3. Additionally, I discuss the role of recordists, their unorthodox processes, attitudinal factors and *maverick methods* – as evaluated in Chapters 4, 5 and 6 – which are foregrounded in these recordings. Before moving on to demonstrating how the main themes of this book are sonically discernible across a range of recordings, I will address my methodology.

Indeed, much progress has been made in this regard, with works by Gibson[1] and Dockwray and Moore[2] using visual indicators to represent analytical findings. However, these analyses are the exception rather than the rule; most phonomusicological analysis is situated within sociocultural contexts and/or musical frameworks. Zak critiqued dependence on a music-based analytical method, as he states:

> Among the problems inherent in establishing an academic discipline aimed at illuminating record production, then, is the need for a fundamental aesthetic reorientation as well as new modes of analytic description. We must resist reducing musical meaning to matters of musical syntax, which stipulates a de facto hierarchy of aesthetic value.[3]

Despite Zak's assertion, only a few instances exist where attempts have been made to analyse popular music recordings as productions, whereby the recording, processing and mixing attributes have been the object of focus as opposed to the musical elements. In *The Ghost in the Machine,* Warner stated:

Accepting that much popular music only exists as a direct result of technological manipulation by artists in the recording studio, necessarily leads the analyst to consider specifically the relationship between technological processes and the product.[4]

Indeed, it is this methodology that Warner applies in his analytical work in *Pop Music – Technology and Creativity*,[5] wherein Warner analyses seven individual tracks produced by Trevor Horn. These analyses are discursive in the main part, with accompanying illustrative tables detailing song sections and 'characteristics'. Whilst some of these analyses acknowledge production aesthetics, the majority consider musical characteristics such as vocal lines, lyrics, song structure and instrument patterns. In *Capturing Sound*,[6] Katz analyses Public Enemy's 'Fight the Power' and Fatboy Slim's 'Praise You', amongst other tracks. These analyses concentrate on cultural and theoretical aspects of these productions and – apart from acknowledging the use of sampling – do not look any deeper at production elements. This is not to say such analyses are not useful; there are very good reasons as to why musical and cultural attributes are privileged in analytical work. After all, recordings are carriers of musical performances and/or constructions, and as such it makes sense that the analytical focus should be the music itself. From a general reception perspective, listening to a recording is inextricable from listening to music; recordings are often positioned as primary texts, particularly in popular music analysis.[7] The situating of recorded texts in their wider sociocultural context is important too, as it allows us to illustrate key interplay(s) between music and socioeconomic and/or class background, political climate,[8] locality, gender and sexuality,[9] and other areas. To that end, it is easy to see why and how musical attributes and cultural contexts have been – and continue to be – privileged in popular music analysis. The problem is, as applications of sound recording technology have been increasingly foregrounded in musical performances, the *presence* of technological intervention and the resulting impact on what we eventually hear become equally important to matters of musical syntax, as Zak rightly suggests. This has been addressed in extensive works on rhythm by Mark Butler in *Unlocking the Groove*[10] and by Anne Danielsen in both *Presence and Pleasure: The Funk Grooves of James Brown and Parliament*[11] and *Musical Rhythm in the Age of Mechanical Reproduction*.[12] These are benchmark studies on the specificities of rhythm in popular music and go a long way in furthering our understanding of dance and funk grooves. There is, however, a clear gap in studies of recording and production generally and particularly in 1980s and 1990s popular music. Additionally, the choices made by artists and industry personnel when appointing recordists and workplaces to musical productions are important barometers when considering musical aesthetics. Recordists and workplaces have their own histories, associations and meanings and can, therefore, impact greatly on what we eventually hear.

Establishing a mode of analysis that not only deals with the sonically discernible production elements but also the context(s) of technology, recordist agency and workplace is, therefore, imperative.

This chapter implements a *tech-processual* analytical methodology to illuminate the impact of matters of technological and processual potential on what is eventually heard. It is not my intention to consider the meaning of these recordings from musical, lyrical or cultural perspectives (although such issues are acknowledged and are indeed at times inextricable from matters of production), but rather to examine the contribution made by technology and process to the overall aesthetic of the recording. That said, foregrounding the context in which the recording was made is essential: tech-processual matters are best illuminated when situated in their wider musical genre and aesthetic contexts; otherwise, we would end up with a simple linear breakdown of sonically discernible events. More concise tech-processual analyses formed the basis of three recent publications: 'Never Mind the Bollocks ... A Tech-Processual Analysis';[13] 'Gus Dudgeon's Super Sonic Signature';[14] and 'Songs About Fucking'.[15] The aforementioned articles feature applied tech-processual analysis to rock recordings of the 1970s and alternative rock recordings of the 1980s. This chapter deals with later recordings, illuminating many of the issues contained within this book, the idea being to demonstrate how the technologies and processes featured in the earlier chapters of this book manifest in popular music recordings. And so on to tech-processual analysis. Four cornerstones of record production study are now well established in phonomusicological discourse, those being:

- The recording and production workplace: studios, acoustic spaces, (bed)rooms, halls and venues, location[16]
- Sound recording and production technology[17]
- Sound recordists[18]
- Processes and techniques[19]

I am not so much interested in these matters taken alone, but the *evidence* and *impact* of such matters as sonically discernible in the recording. In order to ascertain this, contextual information surrounding the artist and recordist(s) needs to be established first: What was the context in which the artist entered into the recording process? If this is known, we can construe the intention on the part of the artist: Did they have any choice in terms of workplace, recordist and/or technology? If so, then how and why did they make such decisions? Secondly, the workplace is established: Where was this recording made and why? Thirdly, the sound recording and production technology is ascertained: Who made these choices and which technologies were used in the recording process and how is this significant? Next, the recordist(s) is considered. Who worked on this recording and why? What is the background of the recordist? Are they aligned with a particular musical genre, form or aesthetic? What was their intention when embarking on the recording project? Following on from these matters, recordist processes are then illuminated. What techniques did the recordist use? How and where in the recording are these techniques, processes and gestures sonically discernible? How do these gestures interact with, complement or otherwise highlight musical, lyrical and/or textural matters? It is important to note that whilst these are questions that guide the analytical work, the answers may not always be fully ascertainable and as such tech-processual analyses may vary in quantity of contextual detail.

In *Song Means*,[20] Allan Moore suggested that whilst we need to illuminate the 'what', the 'so what?' is more important. Moore is right: Why is this an important and necessary mode of analysis? There are several reasons. Firstly, by analysing technological and processual content, a layer of complexity is illuminated. By delving deeper into the construction of a recording, we can ascertain what and who are we listening to aside from music and musicians. Secondly, such analysis allows us to understand the interplay between the aforementioned tech-processual matters and musicality – particularly how such matters contribute to overall texture and shape, lyrics, performance and cultural context: How does technology and process reveal itself in the music, and how are these important factors used to influence, exaggerate or otherwise synergize with musical matters? Thirdly, to assist in establishing overall meaning: if sound recording technologies and processes are loaded with historical contexts, aesthetic value and meanings of their own, then how do they align (or not) with the recordings' musical components? We can also examine the interplay between the known attitudes and standpoints of recordists and the 'presence' of such matters in the recording. Finally, such an analytical mode simply enhances our understanding of the recording from an oft-overlooked perspective.

So what about the analytical process? Whilst it is useful to consider production elements alongside temporal guidelines including song timeline, structure and form, the focus here is to move beyond cultural and musicality-centred analytical models and concentrate as much on production aesthetics as possible. In saying that, the difficulties in 'separating out' production techniques from musical attributes are acknowledged – for example, where a guitarist has applied effects to the instrument at source in order to create a signature 'sound', as opposed to the recordist applying effects later on in the production process. These instances are noted where possible.

To begin, notes were taken against track time point location and corresponding arrangement and noteworthy aspects of the recording and production. These production aspects were split into five separate areas of focus: use of overdubs, effects processing, spatial positioning of instruments and other production aspects, and critical commentary. In order to carry out the analyses as accurately as possible, all listening took place in a fully acoustically treated post-production facility. All songs were transported as lossless, stereo AIFF2 files into AVID Pro Tools and listened to through DynAudio studio monitoring. Key aspects of each production were then listened for during extensive, iterative listening analyses. To elaborate, points of focus included the sonically discernible: use of microphones and technique (i.e. close or ambient microphone placement), technologies used in the signal chain, for example mixing consoles and effects processors, the use of multitracking and/or overdubs, stereo positioning and frequency spread. Other aspects such as instrument placement in the mix, as well as the inclusion of noise, mistakes or other discrepancies, were also noted accordingly on the timing sheets. Once all listening was completed, the Waves 'Paz' psychoacoustic analyser plug-in was applied to all tracks in order to view the stereo image, frequency spread and overall levels. This was an important aspect of the methodology in order to substantiate observations relating to overall compression and loudness, stereo imaging and frequency spread. Such observations were then cross-referenced with other source information including primary and secondary interview material, as well as theoretical texts. Once the analysis was complete, the critical and contextual account of the recording was compiled, focusing on the aforementioned tech-processual attributes.

Aligning the choice of tracks with the historical focus of this book, six popular music recordings were analysed implementing this tech-processual analytical mode: Beastie Boys' '(You Gotta) Fight for Your Right (to Party)' (1986); Madonna's 'Ray of Light' (1997); U2's 'Mofo' (1997); Blur's 'Song 2' (1997); Fatboy Slim's 'Praise You' (1997) and MGMT's 'Electric Feel' (2007). There are key reasons as to why these tracks were chosen. The Beastie Boys' track exemplifies a sideways shift in mid-1980s record production and is an early example of recordist Rick Rubin's recognizable sonic signature. Here, the track is not indicative of technology-driven record production neither is it a reaction against it, but is a strong example of hybrid methodology. There are a number of reasons why I chose to analyse four tracks from the same year in the late 1990s. Firstly, they exemplify 'technological mash-up' as described in Chapter 3 – all these tracks feature music production technologies more at home in the 1980s than in the 1990s. Secondly, whilst they illustrate contrasting musical recordings in terms of genre, all signify a commercial sound recording industry grappling with technological change. Thirdly, the realization of technological hybridity (as opposed to analogue or digital popular music recording processes) is exemplified in all four recordings. I should note that the album version of 'Mofo' is used for analysis here and not any of the remixes featured on the single release. The decision to include a tech-processual analysis of MGMT's 'Electric Feel' (2007) is to demonstrate the progression of maverick methodologies beyond the era detailed in this book. To put it simply, the types of technologies and processes featured here are part of a continuum that proceeds mid-twentieth-century recording and precedes twenty-first-century recording. There are many commonalities between all six recordings making them ideal for tech-processual analysis. All these recordings were commercially successful, in terms of both their single releases and the albums from which they derive. In terms of technology, these modern records feature sound recording and production technologies that were not considered 'industry standard' or 'cutting edge' at the time of the recording. There are also common features amongst the recordists: all of them had been involved in commercially successful popular music recordings both before and after their involvement with the track in question. Additionally, all these recordings are representational of the 'grey area' section in Figure 6.1; neither traditionalist or technophiliac, positive or negative, these recordings exhibit what I call *maverick* methodologies.

This is a tight selection of recordings from a narrowly defined era, but detailed analysis of these modern records goes a long way in highlighting the impact of technology and process in an understudied era of record production and, therefore, act as a foundation upon which more work can be built.

I strongly encourage readers to listen to the proceeding examples when reading the analyses; these analytical accounts are designed to be read whilst listening to the track and, therefore, are unlikely to work as well if read in isolation.

The Beastie Boys

Taken from the biggest-selling rap album in popular music history, the multi-platinum *Licensed to Ill*, '(You Gotta) Fight for Your Right (To Party)' by the Beastie Boys was produced by Rick Rubin, engineered by Steve Ett[21] and released in 1986. The extraordinary production process used to create this record fits neither traditional nor technology-driven modes in either the use of recording equipment, the production methods or the mixing technique. The intention of Rubin was to record a parody of a metal song, emphasizing confrontation to maximize controversy, as he pointed out in *The Men Behind Def Jam*: 'The less going on in a record and the clearer and more in-your-face it is, the better.'[22] This loud, yet simplistic style was unusual for its time and indicative of Rubin's 'music first' attitude as discussed in Chapter 6. The emphasis on 'clearer' suggests a rejection of effects processing and the reference to a 'less is more' approach suggests a 'minimalist' approach to instrumentation and the avoidance of techniques such as double tracking or multiple backing vocal parts. This intention represents a diversion from the 'construction' approaches employed at the time by other mainstream rock recordists including Hugh Padgham and Kevin Killen. With 'Fight for Your Right' the 'up-front' production style is clear from the outset; the tech-processual attributes are commensurate with both the lyrical and musical content, as will be elucidated.

'Fight for Your Right' was the commercial breakthrough single for the independent label Def Jam to which Beastie Boys were signed. The label, established in the early 1980s by Rick Rubin and Russell Simmons and initially run from Rubin's dormitory at New York University,[23] featured a number of promising hip-hop artists including T La Rock & Jazzy Jay and LL Cool J. Chung King Studios was, therefore, an obvious recording workplace for the Beastie Boys' *Licensed to Ill* sessions, since it was the site of many recordings by the aforementioned artists.[24] Situated above its namesake Chinese restaurant on Varick Street, New York, Chung King was founded by John King (formerly of 'Secret Society Records') and recordist Steve Ettinger (later named Steve Ett). Frequented by independent punk and hip-hop acts, by early 1986 the modest studio featured a Neve V-series console in the main control room, as well as a Studer A-827 multitrack tape recorder. In 1986, Chung King was a small facility with one control room and one live room. As well as the central Neve console and Studer 24-track tape machine, Chung King featured three small racks of outboard equipment including vintage Pultec EQ-P1 equalizers, a stereo DBX 160 and DBX 165-A compressors and a vintage Teletronix LA-2A Levelling Amplifier, a revered and 'iconicized' technology. Notably, the outboard equipment at Chung King could be considered vintage in 1986, with the DBX compressor units having been released in 1971, the Teletronix pre-1967 and the Pultec EQs dating back to the late 1950s. This combination of technology is important to the ultimate reception of *Licensed to Ill* – as well as other rap records released on the Def Jam label. Such technologies were used extensively throughout the 1970s in classic rock record production; the combination of large-format Neve console with tube outboard equipment renowned for overall 'warm' and 'fat' sounding recordings aesthetically aligned with the sonic character of classic rock records. The application of such a technological template to an emergent rap genre partly explains how early Def Jam recordings were so successful amongst predominantly white rock audiences; regardless of the vocal delivery style, these records featured a sonic familiarity consistent with the commercially successful rock of the then recent past. Significantly, whilst John King and the Beastie Boys were renowned for using drum machines such as the Oberheim DMX and later, the E-Mu SP-12, most of *Licensed to Ill* was created with live samples and tape loops, as King[25] suggests:

> I just took the drum beat and Steve Ett and I put it all around the room on mic stands, and put clips, you know, and it was just tape (2" tape). There was a Studer machine in one end of the room, and we had the tape wrapped all the way around the room, so we had about a 30 second loop. And we looped the thing, then we played to it. Then we put some cymbals, and then I got my DMX drum machine … I mean I was the drummer … This was back when Heavy D's first record; this was back when you know The Beastie Boys, you know, *License To ILL* … boomp – pap-bb-boomp boomp … That was those two fingers.[26]

Whilst this quote does not refer specifically to 'Fight for Your Right', much can be construed about common processes in early Def Jam recordings. By 1986, the use of samplers was ubiquitous, yet at the inception of commercial hip-hop, Rubin, Ett and King implemented production techniques more consistent with avant-garde composition. At the time of recording, Chung King Studios had a reputation for creating authentic, East Coast underground punk and hip-hop recordings. Much can be construed about the direction of 'Fight for Your Right' by the controversy surrounding Beastie Boys' first single 'Rock Hard', recorded in 1984 and released in 1985 – the second release by the Def Jam label. The single featured an obvious, repeat looped sample of AC/DC's 'Back in Black' single and was used without sample clearance. Subsequently, the single was withdrawn due to a legal challenge, but the Beastie Boys went on to record *Licensed to Ill* with Rubin, still signed to Def Jam. So, at the time of recording, Beastie Boys had already generated significant controversy with a withdrawn single release of 'Rock Hard'. Rubin and Simmons were co-managers of an emergent Def Jam label to which Beastie Boys were signed and Rubin and Simmons also had a good relationship with John King and Steve Ett, owner and engineer of Chung King Studios, respectively. Label co-manager Russell Simmons said of the track 'Fight for Your Right':

> The only people that we made *Licensed [to Ill]* for were the people they hung out with, the people they thought were fashion-forward. Those guys didn't make records like ' … Fight for Your Right … ' because they thought they'd make any money. It was a fucking joke.[27]

Simmons refers to the intention of the artist, but the label co-owners were more ambitious; Simmons had already signed Def Jam to Columbia Records in order to achieve wider distribution and increase recording budgets.[28] Rubin also suggested of 'Fight for Your Right', 'I really wanted to do a straight-up rock song that incorporated rap, but something that really blurred the line and that's what it did.'[29] 'Fight for Your Right' blurred the lines between these two genres because it successfully combined emergent rap genre with the sonic canvas of classic rock. The length of the track, at 3 minutes 29 seconds, coupled with the absence of swearing, suggests that Rubin and Ett's intention was to aim the song at radio, thus courting further controversy by targeting a youthful mainstream audience with multiple references to consumption of pornography, cigarettes, school truanting and alternative appearance.

From the start, many sampled instruments in the track are audible; these have been looped to create what *sounds* like a live performance, but is not. Four simple rock drum patterns have been played and sampled (presumably to tape, as King previously described), then 'looped' into the song at differing points. The patterns are simple, featuring variations on the kick/snare/hi-hat or kick/snare/ride/crash theme, common in heavy rock music. An electric guitar has been looped, double-tracked and panned hard left and right throughout the song. The bass guitar has been processed with distortion – quite possibly at source – and panned centre. Bass and rhythm guitars play the same chord progression and rhythm throughout, suggesting that these instruments were included to enhance the rhythm section, as opposed to adding melody, since most of the song is structured around three chords. The Beastie Boys[30] comprised three vocalists, all of whom deliver lead vocals on the song, which has been recorded with little compression, no de-essing and a small room reverb. The reverb is almost inaudible, but the tails are audible in places, particularly on the more sibilant words. The song begins with a shout of the word 'yeah' that has been recorded with little processing. The lyrics 'kick it' are then placed high in the mix over a rung-through, single distorted guitar chord prompting the drum loops (0.08). Here, it seems the parody is not just in lyrical form but is also present in the production, since an exaggerated reverb has been applied to the snare drum, typical of much 1980s rock and AOR (adult-oriented rock) music.

Significant low frequency equalization has also been applied to the entire track, again typical of 1980s rock, yet not entirely consistent with Rubin's approach to create a 'clear' sounding recording. These processing decisions would almost certainly not have been made had it not been for the ironic intention – snares featuring lengthy reverb uncommon in rap music. The stereo field is narrow throughout, with the vocals and bass panned centre, typical of most hip-hop music. Perhaps the most interesting aspect of this track is how the drums have been recorded and placed in the song, having been played live and sampled. This gives a highly repetitive sound overall, yet places the rapped lyrics in the context of a heavy rock song. Again, this is entirely paradoxical, yet consistent with the intention of the recordist. Having been recorded in a natural stereo field, the kick and snare are panned centre, the hi-hats centre right and the ride hard left with the crashes panned centre left and centre right, respectively.

Barry Walters, journalist for US magazine *The Village Voice*, had exclusive access to Chung King Studios in late 1986 when the album was in its final recording stages. Walters described the preparations made by the band and producers right at the point the vocals to 'Fight for Your Right' were being recorded:

the Beasties start doing whippets, small metal cylinders of laughing gas. This is how they prepare to work. Rubin reacts to the pandemonium coolly and doesn't partake, nor does he disapprove.[31]

Indeed the rapping, particularly the lines performed by Adam Yauch, is consistent with this observation and especially audible at 0.37 on, 'you missed two classes'. During Verse 1 (0.23), all 'p', 't' and 's' sounds are particularly prominent suggesting a lack of de-essing and a dry, natural vocal recording. A significant plosive occurs on the word 'please' (0.31), suggesting a dynamic vocal delivery and the need to bring this under control with compression. Additionally, this is entirely consistent with the recordists' intention to generate an aggressive and up-front performance. Similar instances of sibilance and plosives occur on 'packs' (1.11) and 'busted' (1.29), suggesting the earlier plosive on 'please' is not a 'one-off', but an intentional aspect of the entire vocal performance. Walters described Rubin's demeanour throughout the recording process as '[he] lay spread out on a couch, not appearing to care what they got up to'. This is a significant observation, as it implies that Beastie Boys' behaviour, their haphazard vocal performances and inhalation of 'whippets' were precisely the aesthetic Rubin was intending to capture.

One of the main issues with 'Fight for Your Right' can be heard in the choruses, where the loops do not stop and start in time on the pauses. The synchronization issues suggest how painstaking the production process must have been and is entirely consistent with the six-month recording process of *Licensed to Ill*. It is highly unlikely that the drums, bass and guitar would have been played at the same time when they were sampled; the bass and guitar tracks have been played against the looped drum recording. This is also consistent with the manual construction of tape loops as opposed to quantized or sequenced loops. It is, however, likely these performances were played to a click track so the tempo would be consistent in all three loops. However, this does not account for differences in groove and it is here that audible issues occur. The drums, bass and guitar are very much in time but they lack the cohesion normally associated with a heavy rock track. The 'release' section of the cymbal crash envelope has been cut – consistent with a tape loop recording – so they do not feature a natural fade to silence. This has only added to the awkward, uncomfortable result – there is something about it that does not sound quite *right*. In *The Village Voice*, Walters described how Rubin and Ett used the mixing console as a sequencer on *Licensed to Ill*:

> Each of the board's 24 tracks contains a separately recorded percussion element, which repeats a phrase dozens of times. Rubin and Ett press buttons to make each cowbell, hi-hat, snare and bass drum track pop in and out at the precise moment. The mixing board itself acts as a polymorphic drumset, which allows an enormous amount of freedom to alter a song.[32]

What Walters is describing here is the continual 'soloing' and 'muting' of alternative mixing console channels in order to 'punch in' the required loop at the correct point – a process founded in Jamaican dub music of the 1970s. This is almost certainly witnessed at the point where Rubin and Ett are creating the drum tracks from the drum loops. This production method would have been painstakingly slow and would have relied upon Rubin and Ett's sense of rhythm as well as production skills. In an era when samples were being looped inside a sampler and could be 'played back' through a MIDI keyboard, Rubin and Ett chose a different, arguably more laborious method. It certainly explains how they 'chopped in' the four different drum loops on 'Fight for Your Right' and also goes some way to explaining the synchronization issues. However, their chosen method further reinforces and justifies *Licensed to Ill's* six-month recording and production process.

The guitar solo (1.48) is an exaggerated parody of heavy rock, where the choice of guitar (a Gibson Les Paul), tonality and reverb applied allude to that of Billy Gibbons of ZZ Top. The double chorus (2.31) features yet more synchronization issues with the loops, which are not precisely in time but have been kept in. The guitar and drum loops continue to the end of the song where the only instance of a natural crash cymbal occurs. Here, the cymbal sounds slightly different to the rest of the crashes on the drum loops, and it is suggested this single crash has been played once and then overdubbed into the song at the end point. This is entirely consistent with the process John King described earlier: the 'looping' of the main drum kit with additional 'punching in' of sampled cymbals from drum machine presets.

The irony of 'Fight for Your Right' is that it was supposed to be the 'joke' song from the album, yet it was the most successful and proved extremely lucrative. Rubin achieved everything he set out to – and more – with 'Fight for Your Right'. The song was both hailed and critiqued by the media in both the United States and UK. The controversy surrounding the antics and music of the Beastie Boys only heightened on release of 'Fight for Your Right' and this was largely to do with how the song was produced. The minimal vocal treatment, with no de-essing and just a small room reverb, added to the sharp production. Little to no attempt has been made to 'round off' the edges using EQ. The use of tight loops coupled with aggressively centred drums and vocals, with a large amount of overall compression, created a powerful, 'in your face' result exactly as Rubin intended. Since this powerful production aesthetic was used across many Def Jam recordings, we could argue *Licensed to Ill* was a benchmark for hip-hop and rap recording.

An analysis of both the frequency content and spatial positioning of the track further corroborates the sonic qualities of the track. The Waves Paz Analyser shows a centralized mix with loud overall levels for a track produced in the mid-1980s. Additionally, the frequency content appears to 'tail off' in the low and high ends of the spectrum and appears maximized in the central, audible range. It *sounds* like you are being shouted at by three angry teenagers (you are!) and this makes for uncomfortable listening at a high volume or on headphones.

Rubin and Ett not only recorded this record using unorthodox means but they captured the sound of a young, aggressive band, high on 'whippets' – the sound of mayhem. At the time of recording, samplers and sequencers were freely available and being applied to a broad range of music production processes. Yet Rubin and Ett persisted with loops and the use of the console as a 'polymorphic drum set' to create 'Fight for Your Right'. This is a good example of a maverick methodology; Rubin and Ett did not employ a 'traditionalist' approach to their production; these are not 'whole' performances captured from beginning to end on multitrack tape nor is it a 'live' recording of all musicians performing simultaneously. Neither did the recordists employ a technology-driven approach; they were not using 'cutting edge' technologies or the new digital technologies of the time, but created most of the track simply with analogue tape and mixing console functionality. This unique methodology for its time combined the application of technology as a 'means to an end' with a maverick process befitting of a hybrid rock/hip-hop record in an emergent rap genre.

Madonna – 'Ray of Light'

'Ray of Light' was the second single to be taken from the album of the same name and was released in May 1998, reaching number two in the UK charts. The album, produced by William Orbit and engineered by Pat McCarthy, was received to worldwide critical acclaim, including Grammy awards in 1998 for 'Best Dance Recording' and 'Best Pop Album' amongst others. The late 1990s were a pivotal time for Madonna, who had established herself in the 1980s with multi-platinum selling albums *Like a Virgin* (1984) *True Blue* (1986) and *Like a Prayer* (1989). Having received poor reviews and sales figures for her previous album *Bedtime Stories* (1994) (as well as mixed reception to the controversial 'Girlie Show' (1993) tour), Madonna had also appeared in films such as *Body of Evidence* (1993), which were poorly received by the press and her fans. Her decision to team with William Orbit, who had by the late 1990s built his reputation as a highly sought-after remix producer, was considered and measured. By the early 1990s, Orbit had released four solo albums, including *Strange Cargo* (1987), *Strange Cargo II* (1990) and *Strange Cargo III* (1993), all to critical acclaim and again cementing his reputation as an accomplished electronic musician and composer.

'Ray of Light' is in fact a cover version of 'Sepheryn' (1971), a song by 1970s folk duo Curtiss Maldoon.[33] In the mid-1990s, Clive Maldoon's niece, Christine Leach, decided to record a version of 'Sepheryn' as a tribute to her late uncle. Leach fronted the 1990s indie band Babyfox, and whilst working on their debut album with William Orbit, he started to rearrange 'Sepheryn' with a different tempo. Coincidentally, Orbit placed the rearrangement on a DAT tape, along with a few other demos, to give to Madonna when she requested some of his recent ideas and work to listen to. Madonna then invited Orbit to New York to work through ideas based on the demo – including the version of 'Ray of Light' originally intended for Babyfox.

The album was recorded at The Hit Factory, New York, and Larabee Studios North, California – both highly renowned studios notable for their large-scale productions and associated artists and producers working at the highest levels of the music industry. The album credits multiple engineers and programmers, although it was Pat McCarthy who engineered 'Ray of Light' the single. Madonna is credited as a co-producer along with Orbit on *Ray of Light*; whilst both Madonna and Orbit made reference to her songwriting, performing vocals and working on arrangements and synthesis, Orbit is widely credited as the album's main recordist. His style of production was – and is –

particularly energetic, with emphasis on the use of electronic instruments, especially analogue synthesizers, which are notably absent from Madonna's prior recordings. Orbit's 'sound' could be described as improvisational, implying a freedom and a spontaneity lacking in the clarity and precision of many other dance-genre producers such as Paul Oakenfold or Armand Van Helden. This 'sound' is a prominent feature of his recordings, particularly the *Strange Cargo* series; his recording, production and remix techniques are recognizable to those familiar with the genre and feature multilayered analogue synthesis lines and sparse ambient rhythms. Orbit's 'sound' is instantly recognizable in the production of 'Ray of Light' and this, coupled with the fact that the song is a cover version, raises questions about authorship. Orbit suggests in *Keyboard* magazine, 'Obviously it was Madonna's record, but I'm as proud of it as if I'd done it myself'.[34] Here, Orbit plays down his role in the production of the record; aside from the vocals, Orbit performed many of the musical elements on 'Ray of Light' and the initial idea had come from his collaboration with Christine Leach. 'Ray of Light' is a good example of multi-intertextual form; the amalgamation of Curtiss Maldoon's original song with Leach and Orbit's demo version, as well as Madonna's later addition of a further verse, consolidated the track into a modern hit record.

Orbit has spoken at length about his recording and production methods, as well as the systems he uses, and has made no secret about how he recorded *Ray of Light*; neither was he embarrassed to divulge information about the limitations of using outdated equipment, as described earlier in Chapter 6, when he admitted, 'At one point the thing [the Atari running Cubase] even caught fire'.[35] He went on to say:

> Most of it (equipment) is pretty retro: A Korg MS-20, a Roland Juno 106, a Roland JD-800. Much of the album was done on a Juno 106. Also, a significant amount of it was done on the MS-20 – the more spiky sounds. A few things people think are guitar are actually the MS-20. And then there were a few more bits and pieces: a few modules, a Yamaha DX-7, a Novation Bass Station, a Roland JP-8000, a lot of Roland stuff. I've always liked Roland stuff.[36]

The application of such technologies to the recording and production process is significant. Cubase II on the Atari ST was a common, budget late 1980s system, long surpassed by the sophisticated audio and MIDI sequencers such as Pro Tools, run on powerful Macintosh computers by the late 1990s – such systems would have been available at the time at both The Hit Factory and Larabee. As detailed in Chapter 6, this is an example of risk aversion; Orbit stuck with his 'tried and tested' methodology regardless of technological change or the working practices of his peers.

Initially, Orbit's intention was to produce just one or two tracks on the album. Madonna had enlisted Marius DeVries of British trip-hop group Massive Attack to produce on the record, yet this changed as the process went on. Orbit had more and more involvement in the record until gaining a full 'producer' credit. From this, it could be construed that Orbit's original intention was to make a contribution to the record – to play a small part in a much bigger project. The lengthy recording process is well documented,[37] implying that much thought, experimentation and consideration took place during the process. This is consistent with Orbit's known production methodology, which emphasizes improvisation as opposed to precision and *perfection*. Orbit's attitude is also indicative of trepidation and risk aversion; on 'Ray of Light', he stuck firmly to his accumulated production knowledge and skill set and did not stray either technologically or processually. This is, however, entirely understandable; Madonna hired Orbit for his established production sound, so this was not the time to change working method.

'Ray of Light' is an up-tempo dance record that takes on a very traditional arrangement, featuring an array of dynamic changes, musical interludes and vocal improvisations, justifying its length of well over five minutes. As suggested by earlier comments in *Keyboard* magazine, the instruments used by Orbit included many analogue and digital synthesizers that by 1997 were either obsolete or considered vintage. For example, the Yamaha DX-7 would have been considered out-of-date by 1997, at a time when Korg's 'Trinity' and 'Triton' workstations were the more popular synthesizers, with their large set of presets and on-board sequencing capabilities, not to mention cross-genre appeal. Orbit recorded the analogue synthesizer sounds, mainly from a Korg MS-20 and Roland Juno 106, to tape and then sampled them back from the tape machine. This is an unorthodox, not to mention time consuming, technique, yet goes some way in explaining the length of time taken to make the record, as Orbit suggests:

> I record stuff to tape in a really ad-lib fashion. In other words, I'll get the gear going and just 'perform' it to tape. But the key is, that I would subsequently go back, load the best bits into the sampler, and further manipulate them. You get the best of both worlds that way.[38]

By 'the best of both worlds', Orbit refers to combining sounds from both the analogue and digital domains and references technological hybridity. By recording the analogue synthesizer samples onto tape, he is keeping the sound and all its 'warmth' in the analogue domain, thus retaining analogue aesthetics in a digital production context. However, whilst this technique keeps the analogue synthesizer sounds in the analogue domain, it is problematic as there is no method of 'cleaning up' any tape hiss or noise present in the recording. This is particularly evident in the intro to 'Ray of Light' where tape hiss is particularly noticeable, as well as overspill of conversation or other noise. The entire track was recorded to tape on completion, so the recording features tape hiss from both the synthesizer samples and the master recording. In 1997, when Digidesign's Pro Tools had 'strip silence' capabilities, considered revolutionary by some members of the recording community, it was unusual to leave such obvious tape hiss in, particularly on a dance record. In saying that, the then-emergent UK trip-hop genre (to which DeVries was a key contributor) of the 1990s embraced lo-fidelity aesthetics and such audible technological matters. Here, Madonna has made her own intentions as producer clear: this is a record that must align to the commercial success of the trip-hop genre – to include Portishead and Massive Attack – and not to commercial mainstream pop. In employing Orbit and DeVries, Madonna effectively situates her recording alongside successful, alternative dance records of the era and has avoided the sonic realm of artists such as The Spice Girls.

'Ray of Light's mix is also unusual, with two separate electric guitars – one double-tracked and panned hard left and right, the other panned hard left – beginning the song's introduction. These are more prominent in the mix compared to the initial synthesizers: an analogue filter sweep through a low-pass filter (LPF) placed very low and a digital synth pad fading in very slowly.

The use of the stereo field has been maximized throughout and this is particularly evident once the bass (quite probably a pad on the Novation BassStation) and kick drum enter at 0.23. There are also what sounds like samples of false harmonics played on an electric guitar, processed with reverb and overdubbed at 0.35, although Orbit himself suggested, 'A few things that people think are guitar are actually the MS-20.'[39] The first substantive filter sweep occurs in the intro section, sweeping through highs to lows and back to highs again, placed very high in the mix. A short delay and room reverb has been applied to the largely compressed vocal, which continues throughout, with the analogue sweep settling to a continuing, oscillating tone with a band pass filter (BPF) and low frequency oscillator (LFO) for vibrato.

The chorus at 1.08 features yet more analogue synthesis with a tone heavy in white noise entering hard right. This sound is normally used to create 'wind-like' effects and was uncommon in commercial popular music of this era; the premise behind new digital technology was to eliminate the 'noise' associated with analogue equipment. This coupled with an oscillating tone through a high-pass filter (HPF) lends the chorus significant textural contrast, particularly against the electric guitar riff and open hi-hat loop. It is evident at this point that a full frequency spread has been accounted for with the contrasting instruments, yet this appears to have been achieved naturally, without the forced use of heavy EQ'ing or much in the way of effects processing. At 1.30, the 'white noise' sound is abruptly gated, almost 'sucking' the break into the second verse. This is usually achieved by using a reverse cymbal, commonly heard in dance music production, yet Orbit has used gating, coupled with the kick drum pad placed high in the mix at 1.30, to achieve a similar effect. This demonstrates a highly individualistic method and nonconformity to standardized practices. The electric guitar enters again, hard right at 1.46, but this time it has been looped. This is rather obvious, as the fret board squeaks are audible and repeat in an identical way – something that would have been almost impossible to capture if it had been played live. No attempt has been made to present the guitar as a natural, progressively played piece – it is a loop, electronically manipulated and placed with precision in the mix.

The three sections occurring from 2.39 to 3.39 are the most dynamic and electronically rich parts to the song. An instrumental break occurs at 2.39, with what sounds very much like a Theremin, or a heavily manipulated, time stretched and processed vocal, spread across the section very high in the mix. This sound has been sent to delay with the signal channel and delay channel panned hard left and right. This was a common technique used on guitars and percussion in the 1970s, but with reverb as opposed to delay, so again, whilst precision-applied delays were common in dance music of the era, this particular process was unusual in dance music genre. Here, the illusion of a tempo change has been created. A digital synth pad is dramatically brought up and down in the mix, pushed to the forefront and pulled back against a busy drum loop that enters at 2.47, panned centre. These multiple layers of digital and analogue synthesis, sweeping in and out of frequency ranges and being pushed and pulled in the mix drop out by 2.54, as the track recedes into its quiet third verse. Again, tape hiss is audible to the point of being prominent and no attempt has been made to apply noise reduction or any other processing in order to 'clean' the tracks. In contrast to the preceding section full of electronic instrumentation and digital synthesis, this section is decidedly *analogue* in its sound. The tape hiss, acoustic guitar chucks and riff panned hard left and right, coupled with the noise from the LPF subs on a synth pad entering at 3.16 and then escalating into an eight second sweep, all contribute to a warm, deep and natural sound. These sonic aesthetics align with Orbit's production process mantra – 'Don't gild the lily'[40] – embracing a natural, yet imperfect result.

A large, nine-second filter sweep enters at 3.27 with lots of echo applied to the sweep tails as they fade around 3.36. This is reminiscent of the use of analogue synthesis in video games from the early 1980s and a 'Space Invaders'-style result has been achieved. This would have come from an experimental use of the synthesizer and like Orbit has described, the capturing of a sound performed in an experimental way and placed in an appropriate part of the mix:

> I don't consider myself a keyboardist at all. I'm a two-fingered virtuoso. Wax pencils play a large part in my keyboard playing. I draw on the keys and use them to label what I'm doing – what samples are assigned to what key, and so on. Sequencing plays a large part, obviously.[41]

This 'two-fingered virtuoso' playing is particularly evident in the latter stages of the song, in the digital synth 'stabs'. The final chorus is particularly notable for the vocal performance. This section demonstrates a new-found dynamism to Madonna's vocal delivery, with an aggressive 'and I feel' at 4.24. The final repetition of this line contains a large sweeping note, ascending into a scream. Whilst appearing quite natural at first, it sounds as if the final part has had a dash of auto tuning applied to it or has been sampled in order to extend it a little. This improvised, excited vocal is set against another filter sweep at 4.34 and the Theremin sound entering at 4.28. The synth layers build once more in this section with the 'piano' pad entering hard left and the 'retro' synth 'stabs' brought down in the mix, where they stay until the song ends. There is also a subs-heavy tone, oscillating low in the mix that continues until the end.

This track is a perfect example of *maverick methodology*. In 1997, Apple had released the Power Mac and Digidesign was already up to version 3 of Pro Tools. Emagic's Logic was another popular professional audio and MIDI sequencer and the Korg Triton was the digital synthesizer and workstation of choice. Sampling using a hardware sampler was an all but forgotten art, now the sophisticated capabilities of audio editing within software sequencers were apparent. Yet Orbit used an Atari ST running a version of Cubase more at home in 1987, out-of-date (and, quite probably, out of fashion) synthesizers and techniques that were laborious, unorthodox and time consuming in the height of the time and space saving digital age. These techniques, methods and equipment in the context of making an album with one of the world's biggest popular music artists – especially the album that must turn her career around – are quite paradoxical, to the point of being unimaginable. Yet Orbit was well aware of this, as he stated, 'I mean, picture Madonna, the biggest pop star in the world, playing with this retro gear that you could buy for $50 in the Recycler.'[42] Yet Orbit employed these methods with an unflinching and nonchalant normality, as though it was every other producer and engineer doing it wrong:

> I still use Cubase on an Atari Mega-2. I've got an Akai S3200, and these days I load everything into that and run the whole mix through the stereo outputs and into a couple of valve compressors. I still use my old Trident 80B desk. I love it![43]

This, in 1997, did not conform to recording and production protocol in the professional context, despite how it felt to Orbit. In fact, Orbit's methodology was deliberately nonconformist in that he was well aware of how differently he operated to his peers. At the time, most dance and electronica producers opted for a sequencer-based, tight, clean and precision-timed track with no imperfections or impurities to create a 'perfect' and highly digitized result – nothing would begin in the analogue domain, let alone end up in it. 'Ray of Light' sounds altogether different and I would argue it was this opposition to – what were then – current trends in the production of the genre, this *maverick methodology,* that made 'Ray of Light' stand out in the way that it did.

Often is the case that a producer is employed for their 'sound': their 'sonic signature' that has the potential to 'imprint' on an artist's record. In the 1980s and 1990s, producers often became a marketing tool in the selling of a new artist. This has been particularly evident in the hip-hop genre, where a 'named' producer will always help record sales, particularly in launching new artist careers. Over time, audiences have come to recognize these sounds, but only in the case of a select few producers. Phil Spector was one, with layer upon layer of reverb-saturated vocal and instrumental tracks built into a wall of sound. SAW were another set of producers who achieved a brassy, slick and uber-produced sound for many artists in the late 1980s. Orbit's sound on 'Ray of Light' is obvious, yet I would go further and argue that his work on 'Ray of Light' amounts to more than just production, but a kind of production-led orchestration. Orbit's version bears almost no resemblance to the original; the production showcases a unique electronic composer-recordist tasked with – and succeeding in – Madonna's sonic reinvention.

U2 – 'Mofo'

The consideration of the recording studio as 'musical instrument' and/or 'compositional tool' is an intriguing point of focus in phonomusicological study – a concept first proposed by recordist Brian Eno in 1979.[44] In *The Producer as Composer*, Virgil Moorefield considers this concept further, using Brian Eno and his albums, *Music for Airports* (1978) and *My Life in the Bush of Ghosts* (1981), as case study examples. Arguing that Eno uses the studio as a 'meta-instrument',[45] he states that the studio is 'score and orchestra rolled into one'.[46] A good example of this blurry conflation of the composition and production process lies in this next example – U2's 'Mofo', taken from the 1997 album *Pop*. Recorded during 1995 and 1996 at Windmill Lane, Hanover Quay and The Works studios in Dublin, Ireland, as well as South Beach Studios, Miami, USA, the album was co-produced by London-based Mark Ellis, more commonly known as 'Flood', assisted by Nellee Hooper, formerly of UK R&B act Soul II Soul and Howie B. By the early 1990s, Hooper had already won two Grammy awards for Sinead O'Connor's *I Do Not Want What I Haven't Got* (1990) and Soul II Soul's *Club Classics Volume One* (1989). Howie B had worked on many projects with Icelandic solo artist Bjork, including co-producing her third studio album *Post* (1995). Following early 1980s recording apprenticeships, Flood gained engineering credits on Nick Cave and The Bad Seeds' *From Her to Eternity* (1984), Erasure's *The Circus* (1987) and Depeche Mode's 'Shake the Disease' (1985). In 1986, he engineered U2's *The Joshua Tree* (1987) with Brian Eno and Daniel Lanois as producers. By the mid-1990s, Flood's creative, boundary-pushing production style had already resulted in some of the most sonically distinctive commercial rock recordings of the decade: Nine Inch Nails' *The Downward Spiral* (1994), Smashing Pumpkins' *Mellon Collie and the Infinite Sadness* (1995) and U2's *Zooropa* (1993). All three featured complex combinations of live and programmed rhythm, samples and loops, prominent and processed vocal performances, as well as extensive use of multitracking and overdubs. These records are 'constructed' from multiple performance edits as opposed to 'captured' whole. Yet as a recordist, Flood's outlook does not conform to a 'traditional' or 'technology-driven' production aesthetic, but his unorthodox techniques and commitment to experimentation express freedom from standard methodologies and as such can be considered *maverick*.

Similar to 'Ray of Light' and 'Praise You', 'Mofo' featured the use of technological precursors in conjunction with unorthodox production techniques. Despite vast technological changes in the years since Flood began his career in the late 1970s, Flood committed to the use of analogue tape and did not compromise on *Pop*, as he explained:

> Rock 'n roll isn't about accuracy, rock 'n roll is about feel. Analogue isn't accurate, but it is musical. When you are aware of the fact that analogue isn't accurate, but realise what it can do, you can use the medium as if it's an effect.[47]

This goes some way in explaining his use of analogue tape as both a recording technology and effects processor, but he still refers to 'rock n' roll'; in recording *Pop*, U2 were intending to make a dance record, full of programming, sampling and sequencing.[48] This is a reflection of the strange position U2 found themselves in during the 1990s. Having gained a reputation for roots and blues-based music during the late 1980s, U2 struggled to reposition themselves in a popular music landscape dominated by dance, hip-hop and emergent trip-hop genre. By 1996, U2 had firmly established themselves as one of the world's biggest stadium acts. Having released the multi-platinum selling and multi-award winning albums *Achtung Baby* (1991) and *Zooropa* (1993), U2 were under considerable pressure to reinvent themselves once again, during a time when UK music was dominated by dance music sub-genres including house, drum n' bass, techno and trance, not to mention the post-independent 'Britpop' genre to which U2, as an established Irish stadium rock act, did not belong. U2 had also just finished touring *Zooropa*, with a stadium spectacular entitled 'Zoo TV': an astronomical multimedia event which included live telephone conversations to world leaders, multiple costume and stage set changes and live television footage from war-torn Sarajevo. Such grandiosity was at odds with the UK's musical and political climate of the time, in the context of a New Labour government, 'Cool Britannia' and Britpop, and prompted a change in direction for U2.

As one of the most successful rock recordists of the then recent past, U2's work with Flood – as well as Nellee Hooper and Howie B – suggested an attempt to combine alternative rock and contemporary dance and R&B aesthetics into a 'current' sound, whilst retaining a recordist who knew and had worked on the band's prior material. Flood attempted to explain their direction, '[We wanted to] try to construct a new sound for U2 whilst still making them sound like U2.'[49]

At almost six minutes long, perhaps radio was not the intended direction for 'Mofo', rather the large clubs and DJ sets of the late 1990s dance scenes. The album version was never released; however, the unusual step was taken to release 'Mofo' as a 'single package' double A-side with 'If God Will Send His Angels'. Replacing the album version were remixes of the song from producers such as Roni Size, Alan Moulder and Matthew Roberts, again suggesting a significant contemporary shift for U2. In the case of this chapter, the original album version will be analysed.

In terms of structure, the song parts are unclear in places. A dance track relies heavily upon dynamics, the continuous rise and fall of the rhythm and melodies – a contrast to the A/B/A/B arrangements common in commercial rock music. In 'Mofo', drum loops have been constructed from Larry Mullen Jr's live playing with another industrial-like loop underpinning the entire track. Also, there is no bass guitar – rather, a keyboard bass sound that has been programmed. The bassline is perhaps what separates 'Mofo' from so many U2 tracks; Adam Clayton's loose, root-note oriented playing is decidedly missing, as journalist Paul Tingen explained:

> To change Adam Clayton's bass sound, the team worked a lot with heavy processing, to the extent that several tracks sound as if they feature keyboard bass, but apparently it's all Clayton playing, with the exception of most of 'Mofo', which is indeed a keyboard bass.[50]

There is hardly any guitar 'playing' in the traditional sense, with the majority of the guitars having been reduced to few-second sampled snapshots of the Edge's playing, heavily chopped, gated and 'played' into the mix from a keyboard in varying parts of the song. Contrary to the vocal falsettos so dominant on albums such as *Achtung Baby*, Bono's vocals on 'Mofo' are monotone, direct, lack dynamic contrast (until the coda) and at times almost fall into speech. Undoubtedly, it is the keyboard bassline that carries the main melody of the song as opposed to the lead vocal. A slight distortion has been added to the lead vocal and little de-essing has taken place as sibilance occurs throughout. The vocals are particularly low in the mix, which gives 'Mofo' a rhythm-heavy feel, similar to that of a mid-1990s drum n' bass track.

'Mofo', like the rest of *Pop*, was recorded using samplers and a small amount of sequencing was done using Creator's C-Lab software on an Atari ST. 'We used a Otari MTR90 multitrack (analogue tape machine), with mainly a 1972 Neve desk. Rupert Neve made that for EMI – it was the first 24-buss desk that he made', suggested Howie B.[51] All this equipment was dated – and the Neve desk, vintage – by 1996, which does not explain how Flood managed to edit *Pop* from the mass of recordings that were made. When asked about editing on a digital editor (e.g. Pro Tools or a hard disk recorder), Flood replied, 'You must be joking! I did it on half inch tape!'[52] This explains the lengthy *Pop* recording process of over eighteen months, but also the unusual combination of technologies applied to the recording and production process. The combination of vintage mixing console analogue tape with 1980s MIDI equipment was uncommon in dance music production of the era, yet again is a strong example of technological hybridity in the late 1990s.

'Mofo' starts with an industrial-style drum loop that is panned around the stereo field. Consisting of sharp, percussive overtones, it has been constructed from chopped up and aggressively gated samples. The industrial loop is then joined by a 'live' drum loop. There is a large hall reverb on the kick drum within this loop, which is quite unusual, especially in the context of dance music where a powerful, dry and prominent kick drum is usually positioned to drive the track. Synth pad subs are also audible from the beginning of the track, with another 'filter-style' synth pad panned hard right and placed low in the mix along with a centred, more rhythmic 'noise' based loop. This sparse and industrial-influenced introduction is reminiscent of Nine Inch Nails' *The Downward Spiral* (1994), which situates the track in neither a classic rock or dance music-oriented introduction, but in 'underground', alternative genre and post-industrial rock. The introduction expands (0.27) to include the dominant keyboard bass loop, continuing for the remainder of the track. This loop is particularly high in the mix throughout, reminiscent of drum n' bass acts in the mid-to-late 1990s. Guitars also enter at this point in the track; samples of guitar playing that have been 'played' or 'dropped' in using a MIDI keyboard. At 0.48, some clicks are audible hard left, although it is unclear whether these are highly processed snare samples or noise from the recordings. There are very short, staccato loops that enter for brief periods. For example, a short filter sweep sample enters at 1.02 and a short, rhythmic loop enters between 1.05 and 1.07. The vocals have been placed unusually low in the mix and little de-essing has been applied as they are unusually sibilant, as Flood explained:

> There were many guitar and vocal loops. On 'Mofo' there are little guitar and vocal samples that they played and we sampled. We selected the bits that we liked, and then Edge played them back in off a keyboard. We did that quite a lot, and ended up with maybe 20 or 25 percent of the sounds on the album being loops, samples, or programmed stuff, although these parts were always supplementary; we took great care not to clutter things.[53]

The application of MIDI programming to 'Mofo' once again situates it in dance music genre; such techniques were absent from the majority of U2's earlier recordings and the quantized sequences in 'Mofo' result in a more precise, repetitive track construction. The track also strongly alludes to Nine Inch Nails; the short appearances of half-and one-bar rhythm snippets are a nod to Trent Reznor's production style and almost certainly influenced Flood.

Rhythmically, 'Mofo' is tightly constructed in line with a programmed production method. However, other elements of the track contrast this precision with signs of more experimental, improvisational aesthetics – precisely the '20 or 25 percent' samples and loops Flood referred to. For example, the overdubbed vocal in the verses, 'been around the back, been around the front', has been placed higher in the mix than the lead vocal, thus foregrounding what is traditionally positioned in the background. Some feedback is audible at 2.01, as well as a short burst of speech appearing briefly at 2.16. These performance nuances have been captured within the original sampled material, yet 're-performed' back into the track via MIDI.

One of the key features of 'Mofo' is the treatment of the vocals. On prior albums such as *The Joshua Tree* (1987) and *Rattle and Hum* (1988) Bono's voice is recorded naturally, with plenty of performance nuances indicative of more traditionalist 'performance capture' recording approaches. On *Pop* – and particularly 'Mofo' – Bono's vocal is heavily processed, deconstructed then re-performed, lending him an altogether different voice. Distortion, band pass filtering and heavy use of time-based processing is audible throughout, as Flood explained:

> All his (Bono's) vocals were recorded with a Shure SM58, as usual, and then went through a Neve mic preamp, and had a little bit of valve compression added from an LA2 or a Summit. We only used extreme effects on his voice during the recording, for him to get himself into a different place, and then, gradually, we pulled most effects out. There is a lot of effects processing on the album, but much of it was added during recording.[54]

This quote not only illuminates the presence of vintage technologies on the recording but also points to the clear intention to work destructively and within a predefined set of constraints. This is consistent with Flood's standpoint towards technology as pointed out in Chapter 6. The chorus vocal samples have also been pushed up and down in the mix, which is rather unusual, especially considering the final 'mother', which is aggressively performed yet pushed lower in the mix. Also at 2.19, large, overdriven guitar 'dive-bomb' samples are panned hard left, sent to reverb and returning hard right. Whilst guitarist the Edge is well known for his use of delay as part of his guitar playing style, much of this processing has been added post-recording; otherwise, it would not have been possible to pan the reverb separately. The vocals are at their highest point in the mix (2.43) where the drum loops drop out and the bassline is pulled down in the mix. At this point, the entire mix appears to shift hard left, giving the impression that the track has moved somewhere else. This section is a good example of 'the studio as compositional tool' at work. Considering the placement of certain parts in the mix and how certain tracks are panned around the stereo field, more than one person would had to have operated the console. As Howie B explained:

> Like I said, the desk was a very important instrument in the making of this album, especially the way that me and Flood use it. It's something we can both play, the way that Edge can pick up a guitar and play a fantastic song. I can go onto a desk and use it in a way that no-one else will, and it's the same with Flood.[55]

Flood agreed, as he added: 'When you have two or three people sitting at a desk doing a mix, pushing and pulling and changing the music, it becomes like a performance.'[56] This 'pushing and pulling' is audible throughout 'Mofo', with plenty of manual panning creating a wide stereo field. The second verse begins (3.27) and like the first verse, the vocals are low in the mix with the live drum loop, bass loops and synths creating a very crowded musical backdrop. This is a busy section, drawing attention away from the vocals to the mass of drums and synth pads. Yet the final section of 'Mofo' (4.55) is its most heavily textured, with the industrial drum loop re-entering along with more experimental guitar samples. The guitar samples are panned hard left, with the melodic guitar placed high in the mix and panned hard right. The rhythm guitar chucks are still panned hard right and low in the mix, whilst the keyboard bass loop and synth bass doubler are centred and given prominence. By the track's coda, the pay-off vocal lines are comparatively distant; the low mix position, combined with a large reverb and long delay, has created this effect. The lack of de-essing leaves the vocal naturally sibilant; the application of delay only enhances the sibilance, making it a feature. During the course of a lengthy fade out (5.29), the instruments and samples are pulled down in the mix, as well as pulled down in volume, leaving the vocal more prominent. The guitar samples become more experimental during the fade out with multiple repetitive triggers on the keyboard occurring during the fade.

What has been achieved here is at odds with both the band and producer's original intentions. All members of U2 have commented on *Pop* and how they believe it was unfinished or did not live up to their expectations in other ways, as Bono points out in *U2 by U2*: 'We just couldn't get the fun onto the album. The songs weren't good enough'. Evans draws similar conclusions in the same book: 'The great synthesis between songwriting and dance didn't happen. The two approaches were actually pulling us in opposing directions.'[57]

This is a reasonable conclusion; 'Mofo' has resulted in sounding like a very heavy rock track with clear 'drum and bass' and industrial influences. Indeed, the bass is so prominent in the track that there are unusually high levels of activity present in the subs range, suggesting the application of low end EQ boost.

Work on *Pop* began in the summer of 1995 and the album was released in March 1997. With release dates scheduled for the latter part of 1996, the album was rescheduled multiple times, until *Pop* was finally released.[58] U2 have often cited the early booking of stadiums and the set construction for the 'Pop Mart' tour as the reason for having to release the album unfinished, as Bono explained: '*Pop* never had the chance to be properly finished. It is really the most expensive demo session in the history of music.'[59]

It is also well documented that the band rushed to 'complete' the album, with the Edge suggesting he was still recording backing vocals onto final mixes at the mastering stage. Yet this struggle to finalize the track suggests a lack of confidence pertaining the original musical intention and direction. If the band were not clear about what it was they were trying to achieve, how would they know when they had achieved it? Once again, this is indicative of a group struggling to find their musical place in a changing popular music landscape, but the indecisiveness was not felt by the band alone. Flood said he preferred the 'limitations' of tape and how the medium forces decisiveness, but again, this contradicts what he describes here:

> People ask me when I know a song is finished, and I say: 'when it's finished'. We had three different mixes of 'Mofo', and during mastering in November '97 in New York, I edited a final version of 'Mofo' from these three mixes. So even during mastering, we were trying to push the song to another level. It was a long process of experimentation; the album didn't actually come together until the last few months.[60]

The use of manual mix techniques, the length of time taken to complete the process as well as other aspects such as the inclusion of noise and mistakes in the final mix, all point towards a unique type of recording and production technique. In this instance, Flood and U2's intention was to make a dance record. Dance music production is synonymous with tight, clean edits and precision sequencing, therefore the inclusion of noise and mistakes is out of place in the wider context of this track. In producing 'Mofo', Flood has rejected the technology-driven and labour-saving aspects of dance music production. However, in using samples, sequences and programmed drum loops, he has not employed traditionalist methods either. This is a clear example of a *maverick methodology*, possibly at its most methodical yet paradoxically chaotic point, with many aspects from the original direction, influences, applications of technologies, instruments and mixing method at odds, clashing at every stage of the process.

Fatboy Slim – 'Praise You'

Released in January 1999 and reaching number one in the UK charts, 'Praise You' by Fatboy Slim[61] was taken from the album *You've Come a Long Way, Baby* (1998). Another example of *maverick* production method from the late 1990s, this track features then unorthodox techniques coupled with the application of technological precursors. At this early stage, I'd like to acknowledge Mark Katz's chapter on 'Praise You' in his book *Capturing Sound*.[62] Katz impressively illuminates the politics of sampling in 'Praise You' and reveals much about the origin of Yarborough's 'Take Yo' Praise' and its relationship to Cook's track. The choice to use the same track for analysis in this book is based entirely on the sonically discernible production aesthetics, technological and processual technique present in the recording.

In the late 1990s, commercial dance music was experiencing a newfound, mainstream and 'high fashion' audience. The Balearic island of Ibiza, Cyprus' Ayia Napa, along with the Greek resort of Faliraki proved the ultimate European mainstream house music destinations. 'Superclubs', which regularly booked UK-based 'Superstar DJ's', were one of the main attractions to these resorts, coupled with the hot weather, availability of cheap alcohol and drugs and cheap air fares. Norman Cook often DJ'd in Ibiza and hits from *You've Come a Long Way, Baby* have often appeared on 'Ibiza Anthems'-style compilation records including *The Best Ibiza Anthems ... Ever!* (1999), an indication that the DJ/producer was fundamental to the late 1990s commercial dance music 'peak'.[63]

Featuring vocal samples from Camille Yarborough's 1975 funk/soul record 'Take Yo' Praise', 'Praise You' was the lead single from *You've Come A Long Way Baby* and featured multiple loops, percussion and guitar parts, as well as speech recordings and piano samples. Recorded in Cook's Brighton-based home studio, the album was self-produced with additional engineering and mixing carried out by recordist Simon Thornton. At the time, Cook's studio was a small, modest set-up, as he explained:

> I use an Atari ST running Creator software and two Akai S950s. Those are my staples. I'm just too lazy to learn another system – plus I don't want to get a proper computer in the house because I'd end up on the Internet downloading porn and playing Dungeons & Dragons with people for the next year. The album would have taken much longer if I was on the Web or reading e-mail.[64]

Such technologies were outdated by 1997; Creator had long been superseded by programs such as EMagic's Logic and Digidesign's Pro Tools. Cook also suggests that in sticking with his tried and tested technologies, he avoids distractions and the inevitable learning curves associated with new technologies, once again this is indicative of risk aversion as described in Chapter 6. Whilst the use of AKAI samplers was common amongst hip-hop, dance and other electronic genres during the late 1980s, the use of the samplers had begun to fade in the 1990s, largely due to the emergence and proliferation of software sampling tools. The S950 samplers were particularly outdated by the late 1990s, due to their low memory and floppy disk storage systems.

By 1998, Cook had released one album under his Fatboy Slim moniker, *Better Living Through Chemistry* (1996). Having also achieved commercial success with remixes of Cornershop's 'Brimful of Asha' (1997) and Wildchild's 'Renegade Master '98' (1998), Cook was one of the most sought-after remix producers by the end of the 1990s. Due to Cook's primary role as a remix producer and DJ by the mid-1990s, it is difficult to extrapolate what his intention was in making *You've Come a Long Way, Baby*. As a DJ, he often referred to wanting to make 'good tunes' as he explained, 'To do a good tune, I have to do nine crap ones ... experiment – that's the only way to make interesting music. Just simple gear and knowing what you can do with it.'[65]

Cook's simplistic set-up of an Atari ST and dual AKAI samplers would have been common place during the late 1980s. Ten years on and even home studio production had moved further forward, with Macintosh computers and DAWs with control surfaces the technologies of choice. Technologically, this set-up positioned Cook as an outlier – a recordist working outside of the technological realm of his peer group. Unlike many dance music producers of the 1990s, Cook was clearly not aiming for perfection in his production methodology. He has often referred to his music as 'tracks' or 'tunes'. From this it can be deduced that in producing 'Praise You', Cook's intention was to make a good track, suitable for large dance music audiences. He made no suggestion of aiming his music at radio or other media neither did he suggest he wanted to make a 'hit' record. Suffice to say that the intended direction of 'Praise You' would have been at club and rave audiences.

'Praise You' is an up-tempo dance record, typical of the big-beat sub-genre style. The lead sampled vocal has been sequenced and repetitively looped in places throughout the track. A piano sample is a key component, with time stretching having been applied to the point that it sounds like a warped record. Looped samples of multiple percussion instruments, including bongo drums, wood blocks, tambourine and vibraslap are used throughout, along with bass guitar loops and various drum loops. The entire track is ultimately a *composite*, having been pieced together from various samples, sequenced on a MIDI sequencer and recorded. The repetitive nature of each individual element suggests these are not instrumental sections that have been played continually; rather they are short sections of instrumental playing that have been sampled and looped. The use of time stretching to construct rhythmically synchronous loops is obvious, as 'warping' and audible de-tuning – a common result from time stretching any piece of music – is perceptible throughout the track, as Cook explained, 'I usually end up having to time stretch a few things – which is OK, 'cos the 950's great for that – but my rule is, if it's within three semi-tones, I'll use it.'[66] Even though three semi-tones of detuning results in audible dissonance, Cook is unapologetic; as long as the rhythmic sequences are in place, the harmonic construction of the track is secondary. This emphasis on rhythm was a key musical signature to big-beat genre, with prominent kick drums, bass sequences and quarter-note rhythms.

'Praise You' begins with the isolated piano loop and some sampled conversation. Immediately, the noise, hiss and vinyl crackle is highly present, indicating the piano has been sampled from a record – and a particularly noisy, scratchy record at that. The piano loop is out of tune. This has occurred due to the time stretching applied to it, presumably to fit with the vocal loop. Immediately, multiple unconventional techniques are evident in the production. Firstly, the dance music genre in general has always been noted for its highly polished, 'perfect', noise-free and almost entirely *digitized* sound, so the choice made by Cook to use a sample from such an old noisy record is, in itself, unorthodox. Berk highlights this as follows:

> The dominant dance music subgenres of the late 1990s (trip-hop, drum n' bass, big beat and the like) are more easily defined by their studio production processes than by any readily identifiable sound sources. While no single instrument characterises these genres the way the 303 defined acid house, they depend more heavily on technological progress than any prior post-techno music. While house and techno producers, priced out of their contemporary music technology market, looked

back to older tools that had never been fully exploited, musicians involved in the newer genres are heavily invested in the cutting edge. Their radically cut-and-paste oriented musics are predicated on the existence of studio tools that became available in the late eighties: the sampler and the digital audio workstation.[67]

Berk brushes on the return to older technologies as being economically driven, but the reasoning – as elucidated by Cook's 'Praise You' and others – is of course more nuanced.

In an era where noise reduction and noise minimalization were common tools of production, their use was entirely ignored by Cook. Another aspect of the piano sample is that it contains clicks and overspill, probably from the original recording. The clicks repeat in time with the sampled loops and again the decision was made to include these, rather than eliminate them entirely from the track.

One of the most interesting aspects to the track is that it has been constructed around the vocal, as Katz illuminates in *Capturing Sound*.[68] This goes against common practice in recording and production, where the drums are normally the first instrument to be recorded, setting the tempo, rhythm and time signature. This is a particularly notable aspect of dance music production, yet Cook has turned that practice on its head. Revolving the track around the vocal would have presented timing issues, particularly as Cook rejected the use of quantization,[69] as he explained:

> Quantising is a bit of a weird one with me. Usually, I've got a load of cranky old loops all over the place, so timing is never going to be spot on, but I hate it if things actually start to sound too 'live' or too 'real'. I will specifically change things to make it sound like machine music, like put on some stupid robotic loop or chop up the sample in strange ways. That's what I did with 'Praise You'.[70]

What he is describing here is evident in the first verse of the song (0.16) where the vocal sample begins. More loud vinyl crackle is audible and this is particularly evident, as it is layered on top of the piano sample. There is a loop point at the very last part of the word 'should', which repeats continuously across multiple bars. A bongo drum pattern enters hard right, sent to reverb and returning hard left. A tambourine sample is looped and enters hard right, along with a 'vibraslap'. The bass guitar enters high in the mix (0.52) and is panned centre. At this point, a repeated, short sample of the earlier conversation enters low in the mix and is panned hard left and right. All samples drop out completely (1.10) where a drum sample sounds like it has been time stretched and put through a LPF. This is programmed to sound like a heartbeat; the high frequencies are 'wound in' until an unprocessed kick drum sample enters (1.14). This combination of piano, percussion, drum and bass samples results in a busy track with a wide stereo field and emphasized low frequencies, suggesting the addition of low EQ boost.

Yet 'Praise You' features plenty of dynamic and textural contrast created by the mixture of loops. The use of cymbal samples also occurs throughout the track and result in an unnatural sound, due to the time stretching having extended their natural decay. By 1.35, the song reaches its second verse and the main vocal sample repeats. More time stretching has been applied to the final 'should' in this section, before the original drum loop is dropped (2.10) and replaced with another, more electronic sounding and busier loop with percussive, tambourine-like accentuations on every fourth beat. In dropping the original drum and piano loop, Cook has dropped the main rhythm and melody, replacing them with different loops that create an altogether different texture. The organ and second drum loop samples create some much-needed space in the track, in contrast to the earlier, busier percussive section. The creation of space in this section is also to do with the bass dropping out (2.10) and re-entering at 2.20. This ten-second gap draws attention to the rhythm and gives the impression that the track is somehow being 'drawn in' before being let back out again. Additionally, a time-stretched piano note is wound down and up again in pitch and placed between 2.08 and 2.13. Such dynamic contrast is often created with the use of synthesis – the application of filters to 'suck' lead-in and lead-out segments – yet Cook has gone about this common dance music motif differently, using the bass a means of creating dynamic contrast.

However, later on in the track, the use of filters plays a key role both texturally and dynamically. At 2.45 there is more change in texture as the brass loop, bass and conversation samples drop out, to be replaced with a sample of an electric guitar playing a short riff with added wah-wah. This section is perhaps the most interesting part of the track, particularly in terms of the production or, more precisely, the *lack* of production. All samples and loops drop out (3.03) leaving an oscillating synth pad with a LPF, exposing the subs with the 'mids' and highs gradually being 'wound in.' The synth pad is centred and then suddenly at 3.05, a large burst of noise enters hard left. There is no instrument or sample that appears to have been placed on this channel apart from the almost inaudible digital synth pad that appears momentarily (3.11). However, this does not explain the presence of the noise. Usual dance music production protocol would be to 'tidy up' the channel, either with the use of gates, a very short fade placed just before the required part or a straight cut in order to eliminate the unwanted noise. Additionally, this section demonstrates Cook's manipulation of both texture and dynamics with the bass channel, but textural fluctuations are also a result of the percussion and drum elements. At 3.11 the main vocal sample returns, again with plenty of audible hiss and vinyl crackle. All percussion samples, including the bongos and wood block loop, enter at the same point, with a digital synth pad placed low in the mix, entering hard left. The vocal sample has been cut and looped repeatedly at varying intervals between 3.27 and 3.33, and a large snare drum sample has been repeated as a 'roll' (3.32). The snare hits are programmed in triplets as opposed to on each beat, creating an alternate texture against the other sampled instruments. At 3.53 the piano loop is chopped up into triplets. This 'throws' the track off into a different direction and gives the impression there has been a change in tempo, emphasizing yet another transformation in texture. This use of editing clearly illustrates how changes in musical elements can be achieved with production techniques. Like 'Mofo', this is a good example of the studio as compositional tool.

The final sections of the track demonstrate further *maverick* constructions of common dance music motifs. A new speech sample (it is not clear what the speech sample contains in terms of lyrics, although it could be interpreted as 'get on down to it') enters (4.20) and is repeated and panned hard left. The single snare samples –

along with time-stretched cymbal samples – lead the song into its final section (4.28) where the organ continues along with the brass loops. This section is the busiest in the song, despite the main drum loop dropping out, as it contains all the earlier percussive samples along with the bongos and cymbal samples. The outro is lengthy, between 5.03 and 5.22, and contains just one line of vocal. All the instrument samples drop out by this point and a time-stretched piano sample is put through a LPF exposing the subs and used as a fade out. This is a highly unusual and experimental way of *alluding* to a fade out without actually fading out. In doing so, Cook alludes to past standard recording and production tropes, but goes about this allusion in a unique manner.

The use of samples, such as the time-stretched cymbals, is consistent with Cook's earlier suggestion that he will make certain samples sound more mechanical if he feels they are in danger of sounding too 'live'. What is interesting, however, is that overall this track makes for 'soft' repeated listening. There are no sharp edges or particularly 'loud' parts and the track features a unique 'warmth' for a digitally created recording, due to most of the samples originating from vinyl. This could also be explained by the lack of high frequencies in the overall mix. In attempting to make his track sound like 'machine music', Cook has achieved the opposite – the track sounds remarkably *human*. Far from sounding like a composite, the obvious vinyl crackle and lack of quantization place it somewhere pre-digital formatting and the inclusion of a 1970s vocal sample lends the track a 'retro' appeal. The lack of quantization also adds to the natural flow of the music. The piano loop is immediate and deliberately posited as a catchy 'hook', despite it being out of tune. Yet this is only noticeable in the first few bars where it is isolated; situated in its wider musical context, it blends in with the array of samples and synthesis.

'Praise You' is one of the most recognizable commercial dance records of the 1990s and still features prominently on mainstream radio. Although synonymous with the big-beat genre as a whole, 'Praise You' is a significant record in commercial popular music generally. Its imperfections and rough arrangement and mix, along with the inclusion of all the noise and hiss, position the record in the past. Additionally, the record features motifs from a wide genre spectrum: the vocal lines sampled from a 1970s soul record, and the bass and percussion derived from house music of the then recent past. As such, it is understandable how this record appealed to such a wide audience and, therefore, was so commercially successful.

Cook achieved a number one record in multiple territories and a ubiquitous club hit. It is important to note the track's accompanying, award-winning video. Directed by Spike Jonze, the video was a simple 'home movie' of a group of dancers in a shopping mall, dancing to 'Praise You', with Cook making a cameo as one of the dancers. Once *You've Come a Long Way, Baby* and its multiple single releases had passed, Cook became one of the most sought-after dance music producers in the world, about which he has often expressed amazement. However, the unorthodox, experimental and creative method Cook employed, coupled with his 'luddite' attitude and rejection of then cutting-edge technologies, is what resulted in 'Praise You's unique sonic canvas. Of course, Cook constructed 'Praise You' in an individualistic way and whilst it was not his intention, in making *You've Come a Long Way, Baby*, he became one of the most sought-after dance music DJs and recordists of the era.

Blur – 'Song 2'

'Song 2' by UK indie band Blur, taken from the album *Blur*, was released in 1997 and reached number two in the UK charts. Released in the same year as 'Ray of Light', 'Praise You' and 'Mofo', this track also illustrates the implementation of late 1990s maverick production method. 'Song 2' was produced by Stephen Street, a British recordist renowned for his production work on The Smiths' *Strangeways, Here We Come* (1987), Morrissey's *Viva Hate* (1988) and The Cranberries' *Everybody Else Is Doing It, So Why Can't We?* (1993), as well as multiple Blur albums including *Modern Life Is Rubbish* (1993) and *Parklife* (1994). Whilst Blur emerged at the turn of the 1990s with the largely shoegaze-inspired *Leisure* (1991), the band became one of the most prominent artists in the early-to-mid-1990s Britpop genre. Along with Oasis, Ocean Colour Scene, Elastica, Pulp and Suede, Blur were an intrinsic part of this post-independent British rock sub-genre, which was largely characterized by 'British Invasion'-era rock aesthetics, live performances, observational lyrics culturally local to British life and strong, catchy melodies. For a genre so defined by its British cultural locality, many artists were surprisingly successful in the United States. In 1997, however, Blur were repositioning themselves musically at a time when commercial dance music, particularly the big-beat sub-genre (as described in the Fatboy Slim analysis), began to overshadow Britpop in terms of popularity. Additionally, US grunge music had a major influence on commercial UK popular music of the 1990s, particularly in the earlier part of the decade with globally successful albums such as Nirvana's *Nevermind* (1991) and *In Utero* (1994), Pearl Jam's *Ten* (1991) and *Vs* (1993), Soundgarden's *Badmotorfinger* (1991) and Alice in Chains' *Dirt* (1992).

By 1997, Street was well acquainted with the members of Blur and having worked prolifically as a recordist with many of the genre's defining bands was at least partly responsible for shaping the Britpop sound throughout the 1990s, particularly having produced records for The Smiths. One of the most sought-after recordists of the time, the London-based Townhouse Studios recordist was renowned for crafting independent rock music into radio-friendly pop hits. Street was also well known for his songwriting, having co-wrote many tracks on Morrissey's debut solo album *Viva Hate* (1988).

For Blur's fifth studio album, both recordist and musicians altered their working methods significantly. Firstly, they undertook most of the recording sessions away from Townhouse, instead using Primrose Hill's Mayfair Studios for pre-production. Blur completed the majority of the album out of their comfort zones in an unknown studio in Reykjavik, Iceland. In *Bit of a Blur*, bassist Alex James also noted the change in production techniques:

> Until then (recording of the *Blur* album), everything had been recorded on to tape but Streetie (Street) had a new computer recording system. Songs and parts could be edited, slowed down, speeded up, reversed, quantised and cut and pasted very easily together.[71]

James indicates an affectionate friendship with the recordist and also specifically refers to the Otari RADAR (Random Access Digital Audio Recorder) hard disk recording system used on the sessions. Released in 1994, this particular machine behaved like a 'tape machine without the tape', allowing a recordist up to twenty-four channels of multitracking capability with multiple editing and sequencing functionality, as discussed at length in Chapter 3. Street has discussed his choice to use the RADAR instead of Pro Tools in *Sound on Sound* magazine:

> I know a lot of people that got into Pro Tools because it had a particular plug-in that gave them the ability to pitch up vocals and so on, but I wasn't interested in the Pro Tools way of working so I didn't go down that route.[72]

Whilst the RADAR was a popular technology in the mid-1990s, it was quickly superseded by Pro Tools, particularly as computer processing power and memory capabilities increased towards the end of the 1990s. The RADAR never achieved the same take-up numbers as the ADAT and, as discussed in Chapter 3, acted more as a 'bridge' between analogue tape and DAWs. Street's decision to work with the RADAR instead of a DAW demonstrates his risk aversion; by working with a technology that operated in a similar way to a tape machine, he retained the familiarity of his working practice yet moved into the digital domain without committing to full, computer-based DAW workflows. Street's intention with recording the *Blur* album was to make a strong follow-up to 1995's *Parklife*. Blur, however, wanted to take their music in a different direction. Guitarist Graham Coxon, for example, wanted the songs to be more 'stripped down'.[73] Whilst artists from the Britpop genre, such as Oasis and Pulp, were still attaining commercial success, Blur intended to divert from that scene, particularly as there were signs that the genre had reached its peak. Drummer Dave Rowntree commented on the *Blur* pre-production process: 'We just played together for two weeks in a way we hadn't done since 1991. We wanted to purify the sound, to not have anything there not played by us.'[74]

These references to a 'stripped back', 'purified' sound were somewhat at odds with commercial popular music of the era, which embraced computer-based production methods. Additionally, the quotes suggest a musical intention focused entirely on performances, as opposed to synergizing programmed sequences as featured on *Parklife*.

'Song 2' is an upbeat rock song with grunge influences, particularly noticeable in the overall sonic texture and form. At just 2 minutes and 2 seconds long, the song is short for a commercial popular music recording. Playing on the number two throughout, 'Song 2' features two verses and two choruses 'book ended' with a short intro and coda. 'Song 2' begins with a drum sequence. It is obvious from the start that the drums are unusually centred in the mix, even though a stereo image is present, as Street suggested:

> The drum loop at the beginning of 'Song 2' is Graham and Dave playing together on two separate drum kits in a room. There was just one hanging mic in that room and I happened to be recording while they were playing together. We would do things like that very quickly and without having to stop and sample and blah blah blah.[75]

This quote substantiates the sense of spontaneity clearly embodied in 'Song 2'. Aesthetically, 'Song 2' features an exaggerated, wide dynamic range, following the quiet verse/loud chorus/quiet verse pattern consistent with US grunge acts Pixies and Nirvana. This method of recording drums, hanging one mic to capture all drums and cymbals from two kits, thus picking up the room ambience and varying amounts of each drum, is unorthodox, particularly in the context of late 1990s record production. The drum mic technique, when coupled with the prominent instrument distortion, is also consistent with garage-style punk aesthetics that not only influenced the aforementioned grunge acts but indicated a significant musical change in direction for Blur. With 'Song 2', Blur clearly acknowledged the impact of US grunge on British music, as well as embracing both early 1990s grunge and 1970s US punk aesthetics.

The intro drum loop does, however, foreground a performance featuring clear technological intervention. This is contradictory to the musicians' intention of performance purity. During the drum intro at 0.06, a 'click' consistent with a guitar pickup switch, is audible hard right. Coxon's clean guitar enters with little compression or gain added at 0.07, in contrast to the drum loop; this is a rough and demo-like performance consistent with punk style. The natural performance nuances in Coxon's guitar track are foregrounded in the mix.

At 0.14, all instruments enter in a sudden blast of noise, emphasizing a particularly wide dynamic range. Excessive distortion smothers the bass guitar, which is centred and pushed unusually high in the mix above the guitars. The distorted guitar enters slightly too early, but this timing discrepancy is ignored and kept in. A clean guitar with a subtle distortion repeatedly playing an aggressive, one-note chord is overdubbed and enters hard left. Once again, this is inconsistent with the musical intention; the presence of overdubs does not comply with a 'stripped back', punk-influenced direction. A second drum loop with loud crash cymbals enters during this section with the crash cymbals unusually high in the mix. However, this is entirely consistent with Street's description of the drum recordings: if one mic was hung in the centre of the room, the crash cymbals would be far closer to the mic than the kick or snare drum, thus resulting in a drum loop heavy on overhead signal.

The simple vocal line, 'whoo hoo', repeats four times in this section and is positioned much lower in the mix. This is a common production technique in punk and other loud rock music genres. In order to make a record *appear* as loud as possible it is common practice to place multiple layers of instruments – some with distortion – louder in the mix than the vocal, thus 'submerging' the lead vocal, overpowering it with instruments. However, once again there was an element of spontaneity in the vocal recording, as Street explained in *3862 Days*: 'Damon went "woo hoo" because he had nothing else prepared but it's something everyone understands.'[76] So, like the drum recordings, the featured vocal recording was unintentional. The first verse begins at 0.29 with quiet, nonchalantly sung 'speech' vocals, apparently left natural and uncompressed. There is no reverb on the vocal and sibilance is prominent, particularly on 'it wasn't easy', suggesting the absence of de-essing. Street offered even more insight into the vocal tracks as he suggested, 'The "guide vocal" track was used practically in its entirety, which inadvertently added to the song's most immediate and enduring feature.'[77] A 'guide vocal' track is normally a rough demo – a guide that the other musicians can follow, particularly if the song has an unusual structure. Street offers further explanation in that he was not aiming for a 'perfect' recording:

> I always record vocals with as little EQ as possible and I prefer to use the proper EMT plates, or failing that, a plate setting on a Lexicon. I'd rather have a great vocal slightly dodgily recorded than a pristine version of a bad performance. If someone has captured the moment it doesn't matter if the vocal has a few imperfections.[78]

This is entirely consistent with the vocal recording on 'Song 2', which could be described as 'slightly dodgy', but nonetheless instantly recognizable and memorable. Whilst no audible reverb is present on the 'Song 2' vocal, Street's preference for vintage EMT plate reverberators again suggests a rejection of then cutting-edge systems.

By the first chorus at 0.44, vocal compression is audible. As the chorus enters, the vocals suddenly move from the foreground of the mix to the back, submerged underneath the instruments, which once again enter like a blast of noise in contrast to the preceding verse. In this chorus, the 'whoo hoo' vocals have been overdubbed; the tails from the main vocal lines do not end before the 'whoo hoo' vocals come in; this obvious instance of tech-processual intervention once again contradicts the 'performance purity' intention.

At 1.09, the second verse features some notable production moments, with some frequency masking occurring amongst the vocals and drums. This is particularly evident on the looser, tom-roll parts of the drum loop, particularly where they clash with the word 'problem' that is sung twice in the second verse. There are audible plosives on 'problem' and the sibilance is quite sharp on 'it's not my … '. A second chorus enters at 1.25, which is almost identical to the first with the distorted guitar entering slightly early. Again, the vocals are positioned low in the mix with the highly distorted and overdriven bass guitar pushed to the foreground. Here, the crash cymbals are unusually high in the mix as part of the drum loop. This is, however, not just due to the mix; as previously mentioned, the crash cymbals would have been the closest drum kit voices to the single microphone hanging from the ceiling in the room. Indeed the kick drum, almost certainly the part of the kit furthest away from the microphone, is almost inaudible throughout this track. Entering into its final phase, the outro begins at 1.43 with 'yeah yeah' sung repeatedly three times. However, one guitar ends rather abruptly and is left un-gated, taking the end to precisely 2.02, in line with the song's focus on 'two'.

'Song 2' is a result of a spontaneous recording process. The drums were not intended to be recorded as such; Street just *happened* to record them in that way. The guide vocal was not intended for use as the final track, but Street kept it. Yet 'Song 2' was one of Blur's biggest hits and brought them new-found success in the United States, as Maconie explained:

> A month before the single was released, US computer hardware giants Intel released their Pentium II processor and they instantly fell upon 'Song 2' as their ad

anthem. Nike followed suit. It became the theme music of the USA hockey team, the trailer music for the movie Starship Troopers and was used as a theme for the Sony Playstation game FIFA 98.[79]

'Song 2' exposed Blur to a wider, global audience and brought them recognition from many aspects of the world's media and not just the record industry. The musicians have often expressed bemusement at the success of 'Song 2', as Alex James suggested:

> 'Song 2' was about the simplest thing we'd ever done, and the quickest. The whole thing was done in about fifteen minutes. I had a bad hangover and I felt horrible. It's a nasty record and it wouldn't have sounded so nasty if I'd gone to bed early the night before. We did it without thinking too much about it and felt better afterwards.[80]

James has a point when he refers to 'Song 2' as a 'nasty' record. The use of distortion on the bass guitar coupled with its aggressively foregrounded mix position is rare in modern rock music – and certainly an anomaly in late 1990s Britpop – yet is particularly noticeable throughout 'Song 2' on the choruses. Rarely does such a distorted, noisy record achieve such commercial success; excessive noise and distortion are traditionally associated with alternative artists from subcultural and independent musics, not established, chart-and radio-friendly pop/rock acts. In saying that, the overall frequency distribution on 'Song 2' is quite natural and in line with a four-piece rock band featuring vocals, guitars, bass and drums.

Contrary to the aforementioned process of recording 'Song 2', Street suggested he is a considered decision maker who commits to processed instrumental performances, as he explained:

> It's better to put the effects on as part of the recording process unless you are really not sure about a particular part or about how much delay you want. You know you've got it right and you can't mess around with it later because you are making a production commitment. As a producer, making that kind of commitment is all part of learning how to do the job.[81]

This points to a preference for a destructive process, a certain amount of option anxiety and a preference for using little processing at mix stage, as well as the clear preference for working inside a self-imposed set of limitations. This method conflicts with the kind of equipment available in 1997, as recording and production technologies presented users with increasing options as a priority consideration. Neither traditional nor technology-driven production process has been implemented on this track. There was no plan or methodology in place prior to the recording and it is this lack of formality that lends the track a spontaneous, chaotic overall feel. This capturing of a band in an organic way – Street, for example, could have decisively mic'd up the drums before recording – was achieved via an unorthodox production set-up. Whilst the RADAR was a current hard disk recording system in 1997, higher specification equipment was freely available –

particularly to high-profile recordists such as Street – not to mention computer software that was fast superseding high-end digital recorders. Yet Street rejected these trends at a time when the recording technology market was swamped with an almost unlimited amount of choice and options, instead maintaining a risk-averse attitude towards his technological choices, as well as working with older technologies:

> My other recent purchase was a Zoom 1901 which has some good lo-fi settings and only cost £99 – last of the big spenders, that's me! And, of course, I have an Akai 3000 sampler that I bought a long time ago and still swear by.[82]

By the late 1990s, Stephen Street had gained the reputation as 'The Britpop producer',[83] a recordist capable of sonically packaging independent music for the commercial mainstream. Yet he rejected the notion of a 'sonic signature', as well as the idea that bands sought him out for a particular 'sound', as he explained in *Under the Radar*:

> My job is to be their [the artist's] soundboard as it were. It's not to really change them or to make them sound like my sound. My view is to get a snapshot of them as they are in that period in their history. Nothing more.[84]

A snapshot is exactly what Street achieved in the recording of 'Song 2' as he settled for guide-track takes. A noisy record with all its performance nuances and imperfections kept in; this is a good example of a *maverick* recording methodology in late 1990s record production. The use of the RADAR was not particularly common in 1997 and Street decided to keep performances most producers would not have accepted as demos. He used aggressive, unorthodox mix techniques, positioning the bass guitar – and a distortion pedal – as the centrepiece of the track. Two drum kits, at least twenty channels worth of signals had they been close mic'ed, were recorded with one microphone and almost no EQ, de-essing or reverb has been added to anything. This record has been *captured* as opposed to recorded or produced and Street's technique, or rather *lack* of technique, has only added to its individuality. Yet 'Song 2' is ultimately a contradictory record when the result is considered against the original intention of recordist and musicians. Whilst spontaneous performances were captured, the use of looping within the RADAR, as well as the considered positioning of vocal and guitar overdubs, points to elements of tech-processual intervention inconsistent with 'pure' performance capture methods. Regardless of the demo and punk aesthetics, 'Song 2' still featured intentionally constructed elements in its production.

MGMT – 'Electric Feel'

This final analysis is to illustrate the prevalence of *maverick methods* beyond the main era in this book; indeed, such methods are noticeable long into the twenty-first century. Taken from the album *Oracular Spectacular*, 'Electric Feel' by US electronic duo MGMT was released in 2007. The track – and album – was produced by US recordist Dave

Fridmann, renowned for his work with US indie artists Mercury Rev, Flaming Lips, Sparklehorse and Mogwai. Since the mid-1990s, Fridmann has gained a reputation for creating heavily textured tracks with wide sonic soundscapes featuring innovative uses of effects processing. However, whilst common traits run through his work, he attributes these to the musicians, as opposed to his own 'sonic signature' as he stated, 'I don't know what my sound is, but I don't mind if I have one. It seems more to me indicative of the bands that I work with more so than anything that I've done to them.'[85] Regardless of Fridmann's claim, his reputation is one of an unorthodox recordist that has continually pushed the boundaries of the technologies he works with. Fridmann works from his own studio, Tarbox Road, situated in New York State. The studio is renowned for its unique mix of technologies – as well as its rural location – and features both Logic and Pro Tools on the Apple platform via an Otari Concept Elite mixer. The studio is built into a large shed, comprising a main recording room and control room. Tarbox Road features an impressive range of technologies and instruments, vintage and new, analogue and digital. Fridmann is renowned for his unorthodox microphone techniques, running vocal signals through home-made distortion boxes and modified radio microphones to achieve sonically unique tracks. His blending of analogue and digital equipment at the turn of the 2000s was a key feature of his recording method, as he stated:

> They're [Otari RADAR, Otari 24 track analogue recorder, Alesis A-DAT, Pro Tools] pretty much all on all the time. There's crazy plug-ins available now that do things that are incomprehensible, effectively breaking the laws of physics because once you've digitised your audio, you can look ahead and back in time and make decisions based upon what's going to happen in the future. So I'll need Pro Tools for a sound like that, and then I'll need the analogue to get this extra overdriven analogue sound, and then I'll need the digital because that track is inherently so quiet that if I put it on the analogue it'll be too noisy. It's all this totally weird bunch of tools to use for different situations.[86]

This amalgamation of analogue and digital technologies demonstrates an open-minded attitude towards recording and production systems; Fridmann views his technologies as tools of the trade and does not express a clear preference for one sonic domain or another. Fridmann applies a 'mix and match' approach to his productions, whereby he chooses the tool most suited for the job in hand. In a similar way to William Orbit, Fridmann has cultivated a unique working practice that is inconsistent with the tech-processual methods of his peers. His main clients are commercially successful US indie bands and many of the albums Fridmann has recorded are renowned for their sonic innovation, particularly The Flaming Lips' *Zaireeka* (1997) and *At War with the Mystics* (2007) and Mogwai's *Deserter's Songs* (1998). Fridmann's records are distinctive in their maximizing of frequency spread and stereo field, thick instrumental textures with the presence of large-scale multitracking and overdubs, as well as heavy use of distortion and reverbs. One commonality of Fridmann's records is the presence of the AKG BX20 reverb, a 1970s boxed spring reverb with controllable decay times. By the mid-2000s, many DAW plug-in reverbs featured spring or spring-like settings. The use of a hardware reverberation unit – particularly the BX20 – was unusual and unorthodox at this time, although it could be argued Fridmann used the BX20 as a 'sonic differentiator': 'This [AKG BX20 spring reverb] is the reverb I use on almost everything. I don't know why, I just like it.'[87] This highlights Fridmann's individualized working practice; however, by the end of the decade, Fridmann admitted to using equipment in deliberately unorthodox ways, as he stated:

> But most of the pieces of gear that I have here at the studio all have some special, strange distortion when you use them wrong, like I have a tendency to do. Every piece of gear I have, no matter how nice and pristine it can be, I've figured out how to fuck it up.[88]

Here, Fridmann describes his deliberate intention to use technologies in ways they were not intended, to extract sounds that are not part of their character and to stretch their sonic capabilities. *Oracular Spectacular* was MGMT's debut album and recorded relatively quickly, as Fridmann stated: 'We did the whole record (*Oracular Spectacular*) in less than 3 weeks.' Fridmann also recognized the musical abilities of MGMT musicians Ben Goldwasser and Andrew VanWyngarden, who in early 2007 had just been signed to Columbia Records:

> They are both great musicians. They can both sing any part and play any part on any instruments ... They were having to deal with the realities of being on a major label. I had to talk to them on many occasions, 'guys, you didn't really think they were just going to give you the money without anything in return, did you?' not that we had to compromise on anything in the recording.[89]

This is a good example of Mike Howlett's 'producer as nexus'[90] with Fridmann taking on a business advisory role to a new artist in addition to production duties.

The intention for *Oracular Spectacular* was to record the duo's tracks, with the knowledge that they were signed to a major label and some of the songs would be aimed at mainstream radio. It is not clear how MGMT came to work with Fridmann on their debut album; as an electronic dance music duo, MGMT did not fit Fridmann's usual indie band clientele.

'Electric Feel' begins with a filter sweep on an analogue synthesiser; it is possible to ascertain this due to the hardware noise accompanying the sound at the very beginning of the track. 'Electric Feel' consists of a rhythmic pattern played on a kick and snare drum with the drums placed in the middle of the mix. A tambourine, which is a key feature throughout the track, is panned aggressively from left to right at the forefront of the mix with a centred bass guitar also foregrounded. An electric guitar playing a repetitive staccato chord is double-tracked and panned hard left and right. There are at least two synthesizers present in the introduction: melodic lines emulating a flute are played on one, which has likely been processed with the 'roomy' spring reverb and centred in the stereo field (referred as 'synth 1'). Additionally, there is a synthesizer playing the same individual note, repetitively and placed hard right. At 0.17 two analogue synthesizers enter: one (referred as 'synth 2') playing a low-frequency, square-wave heavy line along with the bass, centred in the stereo field and positioned to the middle ground of the mix; and the other (referred as 'synth 3') playing a much lighter, contrasting high-frequency rich melody (that of the proceeding verse vocal melody) placed to the background of the mix and positioned centre left. From the outset, the intention has been to 'shape' the recording by maximizing activity in the extremities of the frequency spectrum. By taking full advantage of the subs and high-end ranges on the synthesizers, the 'height' of the track is extended; vocals, drums and guitars do not contain much in these frequency ranges. Additionally, the synthesizer aesthetics emulate the lyrics, particularly 'electricity', 'electric feel' and 'shock me like an electric eel'.

A significant textural change occurs at the point of the first verse (0.31). The guitars, tambourine and synthesizers drop out entirely and the drum pattern changes from a kick and snare pattern into a kick, rack and floor tom 'tribal' roll pattern. Another, lengthy reverb has been applied to the toms, whilst the kick drum is treated with a shorter, 'roomier' reverb. It is possible that both reverbs are the BX20 with altered decay times. The drums and bass guitar stay centred in the stereo field and to the fore/middle ground of the mix. The most significant aspect of this verse – and quite possibly the entire track – is the treatment of the vocals. The lead vocal has had only light compression applied and a particularly lengthy reverb with a large amount of diffusion has been applied; this is almost certainly the BX20. Little EQ appears present and the vocal itself is quite natural. Contrary to standard processing practice, Fridmann has not applied any de-essing to the vocal. Instead, these aspects have been enhanced and foregrounded as a feature. This is unusual in popular music, because for decades recordists have refined skills in controlling 'sss' and 'ttt' sounds with processing; such noises are usually unwanted. In 'Electric Feel', an additional delay has been applied to the lead vocal, emphasizing and extending the time of the 'sss' sounds. This is particularly noticeable throughout the verse on the words 'western', 'to receive', 'saw', 'amazon', 'skin', 'standing' and 'swim'. This is usually an unwanted sound, but here, it is intentional and is a good example of a highly creative use of effects processing. Dave Fridmann is renowned for his use of effects processors, as he explained:

> I'll find a certain processor that's in favour with me for this month, or that period of time, or this record or that record, and then it'll be like 'Oh, I'm sick of that one'. But even with that ridiculous array of gear that's up there, in any given two- or three-month period, it's all gotten used for something. Everything makes an appearance. So I don't feel too bad about all the craziness that's up there. It all finds its way into the mix. There's a bunch of gear up there that only does one thing, but does it well, and if you don't want that, don't even bother trying it out, because it doesn't do anything else. There's so much of it because a lot of it is one-trick pony gear.[91]

Despite Fridmann's collection of technologies – many of which feature limited parameters – his application of them has often resulted in richly layered, dense soundscapes. The lead vocal is double-tracked and panned centre left and centre right, filling out a large space both spatially and through depth of field. Additionally, another parallel vocal is audible hard right to the very background of the mix. This vocal sings the same words and melody in unison with the lead, but has been treated entirely differently with a band-pass filter EQ (a classic 'telephone' effect) and some distortion or 'bit crusher' effect; this is in line with Fridmann's earlier comment about creating unique distortions from usually non-distortion-generating equipment. The 'sss' sound from 'swim' repeat delays over the break at 0.57, where the toms, bass and vocals drop out completely exposing the vocal delay and reverberant tails against the kick drum until the chorus at 1.01. Contrary to the verse, this break is left sparse and texturally 'flat'.

Multiple tracks of vocals have been sequenced in the chorus. It is possible to deduce this as MGMT consists of just two vocalists, so they would have had to record multiple parts and sequence them in order to achieve this 'layered', heavily textured result. 'Synth 2' returns with the same square-wave heavy tone from the introduction, centred and pushed to the very foreground of the mix. Once again, the vocals are the key feature throughout the chorus: the double-tracked lead vocal is positioned centre left and centre right in the stereo field and features the same time-based effects processing treatment as in the verse. Backing vocals also enter on the first lines of every other bar (the time signature is an unusual 6/8): 'ooh girl' and 'baby girl'. The backing vocals are also double-tracked with a particularly lengthy reverb with lots of diffusion applied to each. These are positioned at around '10 to 2' in the stereo field, thus broadening the overall width of the vocal. The chorus is unusually bass-heavy with little apart from the hi-hats occupying the higher end of the spectrum. Again, the 'sss' sounds 'said' and 'shock' are emphasized and repeat with the applied delays across the vocal lines. Another backing vocal, positioned hard right and to the very background of the mix, is treated exactly as in the verse with a band pass EQ effect and a little distortion. The lack of de-essing and the amount of multitracked, reverberant vocals present – as well as their positioning to the fore middle ground in the mix – create an 'underwater', 'swamp-like' atmosphere to the recording. No attempt has been made to pull the lead vocal out to the foreground of the mix. Yet this processing synergizes particularly well with the lyrics. 'Electric Feel' references the Amazon rainforest and swimming, the sea and sea shore; the creation of a 'wet' soundscape positions the vocalists in this environment and thus creates a realistic sense of location.

By the break at 1.30, the drums revert back to the verse kick and tom pattern with the bass continuing. An 'egg shaker' percussion instrument enters and pulls the frequency 'height' of the track up, particularly as it is positioned to the foreground of the mix and centred in the stereo field. 'Synth 3' re-enters, positioned to the middle ground of the mix and centre left in the stereo field. A further synthesizer (referred to as 'synth 4') enters to the fore middle ground of the mix and is repeatedly panned around the stereo field from hard right to centre left and back again. This layering of synthesis has created an extraordinary and unusual sonic soundscape; the maximized stereo field and frequency spread have broadened and heightened the track significantly.

At 1.44, the second verse begins, containing the identical sonic elements to verse 1. Once again, the lead vocal processing emphasizes all 'sss' and 'shh' sounds, which are particularly prominent on 'Eastern', 'shore', 'push', 'circuits', 'sea', 'this is', 'electricity', 'change' and 'electric'. Another break at 2.11, exposing only the kick drum and lead vocal reverberant tails, creates another change in texture with the same 'flattening' effect as at 0.57. However, throughout this break some noise is audible to the background of the mix and hard right, possibly attached to a preceding or proceeding synthesizer. Whilst the sequencing of multiple instruments is evident, it is this type of system noise that is indicative of analogue, particularly vintage analogue equipment.

The egg shaker continues into a new phrase at 2.43, where the snare and hi-hats drop to leave the kick drum isolated. The bass guitar plays a disco-inspired groove in unison with a further synthesizer (referred to as 'synth 5'), with the electric guitar returning centre right and to the middle ground of the mix, accentuating part of the bass groove with repeated 'up chucked' chords. Yet another synthesizer – this time, a mid-range rich pad (referred to as 'synth 6') – is brought in for this phrase, centred in the stereo field and to the foreground of the mix. At the end of each bar, a filter sweep effect is added, by which time it becomes apparent that it is the identical synthesizer and filter effect to that at the very beginning of the recording. At 2.58, the tambourine re-enters, fading in from the background to the foreground of the mix, panned alternately hard left to right. Whilst the track is synth-heavy and features a particularly thick texture throughout, much 'room' has been created from the maximizing of the stereo field, as well as volume automation to create a sense of depth.

A snare roll at 2.58 precedes another key part of the track: at 3.02, the kick, snare, hi-hats, egg shaker and synthesizers drop out, a rhythmic floor tom phrase is positioned to the middle ground of the mix and panned hard right, whilst the flute-emulation 'synth 1' that featured in the introduction returns to the very foreground of the mix. 'Synth 3' also returns, this time placed to the background of the mix and centred in the stereo field. The snare drum re-enters at 3.09, this time with just a short reverb applied. Here, the key feature is the tambourine, which is repeatedly panned aggressively around the stereo field from hard left to right. The result is something similar to a 'Leslie loudspeaker' effect, creating the illusion that the sound is 'spinning' around in a circular motion. This does not, however, sound like a manual panning; it is precision timed to synchronize with the drum rhythm patterns and, therefore, is likely to have been automated within a DAW.

The final section of the recording starts at 3.15 with the sound of a radio being tuned (as well as the associated noise as the dial is moved through the frequency bands) moving from centre left to hard right across the stereo field. This section is particularly dense texturally; 'synth 2' re-enters to the very foreground of the mix, whilst the electric guitar appears, double-tracked and panned hard left and hard right, playing the same staccato repetitive chord as in the introduction. Here, all areas of the mix are filled to their extremities: the stereo field is maximized by the continuing tambourine, the frequency range is at its broadest due to the presence of both the high-frequency rich radio tuning and the low-frequency, square-wave heavy 'synth 2'. Depth of field is also fully utilized with the tambourine kept to the foreground, the vocals and backing vocals returning to the fore middle ground, the bass and kick drum to the middle ground with the radio noise and the electric guitar and 'synth 3' flute emulation to the middle background. At 3.34, the track fades to an eventual silence at 3.50.

'Electric Feel' is a good example of unique recording and production techniques matching the aesthetic direction of the artist and the lyrical content of the song in particular. With 'Electric Feel', Fridmann has created a wholly electronic sounding record complementing the contextual elements of the song. The maximization of both the stereo spread and frequency distribution is consistent with a recording being 'pushed' by the technology used to create it. In this case, neither traditional nor technology-driven methods have been implemented; Fridmann's production set-up featuring a mix of analogue and digital, vintage and current systems, is a unique blend of production technologies. The result is a track that sounded like nothing else of its era, a sonically unique creation that 'stood out' in the context of late 2000s commercial dance music. His affirmation at being an artist-led producer – that being working to achieve what the artist has in mind as opposed to intentionally applying a sonic signature – is inconsistent with his results; a Dave Fridmann record is distinctive in its heavy, thick textural make-up, its unusual reverbs and distortion and foregrounding of technological intervention.

Conclusion

The introduction of sound recording in the late nineteenth century and the development of multitrack tape recording in the twentieth century have been rightly cited as key turning points in the history of music.[1] The nexus of technology, recordists and processes on the cusp of the digital age was another critical moment, not least because of the transformative effect on popular music. In 1969, Theodor Adorno stated, 'In the history of technology, it is not all that rare for technological inventions to gain significance long after their inception.'[2] Whilst Adorno was a theorist notorious for his critiques of popular musics and culture, his understanding of the significance of technology is key and relevant to this study, which illuminates the applications of technological precursors and the 'vintage' to contemporary recording. Whilst Timothy Taylor's assertion that digital technology was the most fundamental change in music since the advent of Western notation does not acknowledge the introduction of sound recording, his recognition of this pivotal point in music history is right. As discussed in this book, the advent of digital technologies at the turn of the 1980s converged existing – and created new – recording and production roles, shifted recording practices and forever altered the sonic soundscape of contemporary popular music. Indeed, these are the key findings of this book:

- Digital music and sound recording technologies at the turn of the 1980s did not replace analogue systems overnight; rather, such technologies were integrated into existing recording workplaces resulting in two decades of technological hybridity in popular music recording and production.
- The aforementioned, changing technological landscape greatly impacted on recordists of the era and as such their wide range of responses and attitudes affected the extent to which technologies were adopted and integrated into recording and production sessions.
- Conflations of this technological hybridity and myriad recordist attitudes are evidenced and imbued in many commercial and independent popular music recordings of the era.

One of the most important conclusions to be drawn from this book concerns the conflation of analogue and digital technologies in 1980s and 1990s commercial record production. The advent of digital audio recording and production technologies did not change working practices overnight. On the contrary, more than two decades on at the turn of the millennium, commercial record production existing wholly in the digital domain was still a rarity, with many recording facilities and recordists integrating a blend of analogue and digital tools into their working practices. Not only is this technological conflation evidenced through dozens of wide-ranging recording examples across two decades of record production, but it also appears irrespective of musical genre, independent or major record label association or locality. The manifestation of digital audio in – and the widespread consumer adoption of – the CD format may have skewed perceptions of its prevalence; the consolidation of then new popular music recordings in these shiny new discs obscured multiplex tech-processual practices behind them, as Jonathan Crary pointed out in *Capital Effects*:

> Within the schema of the CD format the perceptual experience of the music is transformed in ways that have nothing to do with audio technology. … one is impelled to listen, beyond the music, for the sound of the product's own justification, for the confirmation that the CD represents authentic 'progress', the elusive evidence that in some way it 'sounds better'.[3]

The complex issues surrounding the study of music and technology have been debated for some time, yet binary frameworks including 'deterministic–pessimistic', 'perfection–imperfection', 'analogue–digital', 'new–old' allude to a discourse focused on extremities as opposed to middle ground,[4] which is partly what this book has sought to address. Beadle alluded to technological renewal in *Will Pop Eat Itself?* suggesting, 'There comes a time in all artistic fields where the tradition of the past weighs so heavily that the only way forward seems to be "rip it up and start again"'.[5] Yet these attitudes were by no means evident amongst the recordists surveyed: very few recordists working in this era suggested such a dramatic approach to adopting new technologies. Christoph Cox argued for the fluid nature of music technology and usage in *Audio Culture* suggesting, 'Music technologies are constantly reappropriated and redirected to ends other than those originally intended.'[6] Cox's statement is certainly more flexible and attributes implementations of music technologies as part of a continuum that includes the pushing of technological boundaries, as opposed to technological usage within strict binary frameworks. In *Analogue Sound in the Age of Digital Tools*, Barlindhaug comments on Bolter and Grusin's theory of 'remediation': that new digital medias 'compete' with their older, analogue counterparts, attempting to replace them by being seen as an improvement. Barlindhaug suggests Bolter and Grusin's theory cannot be applied to music technology as easily as other media, such as journalism:

> In music production, the relationship between new and old media is of a different kind. Software exists alongside its older analogue counterparts, in a relationship much more complex than that of the metaphors and remediations we find in consumer media. These evolutionary contradictions in contemporary electronic music production are to a great extent a result of technology's role in musical aesthetics.[7]

Barlindhaug is absolutely right. However, as evidenced in this book, this complex relationship between old and new media is apparent far beyond electronic music production, across a much greater set of technologies and spanning a broader era.

Every music recording and production process features some degree of technological intervention and decision-making processes on the part of a recordist, whether that individual is the musician or part of a large production team. In writing this book, I hope to have foregrounded the ways in which the sound of recording and production technologies are imbued in popular music recordings and as such are sonically discernible facets of the overall record, equally as much – and in many instances *more so* – than musical elements, instruments and performances. Additionally, recordist agency is a crucial and understudied factor in popular music studies – and in the few phonomusicological analyses focused on extramusical parameters, recordist agency is still largely excluded from the discussion. As the once-concealed tools and techniques of sound recording and (re)production have been slowly demythologized and revealed,[8] it is possible not only to appreciate the impact of recordists but also to illuminate the vast contributions they have made to the history of recorded popular music. Indeed, as Zak suggests, if we expand our musicological horizons above and beyond a 'de facto hierarchy of musical expression',[9] it is possible to elucidate the sonically discernible impact of sound recording technologies and processes on what is eventually heard. The *maverick methods* described in this book are not simply tech-processual means to ends; rather they are foregrounded to the extent that they imbue a sonic identity into a recording that extends beyond orchestration, performance and musicality. Bob Davis described the sonic signature as 'the *potential* for a sound to carry the *identity* of an individual'.[10] Through the examples in this book, such sonic identities are foregrounded, discernible and utterly integral to popular music recordings regardless of genre, artist age or gender, major or independent label or even geographical locality. In some instances, a continuum of sonic aesthetics can be traced through the work of multiple recordists and into a pantheon of techniques – for example, the work of John Loder, Harvey Birrell and Steve Albini is linked by Southern Studios and the construction of an underground punk sonic signature.[11] It is, however, worth noting that rarely do recordists refer to possessing a 'sonic signature' of their own. In the cases of Dave Fridmann and Stephen Street, for example, both stated they did not believe their work exemplified a sonic signature. Yet such sonic identities are a natural result of the repeated implementation of an individual 'tried and tested' set of tech-processual practices.

The era of 1978 through 2000 was a diverse, complex and fascinating time in the continuum of record production, not least due to the proliferation of the digital music technologies that are ubiquitous today. Utopian attitudes towards a new, digital era in music production were clearly embodied in the music of the time, compounded by the realization of then hi-fidelity digital audio in the expensive CD, which was unable to compete with vinyl and cassette at first, but ubiquitous by the turn of the 1990s. This technological utopia was also bound up in exclusivity, expense and decadence aesthetics at the turn of the 1980s.[12] Whilst the Fairlight CMI and Synclavier, like sports cars and mansions, were popular music's very own symbols of economic power, dominance and excess, they were also transformative machines that to some threatened musical tradition. Such aesthetics manifested in the sonic sheen of some of Trevor Horn's cutting-edge productions as well as SAW's 'factory' utilitarianism. Additionally, new initiatives including the SPARS code and new techniques such as Bruce Swedien's 'Acusonic' process epitomized the tech-utopianism surrounding digital audio. The aspiration to achieve such exclusive heights of commercial success was embodied in more accessible, cheaper, sound-a-like systems based on digital sampling, synthesis and sequencing, which – as Théberge has documented – resulted in a new era of music technology consumption.[13] That is not to say that all reactions to new technologies were positive. The negativity surrounding new computer-oriented composition and production processes stemmed from perceptions that programmed music would adversely affect the livelihoods of musicians.[14] Synth-pop artists including the Pet Shop Boys addressed this in the mid-1980s by performing live with computer-based music technologies and synthesizers – something that was normalized by the 1990s.

By the late 1980s and into the 1990s, an increasingly accessible set of music recording and production technologies was available both new and second-hand. To a certain extent, applications of technological precursors are entirely natural; as time passes and more technologies are surpassed, so exists a greater pool of accessible technologies from which to draw. This, to some degree, explains the technological hybridity present in recording and production processes of the era.

Until the 1980s, various instances of recordists' 'pushing the boundaries' with technology and technique have been noted: from Sam Phillips' development of slap-back echo[15] to George Martin's use of multiple tape machines.[16] From Les Paul's use of an additional Ampex tape head[17] to Kraftwerk's drum machine construction,[18] the decades leading up to the 1980s witnessed many recordists' 'one step ahead' of available technologies, pushing the boundaries of technological limitations to create new sounds and implement innovative techniques. The vast spectacle of technological development that ensued at the turn of – and into – the 1980s, as well as its fusing with established tools and techniques, heavily impacted not only on recordists and their working practices but also on the wider audio and music industries. This cannot be attributed only to a move away from the analogue domain and towards the digital. The advent of digital audio, coupled with the musical and recording functionality of MIDI, undoubtedly opened up the prospect of record production to a greater number of people, as scholars such as Paul Théberge have revealed through comprehensive works.[19] However, the professional industry failed to recognize the consequences of this widespread technological dissemination.[20] It is arguable whether the so-called 'democratization of technology' as described by science and technology and philosophy scholars including Andrew Feenberg[21] and Tyler Veak[22] manifested in the recording industry as reality or perception; though new budget digital technologies were aimed at the semi-professional, amateur, musician and enthusiast markets, serious challenges presented by members of these groups to the commercial recording industry were few.[23] Additionally, whilst technology may have become more accessible in the late 1980s, the necessary operational skill sets had not. This is a critical factor when considering the 'democratization of technology' during this era and beyond: access to – and ownership of – the tools of the recording and production trade certainly resulted in more musicians and DJs self-producing commercial releases, but possession of technology alone was not enough to challenge the commercial recording industry. Indeed, this era witnessed the emergence and proliferation of an entirely new music recording and production 'enthusiast' consumer.[24] Incidentally, professional recordists also appeared immune to the aggressive marketing strategies employed by audio technology manufacturers; the new, 'enthusiast' market was their key target.[25]

What *is* evident through studying this era of recording and production practice is a slow demythologization of recording techniques and as a result a power shift away from professional recordists and the wider, professional recording industry. Andrew Leyshon recognized the mid-1990s as an era when 'economic crisis began to emerge within the recording studio sector'.[26] Leyshon indicates a correlation between the rise of software programs such as Pro Tools and the decline of recording budgets as two significant factors impacting on the decline of the recording studio sector. Whilst industry uptake of computer-based software steadily increased through the 1990s, this does not fully explain the impact of digital technologies on the recording industry. As discussed in Chapter 3, the apparently winning combination of Apple computers and Pro Tools software did not result in commercial hit singles until the turn of the 2000s. The decline of the traditional recording studio can be traced much further back to the 1980s: the advent of MIDI, the empowerment of musicians with home recording and production technologies and the resulting reductions in workplace costs. In my ethnographic work, many recordists and audio industry professionals recognized the manifestation of MIDI technologies in musicians' home studios as impacting the professional recording industry from an economic, as opposed to a creative, perspective. Steve Culnane suggested of the late 1980s:

> The A&R departments – with the advent of home studios – started expecting far more from the demos, to the point where they were nearly finished and all they had to do was go to the mastering room for a slight bit of compression and a slight bit of EQ.[27]

This recognition of a greater portion of the production process occurring at 'demo' stage was fully realized in many dance and hip-hop records of the era – in the UK and the United States – as the earlier Warren G example illustrated.[28] During the late 1980s and at the turn of the 1990s, the UK and US charts featured a majority of singles made in professional and independent recording studios, and a minority in home studios and bedrooms.[29] Whilst Leyshon rightly situates Pro Tools as impacting the decline of the traditional recording studio in the 1990s, this only compounded – and possibly increased – the speed of the decline, which was already evident and well underway in the late 1980s. In fact, a key factor in the development of musicians' home and project studios was the far-reaching accessibility and affordability of the ADAT through the 1990s, which resulted in many commercial record releases preceding Pro Tools.

Such fundamental, technological shifts occurring during this era had more to do with the adoption, integration and synchronicity of new systems into then established workplaces, workflows and tech-processual practices. Abbey Road's 1980 'Sale of the Century'[30] presents an exception, in that it was one of very few workplaces of the era that took an 'out with the old, in with the new' approach, selling off their 'old' equipment and transforming their workflow in a relatively short period of time. For many workplaces and recordists, the transition from mechanical to computer-based technologies took much longer,[31] due in part to financial constraints, and resulting in a wide array of hybrid working practices. This tech-processual hybridity was the reality of many 1980s and 1990s recording workplaces and as such presented a unique set of conditions for recordists of the era. Sometimes, a blend of cutting-edge and vintage technologies were applied to the same session, such as Soul II Soul's *Club Classics Vol. I*. The result of this hybridity manifested in an extraordinary – and quite possibly never-to-be-repeated – range of era-defining popular music recordings representing a multitude of genre and style, which not only consolidated traditional popular music forms but also sonically shaped emergent ones. The same might be said of any era of recorded music and the diversity of recordings made within it, but the two decades of practice covered in this book highlight a unique, transitionary period of tech-processual hybridity not evident in the eras preceding nor, arguably, proceeding it. Like all eras in sound recording history, individual recordists operated at a certain point in time. During the 1980s and 1990s, recordists who had experienced the workplaces, technologies and techniques of the 1960s and 1970s were adapting to a diversification of skill sets and the influx of new digital systems to the recording industry. Simultaneously, new recordists began working during this era with no knowledge of 'how things were'. To some extent, this explains the variation in recordist responses and attitudes during the era, but evidently, there is far more at play than simply age. In tracing the volume and speed of technological development in this era, we begin to understand the myriad responses to a changing technological landscape and the de facto blurring of analogue and digital tools so integral to working practices. This technological hybridity is evident in the combinations of systems applied to sessions and, therefore, can be traced through many recordings of the era: William Orbit's winning combination of analogue synthesis and digital sample sequencing on Madonna's 'Ray of Light'; Flood and Howie B's sampling and MIDI programming of acoustic and electronic instruments coupled with a vintage, analogue mixing console 'performance' on U2's 'Mofo'; Fatboy Slim's foregrounding of vinyl aesthetics and the construction of live performance in 'Praise You'; and Stephen Street's live drum loop formations within the Otari RADAR hard disk recorder on Blur's 'Song 2' are four explicit examples of sonically discernible technological hybridity in 1990s commercial record production. Flood sums this up perfectly:

> It's strange; I like both extremes (analogue and digital) for different purposes. All the vintage stuff there is old synths, which have great sounds. But I love high-end digital effects so my whole thing is based on flip-flopping between old and new and getting the best of both worlds. In the last ten years we've had this 'old is bad, new is good' attitude and it's only now that people are starting to realise, there might have been a reason why something worked its way through for 30 years and why people were doing it like that.[32]

Perhaps it is unsurprising that the predominantly digital technological acceleration of the 1980s and 1990s had a divisive effect, with many members of the recording industry expressing scepticism or pessimism and others embracing and anticipating the developments. Whilst such 'black-and-white' recordist attitudes may have related to age and time already spent working in the industry, as well as the steep learning curves associated with new technologies, there is evidence to suggest that such attitudes *were* split broadly along the lines of the analogue–digital binary. This is noted in scholarly discourse by Cunningham,[33] Durant[34] and Bennett,[35] but it is unhelpful at best to frame the range of 1980s and 1990s production modalities within the confines of these polar parameters; the situation was far more complex, as the recordist attitudinal matrix depicts. Moreover, the more revealing results exist in the intersection of these two points, in the mass of 'grey area' where extraordinarily rich and diverse tech-processual practices – *maverick methods* – are not only evident but inextricably embedded in some of the most successful popular music recordings of the era. To that end, it is not possible to ascertain or indeed advocate for the existence of 'standard practice' or 'industry standard' production modalities: contemporary record production of the 1980s and 1990s was individualistic, technologically convoluted and processually diverse. In fact, the presence of patterns and commonalities traced in the tech-processual practice of the era is found not amongst working practices per se, but in the attitudes of recordists towards a transmuting technological landscape. This attitudinal matrix is, therefore, intended as a starting point for further discussion as opposed to a rigid framework and is certainly not essentialist. These are illustrations of patterns evident in the attitudes of recordists across two decades of tech-processual practice. Correlating primary and secondary research sources resulted in a range of evident attitudes, which can be broadly plotted along the traditionalist–technophiliac and positive–negative axes. It is, however, important to note the flexibility of this matrix and that recordist attitudes rarely fit neatly or exactly into one area of it and, indeed, attitudes were found to exist as spanning more than one area, as well as shifting with time. This matrix intends to add to the discourse of recordist agency in its depiction of broad recordist standpoints across two decades of music recording and production history. Risk aversion, rebellion and ignorance often fuse with scepticism, emphasized creativity and nonchalance. Indeed, these views are often complex, sometimes even contradictory. A common theme is that recordists do not view technology within 'analogue–digital' paradigms, nor from linear, historical perspectives, as Flood's quote exemplifies. Moreover, during the 1980s and 1990s, many recordists selected both then new and historical technologies equally and synchronically. Chris Cutler's consideration of new applications of old technologies goes some way in explaining this, as he suggested:

> Applications of a new technology to art are often first inspired by existing art paradigms, frequently simplifying or developing existing procedures. Then new ideas emerge that more directly engage the technology for itself. These arise as a product of use, accident, experiment or cross-fertilisation – but always through hands on interaction. New applications then feed back into new uses of the old technologies and so on.[36]

Indeed, recordists' musical intentions were often bound up with their attitudes towards technology. Whilst Hamilton's acknowledging of the 'perfect–imperfect' binary[37] is an evident production aesthetic, perhaps it was more apparent in the 1970s when emergent 'record construction' approaches proliferated as then current, sonically discernible alternatives to transparent, 'performance capture' intentions. The recordists featured in this book strived to achieve neither 'perfect' nor 'imperfect' results, moreover technologies were largely implemented as tools, in most cases as a 'means to an end' regardless of their place in history, cultural significance, cost or technical specification. In fact, recordists rarely mentioned recording processes or intentions in the context of a perfection–imperfection binary. Rather, features such as usability, creative potential and simplicity were evidenced as being important factors in technological decision making. Whilst nostalgia and sentimentality, as well as technological iconicity,[38] is evident amongst recordists of the era, decisions to implement technological anachronisms in modern recording techniques cannot be attributed to such emotional factors alone.

Throughout the history of sound recording and production, recognized practitioners have often followed 'standard' engineering and production practices, but so too have individuals been known to 'push the boundaries' of technology. To date, most studies of such tech-processual outliers have often been confined to 1960s practitioners and in writing this book, it is hoped the equal contribution made by contemporary recordists to popular music has been asserted. For we hear in the recorded popular music of the 1980s and 1990s extraordinary variations on recording practice, the aurally discernible range of recordists' sonic signatures, as well as evidence of diverse technological implementation. In many instances, tech-processual unorthodoxies – as correlated with recordist attitudes in the centre of the attitudinal matrix – often manifest in the spatial extremities of mixes, in the rough edges and noisy moments, devoid of the production conservatism so associated with traditionalist or technology-driven recording. Nostalgia, technophobia or sentimentalism cannot explain such unorthodoxies; rather, it is the knowledge that music production technologies are creative and musical tools in themselves, which in some cases prompts innovative and individualistic (re)interpretation of their intended purposes. It is quite probable that tech-processual unorthodoxies are simply more reported, revered, documented than their 'business as usual' counterparts – that is certainly the case with this book. Even if that is the case, it is still worth consolidating them as evident and important through popular music history.

To that end, another key finding in this book is the way in which technologies, recordists and commercial recording practices appear to be documented in a parallel historiography: one trajectory that depicts and promotes a largely scientific development-oriented history with an aligning audio engineering pedagogy and set(s) of so-called 'standard' practices; and another that both glorifies and canonizes individuals and examples of their tech-processual unorthodoxies, their *maverick methodologies*. With this in mind, the continuum of historical recording practice as being inextricably linked with popular music recording needs to be asserted in both popular music and audio engineering pedagogy.

Another key conclusion concerns the sonically discernible presence of the featured sound recording and production technologies and techniques on what is eventually heard in final master recordings. In this book, I have focused on then new technologies of the 1980s and 1990s, acknowledged the enduring presence of then technological precursors and the 'vintage', as well as advocated for recordist agency throughout. This serves as a key contextual framework in which to situate the analyses: by understanding the detailed and complex technological climate of the era, as well as mapping recordist responses to it, we better understand the reflections of *maverick methods* as heard in recordings. Furthermore, patterns are elucidated and more informed conclusions can be drawn from the analytical data when it is framed in historical and technical contexts.

Conflating technology and process as major factors influencing recorded music, incorporating and then applying them as a tech-processual analytical methodology goes a long way in elucidating the 'sound of technology' and the 'sound of the recordist' in a musical recording. However, the method does not exist in and of itself and relies upon contextual 'scaffolding'. This methodology is not designed to illustrate tech-processual attributes as separate to – or disconnected from – musical or even lyrical material present in a recording; these components are inextricable. Moreover, this methodology is designed to *illuminate*, to shine a light that reflects a set of previously understudied and less historically foregrounded aspects of a recording. Technologies and recordists have affected recordings to a great extent throughout the era covered in this book, yet understandings and interpretations of such affects have been slow to materialize in popular music studies and musicology. Having devised a tech-processual methodology for analysing popular music recordings, aspects such as volume, multitracking and orchestration, overdubbing, time- and dynamics-based effects processing, frequency distribution and spatial positioning can be acknowledged as major influencing factors on the overall sonic aesthetics of a recording. The inextricable nature of music and production is recognized and as such we can better understand and balance the relevance and effects of production processes on sound recordings by focusing *less* on musical elements and *more* on uses of technology and application of technique. Indeed, by using such a production-centred framework to conduct analyses for this book, the resulting similarities and differences between traditionalist and technology-driven positive and negative tech-processual attitudes are exemplified. From the largely 'performance capture' approaches used by Eno, Lanois, Morris and Costey as well as Albini to the 'record making', new technology-focused techniques of Lange, Absolute and others including SAW, the resulting sonic aesthetics imbued in their recordings mirror the musical, instrumental and performance aesthetics present. It is intended that by building on the work of Tagg,[39] Warner[40] and Dockwray and Moore,[41] this methodology broadens the scope of popular music analysis. Extending music-focused analytical models to include recognizable production tropes adds significant depth to our understandings of recordings. There is of course great potential in using this methodology in conjunction with musical-oriented models, such as those by Everett,[42] Covach[43] and Moore,[44] as well as employing this model in group-oriented analytical work, such as that by von Appen, Doehring, Helms and Moore.[45]

The analyses of six modern records in Chapter 7 exemplify technological unorthodoxies and *maverick methods*. These two decades of extraordinary technological change and workplace flux witnessed the transformation of the recording and production role. To that end, using four well-known, late 1990s tracks as analytical material exemplifies tech-processual practices of the era and allows us to recognize and understand the extent of technological hybridity and recordist agency embedded in the recording. We hear conflations of analogue and digital technologies brought to the fore in Madonna's 'Ray of Light' and U2's 'Mofo', and the use of vintage technologies to mirror the aesthetics of new digital sampling devices in Beastie Boys' 'Fight for Your Right'. In records such as Fatboy Slim's 'Praise You' we hear the enduring resonance of vinyl foregrounded in a dominant digital music era.

What these analyses also reveal is the extent to which the workplace – the 'studio' – is fully realized as compositional tool. In all these examples, we hear the role of technology foregrounded in the compositional process: the use of the console as sequencer in Beastie Boys' 'Fight for Your Right'; the cut-and-paste, sample/sequence reconfiguration of musical performances in both U2's 'Mofo' and Madonna's 'Ray of Light'; the hard-disk-based composition of foundational, rhythmic loops in Blur's 'Song 2'; the technological and temporal adaptation of existing recorded music samples in the construction of Fatboy Slim's 'Praise You'; and the heavy, textural blend of multiple effects processors to fabricate an alternate sonic environment for MGMT's 'Electric Feel'. All these tracks relied heavily – *entirely* – on the sound recording and production technologies used to produce them.

Despite the capability of sophisticated new technologies to construct recordings from existing sound sources – evident in much sample-collage hip-hop in the late 1980s – live performance aesthetics are embodied in digital era recordings in myriad ways, and it is clear from the analyses that these performances cannot be construed as 'perfection': Damon Albarn's 'woo hoo' demo vocal placeholders in 'Song 2', for example, were kept by recordist Stephen Street.

In Beastie Boys' 'Fight for Your Right', we hear Rick Rubin and Steve Ett's classic rock production on an emergent rap track – the illusion of continual performances that have in fact been compiled from loops. The influence of sound recording and production technologies on songwriting processes resulted in a multitude of intertextual forms. Plenty is documented about remixing[46] and sample-collage techniques in hip-hop and dance musics, yet there is plenty of work still to do on multi-intertextual form; Madonna's 'Ray of Light' is a classic example of a reimagined cover version imbued with the sonic signature of the recordist. William Orbit's trademark identity of analogue synthesis-laden textures, two-note rhythms and Cubase-constructed loops is foregrounded. Orbit admitted his preferred equipment was retrograde and at the time was disengaged from then new technological developments. Yet it was this nonchalant attitude that positioned him as a tech-processual outlier: a maverick recordist with a highly sought-after sonic signature.[47] In the wider context of 1990s dance music, Orbit's sound was unique. The composition and production are inextricable, which also reflect the confluence and diversification of recording and production roles and skill sets by the late 1990s, but Cook's methods – and those of others, including Liam Howlett – did not conform to the glossy precision of their dance music peers. In Howlett's case, the foregrounding of analogue tape effects processing with 8-bit synthesis was integral to the commercially successful sound of The Prodigy's 'Firestarter'. This combination of analogue tape effects with digital systems was a winning formula for Flood and Howie B on U2's 'Mofo'; the construction of 'live' performances from sampled snippets created the illusion of performance, an altogether different performance aesthetics indicative of a sonic continuum from 1960s 'constructed' recordings – what Moorefield called 'the illusion of reality'.[48] Similarly, Stephen Street's use of the Otari RADAR to chop up and loop drum performances whilst keeping 'demo' aesthetics highlights a spontaneous approach and fast decision-making: Street's emphasis on commitment, option anxiety and working within self-defined limitations are present in the tech-processual attributes of 'Song 2'. The track is also a good example of underground and alternative music aesthetics brought into the commercial mainstream. The contrasting processes in 'Mofo' and 'Song 2' highlight tech-processual unorthodoxies existing within the extremities of time. In tracks such as 'Praise You', the musical elements are secondary concerns; the precision, quantized tempos and melody lines integral to dance musics of the era do not feature. Instead, pitching issues occur where piano loops have been time stretched: Cook's out-of-tune and out-of-time components are attributable to his intentional *avoidance* of 'liveness' or 'reality'.[49] 'Praise You' is, therefore, a good example of modern record construction where the studio is compositional tool, the songwriter is composer is recordist and where the musical aesthetics are compromised for the overall benefit of the final product – the record.

Having contextualized music and sound recording technologies through the 1980s and 1990s, as well as analysing recordist attitudes, a continuum of technological and processual unorthodoxies in sound recording far beyond the 1960s is elucidated. We hear the innovative techniques and practices of recordists working in a new digital era: the conflations of new and past technologies and recording philosophies imbued in a great range of commercial and independent popular music. New correlations are drawn between historical sound recording practice, new digital technologies, the music and audio industry response and, critically, the manifestation of these matters in recordings. I hope this book encourages others to blend issues present in popular musicology, popular music studies, history and audio engineering; the site of record production in wider academia is a fascinating, interdisciplinary one with plenty of opportunities for further studies. I have only scratched the surface in terms of the research potential in this area; there are so many unexplored lines of enquiry still waiting to investigate, which positions wider phonomusicology as a key area of popular music discourse long into the future.

Notes

Introduction

1. Phillip Tagg, 'Analysing Popular Music – Theory, Method and Practice', *Popular Music* 2 (1982): pp. 37–67; and *Music's Meanings* (MMMSP e-Books, 2013). http://tagg.org/mmmsp/publications.html (Accessed January 2018).
2. Allan Moore, *Song Means* (Farnham: Ashgate, 2012).
3. David Machin, *Analyzing Popular Music* (London: Sage, 2010).
4. Walter Everett, *The Foundations of Rock* (Oxford: Oxford University Press, 2008).
5. Mark Butler, *Unlocking the Groove: Rhythm, Meter and Musical Design in Electronic Dance Music* (Bloomington: Indiana University Press, 2006).
6. Anne Danielsen, *Musical Rhythm in the Age of Digital Reproduction* (Farnham: Ashgate, 2010).
7. John Covach and Graeme M. Boone, *Understanding Rock* (Oxford: Oxford University Press, 2006); John Covach and Mark Spicer, *Sounding Out Pop: Analytical Essays in Popular Music* (Ann Arbour: University of Michigan Press, 2010).
8. Sheila Whiteley, *Sexing the Groove: Popular Music and Gender* (London: Routledge, 1997).
9. Lori Burns and Melisse LaFrance, *Disruptive Divas, Feminism, Identity and Popular Music* (New York: Routledge, 2002).
10. Timothy Warner, *Pop Music, Technology and Creativity: Trevor Horn and the Digital Revolution* (Farnham: Ashgate, 2003), p. 33.
11. Allan Moore, *Rock: The Primary Text*, 2nd ed. (Aldershot: Ashgate, 2001), p. 120.
12. Stephen Cottrell, 'The Rise and Rise of Phonomusicology', in *Recorded Music: Performance, Culture and Technology*, ed. Amanda Bayley (Cambridge: Cambridge University Press, 2010), pp. 15–36.
13. Samantha Bennett, 'Never Mind the Bollocks … A Tech-Processual Analysis', *Popular Music and Society* 38, no. 4 (2015): pp. 466–486.
14. Richard James Burgess, *The History of Music Production* (Oxford: Oxford University Press, 2014).
15. Charlie Gil Gillett, 'The Producer as Artist', in *The Phonograph and Our Musical Life*, ISAM Monograph, No. 14, ed. H. W. Hitchcock (New York: City University, 1977), pp. 51–56.
16. *Popular Music and Society* 14, no. 1 (1990).
17. Steve Jones, 'Technology and the Future of Popular Music', *Popular Music & Society* 14, no. 1 (1990): pp. 19–23.
18. Jari Muikku, 'On the Role and Tasks of a Record Producer', *Popular Music & Society* 14, no. 1 (1990): pp. 25–33.
19. Jeremy Beadle, *Will Pop Eat Itself? – Pop Music in the Soundbite Era* (London: Faber & Faber, 1993).
20. Paul Théberge, *Any Sound You Can Imagine: Making Music/Consuming Technology* (Hanover: Wesleyan University Press, 1997).

21 Mark Katz, *Capturing Sound: How Technology Has Changed Music* (Berkeley and London: University of California Press, 2004).
22 Warner, *Pop Music, Technology and Creativity*.
23 Albin J. Zak III, *The Poetics of Rock: Cutting Tracks, Making Records* (California: University of California Press, 2001).
24 James P. Kraft, *Stage to Studio: Musicians and the Sound Revolution, 1890–1950* (Baltimore, MD: The Johns Hopkins University Press, 1996).
25 Ibid.
26 Susan Schmidt Horning, *Chasing Sound: Technology, Culture & the Art of Studio Recording from Edison to the LP* (Baltimore, MD: The Johns Hopkins University Press, 2012).
27 Simon Zagorski-Thomas, *A Musicology of Record Production* (Cambridge: Cambridge University Press, 2014).
28 Further information on *The Art of Record Production* forum – of which Zagorski Thomas is a founder – is found at www.artofrecordproduction.com.
29 Paul D. Greene and Thomas Porcello, *Wired for Sound: Engineering and Technologies in Sonic Cultures* (Middletown, CT: Wesleyan University Press, 2004).
30 Samantha Bennett and Eliot Bates, eds, *Critical Approaches to the Production of Music and Sound* (London and New York: Bloomsbury Academic, 2018).
31 Dave Grohl, J. Rota and J. Ramsay, *Sound City* (Roswell Films Ltd., 2013).
32 Stevie Nicks, in ibid.
33 Alan Williams, 'Pay Some Attention to the Man Behind the Curtain – Unsung Heroes and the Canonization of Process in the Classic Albums Documentary Series', *Journal of Popular Music Studies* 22, no. 2 (2010): pp. 166–175.
34 The series features documentaries on albums including Bob Marley and the Wailers' *Catch a Fire*, Sex Pistols' *Never Mind the Bollocks … Here's the Sex Pistols* and U2's *The Joshua Tree*.
35 *Classic Albums, Never Mind the Bollocks … Here's the Sex Pistols*. 2002.
36 Liam Watson, *Interview with the author*, 2012.
37 *Classic Albums Black Sabbath Paranoid*, 2010. Directed by Matthew Longfellow. DVD. New York: Red.
38 This can be found in the documentary at 35.12.
39 Dr Dre (1965–) is a US rapper, producer and entrepreneur best known formerly as a member of US rap group NWA, later as a producer for *Snoop Dogg and Eminem* and currently as a producer and founder of Beats by Dre headphones.
40 Phil Ramone (1934–2013) was a South African/US record producer and composer best known for his work with Billy Joel and Frank Sinatra.
41 Sylvia Massy is a US record producer, engineer and recording studio owner best known for her work with Tool, System of a Down and Green Jelly.
42 Brian Eno (1948–) is a musician, producer and artist, best known as synthesist in Roxy Music, his collaborations with David Byrne of Talking Heads and producer of rock bands U2 and Coldplay.
43 Tim Simenon (1967–) is a musician, DJ, producer and remix engineer, and founding member of UK dance act Bomb the Bass.
44 John Loder (1946–2005) was a recording engineer, owner of Southern Studios and owner of Southern Records. He was best known for his work with Crass and The Jesus and Mary Chain.
45 Liam Howlett (1971–) is a producer, programmer and recordist, and founding member of UK big beat/drum n' bass act The Prodigy.

46 Paula Wolfe, 'A Studio of One's Own', *Journal on the Art of Record Production* 7 (2014) [Online], http://arpjournal.com/a-studio-of-one%e2%80%99s-own-music-production-technology-and-gender/ (Accessed January 2018).
47 Zagorski-Thomas, *A Musicology of Record Production*.
48 Mark Savage, 'Why Are Female Record Producers So Rare?' *BBC*, 29 August 2012 [Online], http://www.bbc.com/news/entertainment-arts-19284058 (Accessed January 2018).
49 Steve Haruch, 'Women Account for Less Than 5 Percent of Producers and Engineers – But Maybe Not for Long', *Nashville Scene*, 3 June 2010, http://www.nashvillescene.com/nashville/women-account-for-less-than-5-percent-of-producers-and-engineers-andmdash-but-maybe-not-for-long/Content?oid=1597594 (Accessed September 2015)
50 Timothy Taylor, *Strange Sounds: Music, Technology and Culture* (London and New York: Routledge, 2001), p. 3.
51 Ibid.
52 David Morton, *Sound Recording – The Life Story of a Technology* (Westport, CT: Greenwood Press, 2004).
53 Katz, *Capturing Sound: How Technology Has Changed Music*.
54 Mark Cunningham, *Good Vibrations* (London: Sanctuary Music Publishing, 1998).
55 Greg Milner, *Perfecting Sound Forever: The Story of Recorded Music* (London: Granta Publications, 2009).
56 CD or compact disc is a digital, optical disc format developed by Sony and Phillips individually in the late 1970s and brought to the market as a joint venture in 1982. The CD format was 2-channel, 16-bit with 44.1 KHz sampling rate. The CD became a successful consumer format. Further information and a comprehensive technical specification can be found in Jan Maes and Marc Vercammen, eds, *Digital Audio Technology: A Guide to CD, MINI-DISC, SACD, DVD (A), MP3, DAT* (Oxford: Focal Press, 2001).
57 Musical Instrument Digital Interface. A comprehensive technical specification can be found in Francis Rumsey, *MIDI Systems and Control*, 2nd ed. (Oxford: Focal Press, 1994).
58 The Sony DASH (Digital Audio Stationary Head) machine was released in 1984. The tape recorder was available in 2-track, 24-track and later, 48-track models with a switchable sample rate between 44.1 and 48 KHz. The open-reel tape transport mechanism emulated that of analogue predecessors and supported cut-and-splice editing. Further information can be found in John Borwick, *Sound Recording Practice* (Oxford: Oxford University Press, 2001), pp. 274–275.
59 The Sony PCM-1600 was released in 1978 and was one of the first PCM (pulse code modulation) digital audio recorders. The system utilized a U-matic VCR for storage and playback and was widely used in the professional audio industry as a CD mastering format. 1610 and 1630 models followed soon after and they are still in widespread use. Further information can be found in Borwick, *Sound Recording Practice*, p. 269.
60 Widely recognized as the very first hard-disk-based recording system, the New England Digital Synclavier II was an 8-bit frequency modulation synthesizer (commonly referred to as FM synthesis) that came with a wooden keyboard and additional monitor.
61 The Fairlight CMI was developed by Kim Ryrie and Peter Vogel in Sydney, Australia, during the late 1970s. A computer-based digital sampler, synthesizer and sequencing

device, the Fairlight CMI was used in the recordings of artists including Kate Bush, Frankie Goes to Hollywood, Duran Duran, Peter Gabriel, Tears for Fears and Pet Shop Boys, amongst many others.

62   Including Andrew Goodwin, 'Sample and Hold: Pop Music in the Digital Age of Reproduction', *Critical Quarterly* 30, no. 3 (1988): pp. 34–49 and Beadle, *Will Pop Eat Itself?*.

63   Katz, *Capturing Sound*; and Warner, *Pop Music, Technology and Creativity*.

64   Two examples include Gaute Barlindhaug, 'Analogue Sound in the Age of Digital Tools: The Story of the Failure of Digital Technology', in *A Document (Re) turn – Contributions from a Research Field in Transition*, ed. R. Skare, N. Windfeld Lund and A. Varheim (Frankfurt: Lang, 2007), pp. 73–93; and Mike Berk, 'Analogue Fetishes and Digital Futures', in *Modulations: A History of Electronic Music – Throbbing Words on Sound*, ed. P. Shapiro (New York: Caipirinha Productions Inc., 2000), pp. 188–201.

65   Austin Moore, 'All Buttons In: An Investigation into the Use of the 1176 FET Compressor in Popular Music Production', *Journal on the Art of Record Production* 6 (2012) [Online], http://arpjournal.com/all-buttons-in-an-investigation-into-the-use-of-the-1176-fet-compressor-in-popular-music-production/ (Accessed January 2018).

66   'Technological iconicity' is a term described in Samantha Bennett, 'Endless Analogue', *Journal on the Art of Record Production* 7 (2012) [Online], http://arpjournal.com/endless-analogue-situating-vintage-technologies-in-the-contemporary-recording-production-workplace/ (Accessed January 2018).

67   Steve Albini (1962–) is a US recording engineer. He has spoken prolifically about his dedication to recording and mixing in the analogue domain. He is best known for his work as recording engineer on Nirvana's *In Utero*, PJ Harvey's *Rid of Me* and Pixies' *Surfa Rosa*.

68   Liam Watson is a recording engineer, producer and owner of Toerag studios in Hackney, London. He is best known for his work with The White Stripes, Madness and The Datsuns.

69   Lewis Durham is a UK musician and producer. Along with his sisters, he performs in the band Kitty, Daisy and Lewis and has produced a number of their recordings. He has also produced for Pokey LaFarge and the South City Three.

70   Pete Hutchison is a UK studio owner, producer and owner of Peacefrog Records.

71   Steve Levine is a UK record producer and a former chairman of the Music Producers Guild. He is credited as producer on Culture Club's *Colour by Numbers*, The Honeyz' *Wonder No. 8* and Louise's *Woman in Me*.

72   Elliot Mazer is a US recording engineer and producer best known for his work with Neil Young and Carlos Santana.

73   DAW is a common acronym for digital audio workstation. It usually alludes to an 'all-inclusive' digital sound recording, production, editing and mixing device. AVID's Pro Tools running on an Apple computer is one example of a set-up commonly referred to as a DAW.

74   Three examples of canon studies in musicology include David Dubal, *The Essential Canon of Classical Music* (New York: North Point Press, 1992); Timothy J. Dowd, Kathleen Liddle, Kim Lupo and Anne Borden, 'Organizing the Musical Canon', *Poetics* 30 (2002): pp. 35–61; and Katherine Bergeron and Philip V. Bohlman, *Disciplining Music: Musicology and Its Canons* (Chicago: University of Chicago Press, 1992).

75 For example: Daniel Heartz, *Haydn, Mozart and the Viennese School: 1740–1780* (New York: W. W. Norton & Company, 1995); and Charles Rosen, *The Classical Style: Haydn, Mozart, Beethoven* (New York: W. W. Norton & Company, 1987).
76 Dowd et al., *Organizing the Musical Canon*.
77 Carys Wyn Jones, *The Rock Canon: Canonical Values in the Reception of Rock* (Aldershot: Ashgate, 2008).
78 The 33 1/3 series of books is a good example of this. The first 100 books in the series featured just 14 titles on female artists or bands featuring one or more female performers.
79 Helen Reddington, *The Lost Women of Rock Music: Female Musicians of the Punk Era*, 2nd ed. (Sheffield: Equinox Publishing Ltd, 2012).
80 Williams, 'Pay Some Attention to the Man Behind the Curtain – Unsung Heroes and the Canonization of Process in the Classic Albums Documentary Series'.
81 Eliot Bates, 'What Studios Do', *Journal on the Art of Record Production* 7 (2012) [Online], http://arpjournal.com/what-studios-do/ (Accessed January 2018).
82 Brian Kehew and Kevin Ryan, *Recording the Beatles* (USA: Curvebender Publishing, 2006).
83 Alistair Lawrence, *Abbey Road: The Best Studio in the World* (London: Bloomsbury, 2012).
84 Samantha Bennett, 'Songs About Fucking: John Loder's Southern Studios and the Construction of a Subversive Sonic Signature', *Journal of Popular Music Studies* 29, no. 2 (2017), DOI: 10.1111/jpms.12209.
85 Milner, *Perfecting Sound Forever: The Story of Recorded Music*.
86 Cunningham, *Good Vibrations*.
87 John Repsch, *The Legendary Joe Meek* (London: Cherry Red Books, 1989).
88 Ted Fletcher, in Cunningham, *Good Vibrations*, pp. 88–89.
89 Alexis Petridis, 'Phil Spector and the Myth of the "Mad" Record Producer', *The Guardian*, 14 April 2009 [Online], http://www.theguardian.com/music/musicblog/2009/apr/14/phil-spector-record-producers (Accessed January 2018).
90 Peter O'Hare, 'Steve Albini "In Utero's" Ultra-sound Guy', *The Art of Record Production Conference*, 2007 [Online], http://www.artofrecordproduction.com/arp-conferences/arp-2007/19-arp-conference-archive/arp-2007/126-ohare-2007 (Accessed January 2018).
91 Rebecca Shepherd, 'The Collaborative Recordist', *Musicology Australia* 33, no. 2 (2011): pp. 255–264.
92 Jacques Attali, *Noise* (Minneapolis: University of Minnesota Press, 1985), p. 87.
93 Simon Reynolds, 'Steve Albini: Smoke 'Em If You Got 'Em', *Melody Maker*, 21 November 1992, http://www.rocksbackpages.com/print.html?ArticleID=983 (Accessed January 2018).
94 Camran Afsa Afsari, 'Steve Albini: Nemesis of Corporate Rock', in *Music Producers: Conversations with Today's Top Hitmakers*, ed. Barbara Shultz (New York: Intertec Publishing, 2000).
95 Tom Flint, 'David Gedge, Dare Mason & Steve Albini: Recording Cinarama's Disco Volante', *Sound on Sound* 4, 16, February 2001: pp. 178–185, 181.
96 Louis Miller, 'Band of Brothers', *CMJ*, 26 August 2002, pp. 8–9.
97 Paul Verna, 'For Mercenary Audio, It's Still an Analog World', *Billboard*, 23 September 1995, p. 54.
98 Greg Milner, 'Surfer Rosa Invents the 90s Sound', *SPIN*, May 2010, p. 52.
99 Scott Tennent, *Spiderland* (New York: Continuum, 2011).

100 Paul Brannigan, *This Is a Call: The Life and Times of Dave Grohl* (Cambridge: Da Capo Press, 2011).
101 Tagg, 'Analysing Popular Music – Theory, Method and Practice', pp. 8–9.
102 Ibid, p. 8.
103 Ibid.
104 Moore, *Song Means*.
105 Nicholas Cook, 'Methods for Analysing Recordings', in *The Cambridge Companion to Recorded Music*, ed. N. Cook, E. Clarke, D. Leech-Wilkinson and J. Rink (Cambridge: Cambridge University Press, 2009).
106 William Moylan, *Understanding and Crafting the Mix*, 2nd ed. (Burlington: Focal Press, 2007).
107 David Gibson, *The Art of Mixing: A Visual Guide to Recording, Engineering, and Production* (Boston, MA: ArtistPro Publishing, 2005).
108 Ruth Dockwray and Allan F. Moore, 'Configuring the Sound-Box: 1965–1972', *Popular Music* 29, no. 2 (2010): pp. 181–197.
109 Nicola Dibben, 'Vocal Performance and the Projection of Emotional Authenticity', in *The Ashgate Research Companion to Popular Musicology*, ed. D. B. Scott (Farnham: Ashgate, 2009), p. 319.
110 Serge Lacasse, 'Voice and Sound Processing: Examples of Mise en Scene of Voice in Recorded Rock Music', *Popular Musicology Online*, 2000, http://www.popular-musicology-online.com/issues/05/lacasse.html#fn4 (Accessed January 2018).
111 Peter Doyle, *Echo and Reverb: Fabricating Space in Popular Music Recording 1900–1960* (Middletown, CT: Wesleyan University Press, 2005).
112 Anne Danielsen and Ragnhild Brovig-Hanssen, 'The Naturalised and the Surreal: Changes in the Perception of Popular Music Sound', *Organised Sound* 18, no. 1 (2013): pp. 71–80.
113 Albin J. Zak, 'Editorial – The Art of Record Production', *Journal on the Art of Record Production*, 2 (2007) [Online], http://arpjournal.com/the-art-of-record-production/ (Accessed January 2018).
114 Such as the recent AHRC PiTS project: http://www.artofrecordproduction.com/index.php/ahrc-performance-in-the-studio.
115 For example, René T. A. Lysloff and Leslie C. Gay, eds, *Music and Technoculture* (Middletown: Wesleyan University Press, 2003).
116 Zak, *The Poetics of Rock*.
117 Taylor, *Strange Sounds*.
118 Katz, *Capturing Sound*.
119 Samantha Bennett, 'Revolution Sacrilege! Examining the Technological Divide among Record Producers in the late 1980s', *Journal on the Art of Record Production*, 4 (2009) [Online], http://arpjournal.com/revolution-sacrilege-examining-the-technological-divide-among-record-producers-in-the-late-1980s/ (Accessed January 2018); and Cunningham, *Good Vibrations*.

Chapter 1

1 Zak, *The Poetics of Rock*, p. 181.
2 As discussed in Zak, *The Poetics of Rock*; Taylor, *Strange Sounds*; and Théberge, *Any Sound You Can Imagine*.

3   Pierre Schaeffer, *In Search of a Concrete Music*, trans. Christine North and John Dack (Berkeley and Los Angeles: University of California Press, 2012).
4   See Cunningham, *Good Vibrations*; Durant, 'A New Day for Music?'; Bennett, 'Revolution Sacrilege!'
5   Aside from the work of Timothy Warner, who covers the Fairlight CMI and Trevor Horn in both: Warner, 'The Ghost in the Machine'; and Warner, *Pop Music, Technology and Creativity*.
6   Giles Dawson, 'Machines Alive with the Sound of Music', *New Scientist*, 4 August 1983, pp. 333–335.
7   Zak, *The Poetics of Rock*, p. 181.
8   The Fairlight's system disk was its operating disk, required for booting up the system before use.
9   Trevor Horn quoted in Ian Peel, 'Trevor Horn: 25 Years of Hits', *Sound on Sound* 20, no. 5 (2005): p. 52.
10 The Digeridu is a Western name for the long, cylindrical instrument originating from Australia. The instrument has many indigenous names, including 'Yidaki' from Arnhem Land, Northern Territory.
11 'The Art of Noise' is a reference to 'The Art of Noises', the futurist manifesto of Luigi Russolo (1913). In it, he theorized the normalization of industrial sound sources in the environment required a change in approach to music composition.
12 Such as in Attali, *Noise*; and Watson, *Cultural Production in and Beyond the Recording Studio*.
13 A further example, including The Pet Shop Boys' use of the Fairlight CMI, is discussed in Chapter 5.
14 Phil Collins, *No Jacket Required*. Virgin, 1985.
15 Steve Hills, 'What Makes the Synclavier So Special and Different?' *500 Sound*, 2006, http://www.500sound.com/uniquesync.html (Accessed January 2018).
16 The bitterness New England Digital felt towards the Fairlight CMI is detailed in Milner, *Perfecting Sound Forever: The Story of Recorded Music*, p. 317.
17 Developed in the early 1970s by engineering students Sydney Alonzo, Cameron Jones and Judd Burnham along with Professor Jon Appleton, initially at Dartmouth College, New England, then later with synthesist and sound designer Danny Jaeger as part of the New England Digital Corp.
18 Hills, 'What Makes the Synclavier So Special and Different?'
19 Ibid.
20 Richard Buskin, 'Soft Cell "Tainted Love" Classic Tracks', *Sound on Sound*, 6, 27 April 2012: pp. 124–130.
21 Mike Thorne, in ibid.
22 New England Digital, *New England Digital Archive*, 2010 [Online], http://ned.synthesizers.fr/ (Accessed January 2018).
23 Milner, *Perfecting Sound Forever: The Story of Recorded Music*, p. 323.
24 Genesis, 'Mama' (1982); and New England Digital, *New England Digital Archive*.
25 Ultimate Eurythmics, 'Eurythmics Savage 25: Interview with Dave Stewart', 2013 [Online], http://www.eurythmics-ultimate.com/eurythmics-savage25-interview-with-dave-stewart/ (Accessed January 2018).
26 Christopher Currell, 'The Event Horizon – Synclavier, Music and Michael Jackson', *Headphone Guru*, 31 March 2015, http://headphone.guru/the-event-horizon-synclavier-music-and-michael-jackson/ (Accessed January 2018).
27 Bruce Swedien, *Make Mine Music* (Norway: MIA Musikk, 2004), p. 155.

28 Michael Jackson, *Bad*. Epic, 1987.
29 See Borwick, *Sound Recording Practice*.
30 Steven Dupler, 'Digital over Analog in Two Years', *Billboard*, 9 August 1986, p. 63.
31 Ibid., p. 60.
32 Stephen Hague, in Richard Buskin, 'Classic Tracks: New Order "New Faith"', *Sound on Sound* 5, 20, March 2005: p. 186.
33 SPARS are the Society of Professional Audio Recording Services, a US organization founded in 1979. They collectively developed the SPARS code, a three-letter code that appeared on the reverse of many CDs. The combinations of A (analogue domain) and D (digital domain) included AAD, ADD and the highly coveted DDD. The first letter stood for the recording device, the second letter stood for the mixing device and the third letter stood for the mastering device. Further details can be found at the organization's website at http://www.spars.com
34 Malcom Atkin, *Interview with the Author*, 2009.
35 Steve Culnane, *Interview with the Author*, 2009.
36 Melvyn Toms, *Interview with the Author*, 2009.
37 Chris Lord-Alge, brother of Tom Lord-Alge, is a US producer, recording and mix engineer best known for his work with Green Day, Black Eyed Peas and Muse.
38 Tom Lord-Alge, brother of Chris Lord-Alge, is a US mix engineer best known for his work with Weezer, Santana, The Rolling Stones and Marilyn Manson.
39 Peter Doyle, *Echo and Reverb: Fabricating Space in Popular Music Recording 1900–1960* (Middletown, CT: Wesleyan University Press, 2005).
40 Anne Danielsen and Ragnhild Brovig-Hanssen, 'The Naturalised and the Surreal: Changes in the Perception of Popular Music Sound', *Organised Sound* 18, no. 1 (2013): pp. 71–80.
41 Uncut, 'Uncut Magazine Interviews Tony Visconti', *Uncut*, 1999 [Online], http://www.bowiegoldenyears.com/low.html (Accessed January 2018).
42 Samantha Bennett, 'Never Mind the Bollocks ... A Tech-Processual Analysis', *Popular Music and Society* 38, no. 4 (2015): pp. 466–486.
43 Tony Platt, 'Q&A with Haydn Bendall, Mike Howlett and Tony Platt', *Gearslutz*, 8 June 2007 [Online], https://www.gearslutz.com/board/q-haydn-bendall-mick-glossop-mike-howlett-tony-platt/127182-question-tony-back-black.html (Accessed January 2018).
44 Ian Little, in Richard Buskin, 'Classic Tracks – The Reflex', *Sound on Sound* 9, 19 July 2004: p. 177.
45 Howard Ferstle Ferstler, 'Lexicon Corporation', in *The Encyclopedia of Recorded Sound*, ed. Frank Hoffman (New York: Routledge, 2005), p. 1126.
46 Frank Zappa and Peter Occhiogrosso, *The Real Frank Zappa Book* (New York: Simon & Schuster, 1989), p. 155.
47 Julio d'Escrivan, *Music Technology* (Cambridge: Cambridge University Press, 2012), p. 149.
48 Universal Audio, *Official Website*, 2015 [Online], http://www.uaudio.com (Accessed January 2018).
49 Such as in Theodore Cateforis, 'Isolation: Ambient Reverb and the Spatial Meanings of British Post-Punk', *International Association for the Study of Popular Music – U.S. Chapter*, Iowa City, Iowa, 26 April 2008; and Matthew Bannister, *White Boys, White Noise: Masculinities and 1980s Indie Guitar Rock* (Farnham: Ashgate, 2006).
50 Bannister, *White Boys, White Noise: Masculinities and 1980s Indie Guitar Rock*, p. 74.
51 Joy Division, 'Digital' on: Various. *A Factory Sampler*. Factory FAC-2 (1979).

52. See Bennett, 'Songs About Fucking: John Loder's Southern Studios and the Construction of a Subversive Sonic Signature', *Journal of Popular Music Studies* 29, no. 2 (2017), DOI: 10.1111/jpms.12209.
53. Ray Hitchins, *Vibe Merchants: The Sound Creators of Jamaican Popular Music* (Farnham: Ashgate, 2014), pp. 121–122.

Chapter 2

1. As documented in Goodwin, 'Sample and Hold'; and Beadle, *Will Pop Eat Itself?*.
2. Cunningham, *Good Vibrations*.
3. Harrison Consoles, 'Our History', 2016 [Online], http://harrisonconsoles.com/site/history.html (Accessed January 2018).
4. Burgess, *The History of Music Production*, p. 107.
5. Air Studios, *Custom Neve History*, 2016 [Online], http://www.airstudios.com/the-studios/studio-1/custom-neve-history/ (Accessed January 2018).
6. Malcolm Atkin, *Interview with the Author*.
7. Dave Harries, *Interview with the Author*.
8. Atkin, *Interview with the Author*.
9. Steve Culnane, *Interview with the Author*.
10. Melvyn Toms, *Interview with the Author*.
11. Rick Savage, in *Classic Albums Def Leppard – Hysteria*. Directed by Matthew Longfellow. DVD. New York: Red, 2002.
12. This term was articulated by recordist Steve Albini in *Sidelines – Student Newspaper of Middle Tennessee State University*, USA [Online], http://media.www.mtsusidelines.com/media/storage/paper202/news/2004/03/15/News/Albini.Laments.Age.Of.OverProduction-633200.shtml (Accessed January 2018), and is well articulated by Greg Milner in relation to the SSL console in Milner, *Perfecting Sound Forever: The Story of Recorded Music*, p. 168.
13. Mark Vail, *Vintage Synthesisers* (San Francisco: Backbeat Books, 2000), p. 289.
14. David Mellor, *Interview with the Author*.
15. Hills, 'What Makes the Synclavier So Special and Different?'
16. Mark Coleman, *Playback: From the Victrola to MP3, 100 Years of Music, Machines and Money* (Cambridge, MA: Da Capo Press, 2003), p. 151.
17. Paul White, 'King of the Castle – Paul Hardcastle', *Sound on Sound* 14, no. 12 (1999): pp. 48–54.
18. Phil Harding, *Interview with the Author*.
19. Warner, *Pop Music, Technology and Creativity*, p. 20.
20. Tom Doyle, 'Classic Tracks – "Voodoo Ray" by a Guy Called Gerald', *Sound on Sound* 9, 30, July 2015: pp. 134–140.
21. Mellor, *Interview with the Author*.
22. Tim Simenon, in Paul Tingen, 'Tim Simenon – Bomb the Bass', *Sound on Sound* 10, no. 5 (1995): p. 141.
23. Mick Fleetwood, in Mard Namen, 'Making Tracks with MIDI – Mick Fleetwood of Fleetwood Mac', *Start*, Summer 1988 [Online], http://www.atarimagazines.com/startv3n1/makingtrackswithmidi.html (Accessed January 2018).
24. Goodwin, 'Sample and Hold'; and Beadle, *Will Pop Eat Itself?*

25 For example, Justin Morey, 'The Bridgeport Dimension: Copyright Enforcement and Its Implications for Sampling Practice', in *Music, Law and Business Anthology*, ed. A. V. Kärjä (Helsinki: International Institute for Popular Culture, 5, 2012), pp. 21–45; and Kembrew McLeod and Peter DiCola, *Creative License – The Law and Culture of Digital Sampling* (Durham and London: Duke University Press, 2011).
26 For example, Jeffrey R. Houle, 'Digital Audio Sampling, Copyright Law and the American Music Industry: Piracy or Just a Bad "Rap"?' *Loyola Law Review* 37, no. 4 (1991): pp. 879–902; and Matthew Rimmer, 'The Grey Album: Copyright Law and Digital Sampling', *Media International Australia Incorporating Culture and Policy* 114 (2005): pp. 40–53.
27 Dan LeRoy, *Paul's Boutique* (London: Continuum, 2006); and Christopher Weingarten, *It Takes a Nation of Millions to Hold Us Back* (New York: Bloomsbury Academic, 2010).
28 Including: Steven Best and Douglas Kellner, 'Rap, Black Rage, and Racial Difference', *Enculturation* 2, no. 2 (Spring 1999) [Online], http://www.enculturation.net/2_2/best-kellner.html (Accessed January 2018); and Morey, 'The Bridgeport Dimension'.
29 Including: David Sanjek, 'Don't Have to DJ No More: Sampling and the Autonomous Creator', *Cardozo Arts and Entertainment Law Journal* 607 (1992): pp. 612–615; and S. Hampel, 'Note: Are Samplers Getting a Bum Rap?: Copyright Infringement or Technological Creativity?' *University of Illinois Law Review* 559 (1992): pp. 584–585.
30 Alex Ogg and David Upshall, *The Hip Hop Years – A History of Rap* (London: Channel 4 Books, Macmillan Publishers Ltd, 1999).
31 Ofra Haza's 'Im Nin'Alu' has since been sampled by many artists. Examples of tracks where a sample of Im Nin'Alu features are Public Enemy 'Can't Truss It' (1989); Vanilla Ice 'Hot Sex' (2001); and Fabolous Feat. Meek Mill and Mike Davis' 'Foreigners' (2013).
32 Such as in Venise T. Berry, 'Feminine or Masculine: The Conflicting Nature of Female Images in Rap Music', in *Cecilia Reclaimed: Feminist Perspectives on Gender and Music*, ed. Susan Cook and Judy Tsou (Urbana and Chicago: University of Illinois Press, 1994); and Cheryl Keyes, 'Empowering Self, Making Choices, Creating Spaces: Black Female Identity via Rap Music Performance', *The Journal of American Folklore* 113, no. 449 (2000): pp. 255–269.
33 Brian Eno, in *Classic Albums U2 – The Joshua Tree*. Directed by Bob Smeaton, Philip King and Nuala O' Connor. DVD. New York: Red, 2001.
34 Daniel Lanois, in Mark Prendergast, 'The Magic of Daniel Lanois (Part II)', *Sound on Sound* 2, no. 11 (1987): p. 44.
35 Chris Williams, 'Jazzie B revisits Soul II Soul's debut album "Club Classics Vol. One/Keep On Movin" | #ReturnToTheClassics', *Soul Culture*, 18 May 2012 [Online], http://soulculture.com/music-blog/jazzie-b-revisits-soul-ii-souls-debut-album-club-classics-vol-onekeep-on-movin-returntotheclassics/ (Accessed January 2018).
36 *Club Classics Volume One* was certified triple platinum by the UK's BPI (British Phonographic Industry), double platinum by the US' RIAA (Recording Industry Association of America) and features in numerous 'Best British Albums' lists.
37 Morton, *Sound Recording – The Life Story of a Technology*, p. 172.
38 Mellor, *Interview with the Author*.
39 Harries, *Interview with the Author*.
40 Toms, *Interview with the Author*.
41 Sony/HHB, 'Fiction, Fact' [Advertisement], *Studio Sound* 30, no. 1 (1988): pp. 8–9.

42 Ibid.
43 Tom Rhea, in Vail, *Vintage Synthesisers*, p. 27.
44 As discussed extensively in LeRoy, *Paul's Boutique*; Weingarten, *It Takes a Nation of Millions to Hold Us Back*; and Shawn Taylor, *People's Instinctive Travels and the Paths of Rhythm* (London: Bloomsbury Academic, 2007).
45 Joseph Nunes and Andrea Ordanini, 'I Like the Way It Sounds: The Influence of Which Instruments and How Many Instruments Are Audible on Music Preferences', in *NA – Advances in Consumer Research* 42, ed. June Cotte and Stacy Wood (Duluth, MN: Association for Consumer Research, 2014), pp. 172–176.
46 The implications of technological development on the role of the recordist are fully analysed in Chapters 4, 5 and 6.

Chapter 3

1 See Paul Théberge, *Any Sound You Can Imagine: Making Music, Consuming Technology* (Hanover: Wesleyan University Press, 1997).
2 Jonathan Sterne, 'What's Digital in Digital Music?' in *Digital Media: Transformations in Human Communication*, ed. Paul Messaris and Lee Humphreys (New York: Peter Lang, 2006), p. 102.
3 Bennett, 'Endless Analogue'.
4 Paul Verna, 'Budget Studio Gear Breaks Barriers', *Billboard*, 14 October 1995, p. 1.
5 Ibid.
6 John Strawn, 'Technological Change: The Challenge to the Audio and Music Industries', *Journal of the Audio Engineering Society* 45, no. 3 (1997): p. 182.
7 Dave Simons, *Analog Recording: Using Analogue Gear in Today's Home Studio* (San Francisco: Backbeat Books, 2006), p. 14.
8 Verna, 'Budget Studio Gear Breaks Barriers', p. 1.
9 Investment in new technologies also declined. See Andrew Leyshon, 'The Software Slump? Digital Music, the Democratisation of Technology, and the Decline of the Recording Studio Sector Within the Musical Economy', *Environment and Planning A* 41 (2009): pp. 1309–1331.
10 Michael Talbot-Smith, *Audio Recording & Reproduction: Practical Measures for Audio Enthusiasts* (Oxford: Newnes, 1994).
11 As mentioned in George Petersen, *The Alesis ADAT: The Evolution of a Revolution* (Emeryville, CA: Mix Books, 1998).
12 George Petersen, '10 Technology Movements', *Mix Online*, 2007 [Online], http://www.mixonline.com/news/news-products/10-technology-movements/371292 (Accessed January 2018).
13 Petersen, *The Alesis ADAT: The Evolution of a Revolution*, pp. 2–3.
14 Joe Lambert, in Verna, 'Budget Studio Gear Breaks Barriers', p. 91.
15 Jim Barber, in Verna, 'For Mercenary Audio, It's Still an Analog World', p. 54.
16 Karen Fournier, *The Words and Music of Alanis Morissette* (Santa Barbara: Praeger, 2015), p. 39.
17 Christopher Fogel, in Nigel Humberstone, 'Christopher Fogel: Alanis Morisette's Jagged Little Pill', *Sound on Sound*, March 1997 [Online], http://www.soundonsound.com/sos/1997_articles/mar97/chrisfogel.html (Accessed January 2018).

18 A sample taken from a re-recorded version of an original recording to avoid copyright infringement. See Amanda Sewell, 'How Copyright Affected the Musical Style and Critical Reception of Sample-Based Hip-Hop', *Journal of Popular Music Studies* 2, no. 3 (2014): pp. 295–320.
19 Rebecca Haithcoat, 'A Day with Warren G at Red Bull Studios LA', *Redbull.com*, 24 June 2014 [Online], http://www.redbull.com/us/en/music/stories/1331659882685/interview-with-warren-g-on-20th-anniversary-of-regulate (Accessed January 2018).
20 DJ Shadow, in Eric Stenman, 'DJ Shadow: Samplers, Turntables & Downtime', *Tape Op*, no. 11 (1998) [Online], http://tapeop.com/interviews/11/dj-shadow/ (Accessed January 2018).
21 Hitchins, *Vibe Merchants: The Sound Creators of Jamaican Popular Music*, p. 159.
22 Sterne, 'What's Digital in Digital Music?' p. 103.
23 Simon Langford, *Digital Audio Editing* (Oxon: Focal Press, 2014).
24 Barbara Schultz, 'Colin Fairly and Helioscentric Studios: Producer/Engineer's New Home: Is a Project Room That's Gone Commercial', *Mix Online*, 1999 [Online], http://www.mixonline.com/news/profiles/colin-fairly-and-helioscentric-studios-producerengineers-new-home-project-room-thats-gone-commercial/374213 (Accessed January 2018).
25 Dino Elefante, in Dan Daley, 'Sound Kitchen Carves a Competitive Niche in Outer Nashville', *Billboard*, 26 September 1998, p. 54.
26 Dimebag Darrell, in Jeff Kitts and Brad Tolinski, *Guitar World Presents Nu-Metal* (Milwaukee: Hal Leonard, 2002), p. 34.
27 Sam Inglis, 'XTC: Ideal Studio & Recording Apple Venus Vol. 1 & Wasp Star', *Sound on Sound* 9, 15, July 2000: p. 128.
28 In Chapter 7, I illustrate this with one of the RADAR's most prolific users, UK recordist Stephen Street and his work on Blur's 'Song 2'.
29 Mark Howard, in David J. Farinella, *Producing Hit Records* (London: Schirmer Books), p. 122.
30 Simon Palmskin, in Mike Senior, 'Johnny Dollar & Simon Palmskin: Recording. Gabrielle's "Rise"', *Sound on Sound* 9, 15, July 2000: p. 51.
31 Johnny Dollar, in ibid.
32 Craig Leon, in Sue Sillitoe, 'Craig Leon: Recording the New Blondie Album', *Sound on Sound* 2, 14, December 1998: p. 158.
33 Ibid.
34 Ibid.
35 Ibid.
36 Nicholas Negroponte, *Being Digital* (New York: Vintage, 1995), p. 91.
37 Toms, *Interview with the Author*.
38 Atkin, *Interview with the Author*.
39 Milner, *Perfecting Sound Forever: The Story of Recorded Music*, pp. 295–297.
40 Dave Grohl, in *The Smart Studios Story*. Directed by Butch Vig and Steve Marker. Independent Film, 2014.
41 Butch Vig, in John Vanderslice, 'Butch Vig: Garbage and Smart Studios', *Tape Op* 11, November/December 1998 [Online], http://tapeop.com/interviews/11/butch-vig/ (Accessed January 2018).
42 Butch Vig, in David Weiss, 'Studio Drumming in the Age of Pro Tools', *Drum Magazine*, 26 August 2010 [Online], http://www.drummagazine.com/plugged-in/post/studio-drumming-in-the-age-of-pro-tools/ (Accessed January 2018).

43 Butch Vig, in Vanderslice, 'Butch Vig: Garbage and Smart Studios'.
44 Butch Vig, in Digidesign, 'Pro Tools Takes Our Music into the Next Dimension', *Electronic Musician* 14 (1998): p. 35.
45 Digidesign, 'More Hit Records Are Produced with Pro Tools Than All Other Digital Audio Workstations Combined', *Billboard*, 26 June 1999, p. 43.
46 David Frank, in Mike Senior, 'David Frank: Recording Christina Aguilera's Genie in a Bottle', *Sound on Sound* 6, 15, April 2000: p. 50.
47 David Frank, in Paul Myers, 'Out of the Bottle', *Electronic Musician*, 2001 [Online], http://www.emusician.com/artists/1333/out-of-the-bottle/32050 (Accessed January 2018).
48 See Sue Sillitoe, 'Recording Cher's Believe', *Sound on Sound*, 1999 [Online], https://www.soundonsound.com/sos/feb99/articles/tracks661.htm (Accessed January 2018).
49 Ibid.
50 Including: Bennett, 'Endless Analogue'; Bennett, 'Revolution Sacrilege! Examining the Technological Divide among Record Producers in the Late 1980s', *Journal on the Art of Record Production* 4 (2009); and Bennett, 'Examining the Emergence and Subsequent Proliferation of Anti Production Amongst the Popular Music-Producing Elite' (Doctoral thesis, University of Surrey, 2010).
51 See Bennett, 'Endless Analogue'.
52 In Don Weller, 'Abbey Road Will Hold Studio Sale', *Billboard*, 30 August 1980, p. 64.
53 Including: Durant, 'A New Day for Music?'; Cunningham, *Good Vibrations*; Bennett, 'Revolution Sacrilege!'
54 Brian Hodgson, in Steve Marshall, 'The Story of the BBC Radiophonic Workshop', *Sound on Sound* 6, 23, April 2008: p. 80.
55 See NAMM Official website [Online], http://www.namm.org (Accessed January 2018).
56 Daniel Lanois, in *Classic Albums U2 – The Joshua Tree*, 2001.
57 Phil Brown, *Are We Still Rolling?* (USA: Tape Op Books, 2010).
58 Ibid.
59 For example, Steve Albini has often referred to his decision to stick with analogue tape recording as both a commitment to its sonic aesthetics and a political stand against recording and production in the digital domain.
60 Universal Audio, *Fairchild 670 Legacy Compressor Plug In*, 2015 [Online], http://www.uaudio.com/store/compressors-limiters/fairchild-670.html (Accessed January 2018).
61 Bennett, 'Endless Analogue'.
62 Analogue Tube, *Original Limiters and Compressors*, 2015 [Online], http://www.analoguetube.com (Accessed January 2018).
63 Bennett, 'Endless Analogue'.
64 Universal Audio, *Fairchild 670 Legacy Compressor Plug In*.
65 Alan Parsons and Julian Colbeck, *Alan Parsons' Art & Science of Sound Recording: The Book* (Milwaukee: Hal Leonard, 2014).
66 Sylvia Massy, 'Q&A with Sylvia Massy', *Gearslutz*, 2014 [Online], https://www.gearslutz.com/board/q-sylvia-massy/902697-army-man-compressor.html (Accessed January 2018).
67 Taylor, *Strange Sounds*, p. 3.

Chapter 4

1 Siouxsie Sioux, in Mark Paytress, *Siouxsie & The Banshees: The Authorised Biography* (London: Sanctuary Publishing Ltd, 2003), p. 120.

2   Ibid., p. 120.
3   Including: Andy Keep, 'Does Creative Abuse Drive Developments in Record Production?' *The Art of Record Production Conference*, 2005 [Online], http://www.artofrecordproduction.com/arp-conferences/arp-2005/17-arp-conference-archive/arp-2005/72-keep-2005 (Accessed January 2018); and Mick Glossop, *Interview with the Author*.
4   Peter Martland, *Recording History: The British Record Industry 1888–1931* (London: Scarecrow Press, 2012), p. 238.
5   Francis Rumsey and Tim McCormick, *Sound and Recording: Applications and Theory* (Oxon: Focal Press, 2014), p. 459.
6   Hitchins, *Vibe Merchants: The Sound Creators of Jamaican Popular Music*, pp. 105, 170.
7   This is discussed in Susan Schmidt Horning's book *Chasing Sound*, particularly in the chapter 'When High Fidelity Was New', p. 80.
8   Christopher H. Sterling and Cary O'Dell, *The Concise Encyclopedia of American Radio* (London: Routledge, 2009), p. 348.
9   Schmidt Horning, *Chasing Sound*, p. 79.
10 Ibid., p. 74.
11 EMI Archives, *Walking and Talking*, 2013 [Online], https://www.youtube.com/watch?v=rqaMiDqE6QQ (Accessed January 2018).
12 Peter Hammer, 'In Memoriam', *Journal of the Audio Engineering Society* 42, no. 6 (1994): p. 776.
13 Ibid., p. 777.
14 RCA Victor's microphone research was pivotal, as discussed in Steven E. Schoenherr, 'Microphones part 2 – The Electrical Era', *Audio Engineering Society*, 1999 [Online], http://www.aes-media.org/historical/html/recording.technology.history/microphones2.html (Accessed January 2018).
15 Much research into the LP format was carried out by CBS. This is detailed in Gary Marmorstein, *The Label: The Story of Columbia Records* (New York: Thunder's Mouth Press, 2007), p. 165.
16 Including by tape machine manufacturers such as Ampex. This is documented in John Leslieand Ross Snyer, 'History of the Early Days of Ampex Corporation', *Journal of the Audio Engineering Society*. AES Historical Committee, 2010 [Online], http://www.aes.org/aeshc/docs/company.histories/ampex/leslie_snyder_early-days-of-ampex.pdf (Accessed January 2018).
17 Examples of such textbooks include Borwick, *Sound Recording Practice*; David Huber and Robert Runstein, *Modern Recording Techniques* (Oxon: Focal Press, 2013); and Bruce Bartlett and Jenny Bartlett, *Practical Recording Techniques*, 3rd ed. (Boston, MA: Focal Press, 2002).
18 Such as *Sound on Sound* and *Audio Media*.
19 Such as *Gearslutz*.
20 In the early 1980s, artists such as The Art of Noise who brought avant-garde techniques into the commercial mainstream were in a minority.
21 Zak, *The Poetics of Rock*, p. 192.
22 This is quite evident from many recordist interviews, including those in Howard Massey, *Behind the Glass: Top Record Producers Tell How They Craft the Hits* (New York: BackBeat Books, 2000); Howard Massey, *Behind the Glass: Top Record Producers Tell How They Craft the Hits – Volume II* (New York: BackBeat Books, 2009); and Richard Buskin, *Inside Tracks: A First Hand History of Popular Music from the World's Greatest Record Producers and Engineers* (New York: Avon Books, 1999).

23 As described in Cunningham, *Good Vibrations*; and John Repsch, *The Legendary Joe Meek: The Telstar Man* (London: Cherry Red Books, 2001).
24 Barry Cleveland, *Joe Meek's Bold Techniques* (London: Omnibus Press, 2001).
25 Alan Williams, 'Divide and Conquer: Power, Role Formation and Conflict in Recording Studio Architecture', *Journal on the Art of Record Production* 1 (2011) [Online], http://arpjournal.com/divide-and-conquer-power-role-formation-and-conflict-in-recording-studio-architecture/ (Accessed January 2018).
26 *Telstar – The Joe Meek Story*. Directed by Nick Moran. G2 Pictures, 2008.
27 Mick Glossop, *Interview with the Author*, 2009.
28 Andy Hamilton, 'The Art of Recording and the Aesthetics of Perfection', 2003, p. 347.
29 Ibid., p. 348.
30 Ibid., p. 349.
31 Jamie Sexton, 'Digital Music: Production, Distribution and Consumption', in *Digital Cultures: Understanding New Media* (Maidenhead: McGraw Hill Open University Press, 2009), pp. 92–93.
32 E. R. Kealy, 'From Craft to Art: The Case of Sound Mixers and Popular Music', in *On Record: Rock, Pop and the Written Word*, ed. Simon Frith and Andrew Goodwin (London and New York: Routledge, [1979] 1990), p. 182.
33 Theodore Gracyk, *Rhythm and Noise: An Aesthetics of Rock* (London: Duke University Press, 1996), p. 85; Frank Hoffman, *Encyclopedia of Recorded Sound* (New York: Routledge, 2005), p. 726.
34 Rob Young, *Rough Trade: Labels Unlimited* (London: Black Dog Publishing, 2006), p. 14; Howard, *Sonic Alchemy – Visionary Music Producers and Their Maverick Recordings* (Milwaukee: Hal Leonard, 2004); Moorefield, *The Producer as Composer* (Cambridge, MA and London: The MIT Press, 2005), p. 105.
35 See Timothy Warner, 'Approaches to Analyzing Recordings of Popular Music', in *Ashgate Research Companion to Popular Musicology*, ed. Derek B. Scott (Farnham and New York: Ashgate, 2009), p. 136; and Steve Jones, *Rock Formation: Music Technology and Mass Communication* (Newbury Park, CA: Sage Publications, 1992), p. 59.
36 Williams, 'Pay Some Attention to the Man Behind the Curtain – Unsung Heroes and the Canonization of Process in the Classic Albums Documentary Series'.
37 In Wolfgang Flür, *Kraftwerk: I Was a Robot* (London: Sanctuary, 2000).
38 Such elitism is still evident in the Music Producers Guild (UK).
39 In Arnold Schoenberg, *Letters* (London: Faber & Faber, 1987), p. 241.
40 Ibid.
41 John Borwick, 'The Tonmeister Concept', *46th Convention of the Audio Engineering Society*, 938 (1973)., p. 1–4. [Online] http://www.aes.org/e-lib/browse.cfm?elib=1688&rndx=389321.
42 Tonmeister programs are run by The University of Surrey, UK, and The Royal Danish Academy of Music.
43 Mick Glossop, *Interview with the Author*.
44 Sexton, 'Digital Music', pp. 92–93.
45 See Etienne Wenger, *Communities of Practice: Learning, Meaning and Identity* (Cambridge: Cambridge University Press, 1999).
46 Robert K. Merton, 'Insiders and Outsiders: A Chapter in the Sociology of Knowledge', *American Journal of Sociology* 78, no. 1 (1972): pp. 9–47.
47 Howard Becker, *Outsiders: Studies in the Sociology of Deviance* (New York: The Free Press, 1963).

48. Simon Frith, 'Towards an Aesthetic of Popular Music', in *Music and Society: The Politics of Composition, Performance and Reception*, ed. R. Leppert and S. McClary (Cambridge: Cambridge University Press, 1987), p. 147.
49. Lucy Green, *Music, Gender, Education* (Cambridge: Cambridge University Press, 1997), p. 190.
50. Bannister, *White Boys, White Noise: Masculinities and 1980s Indie Guitar Rock*, p. 118.
51. Keep, 'Does Creative Abuse Drive Developments in Record Production?'
52. Glossop, *Interview with the Author*.
53. The body of scholarly work on both Brian Eno and Trent Reznor is large. Scholars to have covered Eno and Reznor include Bannister, *White Boys, White Noise: Masculinities and 1980s Indie Guitar Rock*; Moorefield, *The Producer as Composer*; and Geeta Dayal, *Another Green World* (New York: Bloomsbury academic, 2009).
54. Brian Eno, in *Classic Albums U2 – The Joshua Tree*.
55. Ibid.
56. Hitchins, *Vibe Merchants: The Sound Creators of Jamaican Popular Music*.
57. Richard Buskin, 'Industrial Revolutionary: Alan Moulder – Recording Nine Inch Nails & Smashing Pumpkins', *Sound on Sound* 15, no. 7 (2000): pp. 106–111.
58. Ibid.
59. Ibid.
60. Simon Emmerson, *Living Electronic Music* (Farnham: Ashgate, 2007), p. 84.
61. The concept of embodied meaning is discussed at length in Allan Moore's 2012 monograph, *Song Means*.
62. Paul Tingen, 'Jim Scott: Recording Red Hot Chili Peppers' Californication', *Sound on Sound* 15, no. 2 (1999): pp. 44–50.
63. The album was subject to an online petition calling for a remaster. See Tim Anderson, 'How CDs Are Remastering the Art of Noise', *The Guardian*, 19 January 2007 [Online], https://www.theguardian.com/technology/2007/jan/18/pop.music (Accessed January 2018).
64. See David Greeves, 'Matt Cox: MIDI Tech for the Chemical Brothers', *Sound on Sound*, December 2011 [Online], https://www.soundonsound.com/people/matt-cox-midi-tech-chemical-brothers (Accessed January 2018).
65. Tom Flint, 'Moby: Recording Moby's "Why Does My Heart Feel So Bad?"' *Sound on Sound* 4, 15, February 2000: pp. 40–45.
66. Paul Nagle, 'Blazing a Trail: Liam Howlett: The Prodigy', *Sound on Sound* 11, 11, September 1996: pp. 92–98.
67. Liam Howlett, in R. Green, 'Playing with Fire – Liam Howlett', *The Mix* 33 (1997), p. 97.
68. Russell Elevado, in Benji B, *Redbull Music Academy – Russell Elevado*, 2007 [Online], http://www.redbullmusicacademy.com/lectures/russell-elevado-elevate-your-mind (Accessed January 2018).
69. Ibid.
70. Ibid.
71. Ibid.

Chapter 5

1. Michael Chanan, *Repeated Takes: A Short History of Recording and Its Effects on Music* (London and New York: Verso, 1995), p. 162.
2. Warner, *Pop Music, Technology and Creativity*, p. 33.

3   Kehew and Ryan, *Recording The Beatles*.
4   The Smiths, 'I Started Something I Couldn't Finish', 1987.
5   Eminem, 'The Way I Am', 2000.
6   Jay Z, '99 Problems', 2003.
7   Eisenberg, *The Recording Angel*, p. 95.
8   See Fred Gaisberg, *Music Goes Round (Opera Bibliographies)* (London: Ayer Co Pub, 1977).
9   Coleman, *Playback: From the Victrola to MP3, 100 Years of Music, Machines and Money*, p. 18.
10 Mike Howlett, *Interview with the Author*, 2009.
11 Williams, 'Divide and Conquer: Power, Role Formation and Conflict in Recording Studio Architecture'.
12 Cunningham, *Good Vibrations*, p. 158.
13 Harding, *Interview with the Author*.
14 Glossop, *Interview with the Author*.
15 *Mix Online*, '1972 MCI JH-400 Series Inline Console', 1 September 2007 [Online], http://www.mixonline.com/news/news-products/1972-mci-jh-400-series-inline-console/377971 (Accessed January 2018).
16 Chris Sheldon, *Interview with the Author*, 2009.
17 Harding, *Interview with the Author*.
18 Howlett, *Interview with the Author*.
19 Tobias Fischer and Lara Cory, 'Fifteen Questions with Stephen Hague', *Fifteen Questions*, n.d. [Online], http://15questions.net/interview/fifteen-question-interview-stephen-hague/page-1/ (Accessed January 2018).
20 Simon Emmerson, *Music, Electronic Media & Culture* (Aldershot: Ashgate Publishing, 2000), p. 213.
21 See Moorefield, *The Producer as Composer*.
22 Chris Michie, 'We Are the Mothers and This Is What We Sound Like!', *Mix*, 1 January 2003, p. 2.
23 Beadle, *Will Pop Eat Itself?* p. 50.
24 Cunningham, *Good Vibrations*, p. 346.
25 Dom Phillips noted the era of the Superstar DJ as being 1992–2000. See Dom Phillips, *Superstar DJs Here We Go! The Rise and Fall of the Superstar DJ* (London: Ebury Press, 2009), p. 3.
26 Beadle, *Will Pop Eat Itself?* p. 51.
27 Goodwin, 'Sample and Hold', p. 266.
28 Stephen Street, *Interview with the Author*, 2009.
29 Harding, *Interview with the Author*.
30 Chanan, *Repeated Takes: A Short History of Recording and Its Effects on Music*, p. 105.
31 See Kevin Crouch and Tanya Crouch, *Sun King: The Life and Times of Sam Phillips, The Man Behind Sun Records* (London: Piakus Books, 2010).
32 Berry Gordy, *To Be Loved: The Music, The Magic, The Memories of Motown – An Autobiography* (New York: Warner Books, 1994).
33 Paul Watson, 'Critical Approaches to Hollywood Cinema: Authorship, Genre and Stars', in *An Introduction to Film Studies*, ed. Jill Nelmes (London: Routledge, 2003), p. 135.
34 Gillett, 'The Producer as Artist'.
35 Eisenberg, *The Recording Angel*.
36 Gillett, 'The Producer as Artist'.
37 Watson, 'Critical Approaches to Hollywood Cinema: Authorship, Genre and Stars', p. 136.

38 Zak, *The Poetics of Rock*, p. 183.
39 Eisenberg, *The Recording Angel*, pp. 94–95.
40 Zak, *The Poetics of Rock*, p. 179.
41 See Catherine Grant, 'Auteur Machines?' in *Film and Television After DVD*, ed. James Bennett and Tom Brown (London: Routledge, 2008).
42 Harding, *Interview with the Author*.
43 Bill Bruce, 'Daniel Miller: Mute Records, Depeche Mode & Home Studio', *Sound on Sound* 2, 14, December 1998: pp. 46–54.
44 Mike Howlett, 'The Record Producer as Nexus: Creative Inspiration, Technology and the Recording Industry' (PhD thesis, University of Glamorgan, 2009), p. 86.
45 Warner, *Pop Music, Technology and Creativity*, p. 18.
46 Andrew Leyshon, 'The Software Slump? Digital Music, the Democratisation of Technology, and the Decline of the Recording Studio Sector Within the Musical Economy', *Environment and Planning A* 41 (2009), p. 27.
47 See Watson, *Cultural Production in and Beyond the Recording Studio*.
48 Glyn Johns, *Sound Man: A Life Recording Hits with The Rolling Stones, The Who, Led Zeppelin, The Eagles, Eric Clapton, The Faces ...* (New York: Blue Rider Press, 2014).
49 Samantha Bennett, 'Revisiting the "Double Production" Industry: Advertising, Consumption and "Technoporn" Surrounding the Music Technology Press', in *Music, Law and Business Anthology*, ed. A.V. Kärjä (Helsinki, FI: International Institute for Popular Culture, 5, 2012).
50 Théberge, *Any Sound You Can Imagine: Making Music/Consuming Technology*, p. 129.
51 Sheldon, *Interview with the Author*.
52 Street, *Interview with the Author*.
53 Théberge, *Any Sound You Can Imagine: Making Music/Consuming Technology*, p. 234.
54 Westminster Exhibitions Ltd, 'Tomorrow's Music Technology – Today. The MIDI Music Show', *Sound on Sound* 5, 4 (1990).
55 David Mellor, *How to Set Up a Home Recording Studio* (Tonbridge: PC Publishing, 1990).
56 Talbot-Smith, *Audio Recording & Reproduction*.
57 Alvin Toffler, *The Third Wave* (New York: Bantam Books, 1980).
58 Axel Bruns, *Blogs, Wikipedia, Second Life, and Beyond: From Production to Produsage* (New York: Peter Lang, 2008).
59 Bennett, 'Revisiting the "Double Production" Industry: Advertising, Consumption and "Technoporn" Surrounding the Music Technology Press'.
60 See Bennett, 'Never Mind the Bollocks ... A Tech-processual Analysis.'
61 Penny Rimbaud, 'John Loder: Sound Engineer Who Founded the Legendary Southern Studios', *The Guardian*, 19 August 2005 [Online], http://www.guardian.co.uk/news/2005/aug/19/guardianobituaries.artsobituaries (Accessed January 2018).
62 See Bennett, 'Songs About Fucking'.
63 Penny Rimbaud, *Interview with the Author*, 2014.

Chapter 6

1 Cunningham, *Good Vibrations*, 282.
2 G. Brock-Nannestad, 'The Influence of Recording Technology on Performers and Listeners – A Review', in *Audio Engineering Society Convention Paper 5533* (MOC Center, München, Germany: 112th Audio Engineering Society Convention, 2002).

3. Durant, *A New Day for Music?*
4. Bennett, 'Revolution Sacrilege!'
5. Steven Jones, *Against Technology – From the Luddites to Neo-Luddism* (London and New York: Routledge, 2006).
6. Andrew Feenberg, *Questioning Technology* (London & New York: Routledge, 1999).
7. Tyler Veak (ed.), *Democratizing Technology* (Albany: State University of New York Press, 2006).
8. Barlindhaug, 'Analogue Sound in the Age of Digital Tools'.
9. Berk, 'Analogue Fetishes and Digital Futures'.
10. Buskin, *Inside Tracks*.
11. Dave Simons, *Studio Stories* (San Francisco: Backbeat Books, 2004).
12. Massey, *Behind the Glass*; and Massey, *Behind the Glass: Top Record Producers Tell How They Craft the Hits – Volume II*.
13. Richard James Burgess, 'Interview with Wendy Page', *Journal on the Art of Record Production* 5 (2011) [Online], http://arpjournal.com/interview-with-wendy-page/ (Accessed January 2018).
14. Ibid.
15. This 'matching' of artist to recordist is detailed in many music industry guides and handbooks, including David Baskerville and Tim Baskerville, *Music Business Handbook and Career Guide* (Los Angeles: Sage, 2012); and Brian M. Jackson, *The Music Producer's Survival Guide: Chaos, Creativity and Career in Independent and Electronic Music* (Boston, MA: Cengage Learning PTR, 2013).
16. Albin. J. Zak, 'Editorial – The Art of Record Production'.
17. Taylor and Rawling, in Sillitoe, 'Recording Cher's Believe'.
18. Zak, 'Editorial – The Art of Record Production'.
19. Williams, 'Pay Some Attention to the Man Behind the Curtain – Unsung Heroes and the Canonization of Process in the Classic Albums Documentary Series'.
20. Cunningham, *Good Vibrations*.
21. Bennett, 'Revolution Sacrilege!'
22. See Taylor, *Strange Sounds: Music, Technology and Culture*; David Toop, *Ocean of Sound: Aether Talk, Ambient Sound and Imaginary Worlds* (London: Serpent's Tail, 2001).
23. Phil Ramone, *Making Records – The Scenes Behind the Music* (New York: Hyperion, 2007).
24. Ibid., p. 54.
25. George Duke, in Terri Stone, *Music Producers: Conversations and Interviews with Some of Today's Top Record Makers* (London: Omnibus Press, 1992), p. 14.
26. Rick Rubin, in Stone, *Music Producers: Conversations and Interviews with Some of Today's Top Record Makers*, p. 97.
27. George Martin, in Massey, *Behind the Glass*, p. 72.
28. Walter Afanasieff, in Massey, *Behind the Glass*, p. 267.
29. Rick Rubin, in Stone, *Music Producers: Conversations and Interviews with Some of Today's Top Record Makers*, p. 96.
30. Dr Dre, in Jake Brown, *Dr Dre in the Studio: From Compton, Death Row, Snoop Dogg, Eminem, 50 Cent* (London: Amber Books, 2007), p. 93.
31. Robbie Adams, in Paul Tingen, 'U2 & Robbie Adams: Recording in Mysterious Ways', *Sound on Sound* 9, 5 (1994), p. 121.
32. Les Paul, in Anthony Savona, *Console Confessions: Insights and Opinions from the Great Music Producers* (San Francisco: Backbeat, 2005), p. 5.
33. Will Mowatt, in Buskin, *Inside Tracks*, p. 313.

34 Hugh Padgham, in Buskin, *Inside Tracks*, p. 244.
35 Steve Levine, in Ralph Denyer, 'Steve Levine – Setting the Record Straight', *Sound on Sound* 2, 8 (1987), p. 44.
36 Steve Levine, *Interview with the Author*, 2009.
37 Mike Howlett, *Interview with the Author*, 2009.
38 Ibid.
39 Théberge, *Any Sound You Can Imagine*.
40 Durant, 'A New Day for Music?'
41 Trevor Horn, in Massey, *Behind the Glass: Top Record Producers Tell How They Craft the Hits – Volume II*, p. 186.
42 Ibid.
43 Mike Stock, *The Hit Factory – The Stock Aitken Waterman Story* (London: New Holland, 2004), p. 82.
44 Harding, *Interview with the Author*.
45 Pete Waterman, in Cunningham, *Good Vibrations*, p. 312.
46 Harding, *Interview with the Author*.
47 Howlett, *Interview with the Author*.
48 Ibid.
49 Harding, *Interview with the Author*.
50 Street, *Interview with the Author*.
51 Bennett, 'Revisiting the "Double Production" Industry'.
52 Steve Albini, in Andrew Young, 'Albini Laments Age of Over Production', *Sidelines – Student Newspaper of Middle Tennessee State University*, 15 March 2004.
53 Such terms are mentioned in Christopher Washburne, and Maiken Derno, *Bad Music: The Music We Love to Hate* (New York: Routledge, 2004); and Young, 'Albini Laments Age of Over Production'.
54 George Martin, in Massey, *Behind the Glass*, p. 72.
55 Neil Postman, *Technopoly – The Surrender of Culture to Technology* (New York: Vintage Books, 1993).
56 Tony Platt, *Interview with the Author*, 2009.
57 Dr Dre, in Brown, *Dr Dre in the Studio: From Compton, Death Row, Snoop Dogg, Eminem, 50 Cent*, p. 93.
58 Sheldon, *Interview with the Author*.
59 Ibid.
60 Stephen Street, in Sue Sillitoe, 'Street Life: At Home with Stephen Street', *Sound on Sound* 14, 10 (1999), p. 103.
61 Levine, *Interview with the Author*.
62 Glossop, *Interview with the Author*.
63 Ramone, *Making Records – The Scenes Behind the Music*, p. 26.
64 Sheldon, *Interview with the Author*.
65 Steve Albini, *Interview with the Author*, 2009.
66 Bennett, 'Revisiting the "Double Production" Industry'.
67 Martin Ware, in Cunningham, *Good Vibrations*, p. 355.
68 William Orbit, in Mark Prendergast, 'Electric Eclectic: William Orbit', *Sound on Sound* 11, no. 3 (1996): p. 170.
69 Strawn, 'Technological Change: The Challenge to the Audio and Music Industries'.
70 Flood, in Savona, *Console Confessions: Insights and Opinions from the Great Music Producers*, p. 131.

71 Flood, in Paul Tingen, 'Pop Art: Flood & Howie B – Recording U2's Pop', *Sound on Sound* 12, 9 (1997), p. 203.
72 Michael Bradford, in Massey, *Behind the Glass: Top Record Producers Tell How They Craft the Hits – Volume II*, p. 276.
73 Walter Afanasieff, in Massey, *Behind the Glass*, p. 269.
74 The concept of 'technostalgia' is discussed in Taylor, *Strange Sounds: Music, Technology and Culture*.
75 Toop, *Ocean of Sound: Aether Talk, Ambient Sound and Imaginary Worlds*.
76 Ibid., p. 263.
77 David Morton, *Off the Record: The Technology and Culture of Sound Recording in America* (New Brunswick, CA: Rutgers University Press, 2000), p. 185.
78 Albini, *Interview with the Author*.
79 Oxford Dictionaries Online [Online], https://en.oxforddictionaries.com/definition/nostalgia (Accessed January 2018).
80 Trevor Pinch and Frank Trocco, *Analog Days – The Invention and Impact of the Moog Synthesiser* (Cambridge, MA: Harvard University Press 2002), p. 318.
81 Barlindhaug, 'Analogue Sound in the Age of Digital Tools', p. 90.
82 See, for example, Peter Diamond and Joseph Stiglitz, 'Increases in Risk and in Risk Aversion', *Journal of Economic Theory* 8, no. 3 (1974): pp. 337–360; Charles Holt and Susan Laury, 'Risk Aversion and Incentive Effects', *American Economic Review* 92, no. 5 (2002): pp. 1644–1655.
83 See, for example, Amos Tversky and Daniel Khanamen, 'The Framing of Decisions and the Psychology of Choice', *Science* 211, no. 4481 (1981): pp. 453–458; George Leowenstein et al., 'Risk as Feelings', *Psychological Bulletin* 127, no. 2 (2001): pp. 267–286.
84 John Stiernberg, *Succeeding in Music: Business Chops for Performers and Songwriters* (Milwaukee, WI: Hal Leonard, 2008), p. 167.
85 Leowenstein et al., 'Risk as Feelings'.
86 Liam Howlett, in Green, 'Playing with Fire – Liam Howlett', p. 94.
87 Street, *Interview with the Author*.
88 Rodney Jerkins, in Massey, *Behind the Glass: Top Record Producers Tell How They Craft the Hits – Volume II*, p. 266.
89 Sheldon, *Interview with the Author*.
90 P. White, *MIDI for the Technophobe* (London: Sanctuary Publishing, 1997).
91 Platt, *Interview with the Author*.
92 Fatboy Slim, in C. Gill, 'Fatboy Slim: Mind in the Gutter', *Remix*, 1 January 2000 [Online], http://remixmag.com/mag/remix_mind_gutter/index.html (Accessed January 2018), p. 94.
93 William Orbit, in Prendergast, 'Electric Eclectic: William Orbit', p. 169.
94 William Orbit, in Greg Rule, 'William Orbit: The Methods and Machinery Behind Madonna's Ray of Light', *Keyboard Magazine* 24, no. 7 (1998): p. 33.
95 Platt, *Interview with the Author*.
96 Daniel Lanois, in Savona, *Console Confessions: Insights and Opinions from the Great Music Producers*, p. 126.
97 Flood, in Dave Robinson, 'Flood Warning', *Future Music* 24 (1994), p. 45.
98 Steve Albini, in Barbara Schultz, 'Steve Albini – Nemesis of Corporate Rock', in *Music Producers: Conversations with Today's Top Hitmakers*, ed. Barbara Schultz (USA: Intertec Publishing, [1994] 2000), p. 71.

Chapter 7

1. Gibson, *The Art of Mixing*.
2. Allan Moore and Ruth Dockwray. 'The Establishment of the Virtual Performance Space in Rock', *Twentieth-Century Music* 5, 2 (2008); and Dockwray and Moore, 'Configuring the Sound-Box'.
3. Zak, 'Editorial – The Art of Record Production'.
4. Timothy Warner, 'The Ghost in the Machine – Video Killed the Radio Star', *Popular Musicology Online*, 3 (2000).
5. Warner, *Pop Music, Technology and Creativity*.
6. Katz, *Capturing Sound: How Technology Has Changed Music*.
7. Moore, *Rock: The Primary Text*.
8. Ian Peddie, *Popular Music and Human Rights: Volume I British and American Music* (Farnham and New York: Ashgate, 2012).
9. Whiteley, *Sexing the Groove*; and Burns and LaFrance, *Disruptive Divas, Feminism*.
10. Butler, *Unlocking the Groove*.
11. Anne Danielsen, *Presence and Pleasure: The Funk Grooves of James Brown and Parliament* (Middletown, CT: Wesleyan University Press, 2006).
12. Danielsen, *Musical Rhythm in the Age of Digital Reproduction*.
13. Bennett, 'Never Mind the Bollocks... A Tech-Processual Analysis'.
14. Samantha Bennett, 'Gus Dudgeon's Super Sonic Signature', in *Global Glam and Popular Music: Style and Spectacle from the 1970s to the 2000s*, ed. I. Chapman and H. Johnson (New York: Routledge, 2015).
15. Bennett, 'Songs About Fucking'.
16. Including: Bates, 'What Studios Do'; Susan Schmidt Horning, *Chasing Sound: Technology, Culture & the Art of Studio Recording from Edison to the LP* (Baltimore, MD: Johns Hopkins University Press, 2013); and Théberge, *Any Sound You Can Imagine*.
17. Including: Zak, *The Poetics of Rock*; David Morton, *Off the Record: The Technology and Culture of Sound Recording in America* (New Brunswick, CA: Rutgers University Press, 2000); and Katz, *Capturing Sound: How Technology Has Changed Music*.
18. Including: Gary Gottileb, *How Does It Sound Now?: Legendary Engineers and Vintage Gear* (Boston, MA: Cengage Learning, 2009); and Samantha Bennett, 'Gus Dudgeon's Super Sonic Signature'.
19. Including: Richard James Burgess, *The Art of Music Production* (London: Omnibus Press, 2005); and Gibson, *The Art of Mixing*.
20. Moore, *Song Means*.
21. Steve Ett (b. Steve Ettinger) is a US recording engineer. He is credited with engineering Steely Dan's *Aja* as well as many Def Jam recordings, including Run DMC's *Tougher than Leather* and *Raising Hell*.
22. Rick Rubin, in Alex Ogg, *The Men Behind Def Jam – The Radical Rise of Russell Simmons and Rick Rubin* (London: Omnibus Press, 2002), p. 32.
23. Ibid.
24. LL Cool J's *I Need a Beat* (1984) and *Radio* (1985) as well as T La Rock and Jazzy Jay's *It's Yours* (1984) had been recorded there in the then recent past.
25. John King, in Amir Said, 'John King and the Story of Chung King Studios', *BeatTips*, October 2010, http://www.beattips.com/beattips/2014/10/john-king-and-the-story-of-chung-king-studios.html (Accessed January 2018).
26. Ibid.

27 Russell Simmons, in Ogg, *The Men Behind Def Jam – The Radical Rise of Russell Simmons and Rick Rubin*, p. 60.
28 Ibid., p. 58.
29 Rick Rubin, in Ogg, *The Men Behind Def Jam – The Radical Rise of Russell Simmons and Rick Rubin*, p. 59.
30 The Beastie Boys, formed in New York in 1979, consist of three vocalists; Adam Yauch (MCA), Michael Diamond (Mike-D) and Adam Horowitz (Ad-Rock). They signed to Rick Rubin and Russell Simmons's Def Jam label in the early 1980s, releasing the critically acclaimed and multi-platinum selling *Licensed to Ill* in 1986. They are also renowned for their albums *Paul's Boutique* (1989) and *Ill Communication* (1994). For further information, see P. Buckley, *The Rough Guide to Rock* (London: Rough Guides, 2003).
31 Barry Walters, 'The King of Rap – Rick Rubin Makes the Music Industry Walk His Way', *The Village Voice* 31 (1986), p. 21.
32 Ibid., p. 22.
33 Curtiss Maldoon were an English folk duo featuring Dave Curtiss and Clive Maldoon (d. 1976). They released one album entitled *Curtiss Maldoon* on Purple Records in 1971, which featured the folk song 'Sepheryn' on which Madonna's 'Ray of Light' is based.
34 William Orbit, in Rule, 'William Orbit: The Methods and Machinery Behind Madonna's Ray of Light', pp. 30–38.
35 Ibid.
36 Ibid.
37 Ibid.
38 Ibid.
39 Ibid.
40 Ibid.
41 Ibid.
42 Ibid.
43 William Orbit, in Prendergast, 'Electric Eclectic: William Orbit', pp. 168–172.
44 1979 lecture reprinted in Brian Eno, 'The Studio as Compositional Tool', in *Audio Culture: Readings in Modern Music*, ed. C. Cox and D. Warner (New York and London: Continuum International Publishing Group, 2004), pp. 127–130.
45 Virgil Moorefield, *The Producer as Composer*, 2005, p. 54.
46 Ibid., p. 54.
47 Flood, in Tingen, 'Pop Art: Flood & Howie B – Recording U2's Pop', p. 191.
48 Neil McCormick, *U2 by U2* (London: Harper Collins, 2006), p. 265.
49 Flood, in Tingen, 'Pop Art: Flood & Howie B – Recording U2's Pop', p. 200.
50 Ibid., p. 202.
51 Howie B, in Tingen, 'Pop Art: Flood & Howie B – Recording U2's Pop'.
52 Flood, in Tingen, 'Pop Art: Flood & Howie B – Recording U2's Pop', p. 196.
53 Ibid., p. 196.
54 Ibid.
55 Howie B, in Tingen, 'Pop Art: Flood & Howie B – Recording U2's Pop', p. 203.
56 Flood, in Tingen, 'Pop Art: Flood & Howie B – Recording U2's Pop', p. 203.
57 Bono, in McCormick, *U2 by U2*, p. 265.
58 Ibid.
59 Ibid., p. 266.
60 Flood, in Tingen, 'Pop Art: Flood & Howie B – Recording U2's Pop', p. 196.

61. Fatboy Slim is the stage name of UK DJ Norman Cook.
62. Katz, *Capturing Sound: How Technology Has Changed Music*.
63. Cunningham, *Good Vibrations*.
64. Fatboy Slim, in Gill, 'Fatboy Slim: Mind in the Gutter'.
65. Fatboy Slim, in Danny Scott, 'Stormin' Norman', *Future Music* 106 (2001): pp. 94–101.
66. Ibid.
67. Berk, 'Analogue Fetishes and Digital Futures', p. 194.
68. Katz, *Capturing Sound: How Technology Has Changed Music*, p. 145.
69. Quantization: a common processing device contained within many audio and MIDI sequencing software packages that places MIDI and/or audio events into exact pre-programmed timing intervals. For further explanation, see White, *MIDI for the Technophobe*.
70. Fatboy Slim, in Scott, 'Stormin' Norman', p. 95.
71. Alex James, *Bit of a Blur* (London: Little Brown, 2007), p. 146.
72. Stephen Street, in Sillitoe, 'Street Life: At Home with Stephen Street', p. 102.
73. Graham Coxon, in James, *Bit of a Blur*, p. 146.
74. Dave Rowntree, in Stuart Maconie, *Blur – 3862 Days – The Official History* (London: Virgin, 1999), p. 234.
75. Stephen Street, in Marcus Kagler, 'Taking Snapshots with Stephen Street or Stephen Street Blah Blah Blah', *Under the Radar* 5 (2003), pp. 92–93.
76. Stephen Street, in Maconie, *Blur – 3862 Days – The Official History*, p. 236.
77. Ibid.
78. Stephen Street, in Sillitoe, 'Street Life: At Home with Stephen Street', p. 102.
79. Maconie, *Blur – 3862 Days – The Official History*, p. 245.
80. James, *Bit of a Blur*, p. 146.
81. Stephen Street, in Sue Sillitoe, 'Streets Ahead – Stephen Street', *Sound on Sound* 9, 9 (1994), p. 112.
82. Stephen Street, in Sillitoe, 'Street Life: At Home with Stephen Street', p. 103.
83. Ibid.
84. Stephen Street, in Kagler, 'Taking Snapshots with Stephen Street or Stephen Street Blah Blah Blah', p. 92.
85. Dave Fridmann, in Mark Redfern, 'The Other Stars, Here's to the Ones in the Control Room', p. 90.
86. Dave Fridmann, in Sam Inglis, 'Mercury Rising – Dave Fridmann: Producing Flaming Lips & Mercury Rev', *Sound on Sound* 15, no. 11 (2000): pp. 204–210, 207.
87. Ibid.
88. Dave Fridmann, in Tom Doyle, 'Flaming Lips', *Sound on Sound* 5, 25 (March 2010): p. 129.
89. Dave Fridmann, in ABC, *Triple J Radio Producer Series Episode 1: Dave Fridmann*, 2009.
90. Howlett, *The Record Producer as Nexus*.
91. Dave Fridmann, in Inglis, 'Mercury Rising – Dave Fridmann', p. 210.

Conclusion

1. See Schmidt Horning, *Chasing Sound*.

2   T. W. Adorno, 'Opera and the Long Playing Record', in *Essays on Music*, ed. R. Leppert (Los Angeles: University of California Press, [1969] 2002), p. 283.
3   Jonathan Crary, 'Capital Effects', *October – High/Low: Art and Mass Culture* 56 (1991): p. 125.
4   This tendency to frame music recording and production in an analogue–digital binary is exemplified in many works, including Barlindhaug, 'Analogue Sound in the Age of Digital Tools', and Berk, 'Analogue Fetishes and Digital Futures'.
5   Beadle, *Will Pop Eat Itself?*, p. 2.
6   Cox, *Audio Culture: Readings in Modern Music*, p. 114.
7   Barlindhaug, 'Analogue Sound in the Age of Digital Tools', p. 74.
8   Williams, 'Pay Some Attention to the Man Behind the Curtain – Unsung Heroes and the Canonization of Process in the Classic Albums Documentary Series', pp. 166–175.
9   Zak, 'Editorial – The Art of Record Production'.
10 Robert Davis, 'Creative Ownership and the Case of the Sonic Signature, or "I'm Listening to This Record and Wondering Who Dunit?"' *Journal on the Art of Record Production* 4 (2009) [Online], http://arpjournal.com/creative-ownership-and-the-case-of-the-sonic-signature-or-'i'm-listening-to-this-record-and-wondering-whodunit'/ (Accessed January 2018).
11 Bennett, 'Songs About Fucking'.
12 Hills, 'What Makes the Synclavier So Special and Different?'
13 Théberge, *Any Sound You Can Imagine*.
14 Martin Cloonan and John Williamson, *The Musician's Union: A Social History*, 2014 [Online], http://www.muhistory.com/contact-us/1971-1980/ (Accessed January 2018).
15 See Albin J. Zak, *I Don't Sound Like Nobody: Remaking Music in 1950s America* (Ann Arbor: University of Michigan Press, 2010), p. 158.
16 See Kehew and Ryan, *Recording the Beatles*.
17 Schmidt Horning, *Chasing Sound*; and Cunningham, *Good Vibrations*.
18 Flür, *Kraftwerk: I Was a Robot*.
19 Théberge, *Any Sound You Can Imagine*.
20 See Strawn, 'Technological Change: The Challenge to the Audio and Music Industries', pp. 170–184.
21 Feenberg, *Questioning Technology*.
22 Veak, *Democratizing Technology*.
23 See Bennett, 'Revisiting the "Double Production" Industry: Advertising, Consumption and "Technoporn" Surrounding the Music Technology Press', pp. 117–145.
24 Ibid. and Théberge, *Any Sound You Can Imagine*.
25 Ibid.
26 Leyshon, 'The Software Slump?' p. 25.
27 Culnane, *Pers. Comms.*
28 See Haithcoat, 'A Day with Warren G at Red Bull Studios LA'.
29 US magazine *Billboard* featured a 'Studio Action' section during the 1980s and 1990s, which listed the studio, recording machine and mixing console used on hit records. Between 1987 and 1992, most hit recordings were made in professional recording houses with analogue or digital tape recorders and large-format mixing consoles.

30 See Weller, 'Abbey Road Will Hold Sale of the Century'; and Bennett, 'Endless Analogue: Situating Vintage Technologies in the Contemporary Recording Workplace'.
31 Melvyn Toms, *Pers. Comms.*
32 Warez, 'Flood – Pro Active Producer', 29 March 2006 [Online], http://magazine.warez.com/interviews/flood-pro-active-producer.html (Accessed January 2018).
33 Cunningham, *Good Vibrations*.
34 Durant, 'A New Day for Music?' pp. 175–196.
35 Bennett, 'Revolution Sacrilege!'
36 Cutler, 'Plunderphonia', p. 151.
37 Hamilton, 'The Art of Recording and the Aesthetics of Perfection', pp. 345–362.
38 Bennett, 'Endless Analogue: Situating Vintage Technologies in the Contemporary Recording Workplace'.
39 Tagg, *Analysing Popular Music: Theory, Method and Practice*, pp. 37–67.
40 Warner, *Pop Music, Technology and Creativity*.
41 Dockwray and Moore, 'Configuring the Sound-Box: 1965–1972', pp. 181–197.
42 Everett, *The Foundations of Rock*.
43 Covach and Boone, *Understanding Rock*.
44 Moore, *Song Means*.
45 Von Appen et al., *Song Interpretation in 21st Century Pop Music* (London and New York: Routledge, 2015).
46 Eduardo Navas, *Remix Theory: The Aesthetics of Sampling* (New York: Springer, 2012) and Navas et al., *The Routledge Companion to Remix Studies* (New York: Routledge, 2014).
47 Orbit went on to produce U2's 'Electrical Storm' and All Saints' 'Pure Shores'. Further discussion on Orbit and mixing can be found in Samantha Bennett, 'The Listener as Remixer: Mix Stems in Online Fan Community and Competition Contexts', in *The Oxford Handbook of Music and Virtuality*, ed. S. Rambarran and S. Whiteley (New York: Oxford University Press, 2016).
48 Moorefield, *The Producer as Composer*.
49 Gill, 'Fatboy Slim: Mind in the Gutter'.

Records Cited

A Flock of Seagulls. *A Flock of Seagulls*. Jive HOP 201 (1982)
A Guy Called Gerald. *Hot Lemonade*. Rham! RA1 (1989)
A Guy Called Gerald. 'Voodoo Ray'. Rham! RS804 (1988)
AC/DC. *Back in Black*. Atlantic. SD 16018 (1980)
AC/DC. 'Back in Black'. Atlantic. 3787 (1980)
Afrika Bambaataa & Soulsonic Force. 'Looking for the Perfect Beat'. Tommy Boy TB-831-7 (1983)
Aguilera, Christina. 'Genie in a Bottle'. RCA 07863-65813-7 (1999)
Akon. *Trouble*. Universal Records 0602498605004 (2003)
Alice in Chains. *Facelift*. Columbia CK 46075 (1990)
Alice in Chains. *Dirt*. Columbia CK 52475 (1992)
Ashford & Simpson. 'Solid'. Capitol Records B-5397 (1984)
Beastie Boys. *Licensed to Ill*. Def Jam Recordings BFC 40238 (1986)
Beastie Boys. '(You Gotta) Fight for Your Right (To Party)'. Def Jam Recordings 38-06595 (1986)
Beastie Boys. *Paul's Boutique*. Capitol Records. C1-91743 (1989)
Beastie Boys. *Ill Communication*. Capitol Records. 7243 8 28599 2 5 (1994)
Big Black. *Songs About Fucking*. Touch & Go T&G LP #24 (1987)
Blondie. *Blondie*. Private Stock PS 2023 (1976)
Blondie. *No Exit*. Beyond Music 74321641142 (1999)
Blondie. 'Maria'. Beyond Music 74321642132 (1999)
Blur. *Leisure*. Food. FOODLP 6 (1991)
Blur. *Modern Life Is Rubbish*. Food. FOOD LP 9 (1993)
Blur. *Parklife*. Food. FOODLP 10 (1994)
Blur. 'Girls & Boys'. Food. CDFOODS 47 (1994)
Blur. 'Song 2'. Food. CDFOODS 93 (1997)
Bomb the Bass. *Into the Dragon*. Rhythm King Records DOOD LP 1 (1988)
Bomb the Bass. 'Beat Dis'. Mister-Ron Records DOOD 1 (1987)
Bon Jovi. *New Jersey*. Vertigo 836 345-2 (1988)
Bowie, David. 'Fame'. RCA Victor RCA 2579 (1975)
Bowie, David. *Low*. RCA Victor PL 12030 (1977)
Brandy. *Never Say Never*. Atlantic 7567-83039-2 (1998)
Bros. *Push*. CBS CBS 460629 2 (1988)
Brown, James. 'I'm a Greedy Man'. Polydor PD 14100 (1971)
Brown, James. 'There It Is'. Polydor PD 14125 (1972)
Bush, Kate. *The Dreaming*. EMI EMC 3419 (1982)
Bush, Kate. 'The Dreaming'. EMI EMI 5296 (1982)
Cave, Nick and the Bad Seeds. *From Her to Eternity*. Mute STUMM17 (1984)
Chemical Brothers. *Surrender*. Freestyle Dust XDUSTCD4 (1999)
Chemical Brothers. 'Hey Boy, Hey Girl'. Freestyle Dust CHEMSD8 (1999)
Cher. 'Believe'. Warner Bros Records 9 44576-2 (1998)

Coalkitchen. 'Keep on Pushin'. Full Moon 8-50476 (1977)
Collins, Phil. *Face Value*. Virgin. V2185 (1981)
Collins, Phil. 'In the Air Tonight'. Virgin. VS 102 (1981)
Collins, Phil. *No Jacket Required*. Virgin. V2345 (1985)
Collins, Phil. 'Sussudio'. Virgin VS 736 (1985)
Cook, Peter and Moore, Dudley. *Peter Cook & Dudley Moore Present Derek and Clive (Live)*. Island Records ILPS 9434 (1976)
Cornershop. 'Brimful of Asha'. Wiiija WIJ 75 (1997)
Crass. *The Feeding of the Five Thousand*. Small Wonder Records WEENY 2 (1979)
Culture Club. *Kissing to be Clever*. Virgin. V2232 (1982)
Curtiss Maldoon. *Curtiss Maldoon*. Purple Records TPS 3501 (1971)
Daddy, Puff and Evans, Faith. 'I'll be Missing You. Tribute to the Notorious B.I.G'. Arista 74321 48540 2 (1997)
D'Angelo. *Voodoo*. Virgin. 7243 8 48499 1 7 (2000)
Day, Morris and the Time. 'The Bird'. Warner Bros Records 7-29094 (1984)
Dead or Alive. 'You Spin Me Round (Like a Record)'. Epic A4861 (1984)
Dean, Hazell. 'Whatever I Do (Wherever I Go)'. Proto Records ENA(T) 119 (1984)
De La Soul. *3 Feet High and Rising*. Tommy Boy TBCD 1019 (1989)
De La Soul. *De La Soul Is Dead*. Tommy Boy TBCD 1029 (1991)
Def Leppard. *Hysteria*. Bludgeon Riffola/Phonogram 830 675-2 (1987)
Def Leppard. 'Animal'. Bludgeon Riffola LEP 1 (1987)
Depeche Mode. 'Strangelove (Pain Mix)'. Sire 0-20769 (1987)
Depeche Mode. *Violator*. Mute Stumm 64 (1990)
Depeche Mode. 'Shake the Disease'. Mute 7 BONG 8 (1985)
Destiny's Child. *The Writing's on the Wall*. Columbia C2 69870 (1999)
Dido. 'Thank You'. BMG 74321 85890 2 (2001)
Dire Straits. *Brothers in Arms*. Vertigo. VERH 25 (1985)
Dire Straits. 'Money for Nothing'. Vertigo 836 419-2 (1988)
DJ Shadow. *Endtroducing*. Mo Wax MW059CD (1996)
Dollar. 'Give Me Back My Heart'. WEA BUCK 3 (1982)
Dr Dre. 'Nuthin'. But a "G" Thang' Interscope Records A8427 (1993)
Dr Dre. *2001*. Aftermath Entertainment 069490486-2 (1999)
Duran Duran. *Duran Duran*. EMI EMC 3372 (1981)
Duran Duran. *Rio*. EMI EMC 3411 (1982)
Duran Duran. *Seven and the Ragged Tiger*. Capitol Records ST-12310 (1983)
Duran Duran. 'The Reflex'. EMI DURAN 2 (1984)
Edwards, Dennis featuring Garrett, Siedah. 'Don't Look Any Further'. Gordy TMG 1334 (1984)
Eels. *Souljacker*. DreamWorks Records 450 335-1 (2001)
Eels. 'Souljacker Part 1'. DreamWorks Records 450 893-2 (2001)
Eminem. *The Marshall Mathers LP*. Interscope Records 069490629-1 (2000)
Eminem. 'The Way I Am'. Interscope Records INTR-10151-2 (2000)
Eminem. 'Stan'. Interscope Records 497 468-2 (2000)
Eno, Brian and Byrne, David. *My Life in the Bush of Ghosts*. Sire SRK 6093(1981)
Eno, Brian. *Ambient 1 (Music for Airports)*. EG AMB 001 (1978)
Erasure. *The Circus*. Mute STUMM35 (1987)
Erik B. and Rakim. 'Paid in Full (Seven Minutes of Madness – The Coldcut Remix)'. 4th & Broadway 12 BRW 78 (1987)

Erik B. and Rakim. 'I Know You Got Soul'. 4th & Broadway BWAY7438 (1987)
Eurythmics. 'Sweet Dreams (Are Made of These)'. RCA RCALP 6063 (1983)
Eurythmics. *Savage*. RCA PL71555 (1987)
Fabolous Feat. Meek Mill and Mike Davis. 'Foreigners'. *The Soul Tape 3*. No Label (2013)
Farnham, John. 'You're the Voice'. Wheatley Records WRS-034 (1986)
Fatboy Slim. *Better Living Through Chemistry*. Skint BRASSIC 2CD (1996)
Fatboy Slim. *You've Come a Long Way, Baby*. Skint BRASSIC 11CD (1998)
Fatboy Slim. 'Praise You'. Skint SKI 666785 1 (1998)
Feeder. *Polythene*. Echo ECHCD 19 (1997)
Fleetwood Mac. *Tango in the Night*. Warner Bros. Records 9 25471-2 (1987)
Fleetwood Mac. 'Big Love/Seven Wonders'. Warner Bros. Records 7-21943 (1987)
Fleetwood Mac. 'Little Lies'. Warner Bros. Records 7-28291 (1987)
Foo Fighters. *The Colour and the Shape*. Capitol Records CDP 7243 8 55832 2 3 (1997)
Frankie Goes to Hollywood. 'Relax'. ZTT ZTAS 1 (1983)
Frankie Goes to Hollywood. *Welcome to the Pleasuredome*. ZTT IQ1 (1984)
G., Warren and Nate Dogg. 'Regulate'. Interscope Records A 8290 LC (1994)
Gabriel, Peter. 'Shock the Monkey'. Charisma. SHOCK1 (1982)
Gabriel, Peter. *Peter Gabriel*. Charisma. PG4 (1982)
Gabrielle. 'Rise'. Go! Beat RISECDPRO (1999)
Garbage. *Version 2.0*. Mushroom MUSH29LP (1998)
Garbage. 'I Think I'm Paranoid'. Mushroom MUSH35CDS (1998)
Genesis. *Genesis*. Charisma. GEN LP 1 (1983)
Genesis. 'Mama'. Virgin Mama 1 (1983)
Genesis. *Invisible Touch*. Atlantic A1-81641 (1986)
Go West. *Go West* Chrysalis CDP32 1495-2 (1985)
Grand Master Flash and the Furious Five. 'The Message'. Sugar Hill Records SH-584 (1982)
Green Day. *Dookie*. Reprise Records 9 45529-2 (1994)
Guns N' Roses. *Appetite for Destruction*. Geffen Records GHS 24148 (1987)
Hammer, Jan. 'Theme From Miami Vice'. MCA Records MCA 52666 (1985)
Hardcastle, Paul. '19'. Chrysalis CHS 2860 (1985)
Haza, Ofra. 'Im Nin'. Alu (Played in Full Mix) Special Radio Edit' Globe Style NS 122 (1988)
Hell, Richard and the Voidoids. *Blank Generation*. Sire SR 6037 (1977)
Houston, Whitney. *My Love Is Your Love*. Arista 07822 19037 2 (1998)
Iglesias, Enrique. 'Be with You'. Interscope Records 497 294-2 (2000)
INXS. *Kick*. Mercury 832 721-2 (1987)
INXS. 'Never Tear Us Apart'. Mercury 870 488-7 (1987)
Jackson, Michael. 'Rock with You'. Epic EPC 8243 (1979)
Jackson, Michael. *Thriller*. Epic QE 38112 (1982)
Jackson, Michael. 'Beat It'. Epic 34-03759 (1983)
Jackson, Michael. *Bad*. Epic EK 40600 (1987)
Jackson, Michael. 'Smooth Criminal'. Epic 34-08044 (1988)
James, Bob. 'Sign of the Times/Enchanted Forest'. Tappan Zee Records 18-02530 (1981)
Jarre, Jean Michel. *Zoolook*. Disques Dreyfus. FDM 18118 (1984)
Jay Z. *The Blueprint*. Roc-A-Fella Records 314 586 396-2 (2001)
Jay Z. '99 Problems'. Roc-A-Fella Records PROBLEMSCD1 (2003)
Jefferson Starship. 'Rock Music/Lightening Rose'. Grunt Records FB-11961 (1979)

Joel, Billy. *The Nylon Curtain*. Columbia QC 38200 (1982)
Joel, Billy. *An Innocent Man*. Columbia QC 38837 (1983)
Jones, Grace. *Slave to the Rhythm*. ZTT GRACE 1 (1985)
Jones, Grace. 'Slave to the Rhythm'. Manhattan Island Records B500 20-RE1 (1985)
Joy Division. *Unknown Pleasures*. Factory FACT 10 (1979)
Khan, Chaka. 'I Feel for You'. Warner Bros. Records 7-29195 (1984)
Kraftwerk. *Autobahn*. Phillips 6305 231 D (1974)
Kraftwerk. *The Man Machine*. Capitol Records E-ST 11728 (1978)
Kraftwerk. *Electric Café*. Kling Klang 1C 064-24 0654 1 (1986)
L7. *Bricks Are Heavy*. Slash 9 26784-2 (1992)
LL Cool J. 'I Need a Beat'. Def Jam Recordings DJ001 (1984)
LL Cool J. *Radio*. Def Jam Recordings C 40239 (1985)
Lloyd Feat. Lil Wayne. 'Girls Around the World'. Universal Motown BOO1160911 (2008)
Loeb, Lisa and Nine Stories. 'Stay (I Missed You)'. RCA 74321 21252-7 (1994)
Loeb, Lisa and Nine Stories. *Tails*. Geffen Records GEFD-24734 (1995)
Lush. *Spooky*. 4AD CAD 2002 (1992)
Madonna. *Madonna*. Sire 1-23867 (1983)
Madonna. *Like a Virgin*. Sire 9-25157-1 (1984)
Madonna. 'Like a Virgin/Stay'. Sire W-9210 (1984)
Madonna. 'Material Girl'. Sire 7-29083 (1984)
Madonna. *True Blue*. Sire 1-25442 (1986)
Madonna. *Like A Prayer*. Sire W1-25844 (1989)
Madonna. 'Vogue'. Warner Bros. Records W 9851 (1990)
Madonna. *Bedtime Stories*. Maverick 9 45767-2 (1994)
Madonna. *Ray of Light*. Maverick 9362-46847-2 (1998)
Madonna. 'Ray of Light'. Maverick W0444LC (1998)
M/A/R/R/S. 'Pump Up the Volume'. 4AD BAD 707 (1987)
Martha and the Muffins. *Metro Music*. Dindisc DID.1 (1980)
Martin, Ricki. 'Livin La Vida Loca'. C2Records 38K 79124 (1999)
Massive Attack. *Mezzanine*. Circa WBRLP4 (1998)
McDonald, Michael. 'I Keep Forgettin'/Losin' End' Warner Bros. Records K 17992 (1982)
Mel and Kim. 'Respectable'. Atlantic 0-86703 (1987)
Mercury Rev. *Deserter's Songs*. V2 63881-27027-2 (1998)
MGMT. *Oracular Spectacular*. Columbia 88697195122 (2008)
MGMT. 'Electric Feel'. Columbia 88697 32649 2 (2008)
Milli Vanilli. 'Girl You Know It's True'. Arista AS1-9781 (1988)
Ministry. *The Land of Rape and Honey*. Sire 9 25799-2 (1988)
Minogue, Kylie. 'I Should Be So Lucky'. PWL Records PWL 8 (1987)
Mirwais. *Production*. Epic EK 85142 (2000)
Moby. *Play*. V2 63881-27049-2 (1999)
Morissette, Alanis. *Jagged Little Pill*. Maverick 9 45901-2 (1995)
Morrissey. *Viva Hate*. His Masters Voice CSD 3787 (1988)
Mr Mister. 'Broken Wings'. RCA PB49945 (1985)
My Bloody Valentine. *Loveless*. Creation Records crelp 060 (1991)
n'Dour, Youssou and Red, Axelle. 'La Cour Des Grands (A Ton Tour De Jour)'. Work WRK 665595 2 (1998)
New England Digital. *The Incredible Sounds of Synclavier II*. New England Digital Corp. NED 1/NED 2 (1981)

New Order. 'True Faith'. Factory Fac 183 (1987)
Nine Inch Nails. *Pretty Hate Machine*. TVT Records TVT 2610-1 (1989)
Nine Inch Nails. *The Downward Spiral*. Nothing Records intd-92346 (1994)
Nine Inch Nails. *The Fragile*. Nothing Records 0694904732 (1999)
Nine Inch Nails. 'Into the Void'. Nothing Records INT5P-6754 (1999)
Nirvana. *Nevermind*. DGC DGCD-24425 (1991)
Nirvana. *In Utero*. DGC DGCD-24607 (1993)
O'Connor, Sinead. *I Do Not Want What I Haven't Got*. Chrysalis F2 21759 (1990)
Oldfield, Mike. *Tubular Bells*. Virgin V2001 (1973)
Oldfield, Mike. *Earth Moving*. Virgin V 2610 (1989)
Orbit, William. *Strange Cargo*. I.R.S. DMIRF 1030 (1987)
Orbit, William. *Strange Cargo II*. I.R.S. X2-13055 (1991)
Orbit, William. *Strange Cargo III*. I.R.S. 7243 8 27703 29 (1993)
Orchestral Manoevres in the Dark. *Crush*. Virgin. CDV2349 (1985)
Pantera. *Reinventing the Steel*. EastWest Records America 62451-2 (2000)
Parliament. 'Star Child (Mothership Connection)'. Casablanca Records NB 864 (1975)
Pearl Jam. *Ten*. Epic ZK 47857 (1991)
Pearl Jam. *Vs*. Epic ZK 53136 (1993)
Pet Shop Boys. *Please*. Parlophone PCS 7303 (1986)
Pet Shop Boys. 'West End Girls'. Parlophone R 6115 (1985)
Pet Shop Boys 'Opportunities (Let's Make Lots of Money)'. Parlophone R 6129 (1986)
Pink Floyd. *Dark Side of the Moon*. Harvest SHVL 804 (1973)
Pink Floyd. 'Wish You Were Here'.
Pixies. *Surfer Rosa*. 4AD CAD 803 (1988)
Pixies. 'Dig for Fire'. 4AD BAD 0014 (1990)
PJ Harvey. *Rid of Me*. Island Records CID 8002 (1993)
PM Dawn. 'Set Adrift on Memory Bliss'. Gee Street GEE 33 (1991)
Portishead. *Dummy*. Go! Beat 828 522-1 (1994)
Prince. *1999*. Warner Bros. Records 9 23720-1 F (1982)
Prince and the Revolution. *Purple Rain*. Warner Bros. Records 1-25110 (1984)
Prodigy. *The Fat of the Land*. XL Recordings XLLP 121 (1997)
Prodigy. 'Firestarter'. XL Recordings XLS 70 CD (1996)
Public Enemy. *Yo! Bum Rush the Show*. Def Jam Recordings BFC 40658 (1987)
Public Enemy. *It Takes a Nation of Millions to Hold Us Back*. Def Jam Recordings. CK 44303 (1988)
Public Enemy. 'Fight the Power'. Motown MOT-1972 (1989)
Public Enemy. *Fear of a Black Planet*. Def Jam Recordings C 45413 (1990)
Public Enemy. 'Can't Truss It'. Def Jam Recordings 657530 7 (1991)
Ramones. *Ramones*. Sire SASD-7520 (1976)
Radiohead. *Kid A*. EMI 7243 5 29590 2 0 (2000)
Red Hot Chili Peppers. *Californication*. Warner Bros. Records 9 47386-2 (1999)
Rhymes, Busta. 'Woo-Hah!! Got You All in Check'. Elektra EKR 220 T (1996)
Ride. *Nowhere*. Creation Records CRECD 074 (1990)
Run DMC. *Raising Hell*. Profile Records PRO-1217 (1986)
Salt N' Pepa. *Hot, Cool & Vicious*. Next Plateau Records PL1007 (1986)
Salt N' Pepa. *A Salt with a Deadly Pepa*. FFRR 828 364-2 (1988)
Salt N' Pepa. 'Push It'. FFRR FFRRX 2 (1988)
Sex Pistols. *Never Mind the Bollocks … Here's the Sex Pistols*. Virgin. V 2086 (1977)

Simon, Paul. *Graceland*. Warner Bros. Records 1-25447 (1986)
Sinatra, Frank. *Duets*. Capitol Records 7243 8 28067 2 1 (1993)
Sinatra, Frank. *Duets II*. Capitol Records C2 7243 8 28103 2 2 (1994)
Siouxsie and the Banshees. *A Kiss in the Dreamhouse*. Polydor POLD 5064 (1982)
Siouxsie and the Banshees. *Hyaena*. Polydor 821 510-1 (1984)
Siouxsie and the Banshees. *Peepshow*. Polydor 837 240-1 (1988)
Slayer. *Reign in Blood*. Def Jam Recordings 9 24131-2 (1986)
Smashing Pumpkins. *Gish*. Caroline Records CAROL 1705-2 (1991)
Smashing Pumpkins. *Mellon Collie and the Infinite Sadness*. Virgin 7243 8 40861 2 1 (1995)
Soft Cell. 'Tainted Love'. Some Bizzare BZS 2 (1981)
Sonic Youth. *Dirty*. DGC DGCD-24493 (1992)
Soul II Soul. *Club Classics Vol. One*. Ten Records DIX 82 (1989)
Soul II Soul. 'Keep on Movin''. Ten Records TEN 263 (1989)
Soul II Soul Feat. Caron Wheeler. 'Back to Life (However Do You Want Me)'. Ten Records TEN 265 (1989)
Soundgarden. *Badmotorfinger*. A&M Records 75021 5374 1 (1991)
Soundgarden. *Superunknown*. A&M Records 31454 0198 2 (1994)
System of a Down. *System of a Down*. American Recordings CK 68924 (1998)
T La Rock and Jazzy Jay. 'It's Yours'. Def Jam Recordings JAM 1 (1984)
T Pain. *Epiphany*. Jive 88697-08719-2 (2007)
T Pain. *Thr33 Ringz*. Jive 88697 38526 2 (2008)
Talk Talk. *It's My Life*. EMI EMC 2400021 (1984)
Talk Talk. *Spirit of Eden*. Parlophone PCSD 105 (1988)
Tears for Fears. 'Shout'. Mercury. IDEA 8 (1984)
Tears for Fears. *Songs from the Big Chair*. Mercury. MERH 58 (1985)
The 2 Live Crew Feat. KC (from KC and the Sunshine Band) and Freak Nasty. '2 Live Party'. Lil' Joe Records LJR 897 (1998)
The Art of Noise. 'Close (To The Edit)'. ZTT ZTPS01 (1984)
The Art of Noise. *(Who's Afraid of?) The Art of Noise*. ZTT IQ2 (1984)
The Beatles. *Sgt Pepper's Lonely Hearts Club Band*. Parlophone 0602498605004 (1967)
The Breeders. *Last Splash*. 4AD 9 61508-2 (1993)
The Buggles. 'Video Killed the Radio Star'. Island Records 100 924 (1979)
The Buggles. *The Age of Plastic*. Island Records ILPS 9585 (1980)
The Charlatans. *Us And Us Only*. Universal MCD 60069 (1999)
The Cranberries. *Everybody Else Is Doing It So Why Can't We?* Island Records CID 8003 (1993)
The Cure. *Disintegration*. Fiction Records FIXH 14 (1989)
The Evasions. 'Wikka Wrap'. Groove Production GP 107 (1981)
The Flaming Lips. *Zaireeka*. Warner Bros. Records 9 46804-2 (1997)
The Flaming Lips. *At War with the Mystics*. Warner Bros. Records 49966-2 (2006)
The Human League. *Crash*. Virgin V2391 (1986)
The Jesus and Mary Chain. *Psychocandy*. Blanco Y Negro BYN 7 (1985)
The Jesus and Mary Chain. 'Just Like Honey'. Blanco Y Negro NEG 17(T) (1985)
The Kinks. 'You Really Got Me'. Pye Records 7N.15673 (1964)
The Normal. 'T.V.O.D./Warm Leatherette'. Mute MUTE 001 (1978)
The Police. *Ghost in the Machine*. A&M Records SP-3730 (1981)
The Police. *Synchronicity*. A&M Records SP-3735 (1983)

The Smiths. *Strangeways, Here We Come*. Rough Trade ROUGH 106 (1987)
The Smiths. 'I Started Something I Couldn't Finish'. Rough Trade RT 198 (1987)
The Soul Searchers. *Salt of the Earth*. Sussex SRA 8030 (1974)
The Spice Girls. *Spice*. Virgin CDV 2812 (1996)
The Sugarhill Gang. 'Rappers Delight'. Sugar Hill Records SH-542 (1979)
The Treacherous Three. 'The Body Rock'. Enjoy Records ER-6007 (1980)
Therapy? *Nurse*. A&M Records 540 044-2 (1992)
Therapy? *Pleasure Death*. Southern Records 18508-2 (1992)
Therapy? *Troublegum*. A&M Records 540 196-2 (1994)
Tool. *Undertow*. Zoo Entertainment 72445-11052-2 (1993)
Tricky. *Maxinquaye*. 4th & Broadway BRLP 610 (1995)
Tubeway Army. *Replicas*. Beggars Banquet BEGA 7 (1979)
Tubeway Army. 'Are Friends Electric?'. Beggars Banquet BEG 18 (1979)
Turner, Ike and Tina. 'River Deep, Mountain High'. Philles Records 131 (1966)
U2. *The Unforgettable Fire*. Island Records. 90231-1 (1984)
U2. *Achtung Baby*. Island Records 212 110 (1991)
U2. *The Joshua Tree*. Island Records 208-219 (1987)
U2. *Rattle and Hum*. Island Records 303 400 (1988)
U2. 'Where the Streets Have No Name'. Island Records IS 340 (1987)
U2. *Lemon (Remixes)* Island Records 422-862 957-1 (1993)
U2. *Zooropa*. Island Records 314-518 047-2 (1993)
U2. *Pop*. Island Records CIDU210 (1997)
U2. *Mofo Remixes*. Island Records CIDX 684 (1997)
U2. 'The Sweetest Thing'. Island Records CIDX 727 (1998)
Vanilla Ice. 'Hot Sex'. *Hot Sex*. Liquid 8 Records LIQ 12117 (2003)
Various. *A Journey into Stereo Sound*. Decca SKL 4001 (1958)
Various. *A Factory Sampler*. Factory FAC-2 (1979)
West, Kanye. *808s and Heartbreak*. Roc-A-Fella Records B0012198-01 (2008)
Winwood, Steve. 'Higher Love'. Island Records 108 317 (1986)
Whitesnake. *Whitesnake*. Geffen Records 9 24099-2 (1987)
Winehouse, Amy. 'Rehab'. Universal AMYCDPRO4 (2006)
Wonder, Stevie. 'Happy Birthday'. Motown. 4517 MG (1980)
Yarborough, C. *The Iron Pot Cooker*. Vanguard VSD 79356 (1975)
Yazoo. *You and Me Both*. Mute. STUMM 12 (1983)
Zappa, Frank. *London Symphony Orchestra Vol. I*. Barking Pumpkin Records (1983)
Zappa, Frank. *Francesco Zappa – The Barking Pumpkin Digital Gratification Consort*. Barking Pumpkin Records. ST-74202 (1984)

Bibliography

ABC. 2009. *Triple J Radio Producer Series Episode 1: Dave Fridmann*. Accessed January 2018 http://www.abc.net.au/triplej/media/s2706439.htm.

Adorno, T. W. [1969] 2000. 'Opera and the Long Playing Record'. In: Leppert, R. (ed.) *Essays on Music*. Los Angeles, CA: University of California Press.

Afsari, Camran. 2000. 'Steve Albini: Nemesis of Corporate Rock'. In: Shultz, Barbara (ed.) *Music Producers: Conversations with Today's Top Hitmakers*. New York: Intertec Publishing.

Air Studios. 2016. *Custom Neve History*. Accessed April 2016 http://www.airstudios.com/the-studios/studio-1/custom-neve-history/.

Albini, Steve. *Interview with the Author*. 4 August 2009.

Analogue Tube. 2015. *Original Limiters and Compressors*. Accessed January 2018 http://www.analoguetube.com

Atari. 2010. *Atari Historical Society*. Accessed January 2018 http://www.atarimuseum.com

Atkin, Malcolm. *Interview with the Author*. 1 July 2009.

Attali, Jacques. 1985. *Noise*. Minneapolis: University of Minnesota Press.

Audio Engineering Society. 2010. Official website. Accessed January 2018 http://www.aes.org

B, Benji. 2007. *Russell Elevado*. Redbull Music Academy. Accessed January 2018 http://www.redbullmusicacademy.com/lectures/russell-elevado-elevate-your-mind.

Bannister, Matthew. 2006. *White Boys, White Noise: Masculinities and 1980s Indie Guitar Rock*. Farnham, NY: Ashgate.

Barlindhaug, Gaute. 2007. 'Analogue Sound in the Age of Digital Tools: The Story of the Failure of Digital Technology'. In: Skare, R., Windfeld Lund, N. and Varheim, A. (eds) *A Document (Re) turn – Contributions from a Research Field in Transition*. Frankfurt: Lang, 73–93.

Bartlett, Bruce and Bartlett, Jenny. 2002. *Practical Recording Techniques*. 3rd Ed. Boston, MA: Focal Press.

Baskerville, David and Baskerville, Tim. 2012. *Music Business Handbook and Career Guide*. Los Angeles, CA: Sage.

Bates, Eliot. 2012. 'What Studios Do'. *Journal on the Art of Record Production*, 7. Accessed January 2018 www.arpjournal.com

Beadle, Jeremy. 1993. *Will Pop Eat Itself? – Pop Music in the Soundbite Era*. London: Faber & Faber.

Becker, Howard. 1963. *Outsiders: Studies in the Sociology of Deviance*. New York: The Free Press.

Benjamin, Walter. 2008 [1936]. *The Work of Art in the Mechanical Age of Reproduction*. London: Penguin.

Bennett, Samantha. 2009. 'The Emergence and Subsequent Proliferation of Anti-Production Amongst the Popular Music-Producing Elite – An Overview of Doctoral Study'. In: Proceedings of the 2nd International Conference for PhD Music Students. Department of Music Studies, Aristotle University of Thessaloniki: 2nd International Conference for PhD Music Students, 165–172.

Bennett, Samantha. 2009. 'Revolution Sacrilege! Examining the Technological Divide among Record Producers in the Late 1980s'. *Journal on the Art of Record Production*, 4. Accessed January 2018 www.arpjournal.com

Bennett, Samantha. 2012. 'Endless Analogue: Situating Vintage Technologies in the Contemporary Recording Workplace'. *Journal on the Art of Record Production*, 7. Accessed January 2018 www.arpjournal.com

Bennett, Samantha. 2012. 'Revisiting the "Double Production" Industry: Advertising, Consumption and "Technoporn" Surrounding the Music Technology Press'. In: Kärjä, A. V. (ed.) *Music, Law and Business Anthology*. Helsinki, FI: International Institute for Popular Culture, 5, 117–145.

Bennett, Samantha. 2015. 'Never Mind the Bollocks … A Tech-Processual Analysis'. *Popular Music and Society*, 38, 4 466–486.

Bennett, Samantha. 2015. 'Gus Dudgeon's Super Sonic Signature.' In: Chapman, I. and Johnson, H. (eds.) *Global Glam and Popular Music: Style and Spectacle from the 1970s to the 2000s*. New York: Routledge.

Bennett, Samantha. 2016. *Songs About Fucking: Southern Studios and the Construction of Punk's Subversive Sonic Signature*. At: Keep It Simple, Make It Fast! DIY Cultures, Spaces, Places: Faculdade de Letras da Universidade do Porto, Portugal, 18 July 2016.

Bennett, Samantha. 2016. 'The Listener as Remixer: *Mix Stems in Online Fan* Community *and* Competition Contexts'. In: Rambarran, S. and Whiteley, S. (eds.) *The Oxford Handbook of Music and Virtuality*. New York: Oxford University Press.

Bennett, Samantha. 2017. 'Songs About Fucking: John Loder's Southern Studios and the Construction of a Subversive Sonic Signature'. *Journal of Popular Music Studies*, 29, 2, DOI: 10.1111/jpms.12209.

Bergeron, Katherine and Bohlman, Philip V. 1992. *Disciplining Music: Musicology and Its Canons*. Chicago: University of Chicago Press.

Berk, Mike. 2000. 'Analogue Fetishes and Digital Futures'. In: Shapiro, P. (ed.) *Modulations: A History of Electronic Music – Throbbing Words on Sound*. New York: Caipirinha Productions Inc., 188–201.

Berry, Venise T. 1994. 'Feminine or Masculine: The Conflicting Nature of Female Images in Rap Music'. In: Cook, Susan and Tsou, Judy (eds.) *Cecilia Reclaimed: Feminist Perspectives on Gender and Music*. Urbana and Chicago: University of Illinois Press.

Best, Steven and Kellner, Douglas. 1999. 'Rap, Black Rage, and Racial Difference'. *Enculturation*, 2, 2. Accessed April 2016. http://www.enculturation.net/2_2/best-kellner.html

Black, J. 2002. 'Making Ray of Light'. *Q Magazine*, 193, 102–104.

Borwick, John. 1973. 'The Tonmeister Concept'. *46th Convention of the Audio Engineering Society*, 938. Accessed January 2018 http://www.aes.org/e-lib/browse.cfm?elib=1688&rndx=389321

Borwick, John. (ed.) 2001. *Sound Recording Practice*. Oxford: Oxford University Press.

Brannigan, Paul. 2011. *This Is a Call: The Life and Times of Dave Grohl*. Cambridge, MA: Da Capo Press.

Brock-Nannestad, G. 2002. 'The Influence of Recording Technology on Performers and Listeners – A Review'. In: *Audio Engineering Society Convention Paper 5533*. MOC Center, München, Germany: 112th Audio Engineering Society Convention.

Brown, Jake. 2007. *Dr Dre in the Studio: From Compton, Death Row, Snoop Dogg, Eminem, 50 Cent*. London: Amber Books.
Brown, Mick. 2008. *Tearing Down the Wall of Sound: The Rise and Fall of Phil Spector*. London: Bloomsbury Publishing.
Brown, Phil. 2010. *Are We Still Rolling?* Venice, CA: Tape Op Books.
Bruce, Bill. 1998. 'Daniel Miller: Mute Records, Depeche Mode & Home Studio'. *Sound on Sound*, 2, 14, 46–54..
Bruns, Axel. 2008. *Blogs, Wikipedia, Second Life, and Beyond: From Production to Produsage*. New York: Peter Lang.
Buckley, P. 2003. *The Rough Guide to Rock*. London: Rough Guides.
Burgess, Richard James. 2005. *The Art of Music Production*. London: Omnibus Press.
Burgess, Richard James. 2014. *The History of Music Production*. Oxford: Oxford University Press.
Burns, Lori and LaFrance, Melisse. 2002. *Disruptive Divas, Feminism, Identity and Popular Music*. New York: Routledge.
Buskin, Richard. 1997. 'Talking Garbage: Butch Vig'. *Sound on Sound*, 12, 5, 186–191.
Buskin, Richard. 1999. *Inside Tracks: A First Hand History of Popular Music from the World's Greatest Record Producers and Engineers*. New York: Avon Books.
Buskin, Richard. 2000. 'Industrial Revolutionary: Alan Moulder – Recording Nine Inch Nails & Smashing Pumpkins'. *Sound on Sound*, 15, 7, 106–111.
Buskin, Richard. 2004. 'Classic Tracks – The Reflex'. *Sound on Sound*, 9, 19, 174–180.
Buskin, Richard. 2005. 'Classic Tracks: New Order "New Faith"'. *Sound on Sound*, 5, 20, 182–188.
Buskin, Richard. 2012. 'Soft Cell "Tainted Love" Classic Tracks'. *Sound on Sound*, 6, 27, 124–130.
Butler, Mark. 2006. *Unlocking the Groove: Rhythm, Meter and Musical Design in Electronic Dance Music*. Bloomington: Indiana University Press.
Carter, Chris. 1997. '808 Statement – Roland TR-808 Rhythm Composer'. *Sound on Sound*, 12, 7, 258–261.
Cascone, Kim. 2000. 'The Aesthetics of Failure: 'Post-Digital' Tendencies in Contemporary Computer Music'. *Computer Music Journal*, 24, 4, 12–18.
Cateforis, Theodore. 2008. 'Isolation: Ambient Reverb and the Spatial Meanings of British Post-Punk'. In: *International Association for the Study of Popular Music – U.S. Chapter*. Iowa City, Iowa, 26 April 2008.
Chadabe, Joel. 1997. *Electric Sound: The Past and Promise of Electronic Music*. New Jersey, NJ: Prentice Hall.
Chadabe, Joel. 2000. 'Remarks on Computer Music Culture'. *Computer Music Journal*, 24, 4, 9–11.
Chanan, Michael. 1994. *Musica Practica: The Social Practice of Western Music from Gregorian Chant to Postmodernism*. London & New York: Verso.
Chanan, Michael. 1995. *Repeated Takes: A Short History of Recording and Its Effects on Music*. London & New York: Verso.
Cleveland, Barry. 2001. *Joe Meek's Bold Techniques*. London: Omnibus Press.
Cloonan, Martin and Williamson, John. 2014. *The Musician's Union: A Social History* [Online]. Accessed January 2018 http://www.muhistory.com/contact-us/1971-1980/
Coleman, Mark. 2003. *Playback: From the Victrola to MP3, 100 Years of Music, Machines and Money*. Cambridge, MA: Da Capo Press.

Cook, Nicholas. 2009. 'Methods for Analysing Recordings'. In: Cook, N., Clarke, E. Leech-Wilkinson, D. and Rink, J. (eds.) *The Cambridge Companion to Recorded Music*. Cambridge: Cambridge University Press.

Cottrell, Stephen. 2010. 'The Rise and Rise of Phonomusicology'. In: Bayley, Amanda (ed.) *Recorded Music: Performance, Culture and Technology*. Cambridge: Cambridge University Press, 15–36.

Covach, John and Boone, Graeme M. 2006. *Understanding Rock: Essays in Musical Analysis*. Oxford: Oxford University Press.

Covach, John and Spicer, Mark (eds.) 2010. *Sounding Out Pop: Analytical Essays in Popular Music*. Ann Arbour: University of Michigan Press.

Cox, Christoph and Warner, Daniel (eds.) 2004. *Audio Culture: Readings in Modern Music*. London & New York: Continuum International Publishing Group.

Crary, Jonathan. 1991. 'Capital Effects'. *October – High/Low: Art and Mass Culture*, 56, 121–131.

Creeber, Glen and Martin, Royston. (eds.) 2009. *Digital Cultures – Understanding New Media*. Maidenhead: McGraw Hill/Open University Press.

Crouch, Kevin and Crouch, Tanya. 2010. *Sun King: The Life and Times of Sam Phillips, The Man Behind Sun Records*. London: Piaktus Books.

Culnane, Steve. 2009. *Interview with the Author*. 21 May.

Culshaw, John. 1981. *Putting the Record Straight: Autobiography*. London: Secker & Warburg.

Cunningham, Mark. 1998. *Good Vibrations*. London: Sanctuary Music Publishing.

Currell, Christopher. 2015. 'The Event Horizon – Synclavier, Music and Michael Jackson'. *Headphone Guru*. 31 March. Accessed January 2018 http://headphone.guru/the-event-horizon-synclavier-music-and-michael-jackson/

Cutler, Chris. 2004. 'Plunderphonia'. In: Cox, C and Warner, D. (eds.) *Audio Culture: Reading in Modern Music*. London & New York: Continuum International Publishing Group, 138–156.

d'Escrivan, Julio. 2012. *Music Technology*. Cambridge: Cambridge University Press.

Daley, Dan. 1998. 'Sound Kitchen Carves a Competitive Niche in Outer Nashville'. *Billboard*, 110, 39. 26 September, 54.

Daley, Dan. 2004. 'The Engineers Who Changed Recording – Fathers of Invention'. *Sound on Sound*, 19, 12, 84–89.

Danielsen, Anne. 2006. *Presence and Pleasure: The Funk Grooves of James Brown and Parliament*. Middletown, CT: Wesleyan University Press.

Danielsen, Anne. 2010. *Musical Rhythm in the Age of Digital Reproduction*. Farnham: Ashgate.

Danielsen, Anne and Brovig-Hanssen, Ragnhild. 2013. 'The Naturalised and the Surreal: Changes in the Perception of Popular Music Sound'. *Organised Sound*, 18, 1, 71–80.

Davis, Robert. 2009. 'Creative Ownership and the Case of the Sonic Signature, or "I'm Listening to This Record and Wondering Who Dunit?"'. *Journal on the Art of Record Production*, 4 [Online]. Accessed January 2018 http://arpjournal.com/creative-ownership-and-the-case-of-the-sonic-signature-or-"i'm-listening-to-this-record-and-wondering-whodunit"/

Dawson, Giles. 1983. 'Machines Alive with the Sound of Music'. *New Scientist*, 4 August, 333–335.

Dayal, Geeta. 2009. *Another Green World*. New York: Bloomsbury Academic.

Denyer, Ralph. 1987. 'Steve Levine – Setting the Record Straight'. *Sound on Sound*, 2, 8, 40–46.
Diamond, Peter and Stiglitz, Joseph. 1974. 'Increases in Risk and in Risk Aversion'. *Journal of Economic Theory*, 8, 3, 337–360.
Dibben, Nicola. 2009. 'Vocal Performance and the Projection of Emotional Authenticity'. In: Scott, D. B. (ed.) 2009. *The Ashgate Research Companion to Popular Musicology*. Farnham: Ashgate. 317–334.
Digidesign. 1998. 'Pro Tools Takes Our Music into the Next Dimension'. *Electronic Musician*, 14, 35.
Digidesign. 1999. 'More Hit Records Are Produced with Pro Tools Than All Other Digital Audio Workstations Combined'. *Billboard*, 26 June, 43. Digidesign. Official website. Accessed January 2018. http://www.digidesign.com
Dockwray, Ruth, and Moore, Allan F. 2010. 'Configuring the Sound-Box: 1965–1972'. *Popular Music*, 29, 2, 181–197.
Dowd, Timothy J. et al. 2002. 'Organising the Musical Canon'. *Poetics*, 30, 35–61.
Doyle, Peter. 2005. *Echo and Reverb: Fabricating Space in Popular Music Recording 1900–1960*. Middletown, CT: Wesleyan University Press.
Doyle, Tom. 2010. 'Flaming Lips'. *Sound on Sound*, 5, 25, 128–133.
Doyle, Tom. 2015. 'Classic Tracks – "Voodoo Ray" by A Guy Called Gerald'. *Sound on Sound*, 9, 30, 134–140.
Droney, Maureen. 2000. 'Rick Rubin – Life Among the Wildflowers'. *Mix*. 1 October 2000. Accessed January 2018 http://mixonline.com/mag/audio_rick_rubin/
Dubal, David. 1992. *The Essential Canon of Classical Music*. New York: North Point Press.
Dupler, Steven. 1986. 'Digital over Analog in Two Years'. *Billboard*. 9 August, 63.
Dupler, Steven. 1986. '1986 The Year in Music and Video'. *Billboard*. 27 December, 60.
Durant, Alan. 1990. 'A New Day for Music? Digital Technologies in Contemporary Music Making'. In: Hayward, P. (ed.) *Culture, Technology & Creativity in the Late Twentieth Century*. London: John Libbey, 175–196.
Eisenberg, Evan. 2005. *The Recording Angel*. New Haven & London: Yale University Press.
Emerick, Geoff. 2007. *Here, There and Everywhere: My Life Recording the Beatles*. New York: Gotham Books.
EMI Archives. 2013. *Walking and Talking*. Accessed January 2018 https://www.youtube.com/watch?v=rqaMiDqE6QQ
Emmerson, Simon. 2000. *Music, Electronic Media & Culture*. Aldershot: Ashgate Publishing.
Emmerson, Simon. 2007. *Living Electronic Music*. Farnham: Ashgate.
Eno, Brian. 2004. 'The Studio as Compositional Tool'. In: C. Cox and D. Warner (eds.) *Audio Culture: Readings in Modern Music*. New York and London: Continuum International Publishing Group, 127–30.
Everett, Walter. (ed.) 2000. *Expression in Pop-Rock Music – A Collection of Critical and Analytical Essays*. New York: Garland Publishing.
Everett, Walter. 2008. *The Foundations of Rock*. Oxford: Oxford University Press.
Farinella, David J. *Producing Hit Records*. London: Schirmer Books.
Feenberg, Andrew. 1999. *Questioning Technology*. London & New York: Routledge.
Ferstler, Howard. 2005. 'Lexicon Corporation'. In: Hoffman, Frank (ed.) *The Encyclopedia of Recorded Sound*. New York: Routledge, 1126.

Fischer, Tobias and Cory, Lara. n.d. "Fifteen Questions with Stephen Hague". *Fifteen Questions*. Accessed January 2018 http://15questions.net/interview/fifteen-question-interview-stephen-hague/page-1/

Flint, Tom. 2000. 'Moby: Recording Moby's "Why Does My Heart Feel So Bad?"'. *Sound on Sound*, 4, 15, 40–45.

Flint, Tom. 2001. 'David Gedge, Dare Mason & Steve Albini: Recording Cinarama's Disco Volante' *Sound on Sound*, 4, 16, 178–185.

Flür, Wolfgang. 2000. *Kraftwerk: I Was a Robot*. London: Sanctuary.

Fournier, Karen. 2015. *The Words and Music of Alanis Morissette*. Santa Barbara, CA: Praeger.

Frith, Simon. 1987. 'Towards an Aesthetic of Popular Music'. In: Leppert, R. and McClary, S. (eds.) *Music and Society: The Politics of Composition, Performance and Reception*. Cambridge: Cambridge University Press.

Frith, Simon. 2001. 'Pop Music'. In: Frith, S., Straw, W. and Street, J. (eds.) *The Cambridge Companion to Pop and Rock*. Cambridge: Cambridge University Press, 93–108.

Frith, Simon and Goodwin, Andrew (eds.) 1990. *On Record: Rock, Pop and the Written Word*. London & New York: Routledge.

Frith, Simon, Straw, Will, and Street, John (eds.) 2001. *The Cambridge Companion to Pop and Rock*. Cambridge: Cambridge University Press.

Gaisberg, Fred. 1977. *Music Goes Round (Opera Bibliographies)*. London: Ayer Co Pub.

Gibson, David. 2005. *The Art of Mixing: A Visual Guide to Recording, Engineering, and Production*. Boston, MA: ArtistPro Publishing.

Gill, C. 2001. 'Fatboy Slim: Mind in the Gutter'. *Remix*. 1 January 2000. Accessed January 2018 http://remixmag.com/mag/remix_mind_gutter/index.html

Gillett, Charlie. 1977. 'The Producer as Artist'. In: Hitchcock, H. W. (ed.) *The Phonograph and Our Musical Life*, ISAM Monograph, No. 14. New York: City University, 51–56.

Glossop, Mick. 2009. *Interview with the Author*. 15 July.

Gold, Sue, Benjamin, Brad Leigh, Cheshire, Godfrey et al. 2002. *Music Producers: Conversations with Today's Top Record Makers*. Milwaukee, WI: Hal Leonard.

Goodwin, Andrew. 1988. 'Sample and Hold: Pop Music in the Digital Age of Reproduction'. *Critical Quarterly*, 30, 3 34–49.

Goodwin, Andrew. 1990. 'Sample and Hold: Pop Music in the Digital Age of Reproduction'. In: Frith, Simon and Goodwin, Andrew (eds.) *On Record: Rock, Pop & the Written Word*. London & New York: Routledge. 258–273.

Gordy, Berry. 1994. *To Be Loved: The Music, The Magic, The Memories of Motown – An Autobiography*. New York: Warner Books.

Gottlieb, Gary. 2009. *How Does It Sound Now?: Legendary Engineers and Vintage Gear*. Boston, MA: Cengage Learning.

Gracyk, Theodore. 1996. *Rhythm and Noise: An Aesthetics of Rock*. London: Duke University Press.

Grant, Catherine. 2008. 'Auteur Machines?' In: Bennett, J. and Brown, T. (eds.) 2008. *Film and Television After DVD*. London: Routledge.

Green, Lucy. 1997. *Music, Gender, Education*. Cambridge: Cambridge University Press.

Green, R. 1997. 'Playing with Fire – Liam Howlett'. *The Mix*, 33, 92–97.

Greene, Paul D., and Porcello, Thomas. 2004. *Wired for Sound: Engineering and Technologies in Sonic Cultures*. Middletown, CT: Wesleyan University Press.

Greeves, David. 2011. 'Matt Cox: MIDI Tech for the Chemical Brothers'. *Sound on Sound*, December [Online]. Accessed January 2018 https://www.soundonsound.com/people/matt-cox-midi-tech-chemical-brothers

Haithcoat, Rebecca. 2014. 'A Day with Warren G at Red Bull Studios LA'. *Redbull. com*, 24 June. Accessed January 2018. http://www.redbull.com/us/en/music/stories/1331659882685/interview-with-warren-g-on-20th-anniversary-of-regulate http://www.soundonsound.com/sos/dec11/articles/chem-bros.htm
Hamilton, Andy. 2003. 'The Art of Recording and the Aesthetics of Perfection'. *The British Journal of Aesthetics*, 43, 4, 345–362.
Hammer, Peter. 1994. 'In Memoriam'. *Journal of the Audio Engineering Society*, 42, 6, 777.
Hampel, S. 1992. 'Note: Are Samplers Getting a Bum Rap?: Copyright Infringement or Technological Creativity?' *University of Illinois Law Review*, 559, 584–585.
Harding, P. 2009. *PWL – From the Factory Floor*. Bury St Edmunds: WB Publishing.
Harding, Phil. 2009. *Interview with the Author*. 22 May.
Harries, Dave. 2009. *Interview with the Author*. 11 May.
Harrison Consoles. 2016. 'Our History'. Accessed April 2016 http://harrisonconsoles.com/site/history.html
Haruch, Steve. 2010. 'Women Account for less Than 5 Percent of Producers and Engineers – But Maybe Not for Long'. *Nashville Scene*, 3 June. Accessed January 2018 http://www.nashvillescene.com/nashville/women-account-for-less-than-5-percent-of-producers-and-engineers-andmdash-but-maybe-not-for-long/Content?oid=1597594
Heartz, Daniel. 1995. *Haydn, Mozart and the Viennese School: 1740–1780*. New York: W. W. Norton & Company.
Hills, Steve. 2006. 'What Makes the Synclavier So Special and Different?' *500 Sound*. Accessed January 2018 http://www.500sound.com/uniquesync.html
Hitchins, Ray. 2014. *Vibe Merchants: The Sound Creators of Jamaican Popular Music*. Farnham: Ashgate.
Hoffman, Frank. 2005. *Encyclopedia of Recorded Sound*. New York: Routledge.
Holt, Charles and Laury, Susan. 2002. 'Risk Aversion and Incentive Effects'. *American Economic Review*, 92, 5, 1644–1655.
Homer, Matthew. 2009. 'Beyond the Studio: The Impact of Home Recording Technologies on Music Creation and Consumption'. *Nebula*, 6, 3, 85–99.
Houle, Jeffrey R. 1991. 'Digital Audio Sampling, Copyright Law and the American Music Industry: Piracy or Just a Bad "Rap"?' *Loyola Law Review*, 37, 4, 879–902.
Howard, David N. 2004. *Sonic Alchemy – Visionary Music Producers and Their Maverick Recordings*. Milwaukee, WI: Hal Leonard.
Howlett, Mike. 2009. *Interview with the Author*. 16 July.
Howlett, Mike. 2009. *The Record Producer as Nexus: Creative Inspiration, Technology and the Recording Industry*. PhD thesis, University of Glamorgan.
Huber, David and Runstein, Robert. 2013. *Modern Recording Techniques*. Oxon: Focal Press.
Humberstone, Nigel. 1997. 'Christopher Fogel: Alanis Morrisette's Jagged Little Pill'. *Sound on Sound*, 12, 5, 70–76.
Inglis, Sam. 2000. 'Mercury Rising – Dave Fridmann: Producing Flaming Lips & Mercury Rev'. In: *Sound on Sound*, 15, 11, 204–210.
Inglis, Sam. 2000. 'XTC: Ideal Studio & Recording Apple Venus Vol. 1 & Wasp Star'. *Sound on Sound*, 9, 15, 120–129.
Jackson, Brian M. 2013. *The Music Producer's Survival Guide: Chaos, Creativity and Career in Independent and Electronic Music*. Boston, MA: Cengage Learning PTR.
James, Alex. 2007. *Bit of a Blur*. London: Little Brown.

Jensen, Joli. 1990. 'Technology/Music: Understanding Processual Relations'. *Popular Music & Society*, 14, 1, 7–12.

Johns, Glyn. 2014. *Sound Man: A Life Recording Hits with The Rolling Stones, The Who, Led Zeppelin, The Eagles, Eric Clapton, The Faces* .... New York: Blue Ryder Press.

Jones, Carys Wyn. 2008. *The Rock Canon: Canonical Values in the Reception of Rock*. Aldershot: Ashgate.

Jones, Steve. 1990. 'Technology and the Future of Popular Music'. *Popular Music & Society*, 14, 1, 19–23.

Jones, Steve. 1990. 'The Intro and the Outro: Technology and Popular Music Practice'. *Popular Music & Society*, 14, 1, 1–6.

Jones, Steve. 1992. *Rock Formation: Music Technology and Mass Communication*. Newbury Park, CA: Sage Publications.

Jones, Steven. 2006. *Against Technology – From the Luddites to Neo-Luddism*. London & New York: Routledge.

Kagler, Marcus. 2003. 'Taking Snapshots with Stephen Street or Stephen Street Blah Blah Blah'. *Under the Radar*, 5, 92–92.

Katz, Mark. 2004. *Capturing Sound: How Technology Has Changed Music*. Berkeley & London: University of California Press.

Kealy, E. R. 1979. 'From Craft to Art: The Case of Sound Mixers and Popular Music'. *Sociology of Work and Occupations*, 6, 1, 3–29.

Keep, Andy. 2005. 'Does Creative Abuse Drive Developments in Record Production?' *Journal on the Art of Record Production*. Accessed January 2018 http://:www.arpjournal.com

Kehew, Brian. and Ryan, Kevin. 2006. *Recording The Beatles*. USA: Curvebender Publishing.

Keyes, Cheryl. 2000. 'Empowering Self, Making Choices, Creating Spaces: Black Female Identity via Rap Music Performance'. *The Journal of American Folklore*, 113, 449, 255–269.

Kitts, Jeff and Tolinski, Brad. 2002. *Guitar World Presents Nu-Metal*. Milwaukee, WI: Hal Leonard.

Kraft, James P. 1996. *Stage to Studio: Musicians and the Sound Revolution, 1890–1950*. Baltimore, MD: The Johns Hopkins University Press.

Lacasse, Serge. 2000. 'Voice and Sound Processing: Examples of mise en scene of Voice in Recorded Rock Music'. *Popular Musicology Online*. http://www.popular-musicology-online.com/issues/05/lacasse.html#fn4

Langford, Simon. 2014. *Digital Audio Editing*. Oxon, Focal Press.

Lanois, Daniel. 2011. *Soul Mining: A Musical Life*. London: Faber & Faber.

Lawrence, Alistair. 2012. *Abbey Road: The Best Studio in the World*. London: Bloomsbury.

Leete, Norm. 1999. 'The Fun of the Fairlight'. *Sound on Sound*, 14, 6, 254–259.

Leowenstein, George, Weber, Elke, Hsee, Christopher et al. 2001. 'Risk as Feelings'. *Psychological Bulletin*, 127, 2, 267–286.

LeRoy, Dan. 2006. *Paul's Boutique*. London: Continuum.

Leslie, John and Snyer, Ross. 2010. 'History of the Early Days of Ampex Corporation'. *Journal of the Audio Engineering Society*. AES Historical Committee. Accessed January 2018 http://www.aes.org/aeshc/docs/company.histories/ampex/leslie_snyder_early-days-of-ampex.pdf

Levine, Steve. 2009 *Interview with the Author*. 25 August.

Lexicon. 2010. *Lexicon by Harman – Official Website*. Accessed January 2018 http://www.lexiconpro.com
Leyshon, Andrew. 2009. 'The Software Slump? Digital Music, the Democratisation of Technology, and the Decline of the Recording Studio Sector Within the Musical Economy'. *Environment and Planning A*, 41, 1309–1331.
Leyshon, Andrew. 2014. *Reformatted: Code, Networks and the Transformation of the Music Industry*. New York: Oxford University Press.
Lysloff, Rene and Gay, Leslie (eds.) 2003. *Music and Technoculture*. Middletown, CT: Wesleyan University Press.
Machin, David. 2010. *Analysing Popular Music*. London: Sage.
Maconie, Stuart. 1999. *Blur – 3862 Days – The Official History*. London: Virgin.
Maes, Jan, and Vercammen, Marc (eds.) 2001. *Digital Audio Technology: A Guide to CD, MINI-DISC, SACD, DVD (A), MP3, DAT*. Oxford: Focal Press.
Marmorstein, Gary. 2007. *The Label: The Story of Columbia Records*. New York: Thunder's Mouth Press.
Marshall, Steve. 2008. 'The Story of the BBC Radiophonic Workshop'. *Sound on Sound*, 6, 23, 78–91.
Martin, George. 1979. *All You Need Is Ears*. London: St Martins Press.
Martland, Peter. 2012. *Recording History: The British Record Industry 1888–1931*. London: Scarecrow Press.
Marx, Leo and Smith, Merritt Roe (eds.) 1994. *Does Technology Drive History? The Dilemma of Technological Determinism*. Cambridge, MA: The MIT Press.
Massey, Howard. 2000. *Behind the Glass: Top Record Producers Tell How They Craft the Hits*. New York: BackBeat Books.
Massey, Howard. 2009. *Behind the Glass: Top Record Producers Tell How They Craft the Hits – Volume II*. New York: BackBeat Books.
Massey, Sylvia. 2014. 'Q&A with Sylvia Massy'. *Gearslutz*. Accessed January 2018 https://www.gearslutz.com/board/q-sylvia-massy/902697-army-man-compressor.html
McCormick, Neil. 2006. *U2 by U2*. London: Harper Collins.
McLeod, Kembrew and DiCola, Peter. 2011. *Creative License – The Law and Culture of Digital Sampling*. Durham and London: Duke University Press.
Mellor, David. 1990. *How to Set Up a Home Recording Studio*. Tonbridge: PC Publishing.
Mellor, David. 2009. *Interview with the Author*. 1 August.
Merton, Robert K. 1972. 'Insiders and Outsiders: A Chapter in the Sociology of Knowledge'. *American Journal of Sociology*, 78, 1, 9–47.
Micallef, K. 2004. 'Fatboy Slim: Devil May Care'. *Remix* [Online] 1 October. Accessed January 2018 http://emusician.com/remixmag/artists_interviews/musicians/remix_devil_may_care/
Michie, Chris. 2003. 'We Are the Mothers and This Is What We Sound Like!' *Mix: Professional Audio and Music Production*. 1 January. Accessed January 2018 http://mixonline.com/recording/business/audio_mothers_sound/
Miller, Louis. 2002. 'Band of Brothers'. *CMJ*, 26 August, 8–9.
Milner, Greg. 2009. *Perfecting Sound Forever: The Story of Recorded Music*. London: Granta Publications.
Milner, Greg. 2010. 'Surfer Rosa Invents the 90s Sound'. *SPIN*, May, 52.
Mix Online. 2007. '1972 MCI JH-400 Series Inline Console'. *Mix Online*, 1 September. Accessed January 2018 http://www.mixonline.com/news/news-products/1972-mci-jh-400-series-inline-console/377971

MGMT. 2010. Official website. Accessed January 2018 http://www.whoismgmt.com
Moore, Allan. 2001. *Rock: The Primary Text*. 2nd ed. Aldershot: Ashgate.
Moore, Allan. 2004. *Analyzing Popular Music*. Cambridge: Cambridge University Press.
Moore, Allan. 2007. *Critical Essays in Popular Musicology*. Aldershot: Ashgate.
Moore, Allan. 2012. *Song Means: Analyzing and Interpreting Recorded Popular Song*. Farnham, NY: Ashgate.
Moore, Allan and Dockwray, Ruth. 2008. 'The Establishment of the Virtual Performance Space in Rock'. *Twentieth-Century Music*, 5, 2, 219–241.
Moore, Austin. 2012. 'All Buttons In: An Investigation into the Use of The 1176 FET Compressor in Popular Music Production'. *Journal on the Art of Record Production*, 6. Accessed January 2018 www.arpjournal.com
Moorefield, Virgil. 2005. *The Producer as Composer*. Cambridge, MA and London: The MIT Press.
Morey, Justin. 2012. 'The Bridgeport Dimension: Copyright Enforcement and Its Implications for Sampling Practice' In: Kärjä, A. V. (ed.) *Music, Law and Business Anthology*. Helsinki: International Institute for Popular Culture, 5, 21–45.
Morton, David. 2000. *Off the Record: The Technology and Culture of Sound Recording in America*. New Brunswick, CA: Rutgers University Press.
Morton, David. 2004. *Sound Recording – The Life Story of a Technology*. Westport: Greenwood Press.
Moylan, William. 2007. *Understanding and Crafting the Mix*. 2nd ed. Burlington: Focal Press.
Mugan, Chris. 2009. 'William Orbit – Coming Back to Earth'. *The Independent*, 7 August. Accessed January 2018 http://www.independent.co.uk/arts-entertainment/music/features/william-orbit-coming-back-to-earth-1768111.html
Muikku, Jari. 1990. 'On the Role and Tasks of a Record Producer'. *Popular Music & Society*, 14, 1, 25–33.
Music Producers Guild. Official website. Accessed January 2018 http://www.mpg.org
Musicians' Union. 2008. Official website. Accessed January 2018 http://www.musiciansunion.org.uk
Myers, Paul. 2001. 'Out of the Bottle'. *Electronic Musician*. Accessed January 2018 http://www.emusician.com/artists/1333/out-of-the-bottle/32050
Nagle, Paul. 1996. 'Blazing a Trail: Liam Howlett: The Prodigy'. *Sound on Sound*, 1, 11, 92–98.
Namen, Mard. 1988. 'Making Tracks with MIDI – Mick Fleetwood of Fleetwood Mac'. *Start* 3, 1. Accessed January 2018 http://www.atarimagazines.com/startv3n1/makingtrackswithmidi.html
NAMM. Official website. Accessed January 2018 http://www.namm.org
Navas, Eduardo. 2012. *Remix Theory: The Aesthetics of Sampling*. New York: Springer.
Navas, Eduardo, Gallagher, Owen and Burrough, xtine. (eds.) 2014. *The Routledge Companion to Remix Studies*. New York: Routledge.
Negroponte, Nicholas. 1995. *Being Digital*. New York: Vintage.
New England Digital. 2010. *New England Digital Archive*. Accessed January 2018 http://www.ned.synthesizers.fr
Northrop Moore, Jerrold. 1999. *Sound Revolutions: A Biography of Fred Gaisberg, Founding Father of Commercial Sound Recording*. London: Sanctuary Publishing.

Nunes, Joseph and Ordanini, Andrea. 2014. 'I Like the Way It Sounds: The Influence of Which Instruments and How Many Instruments Are Audible on Music Preferences'. In: Cotte, June and Wood, Stacy (eds.) *NA – Advances in Consumer Research*, 42. Duluth, MN: Association for Consumer Research, 172–176.

O'Hare, Peter. 2007. 'Steve Albini "In Utero's" Ultra-sound Guy'. In: *The Art of Record Production Conference*. Brisbane, Australia: Queensland University of Technology. Available at: http://artofrecordproduction.com/arp-conferences/arp-2007/19-arp-conference-archive/arp-2007/21-arp-2007-cfp

O'Hare, Peter. 2011. 'Radio Unfriendly: Unacceptable Sounds and Corporate Hounds'. Paper presented at The Unacceptable Conference, Macquarie University, 30 April – 1 May.

Ogg, Alex. 2002. *The Men Behind Def Jam – The Radical Rise of Russell Simmons and Rick Rubin*. London: Omnibus Press.

Ogg, Alex and Upshall, David. 1999. *The Hip Hop Years – A History of Rap*. London: Channel 4 Books, Macmillan Publishers Ltd.

Olsen, Eric and Verna, Paula (eds.) 1999. *The Encyclopaedia of Record Producers: An Indispensable Guide to the Most Important Record Producers in Music History*. New York: Billboard Books.

OTARI Inc. 2010. Official website. Accessed January 2018 http://www.otari.com

Parsons, Alan and Colbeck, Julian. 2014. *Alan Parsons' Art & Science of Sound Recording: The Book*. Milwaukee: Hal Leonard.

Paytress, Mark. 2003. *Siouxsie & The Banshees: The Authorised Biography*. London: Sanctuary Publishing Ltd.

Peddie, Ian. 2012. *Popular Music and Human Rights: Volume I British And American Music*. Farnham and New York: Ashgate.

Peel, Ian. 2005. 'Trevor Horn: 25 Years of Hits'. *Sound on Sound*, 20, 5, 50–57.

Perks, Robert. 1989. *Developments in Recorded Sound – A Catalogue of Oral History Interviews*. London: The British Library Board.

Petersen, George. 1998. *The Alesis ADAT: The Evolution of a Revolution*. Emeryville, CA: Mix Books.

Petersen, George. 2007. *10 Technology Movements*. Mix Online. Accessed April 2016 http://www.mixonline.com/news/news-products/10-technology-movements/371292

Petridis, Alexis. 2009. 'Phil Spector and the Myth of the "Mad" Record Producer'. *The Guardian*, 14 April. Accessed January 2018 http://www.theguardian.com/music/musicblog/2009/apr/14/phil-spector-record-producers

Phillips, Dom. 2009. *Superstar DJs Here We Go! The Rise and Fall of the Superstar DJ*. London: Ebury Press.

Pinch, Trevor and Trocco, Frank. 2002. *Analog Days – The Invention and Impact of the Moog Synthesiser*. Cambridge, MA: Harvard University Press.

Platt, Tony. 2007. 'Q&A with Haydn Bendall, Mike Howlett and Tony Platt'. *Gearslutz*, 8 June. Accessed January 2018 https://www.gearslutz.com/board/q-haydn-bendall-mick-glossop-mike-howlett-tony-platt/127182-question-tony-back-black.html

Platt, Tony. 2009. *Interview with the Author*. 15 May.

Postman, Neil. 1993. *Technopoly – The Surrender of Culture to Technology*. New York: Vintage Books.

Prendergast, Mark. 1987. 'The Magic of Daniel Lanois (Part II)'. *Sound on Sound*, 2, 11, 42–46.

Prendergast, Mark. 1996. 'Electric Eclectic: William Orbit'. *Sound on Sound*, 11, 3, 168–173.
Publison. 2010. *Publison Systems – Official Website*. Accessed January 2018 http://pagesperso-orange.fr/.publison/_english/index.htm
Ramone, Phil. 2007. *Making Records – The Scenes Behind the Music*. New York: Hyperion.
Reddington, Helen. 2012. *The Lost Women of Rock Music: Female Musicians of the Punk Era*. 2nd ed. Sheffield: Equinox Publishing Ltd.
Redfern, Mark. 2004. 'The Other Stars, Here's to the Ones in the Control Room'. *Under the Radar*, 5, 90.
Reid, Gordon. 2002. '40 Years of Korg Gear: The History of Korg Part 1'. *Sound on Sound*, 17, 12, 194–203.
Reid, Gordon. 2004. 'Designing the Future: The History of Roland – Part 1: 1930 – 1978'. *Sound on Sound*, 20, 1, 106–121.
Reid, Gordon. 2004. 'The History of Roland – Part 2: 1979–1985'. *Sound on Sound*, 20, 2, 129–145.
Repsch, John. 2001. *The Legendary Joe Meek: The Telstar Man*. London: Cherry Red Books.
Reynolds, Simon. 1992. 'Steve Albini: Smoke 'Em If You Got 'Em'. *Melody Maker*, 21 November. Accessed January 2018 http://www.rocksbackpages.com/print.html?ArticleID=983
Rimbaud, Penny. 2005. 'John Loder: Sound Engineer Who Founded the Legendary Southern Studios'. *The Guardian*, 19 August. Accessed January 2018 http://www.guardian.co.uk/news/2005/aug/19/guardianobituaries.artsobituaries
Rimbaud, Penny. 2014. *Interview with the Author*. 5 September.
Rimmer, Matthew. 2005. 'The Grey Album: Copyright Law and Digital Sampling'. *Media International Australia Incorporating Culture and Policy*, 114, 40–53.
Robertson, Alex. 2006. *William Orbit Interview. Virgin Media*. Accessed January 2018 http://www.virginmedia.com/music/interviews/williamorbit.php
Robinson, Dave. 1994. 'Flood Warning'. *Future Music*, 24, 45–46.
Roger Linn Design. 2010. Official website. Accessed January 2018 http://www.rogerlinndesign.com
Rosen, Charles. 1987. *The Classical Style: Haydn, Mozart, Beethoven*. New York: W. W. Norton & Company.
Rule, Greg. 1998. 'William Orbit: The Methods and Machinery Behind Madonna's Ray of Light'. *Keyboard Magazine*, 24, 7, 30–38.
Rumsey, Francis. 1994. *MIDI Systems and Control*. 2nd ed. Oxford: Focal Press.
Rumsey, Francis and McCormick, Tim. 2014. *Sound and Recording: Applications and Theory*. Oxon: Focal Press.
Russolo, Luigi. 1967 [1913]. *The Art of Noise (Futurist Manifesto, 1913)*. A Great Bear Pamphlet. Something Else Press.
Said, Amir. 2010. 'John King and the Story of Chung King Studios'. *BeatTips*, October. Accessed January 2018 http://www.beattips.com/beattips/2014/10/john-king-and-the-story-of-chung-king-studios.html
Sanjek, David. 1992. 'Don't Have to DJ No More: Sampling and the Autonomous Creator'. *Cardozo Arts and Entertainment Law Journal*, 607, 612–615.
Savage, Mark. 2012. 'Why Are Female Record Producers So Rare?' *BBC*, 29 August. Accessed January 2018. http://www.bbc.com/news/entertainment-arts-19284058
Savona, Anthony. 2005. *Console Confessions: Insights and Opinions from the Great Music Producers*. San Francisco: Backbeat.

Schaeffer, Pierre. 2012. *In Search of a Concrete Music*. Translated by North, Christine and Dack, John. Berkeley and Los Angeles, CA: University of California Press.

Schmidt Horning, Susan. 2002. *Chasing Sound: The Culture and Technology of Recording Studios in America, 1877 to 1977*. PhD thesis, Case Western Reserve University, Cleveland.

Schmidt Horning, Susan. 2013. *Chasing Sound: Technology, Culture & the Art of Studio Recording from Edison to the LP*. Baltimore, MD: The Johns Hopkins University Press.

Schoenberg, Arnold. 1987 *Letters*. London: Faber & Faber.

Schoenherr, Steven E. 1999. 'Microphones part 2 – The Electrical Era'. *Audio Engineering Society*. Accessed January 2018 http://www.aes.org/aeshc/docs/recording.technology.history/microphones2.html

Schultz, Barbara. [1994] 2000. 'Steve Albini – Nemesis of Corporate Rock'. In: *Music Producers: Conversations with Today's Top Hitmakers*, ed. Barbara Schultz. USA: Intertec Publishing.

Schultz, Barbara. 1999. 'Colin Fairly and Helioscentric Studios: Producer/Engineer's New Home: Is a Project Room That's Gone Commercial'. *Mix Online*. Accessed January 2018 http://www.mixonline.com/news/profiles/colin-fairly-and-helioscentric-studios-producerengineers-new-home-project-room-thats-gone-commercial/374213

Schultz, Barbara. 2000. *Mix ProAudio Series – Music Producers: Conversations with Today's Top Hitmakers*. New York: Intertec Publishing.

Scott, Danny. 2001. 'Stormin' Norman'. *Future Music*, 106, 94–101.

Scott, Ken and Owsinski, Bobby. 2012. *Abbey Road to Ziggy Stardust: Off the Record with the Beatles, Bowie, Elton & So Much More*. Los Angeles, CA: Alfred Music Publishing.

Senior, Mike. 2000. 'David Frank: Recording Christina Aguilera's Genie in a Bottle'. *Sound on Sound*, 6, 15, 48–56.

Senior, Mike. 2000. 'Johnny Dollar & Simon Palmskin: Recording Gabrielle's "Rise"' *Sound on Sound*, 9, 15, 46–52.

Sewell, Amanda. 2014. 'How Copyright Affected the Musical Style and Critical Reception of Sample-Based Hip-Hop'. *Journal of Popular Music Studies*, 2, 3, 295–320.

Sexton, Jamie. 2009. 'Digital Music: Production, Distribution and Consumption'. In: *Digital Cultures: Understanding New Media*. Maidenhead: McGraw Hill Open University Press, 92–101.

Shapiro, Peter (ed.) 2000. *Modulations: A History of Electronic Music – Throbbing Words on Sound*. New York: Caipirinha Productions Inc.

Sheldon, Chris. 2009. *Interview with the Author*. 27 July.

Shepherd, Rebecca. 2007. 'Stephen Street and the Art of Man Management'. *Journal on the Art of Record Production*, 2. Accessed January 2018 http://www.arpjournal.com

Shepherd, Rebecca. 2011. 'The Collaborative Recordist'. *Musicology Australia*, 33, 2, 255–264.

Sillitoe, Sue. 1994. 'Production Lines – Mike Stock'. *Sound on Sound*, 9, 10, 208.

Sillitoe, Sue. 1994. 'Streets Ahead – Stephen Street'. *Sound on Sound*, 9, 9, 108–114.

Sillitoe, Sue. 1998. 'Craig Leon: Recording the New Blondie Album'. *Sound on Sound*, 2, 14, 158–165.

Sillitoe, Sue. 1999. 'Street Life: At Home with Stephen Street'. *Sound on Sound*, 14, 10, 98–103.

Sillitoe, Sue. 1999. 'Recording Cher's Believe'. *Sound on Sound*, 4, 14, 34–40.

Sillitoe, Sue. 2008. 'MPG Producers of All Time'. 18 December 2008. Accessed January 2018 http://www.mpg.org.uk/news_stories/104
Simons, Dave. 2004. *Studio Stories*. San Francisco: Backbeat Books.
Simons, Dave. 2006. *Analog Recording: Using Analogue Gear in Today's Home Studio*. San Francisco: Backbeat Books.
Skare, Roswitha, Windfeld Lund, Niels and Vårheim, Andreas (eds.) 2007. *A Document (Re)turn: Contributions from a Research Field in Transition*. Frankfurt: Peter Lang.
Society of Professional Audio Recording Services. 2010. Official website. Accessed January 2018 http://www.spars.com
Solid State Logic. 2010. Official website. Accessed January 2018 http://www.solid-state-logic.com
Sony/HHB. 1988. 'Fiction, Fact'. Advertisement. *Studio Sound*, 30, 1, 8–9.
Sony. 2010. Official website. Accessed January 2018 http://www.sony.com
Stapley, Patrick. 1994. 'Otari Radar'. *Studio Sound*, 36, 10, 53–60.
Steinberg. 2010. Official website. Accessed January 2018 http://www.steinberg.net
Stenman, Eric. 1998. 'DJ Shadow: Samplers, Turntables & Downtime'. *Tape Op*. 11. Accessed April 2016 http://tapeop.com/interviews/11/dj-shadow/
Sterling, Christopher H. and O'Dell, Cary. 2009. *The Concise Encyclopedia of American Radio*. London: Routledge.
Sterne, Jonathan. 2006. 'What's Digital in Digital Music?' In Messaris, Paul and Humphreys, Lee (eds.) *Digital Media: Transformations in Human Communication*. New York: Peter Lang.
Stiernberg, John. 2008. *Succeeding in Music: Business Chops for Performers and Songwriters*. Milwaukee, WI: Hal Leonard.
Stock, Mike. 2004. *The Hit Factory – The Stock Aitken Waterman Story*. London: New Holland.
Stone, Terri. 1992. *Music Producers: Conversations and Interviews with Some of Today's Top Record Makers*. London: Omnibus Press.
Strawn, John. 1997. 'Technological Change: The Challenge to the Audio and Music Industries'. *Journal of the Audio Engineering Society*, 45, 3, 170–184.
Street, Stephen. 2009. *Interview with the Author*. 7 September.
Streicher, Ron. 2003. 'The Decca Tree'. *Mix*. Accessed January 2018 http://mixonline.com/recording/applications/audio_decca_tree/
Studer. 2010. *Studer by Harman – Official Website*. Accessed January 2018 http://www.studer.ch
Sutcliffe, Phil. 1987. 'Sound Wars: M/A/R/R/S Vs. Stock, Aitken, Waterman'. *Q Magazine*, 2, 3, 10–12.
Swedien, Bruce. 2004. *Make Mine Music*. Norway: MIA Musikk.
Swedien, Bruce. 2009. *In the Studio with Michael Jackson*. Milwaukee: Hal Leonard Corporation.
Tagg, Philip. 1982. 'Analysing Popular Music – Theory, Method and Practice'. *Popular Music*, 2, 37–67.
Tagg, Philip. 2000. '"The Work": An Evaluative Charge'. In: Talbot, M. (ed.) *The Musical Work – Reality or Invention?* Liverpool: Liverpool University Press. 153–167.
Tagg, Philip. 2013. *Music's Meanings*. MMMSP e-Books. Accessed January 2018 http://tagg.org/mmmsp/publications.html
Talbot-Smith, Michael. 1994. *Audio Recording & Reproduction: Practical Measures for Audio Enthusiasts*. Oxford: Newnes.

Taylor, Shawn. 2007. *People's Instinctive Travels and the Paths of Rhythm*. London: Bloomsbury Academic.
Taylor, Timothy. 2001. *Strange Sounds: Music, Technology and Culture*. London & New York: Routledge.
Taylor, Timothy. 2007. *Beyond Exoticism: Western Music and the World*. Durham: Duke University Press.
Tennent, Scott. 2011. *Spiderland*. New York: Continuum.
Théberge, Paul. 1989. 'The "Sound" of Music: Technological Rationalization and the Production of Popular Music'. *New Formations*, 8, 99–111.
Théberge, Paul. 1990. 'Musicians as Market – Consumers of Technology'. *One Two Three Four*, 9, 53–60.
Théberge, Paul. 1997. *Any Sound You Can Imagine: Making Music/Consuming Technology*. Hanover: Wesleyan University Press.
Théberge, Paul. 2001. '"Plugged in": Technology and Popular Music'. In: Frith, Simon, Straw, Will and Street, John (eds.) *The Cambridge Companion to Pop and Rock*. Cambridge: Cambridge University Press, 3–5.
Théberge, Paul. 2004. 'The Network Studio: Historical and Technological Paths to a New Ideal in Music Making'. *Social Studies of Science*, 34, 5, 759–781.
Tingen, Paul. 1994. 'Daniel Lanois – Canada Dry'. *Sound on Sound*, 9, 11, 130–136.
Tingen, Paul. 1994. 'U2 & Robbie Adams: Recording in Mysterious Ways'. *Sound on Sound*, 9, 5, 112–121.
Tingen, Paul. 1995. 'Tim Simenon – Bomb the Bass'. *Sound on Sound*, 10, 5, 136–141.
Tingen, Paul. 1997. 'Pop Art: Flood & Howie B – Recording U2's Pop'. *Sound on Sound*, 12, 9, 188–203.
Tingen, Paul. 1999. 'Jim Scott: Recording Red Hot Chili Peppers' Californication'. *Sound on Sound*, 15, 2, 44–50.
Tingen, Paul. 2005. 'Phil Ramone: Managing People & Technology'. *Sound on Sound*, 20, 6, 142–147.
Tingen, Paul. 2005. 'Steve Albini: Sound Engineer Extraordinaire'. *Sound on Sound*, 20, 6, 98–105.
Toffler, Alvin. 1980. *The Third Wave*. New York: Bantam Books.
Toms, Melvyn. 2009. *Interview with the Author*. MP3 recording in possession of the author, 3 July.
Toop, David. 2001. *Ocean of Sound: Aether Talk, Ambient Sound and Imaginary Worlds*. London: Serpent's Tail.
Tversky, Amos and Khanamen, Daniel. 1981. 'The Framing of Decisions and the Psychology of Choice'. *Science*, 211, 4481, 453–458.
Ultimate Eurythmics. 2013. 'Eurythmics Savage 25: Interview with Dave Stewart'. Accessed January 2018 http://www.eurythmics-ultimate.com/eurythmics-savage25-interview-with-dave-stewart/
Uncut. 1999. 'Uncut Magazine Interviews Tony Visconti. *Uncut*. Accessed January 2018 http://www.bowiegoldenyears.com/low.html
Universal Audio. 2015. *Fairchild 670 Legacy Compressor Plug In*. Accessed January 2018 http://www.uaudio.com/store/compressors-limiters/fairchild-670.html
Universal Audio. 2015. Official website. Accessed January 2018 http://www.uaudio.com
Vail, Mark. 2000. *Vintage Synthesisers*. San Francisco: Backbeat Books.
Vail, Mark. 2002. 'Working Class Korg M1'. *Sound on Sound*, 17, 4, 258–263.

Vanderslice, John. 1998. 'Butch Vig: Garbage and Smart Studios'. *Tape Op*, 11, November/December. Accessed January 2018 http://tapeop.com/interviews/11/butch-vig/
Veak, Tyler. (ed.) 2006. *Democratizing Technology*. Albany: State University of New York Press.
Verna, Paul. 1995. 'Budget Studio Gear Breaks Barriers'. *Billboard*, 14 October, 1–91.
Verna, Paul. 1995. 'For Mercenary Audio, It's Still an Analog World'. *Billboard*, 23 September. 54.
Von Appen, Ralf, Doehring, André, Helms, Dietrich and Moore, Allan (eds.) 2015. *Song Interpretation in 21st Century Pop Music*. London and New York: Routledge.
Walters, Barry. 1986. 'The King of Rap – Rick Rubin Makes the Music Industry Walk His Way'. *The Village Voice*, 31, 19–25.
Warez. 2006. 'Flood – Pro Active Producer'. 29 March [Online]. Accessed January 2018 http://magazine.warez.com/interviews/flood-pro-active-producer.html
Warner, Timothy. 2000. 'The Ghost in the Machine – Video Killed the Radio Star'. *Popular Musicology Online*, 3. Accessed January 2018 http://www.cyberstudia.com/popular-musicology-online/papers-4/warner.html
Warner, Timothy. 2003. *Pop Music, Technology and Creativity: Trevor Horn and the Digital Revolution*. Aldershot: Ashgate.
Warner, Timothy. 2009. 'Approaches to Analyzing Recordings of Popular Music' In: Scott, Derek B. (ed.) *Ashgate Research Companion to Popular Musicology*. Farnham and New York: Ashgate.
Washburne, Christopher and Derno, Maiken. 2004. *Bad Music: The Music We Love to Hate*. New York: Routledge.
Waterman, Pete. 2000. *I Wish I Was Me – The Autobiography*. London: Virgin.
Watson, Allan. 2015. *Cultural Production in and Beyond the Recording Studio*. New York: Routledge.
Watson, Liam. 2012. *Interview with the Author*. February.
Watson, Paul. 2003. 'Critical Approaches to Hollywood Cinema: Authorship, Genre and Stars'. In: Nelmes, Jill (ed.) *An Introduction to Film Studies*. London: Routledge.
Weingarten, Christopher. 2010. *It Takes a Nation of Millions to Hold Us Back*. New York: Bloomsbury Academic.
Weiss, David. 2010. 'Studio Drumming in the Age of Pro Tools'. *Drum Magazine*, 26 August. Accessed January 2018 http://www.drummagazine.com/plugged-in/post/studio-drumming-in-the-age-of-pro-tools/
Weller, Don. 1980. 'Abbey Road Will Hold Studio Sale'. *Billboard*, 30 August, 64.
Wenger, Etienne. 1999. *Communities of Practice: Learning, Meaning and Identity*. Cambridge: Cambridge University Press.
Westminster Exhibitions Ltd. 1990. 'Tomorrow's Music Technology – Today. The MIDI Music Show' [Advertisement]. *Sound on Sound*, 5, 4, 68.
White, P. 1997. *MIDI for the Technophobe*. London: Sanctuary Publishing.
White, Paul. 1999. 'King of the Castle – Paul Hardcastle'. *Sound on Sound*, 14, 12, 48–54.
Whiteley, Sheila. 1997. *Sexing the Groove: Popular Music and Gender*. London: Routledge.
Whiteley, Sheila. 2000. *Women and Popular Music: Sexuality, Identity and Subjectivity*. New York: Routledge.
Williams, Alan. 2010. 'Pay Some Attention to the Man Behind the Curtain – Unsung Heroes and the Canonization of Process in the Classic Albums Documentary Series'. *Journal of Popular Music Studies*, 22, 2, 166–175.

Williams, Alan. 2011. 'Divide and Conquer: Power, Role Formation and Conflict in Recording Studio Architecture'. *Journal on the Art of Record Production*. Accessed January 2018 http://www.arpjournal.com

Williams, Chris. 2012. 'Jazzie B Revisits Soul II Soul's Debut Album "Club Classics Vol. One/Keep On Movin" | #ReturnToTheClassics'. *Soul Culture*, 18 May. Accessed January 2018 http://soulculture.com/music-blog/jazzie-b-revisits-soul-ii-souls-debut-album-club-classics-vol-onekeep-on-movin-returntotheclassics/

Wolfe, Paula. 2012. 'A Studio of One's Own'. *Journal on the Art of Record Production*, 7 [Online]. Accessed January 2018 http://arpjournal.com/technology-time-and-place/

Young, Andrew. 2004. 'Albini Laments Age of Over Production'. *Sidelines – Student Newspaper of Middle Tennessee State University*, 15 March. Accessed January 2018 http://media.www.mtsusidelines.com/media/storage/paper202/news/2004/03/15/News/Albini.Laments.Age.Of.OverProduction-633200.shtml

Young, Rob. 2006. *Rough Trade: Labels Unlimited*. London: Black Dog Publishing.

Zagorski-Thomas. 2014. *A Musicology of Record Production*. Cambridge: Cambridge University Press.

Zak, Albin J. III 2001. *The Poetics of Rock: Cutting Tracks, Making Records*. California: University of California Press.

Zak, Albin J. 2007. 'Editorial – The Art of Record Production'. *Journal on the Art of Record Production*, 2 [Online]. Accessed January 2018 http://arpjournal.com/the-art-of-record-production/

Zak, Albin J. 2010. *I Don't Sound Like Nobody: Remaking Music in 1950s America*. Ann Arbor, MI: University of Michigan Press.

Zappa, Frank and Occhiogrosso, Peter. 1989. *The Real Frank Zappa Book*. New York: Simon & Schuster.

Filmography

Classic Albums U2 – The Joshua Tree. 2001. Directed by Bob Smeaton, Philip King and Nuala O' Connor. DVD. New York: Red.
Classic Albums Def Leppard – Hysteria. 2002. Directed by Matthew Longfellow. DVD. New York: Red.
Classic Albums Black Sabbath Paranoid. 2010. Directed by Matthew Longfellow. DVD. New York: Red.
Classic Albums The Sex Pistols – Never Mind the Bollocks … Here's the Sex Pistols. 2002. Directed by Matthew Longfellow. DVD. New York: Red.
Grohl, Dave, Rota, J. and Ramsay, J. 2013. *Sound City*. Roswell Films Ltd.
Phil Spector. 2013. Directed by David Mamet. HBO Films.
Telstar – The Joe Meek Story. 2008. Directed by Nick Moran. G2 Pictures.
The Smart Studios Story. 2014. Directed by Butch Vig and Steve Marker. Independent Film. Accessed January 2018. Available at: http://www.smartstudiosdocumentary.com
The Agony and the Ecstacy of Phil Spector. 2010. Directed by Vikram Jayanti. BBC.

Index

Abbey Road Studios 13, 65, 69–70, 72, 93, 178
'ABLE' computer 24
Absolute 93
AC/DC 31, 139
Achtung Baby (U2) 149, 150
'Acusonic' process 176
Adams, Robbie 116
ADAT (Alesis Digital Audio Tape) 55, 57–60, 62, 70, 73, 161, 177
Adorno, Theodore 173
Afanasieff, Walter 115, 124, 125
Afrika Bambaataa 46
Against Technology (Jones) 111
Age of Plastic, The (Buggles) 8
Agnello, Anthony 31
Aguilera, Christina 67–8
AIR Montserrat Desk 38
Aitken, Matt 99, 119
AKAI 42, 155
    MPC-60 43–4, 59, 73
    S-900 43, 45, 47
    S-950 155
    S-1000 43
    S-1100 42, 43
    S-3000 43, 165
    S-3200 148
    S series 43
AKG
    BX-20 reverb 166–8
    C12 microphone 70
Akon 68
Albarn, Damon 182
Albini, Steve 13–14, 82, 109, 120, 123, 126, 131, 175
Alesis 42, 55, 57
    A-DAT 166
Alice in Chains 71
Allen, Rick 40
Ampex 77
AMS
    DMX-15-80 33, 34
    RMX-16 Digital Reverberator 30–1, 33–4
anachronisms 89–91
Analogue Fetishes and Digital Futures (Berk) 111
analogue recording 68–73
Analogue Sound in the Age of Digital Tools (Barlindhaug) 111, 126–7, 174
analogue synthesis, decline of 52–3
Antares Autotune 32, 68, 113
Any Sound You Can Imagine (Théberge) 4
Appetite for Destruction (Guns n' Roses) 87
Apple 64–8, 87, 147, 166, 177
APRS (Association of Professional Recording Services) 38
'Army Man' compressor 72
ARP synthesizers 52–3
'artist-producer' 98–101
Art of Mixing, The (Gibson) 15
Art of Noise, The 23, 90
Art of Recording and Aesthetics of Perfection, The (Hamilton) 82
Art of Record Production forum 5
Art of Record Production (Zagorski-Thomas) 5
Atari 121
    1040ST 45–6, 55, 106, 129–31, 144, 147, 151, 155
    Mega-2 148
Atkin, Malcolm 28–9, 38–9, 65
Attali, Jaques 13
Audio Culture (Cox) 174
Audio Engineering Society 56, 59–60, 77, 78, 83
Audio Home Recording Act 52
Audio Recording and Reproduction for Audio Enthusiasts (Talbot-Smith) 108
auteurism 103–6
Autobahn (Kraftwerk) 8

Babyfox 143
'Back in Black' (AC/DC) 139
Back in Black (AC/DC) 31
Bad (Jackson) 26
Baker, Roy Thomas 95
Ballard, Glen 58
Bannister, Matthew 84
Barber, Jim 58
Barlindhaug, Gaute 111, 126–7, 174–5
Bates, Eliot 5
BBC Redundant Plant 70
Beadle, Jeremy 4, 99–101, 174
Beastie Boys 47, 79, 137, 138–43, 182
'Beat It' (Jackson) 25
Beatles 12, 69, 72, 93
Becker, Howard 84
Behind the Glass Volumes I and II (Massey) 112
'Believe' (Cher) 68, 113
Bennett, Samantha 13, 111, 113, 179
Berk, Mike 111, 156–7
Better Living Through Chemistry (Fatboy Slim) 155
Be With You (Iglesias) 61
Big Black 10, 13, 109, 120
binaries 81–2
'binaural recording' (stereo) 77
Birrell, Harvey 109, 175
Bit of a Blur (James) 160
'Black Hole Sun' (Soundgarden) 89
Black Sabbath 6
Blank Generation (Richard Hell and the Voidoids) 63
blended technologies 8–10
Blondie 62–4
Blondie (Blondie) 63
Blumlein, Alan 77
Blur 127–8, 137, 160–5, 178, 182, 183
Blur (Blur) 160
Bolter 174
Bomb the Bass 46, 47, 100
Bon Jovi 87
Bono 150, 152, 153
Borwick, John 83
boundary pushing 76, 176, 180
Bowie, David 31, 44, 95
Bradford, Michael 124
Breeders, The 90

Bricks Are Heavy (L7) 66
'brick wall limiting' 89
Briscoe, Desmond 70
Brock-Nannestad, G. 111
Bros 79
Brothers in Arms (Dire Straits) 28
Brovig-Hanssen, Ragnhild 15
Brown, Errol 59
Brown, James 48
Brown, Mick 13
Brown, Phil 71
Bruns, Axel 108
Buggles, The 8, 98
Burgess, Richard James 2, 112
Burns, Lori 1
Bush, Kate 22
Buskin, Richard 112
Busta Rhymes 71
Butler, Mark 1, 134

Cadac 37, 96
Californication (Red Hot Chilli Peppers) 89
canon 11–14
Capital Effects (Crary) 174
Capturing Sound (Katz) 4, 5, 134, 154, 157
Casio FZ-1 48
Cattini, Clem 81
Caughty, Jimmy 100
Cavallo, Rob 71
CDs 50–1, 78, 174
Chanan, Michael 93, 102
Charlatans, The 61
Chasing Sound (Schmidt Horning) 4
Chemical Brothers 90, 100
Cher 68, 113
Chung King 138–40
C-Lab 45, 48, 128, 151
Classic Albums documentary 6
Clayton, Adam 49, 150
'Close (To the Edit)' (The Art of Noise) 23
Club Classics Volume One (Soul II Soul) 50
Coldcut 47–8, 100
Coleman, Mark 42
Collier, Nicola 45
Collins, Phil 23, 33, 41
competitiveness/ambition 117, 119–20

computer-based sequencers 45–6
computer-based workstations 65. *See also* Apple
consoles 37–40
'construction' 81–3, 111, 120, 138, 180
Cook, Nicholas 14
Cook, Norman 100, 129, 155–9, 182–3
Cook, Peter 45
Cornershop 100
Cottrell, Stephen 1
Covach, John 1, 181
Cox, Christoph 174
Coxon, Graham 161, 162
Crary, Jonathan 174
Crash (Human League) 41
Crass 13, 109
Creation Technologies 60
Creator software 45, 155
Critical Approaches to the Production of Music and Sound (Bennett and Bates) 5
Crush (OMD) 97
Cubase 90, 147–8
Cubase II 144
Cubase Version 1 45
Culnane, Steve 29, 39, 177
Culshaw, John 94, 104
Culture Club 25
Cunningham, Mark 13, 100, 111, 113, 179
Curnow, Ian 105
Currell, Christopher 26
Curtiss Maldoon 143, 144
Cutler, Chris 179

Daddy's House Studios and Music Palace 71
D'Angelo 90–1
Danielsen, Anne 1, 15, 134
Dark Side of the Moon (Pink Floyd) 98
Dartmouth Digital Synthesizer 24
DASH 27–30, 35, 55, 57, 60, 66, 97, 119
DAT format 50, 51–2
Davis, Bob 175
Day, Morris 48
DBX 160 compressor 138
DBX 165-A compressor 138
Dead or Alive 79, 99–100
Dean, Hazel 99

Death Row studios 71
'Decca tree' technique 94
Def Jam 138–9
Def Leppard 10, 39–40
De La Soul 47, 79, 99
De La Soul Is Dead (De La Soul) 99
'democratization of technology' 176–7
Democratizing Technology (Veak) 111
Depeche Mode 44, 79, 105
deviance 84–6
DeVries, Marius 144, 145–6
Dibben, Nicola 15
Dido 88
Digidesign 64, 65, 67, 70, 100, 116, 121, 130, 145, 147, 155
digital effects processors 30–4
digital formats 50–2
digital tape recorders 27–30
digital technologies. *See also individual technologies*
    emergence of 7–9
    move to 55–6
Dimebag Darrell 61
Dire Straits 28, 35
Dirty (Sonic Youth) 66
diversification of skill sets 96–7
DJs 99
DJ Shadow 59
Dockwray, Ruth 15, 133, 181
documentation 78
Doehring, André 181
Dolby, Ray 78
Dollar, Johnny 62
Dookie (Green Day) 71
Dowd, Tom 92
Downward Spiral, The (Nine Inch Nails) 149, 151
Doyle, Peter 15
Dr Dre 44, 71, 94, 116, 121
Dreaming, The (Bush) 22
Drony, Maureen 115
Drummond, Bill 100
Dudgeon, Gus 95, 106
Duke, George 115
Dummy (Portishead) 88
Dunne, Phil 95
Duran Duran 8, 31, 53
Duran Duran (Duran Duran) 8

Durant, Alan 111, 117, 179
Dust Brothers 47

Earth Moving (Oldfield) 46
eBay 70
Echo and Reverb (Doyle) 15
Edge, The 49, 150, 152–4
Eels 89
808s and Heartbreak (West) 68, 73
Eisenberg, Evan 94, 104
Electric Café (Kraftwerk) 79
'Electric Feel' (MGMT) 137, 182
Electronic Media and Culture (Emmerson) 97
Elefante, Dino 61
Elevado, Russell 90–1
Ellis, Mark *see* Flood
Emagic Logic 67, 87, 90, 147, 155
EMI 77
Eminem 88, 94
Emmerson, Simon 88, 97
E-Mu 44
    Emulator 42
    Emulator II 43, 79, 97, 101
    SP-12 47, 139
    SP-1200 50
Endtroducing (DJ Shadow) 59
Eno, Brian 32, 49, 84, 86–7, 91, 148–9
Ensoniq Mirage 42
'enthusiasts' 108, 177
Epiphany (T-Pain) 68
Erasure 105
Erik B and Rakim 47, 48
Ett (formerly Ettinger), Steve 138–43, 182
Euphonix 58
Eurythmics 25, 98
Evans 153
Evans, Faith 71
Evasions, The 59
Eventide Harmonizer 30–2
Everett, Walter 1, 181
Evolution Synthesis 42
Experience (Prodigy) 127

Facelift (Alice in Chains) 71
Fairchild 670 limiter 72
Fairlight CMI (Computer Music Instrument) 8, 20–3, 35, 40, 42, 56, 98, 101, 102, 119, 121, 175–6

Fairly, Colin 61
Farnham, John 22
Fatboy Slim 89, 100, 134, 137, 154–9, 178, 182, 183
Fat of Land, The (Prodigy) 90
faults and flaws 88–9
Fear of a Black Planet (Public Enemy) 99
Feeding of the Five Thousand, The (Crass) 109
Feenberg, Andrew 111, 176
'Fight the Power' (Public Enemy) 134
'Firestarter' (Prodigy) 90, 183
flaws, embracing of 85, 88–9
Flea 89
Fleetwood Mac 46
Fleetwood, Mick 46
Fletcher, Ted 13
Flood (Mark Ellis) 124, 131, 149–54, 178
Fogel, Christopher 58
Fragile, The (Nine Inch Nails) 87–8
Francesco Zappa (Zappa) 25
Frank, David 67
Fraunhofer institute 78
freelancing 106–8
Fridmann, Dave 61, 165–71, 175
Frith, Simon 84
Frusciante, John 89
Furse, Tony 20

Gabrielle 62
Gaisberg, Fred 94
Garbage 66–7
Garrett, Siedah 47
Geffen Records 58
Genesis 25, 41
Genesis (Genesis) 41
'Genie in a Bottle' (Aguilera) 67–8
genre 7
Gertzenauer, Greg 58
Ghost in the Machine, The (Warner) 133–4
Gibbons, Billy 142
Gibson, David 15, 133
Gillett, Charlie 4, 103
Gish (Smashing Pumpkins) 66
Glossop, Mick 81, 84–6, 95–6, 122, 131
Goldwasser, Ben 167
Good Vibrations (Cunningham) 13, 100, 111
Goodwin, Andrew 4, 101

Gordy, Berry Jr 92, 103
Go West 53
Go West (Go West) 53
Graceland (Simon) 25
Graham, Nicky 79
Grandmaster Flash and the Furious Five 99
Green, Lucy 84
Green, Nigel 131
Green Day 71
Greene, Paul D. 5
Grohl, Dave 5–6
Ground Zero Studios 58
Grusin 174
Guns n' Roses 87
Guy Called Gerald, A 100

Hague, Stephen 27–8, 97
Hamilton, Andy 82, 180
Hammer, Jan 22
Hannett, Martin 34
'Happy Birthday' (Wonder) 22
Hardcastle, Paul 43
Harding, Phil 44, 95–7, 102, 105, 118–19
Harries, Dave 38, 39, 51
Harrison, Dave 38
Harrison (manufacturer) 96
Harvey, PJ 109, 131
Haza, Ofra 48
headroom 38
Hedges, Mike 75–6
Hell, Richard 63
Helms, Dietrich 181
Hewitt, Karen 105
'high fidelity' 77–8
Hills, Steve 24
historical conventions and 'standards' 76–80
Hit Factory 71, 143
Hit Factory, The (Stock) 118
Hitchens, Ray 59, 76
Hodgson, Brian 70
Hooper, Nellee 149, 150
Horn, Trevor 9, 22, 98, 117, 119, 134, 176
Hot, Cool and Vicious (Salt N' Pepa) 99
Howard, Dennis 47
Howard, Mark 61
Howie B 149–51, 153, 178, 183
Howlett, Liam 90, 100, 127–8, 182–3

Howlett, Mike 94–5, 97, 105, 108, 117, 119, 167
How to Set up a Home Recording Studio (Mellor) 108
Human League 41
Hurby Luv Bug 48, 99
Hutchins, Robert 83
Hysteria (Def Leppard) 10, 39–40, 87

Iglesias, Enrique 61
imperfectionist approach 82
'industry standard' 76–7
'in-line' consoles 96
Inside Tracks (Buskin) 112
'In the Air Tonight' (Collins) 33
Into the Dragon (Bomb the Bass) 46
In Utero (Nirvana) 109
Invisible Touch (Collins) 41
INXS 43
isolation 107
'I Think I'm Paranoid' (Garbage) 66
It's My Life (Talk Talk) 53
It Takes a Nation of Millions to Hold Us Back (Public Enemy) 47, 79

Jackson, Michael 25, 26, 35, 40, 79
Jagged Little Pill (Morrisette) 58
James, Alex 164
James, Bob 59
Jam Master Jay 99
Jay-Z 94
Jazzie B 50
Jerden, Dave 71
Jerkins, Rodney 128
Jesus and Mary Chain, The 13, 109
John, Elton 95
Johns, Glyn 11, 106
Jones, Quincy 26
Jones, Steven 4, 111
Jonze, Spike 159
Joshua Tree, The (U2) 10, 49–50, 71, 86, 152
Journal on the Art of Record Production 112
Journey into Stereo Sound, A (Sumner) 46
Joy Division 34

Katz, Mark 4, 5, 134, 154, 157
Keep, Andy 85, 86

'Keep Music Live' campaign 101
Kehew, Brian 12, 93
Keidis, Anthony 89
King, John 138–9, 142
Kinks, The 48–9
Kiss in the Dreamhouse, A (Siouxsie and the Banshees) 75
Kissing to be Clever (Culture Club) 25
'Kiss' (Prince) 33
KLF, The 100
Kling Klang 83, 98
Korg 42
    M1 42
    MS-20 144–6
    Trinity 145
    Triton 145, 147
    Vocoder 68
Kraft, James P. 4
Kraftwerk 8, 79, 83, 98, 176

L7 66
Lacasse, Serge 15
Lambert, Joe 58
Land of Rape and Honey, The (Ministry) 109
Lange, Robert 'Mutt' 10, 39–40, 87
Langford, Simon 60
Lanois, Daniel 32, 49, 71, 87, 131
Larabee Studios North 143
Lawrence, Alistair 12
Leach, Christine 143, 144
Le Bon, Simon 31–2
Leckie, John 95
Legendary Joe Meek, The (Repsch) 13
Legge, Walter 94, 104
Leon, Craig 63–4
Leslie Loudspeaker cabinet 89
Levine, Ian 99
Levine, Steve 117, 120, 122
Lexicon 224X and 224XL 30–3
Leyshon, Andrew 106, 177
Licensed to Ill (Beastie Boys) 138–9, 141–3
'light pen' 21
Like a Virgin (Madonna) 25, 30, 79
Lillywhite, Steve 86
limitations-options anxiety 123–5
Line 6 'Echo Farm' 85
Linn, Roger 40–1, 43

LinnDrum machine 40–1, 43, 53
Little, Ian 31–2
Living Electronic Music (Emmerson) 88
'Livin' La Vida Loca' (Martin) 65
Loder, John 9, 10, 12–13, 34, 93, 108–9, 175
Loeb, Lisa 58
Logic 67, 87, 90, 147, 155, 166
London Symphony Orchestra 32–3
Lord-Alge, Chris 30
Lord-Alge, Tom 30
'loudness war' 81, 89
Low (Bowie) 31
Lowe, Chris 101

Machin, David 1
Macintosh 64
Maconie, Stuart 163–4
Madonna 25, 30, 35, 40, 79, 82, 130–1, 137, 143–8, 178, 182
Madonna (Madonna) 40
'Magnetophon' tape machine 77
Making Records (Ramone) 115, 122
Maldoon, Clive 143
'Mama' (Genesis) 25
Man Machine, The (Kraftwerk) 8
Marcato Strings 43
'Maria' (Blondie) 62–4
M/A/R/R/S 47, 79
Marshall Mathers LP, The (Eminem) 88
Martin, George 11, 12, 38, 81, 82, 115, 120–1, 124, 176
Martin, Ricky 65
Martland, Peter 76
Massey, Howard 112
Massive Attack 88
Massy, Sylvia 72–3
maverick methods 10, 75–92, 130, 133, 137, 142, 147, 148, 154, 165, 175, 179, 180–2
Maxinquaye (Tricky) 88
Mayfair Studios 160
McCarthy, Pat 143
McDonald, Michael 58–9
MCI 37–9
    JH-400 'in-line' mixing console 96
    JH-600 38
Meek, Joe 13, 81–2, 84

Mel & Kim 79
Mellon Collie and the Infinite Sadness (Smashing Pumpkins) 149
Mellor, David 41, 45, 51, 52, 108
Mellotron 69, 89
Men Behind Def Jam, The (Ogg) 138
Merton, Robert K. 84
Mezzanine (Massive Attack) 88
MGMT 137, 165–71, 182
Michie, Chris 98
MIDI for the Technophobe (White) 129
MIDI (Musical Instrument Digital Interface) 25, 41–5, 64, 66, 76–9, 89–90, 117, 119, 121, 152, 176, 177
MIDI Music Show 108
Miller, Daniel 102, 105
Miller, Keith 25
Milner, Greg 65, 77
Ministry 13, 109
Minogue, Kylie 79
Mirwais 68
Mister Mister 79
Mitsubishi 27
    ProDigi 56, 57, 60
Moby 90, 100
'Mofo' (U2) 137, 148–54, 178, 182–3
Moog synthesizer 50, 52–3
Moore, Allan 1, 3, 14, 15, 88, 133, 136, 181
Moore, Dudley 45
Moorefield, Virgil 98, 148–9, 183
Morisson, Van 81
Morrisette, Alanis 58
Morrissey 94, 160
Morton, David 50–1, 125
MOTU 45, 97
    Digital Performer 45
    Performer software 100
Moulder, Alan 87–8
Moulding, Colin 61
Mowatt, Will 116, 125
Moylan, William 14–15
Muikku, Jari 4
Mullen, Larry Jr 150
Mullin, John 77
'multitasking' 101–3
multitrack recording/capabilities 8, 123–5
Musical Rhythm in the Age of Mechanical Reproduction (Danielson) 134
'music first' attitude 115–16
Music for Airports (Eno) 86, 148–9
Music for the Jilted Generation (Prodigy) 127
Musicology of Record Production, A (Zagorski-Thomas) 4–5
Mute record label 105
My Life in the Bush of Ghosts (Eno) 86, 149

NAMM (National Association of Music Merchants) 57, 70
Nate Dogg 58
'National Anthem, The' (Radiohead) 89
n'Dour, Youssou 61
Necam (Neve Computer Assisted Mixdown) 38
Negroponte, Nicholas 64
neo-Luddite 127–30
Neumann microphones 72
Neve 37–8, 39, 71, 80, 96, 151, 152
    8038 89
    8068 72
    8078 90
    V-series 138
Neve, Rupert 151
Never Mind the Bollocks . . . (Sex Pistols) 31, 109
Nevermind (Nirvana) 66
New England Digital (NED) 8, 24–6, 70
New Jersey (Bon Jovi) 87
New Order 97
Nine Inch Nails 87–8, 149, 151, 152
'19' (Hardcastle) 43
1999 (Prince) 40
Nirvana 66, 109
No Exit (Blondie) 62–3
Noise (Attali) 13
No Jacket Required (Collins) 23, 41
nonchalance 127–30
nostalgia 125–7
Notator software 45
Novation Bass Station 144
Numan, Gary 98

Oakenfold, Paul 100
Oberheim 52–3
    DMX 139
Ocean of Sound (Toop) 125

Ocean Way 89
Ogg, Alex 47
O'Hare, Peter 13
Oldfield, Mike 46
Olsen, Keith 87
OMD 97
Ondes Martenot 89
'Opportunities (Let's Make Lots of Money)' (Pet Shop Boys) 101
option anxiety 123–5
Oracular Spectacular (MGMT) 165, 167
oral histories, problems with reliance on 112–13
Orbit, William 82, 123, 129–31, 143–8, 166, 178, 182
ORK (Original Keyboard) 24
Otari
    24 track analogue recorder 166
    Concept Elite mixer 166
    MTR89 multitrack 151
    RADAR (Random Access Digital Audio Recorder) 60–4, 73, 80, 122, 160–1, 164, 165, 166, 178, 183

Padgham, Hugh 33, 116, 118
Page, Wendy 112
Palmskin, Simon 62
Pantera 61
Parklife (Blur) 127–8, 161
Parliament 59
Partridge, Andy 61
Pasrons, Alan 98
Patiño, Juan 58
Paul, Les 116, 176
Paul's Boutique (Beastie Boys) 47, 79
PCM coder/decoder 50–1
PCM-501ES 29
PCM-1600 digital audio recorder 8, 27
perfectionist approach 82
'performance capture' techniques 71, 81–2, 111, 180, 181
Performer software 45
Perry, Linda 112
pessimism 113, 120–1, 132
Petersen, George 57
Petridis, Alexis 13
Pet Shop Boys 43, 61, 97, 101, 176

Phillips, Sam 13, 92, 103, 176
phonomusicology 1
Pinch, Trevor 126
Pink Floyd 93, 98
pitch-shifting 31–2, 68
Pixies 82, 109
Platt, Tony 121, 129, 131
Play (Moby) 90, 100
Please (Pet Shop Boys) 97, 101
Pleasure Death (Therapy?) 109
plug-ins 68
Poetics of Rock, The (Zak) 1, 4, 19, 80, 104
Pop Music, Technology and Creativity (Warner) 1, 4, 5, 22, 93, 106, 134
Pop (U2) 149, 151, 152, 153–4
Porcello, Thomas 5
Portishead 88
Postman, Neil 121
Power Mac 147
'Praise You' (Fatboy Slim) 89, 134, 137, 154–9, 178, 182, 183
Presence and Pleasure (Danielson) 134
Price, Bill 109
Prince 26, 33, 40
Prince Paul 99
Pro Audio Europe 70
processes 86–8
process, as term 2
ProDigi 27, 29
Prodigy, The 90, 100, 127, 183
'Producer as Artist, The' (Gillett) 103
Producer as Composer, The (Moorefield) 98, 148
producers, role of 94–5
production-aware artists 98
Production (Mirwais) 68
'product mix' 56
'Produser' 108
programmers, role of 97
ProLogic 55
'Prosumer' 108
Pro Tools software 61, 64–8, 70, 76, 89, 96, 102, 121, 128–9, 144, 145, 147, 155, 161, 166, 177
Pro-24 software 46
Psychocandy (The Jesus and Mary Chain) 109
Public Enemy 47, 79, 99, 134

Publison 44
Puff Daddy 71
Pultec EQP-1A equalizers 138
Purple Rain 48
Push (Bros) 79
'Push It' (Salt N' Pepa) 48–9
PWL 13, 44, 99, 105, 118

Qasar M8 synthesizer 20
quantization 157
Queen 95
Questioning Technology (Feenberg) 111

Radiohead 89
Radiophonic Workshop 70
Ramone, Phil 115, 118, 122
Ramones 63
Ramones (Ramones) 63
Rattle and Hum (U2) 152
Rawling, Brian 68, 113
'Ray of Light' (Madonna) 137, 143–8, 178, 182
Ray of Light (Madonna) 130–1, 144
rebellion 130–2
recall consoles 38–9
Recorded Music (Cottrell) 1
recording and production role, historical context of 94–5
Recording Angel, The (Eisenberg) 94, 104
recordings, analysing 14–16, 133, 137. *See also individual recordings*
recordist. *See also individual people*
    autobiographies of 12
    canon and 11–14
    focus on 4
    role of 11–14, 175
    'technophiliac' 16, 111–12, 115, 117, 119–20, 125, 132
    as term 1
    'traditionalists' 16, 111–12, 115, 117, 125, 132
recordist attitudes 113, 114. *See also individual attitudes*
Reddington, Helen 11
Red Hot Chilli Peppers 89
'Regulate' (Warren G and Nate Dogg) 58–9
Reinventing the Steel (Pantera) 61

'remediation' theory of 174
Repeated Takes (Chanan) 102
Replicas (Tubeway Army) 8
Repsch, John 13
reverb 30, 32–3
Reznor, Trent 86–8, 152
RGM Sound 81
Rhea, Tom 52
Richard Hell and the Voidoids 63
Rid of Me (Harvey) 109, 131
Rimbaud, Penny 109
Rio (Duran Duran) 53
'Rise' (Gabrielle) 62
risk aversion 127–30
'Rock Hard' (Beastie Boys) 139
Rock: The Primary Text (Moore) 1
Rogers, Nile 25, 30
Roland 24, 41, 42
    D-50 42, 119
    JD-800 144
    JP-8000 144
    Juno 106 42, 144, 145
    Jupiter 8 53
    SH-101 45
    TR-808 45, 46, 53, 73, 111
    TR-909 10, 42, 45, 46, 53, 73, 111
    W-30 90, 127
Romo, Olle 25
'Root, The' (D'Angelo) 90–1
Rowntree, Dave 161
Rubin, Rick 89, 94, 99, 115, 116, 118, 120, 131, 137, 138–43, 182
rule breaking 75, 84–6
Rumsey, Francis 76
Run DMC 99
Ryan, Kevin 12, 93
Ryrie, Kim 20

Sadkin, Alan 31–2
'Sale of the Century' (Abbey Road) 69–70, 178
Salsoul Orchestra 48
Salt N' Pepa 48–9, 99
Salt of the Earth (Soul Searchers) 47
Salt with a Deadly Pepa, A (Salt N' Pepa) 99
Sample and Hold (Goodwin) 101
samplers 42, 47–9

Savage (Eurythmics) 25
Savage, Rick 40
scepticism 121–2
Schaeffer, Pierre 20
Schmidt Horning, Susan 4, 77
Schoenberg, Arnold 83
Scott, Jim 89
'Sepheryn' (Curtiss Maldoon) 143
Sequential Circuits 41, 53
Serial Copy Management System (SCMS) 52
Seven and the Ragged Tiger (Duran Duran) 31
Sex Pistols 6, 31, 84, 109
Sexton, James 82–3, 86
Sheldon, Chris 96, 107–8, 121–3, 128–9
Sheppard, Rebecca 13
'Shout' (Tears for Fears) 21–2
Shure SM58 152
Simenon, Tim 46, 91, 100
Simmonds STS and SDX 122
Simmons, Russell 99, 138, 139
Simon, Paul 25
Simons, Dave 56, 112
Simpson, Gerald 44–5
Sioux, Siouxsie 75
Siouxsie and the Banshees 75–6
slap-back echo 176
Smashing Pumpkins 66, 149
Smiths, The 94
Society for Professional Recording Services 57
'Software Slump, The' (Leyshon) 106
'Song 2' (Blur) 137, 160–5, 178, 182, 183
Song Means (Moore) 3, 136
Songs About Fucking (Big Black) 10, 109, 120
'sonic alchemy' 84
'sonic continuum' 108–10
'sonic imprint' 93–4
'sonic signature' 93, 175
Sonic Youth 66
Soul Searchers 47
Soul II Soul 50
'Souljacker Part 2' (Eels) 89
Soulsonic Force 46
'Soundbox' (Dockwray and Moore) 15
Sound City (Grohl) 5–6

Sound Designer software 64–5
Soundgarden 89
Sound Recording (Morton) 125
Sound Tools 64, 100, 130
SPARS (Society of Professional Audio Recording Services) 51, 78, 176
Spector, Phil 13, 81, 82, 92, 93, 148
Spencer, Jim 61
Spice (Spice Girls) 80
Spinderella 99
Spirit of Eden (Talk Talk) 71
SSL 37–9, 80, 96
    4000 E-Series 33, 38, 70
    G-series 50
Stage to Studio (Kraft) 4
'Stan' (Eminem) 88
'standards' historical conventions and 76–80
Stein, Chris 62–3
Steinberg 45, 46, 90
Sterne, Jonathan 55, 60
Stewart, Dave 25, 98
Stiernberg, John 127
Stock, Aitken and Waterman (SAW) 10, 30, 44, 79, 99–100, 105, 118–19, 132, 148, 176
Stock, Mike 99, 118, 119
Stone, Mike 87
Strange Cargo series (Orbit) 143, 144
Strawn, John 56, 59–60, 124
Street, Stephen 94, 102, 107–8, 120, 122, 127–8, 160–5, 175, 178, 183
Studer
    A800 71–2
    A827 analogue recorder 66, 72, 73, 138
'studio magic' 83
Studio Stories (Simons) 112
Succeeding in Music (Stiernberg) 127
Sugarhill Gang 99
Sumner, Geoffrey 46, 48
superstar DJs 100, 155
Surfer Rosa (Pixies) 82, 109
Surrender (Chemical Brothers) 90, 100
Swedien, Bruce 26, 176
Synclavier 8, 24–6, 35, 98, 102, 121, 175–6
System of a Down 72–3
System of a Down (System of a Down) 72–3

Tagg, Philip 1, 14, 181
'Take Yo Praise' (Yarborough) 154, 155
Talbot-Smith, Michael 108
Talk Talk 53, 71
Tango in the Night (Fleetwood Mac) 46
tape manipulation 90–1
tape-op 95–6
Tarbox Road Studios 166
Taylor, Mark 68, 112–13
Taylor, Timothy 8, 73, 125, 173
Tearing Down the Wall of Sound (Brown) 13
Tears for Fears 21–2
TEC foundation 70
Technics PX1 101
technique, mythologization of 80–1, 82–4
technological anachronisms 85
'technological arms race' 27, 119–20
technological iconicity 68–73, 180
technology. *See also individual technological devices and processes*
    analogue versus digital 7–11
    as session hindrance 122–3
    term 1–2
technological hybridity 10, 55–74, 178
'technophiliac' recordists 16, 111–12, 115, 117, 119–20, 125, 132
technophobia 129
Technopoly (Postman) 121
tech-processual analytical methodology 2–3, 6,–7, 8, 10, 11–12, 15, 134–7
Teletronix LA-2A Leveling Amplifier 138
'Telstar' 81
Telstar: The Joe Meek Story 13
Temptations 47
Tennant, Neil 101
Terminator-X 99
terminology 1–2
Théberge, Paul 4, 106, 107, 110, 117, 176
'Theme From Miami Vice' (Hammer) 22
Therapy? 109
Thomas, Chris 98, 107, 109
Thorne, Mike 24
Thornton, Simon 155
Thr33 Ringz (T-Pain) 68
3 Feet High and Rising (De La Soul) 47, 79, 99
3862 Days 162

Thriller (Jackson) 25, 26, 40, 79
Thunderbirds 46
Time, The 48
Tingen, Paul 150
Toffler, Alvin 108
Toms, Melvyn 29, 39, 51–2, 65
Tool 72
Toop, David 125
Townhouse Studios 160
T-Pain 68
Track Record Studios 58
'traditionalists' 16, 111–12, 115, 117, 125, 132
Tricky 88
Trident
    80B 148
    ADC mixing console 66
Trocco, Frank 126
Trouble (Akon) 68
'True Faith' (New Order) 97
Tubeway Army 8, 98
2 Live Crew 61–2
2 Live Party (2 Live Crew) 61–2
2001 (Dr Dre) 44

U2 10, 32, 49–50, 62, 71, 86–7, 100, 137, 148–54, 178, 182–3
U2 by U2 153
U-matic 27
unconventionality 130–2
Under the Radar (Street) 165
underground 108–10
Understanding and Crafting the Mix (Moylan) 14–15
Undertow (Tool) 72
Unforgettable Fire, The (U2) 32
Unlocking the Groove (Butler) 134
unorthodoxies 130–2, 180
Urei
    1176 compressor 72
    1178 compressor 72
Us and Us Only (Charlatans) 61
utopianism 113, 116–19, 123, 132, 175–6

VanWyngarden, Andrew 167
Veak, Tyler 111, 176
Velocity Pressure Keyboard (VPK) 25
Verna, Paul 55

Version 2.0 (Garbage) 66
Vibe Merchants (Hitchins) 59
Vig, Butch 66–7, 116
Vintage King 70
'vintage' systems 68–73, 90, 111, 113, 181
Violator (Depeche Mode) 79
Visconti, Tony 31, 95
Viva Hate (Morrissey) 160
Vogel, Peter 20
voice
    effects of sound processing on 15
    Eventide Harmonizer and 31–2
von Appen, Ralf 181
Voodoo (D'Angelo) 90–1
'Voodoo Ray' (A Guy Called Gerald) 45

Walking and Talking 77
Walters, Barry 140–1
Ware, Martin 123
Warner, Timothy 1, 4, 5, 22, 44, 93, 106, 133–4, 181
Warren G 58, 59, 177
Waterman, Pete 99, 118, 119
Watson, Paul 103
wave-form editing 21
Waves Paz Analyser 142
Weller, Don 69
West, Kanye 68
Western Electric RA-1217 limiting amplifier 72, 73
What the Fuck Is Going On? (KLF) 100
What's That Noise (Coldcut) 100
'Where the Streets Have No Name' (U2) 86–7
White, Paul 129
White Boys, White Noise 34
Whiteley, Sheila 1
White Room, The (KLF) 100

Whitesnake 87
Whitesnake (Whitesnake) 87
Williams, Alan 6
Will Pop Eat Itself? (Beadle) 4, 99–101, 174
Wilson, Brian 81, 82
Wired for Sound (Greene and Porcello) 5
Wonder, Stevie 22, 115
workplace canon 13
Works, The 149
Wyn Jones, Carys 11

X-800 ProDigi 27
X-80 recorder 27
XTC 61

Yamaha 42, 52
    DX-7 42, 101, 117, 144, 145
    QX1 hardware sequencer 97
    SPX-90 33
Yarborough, Camille 154, 155
Yauch, Adam 141
Yazoo 105
Yo! Bum Rush the Show (Public Enemy) 99
'(You Gotta) Fight for Your Right (to Party)' (Beastie Boys) 137–43, 182
Young Guns 59
'You're the Voice' (Farnham) 22
You've Come a Long Way, Baby (Fatboy Slim) 154–5, 159

Zagorski-Thomas, Simon 4–5
Zak, Albin 1, 4, 15, 19, 80, 103–4, 112–13, 133, 175
Zappa, Frank 25, 32–3, 92, 98
Zero Hour Records 58
Zoom 1901 165
Zooropa (U2) 149–50
ZZ Top 142

www.ingramcontent.com/pod-product-compliance
Lightning Source LLC
Chambersburg PA
CBHW071824300426
44116CB00009B/1424